WITNESS

WITNESS

An investigation
into the brutal cost
of seeking justice

LOUISE
MILLIGAN

hachette
AUSTRALIA

hachette
AUSTRALIA

Published in Australia and New Zealand in 2020
by Hachette Australia
(an imprint of Hachette Australia Pty Limited)
Level 17, 207 Kent Street, Sydney NSW 2000
www.hachette.com.au

10 9 8 7 6 5 4 3 2 1

A catalogue record for this
book is available from the
National Library of Australia

ISBN: 978 0 7336 4463 4 (paperback)

Cover design by Christabella Designs
Cover image courtesy of Getty Images
Typeset in Sabon LT Std by Kirby Jones
Printed and bound in Australia by McPherson's Printing Group

For my husband, for always being there.

And for my two beautiful children, for reminding me, every single day, how important this work is.

CONTENTS

PROLOGUE

You don't sleep the night before that first day in court.

You spend it tossing and turning, bathed in a slick sweat you had never felt before, glistening like a pallid chicken about to be shoved into the oven and roasted.

You vomit. Your heart feels so close to the palm of the hand that's clasped to your chest that it might jump on out and tumble off the bed, still pulsing in the moonlight.

Your mind spins, processing and reprocessing questions you might be asked, retorts you might deliver, then remorse that those retorts might sound *too much*. 'Don't be an angry ant,' one of the lawyers had said. 'That's what he wants. Angry ants are always the worst witnesses.'

You think of the others who are also about to give their evidence. How tormented they must be. Of their poor families, struggling to know how to make it okay for them. And you think of those in their premature graves.

You cry.

You get up stupidly early as there is no point lying in that stupid bed. As the shower water pelts down, you will it to wash away the fear and the signs of insomnia. And then you get out, blow-dry your hair within an inch of its life and look in the mirror.

And somehow, at that moment, a deathly calm descends over the room like an opium cloud, your heart slows down to a dull thrum.

'This man is not going to fuck with me.'

And that is your mantra, your prayer, as you make your way to the Melbourne Magistrates' Court that March morning.

'This man is not going to fuck with me.'

* * *

My experience as a witness was illuminating, traumatic and, ultimately, politicising. This book recounts that experience but it is not about me. It is about and for the people I have come to know who wanted to tell their story about men, some in the highest echelons of power, only to be met with a paternalistic, disappointing and bruising system that often made them regret their decision to come forward.

A system where, even if they received what is considered to be justice, they came away from the experience worse than when they went into it.

It's about those who made it, and those who never got there in the first place.

It's about people who died because they were afraid, because they were traumatised by what happened to them, because they were traumatised by the criminal justice process itself.

It is about the disservice we have done them and others across the country, every day.

I AM THAT GIRL

One week after my day in the witness box at Melbourne Magistrates' Court, I flew to Sydney to meet a source for a story. The young woman I was flying to meet had also been a witness in a trial.

Saxon Mullins still called herself a girl. Her curial ordeal had been far more profound than mine. It had been going, at that stage, for four years. She was twenty-two. I met her in the back corner of a dark and nondescript bar in Sydney's CBD.

For the public, to that point, Saxon's name and her face had been hidden, but her story had not. Until that time, the narrative had been dominated by the young man who had changed her life in ways most of us would struggle to comprehend.

His name was Luke Lazarus. His story is complicated – from being convicted by a jury, to being acquitted by a judge, to having that judge's decision questioned by an appeal court, to legal limbo.

But back when the case first began, as Lazarus jostled past news crews and reporters jabbing microphones at him – 'Luke! Do you have anything to say?' – the indeterminate spectre of Saxon floated, faceless and nameless, above the chases to the car, the camera flashes, the bold-type tabloid headlines.

'*Sydney man jailed for rape of 18-year-old girl in an alleyway behind his father's nightclub.*'

'*Alleged rapist kept trophy list of women.*'

'*Rapist says his life was destroyed by conviction after alleyway assault.*'

The only picture I had seen of Saxon before I met her that May afternoon was one which, at that time, like her name, could not be published.

In it, her blonde hair was straightened, she was dressed in a strappy crop top to go clubbing, her head thrown back in a wide smile.

That was Saxon's Facebook photo. As with so many of these things, the profile photo was not really the girl.

The person sitting across from me on a dark bentwood chair was a modestly dressed paralegal. She'd come from a coastal town to work with her big sister in the litigation department of a large city law firm. She was unfailingly polite.

Saxon Mullins had luminous pale skin, unruly dark-blonde curls framing a still babyish face, brown eyes that crinkled up at the edges when she broke into a slightly lopsided smile. Her initially shy, at times halting, demeanour belied a kooky sense of humour and a courage in her convictions. Tattooed on her wrist was an hourglass and, on the back of her neck, L.I.F.E.G.O.E.S.O.N. She sometimes signed her text messages with a saxophone emoji. Saxon could have been anyone's kid sister, any girl's best friend.

To be frank, as a journalist, when you meet someone like Saxon, you wonder 'Where's the catch?' because she seems, as a protagonist, too good to be true. But Saxon was that good and she was that true. Not because she was perfect. Because she was normal.

To think of her, on her hands and knees in gravel in a dark alleyway out the back of a stupid nightclub, anally penetrated as her first sexual experience … To think of her, enduring that, just minutes after meeting the man who didn't pause to ask her if it was okay – a man who later admitted he knew she was a virgin … It was confounding to compute this girl before me and that awful night.

I tried not to fumble my words as I told her what I had planned for our story on *Four Corners*. I could only say what I knew to be true: 'All I can say is, I promise I'll look after you.'

She nodded, chewed her lip a bit and said, 'Okay.'

Not long before I met Saxon, she posted on her personal Facebook page:

There's something I need to get off my chest. I've spent far too long feeling embarrassed and ashamed.

The 18-year-old in the story is me. Those awful things happened to me. I am that girl …

… Two years ago I told my story to a jury of 12 people who believed me. But for legal reasons I don't really understand some judges decided I had to go through it all again. So, back I came to relive everything that happened to me that night. This time, another judge sitting without a jury wasn't convinced by what I said.

The person found guilty by a jury has been found not guilty by a judge. His criminal conviction is erased. He is free to move on with his life.

I feel let down and confused.

I lost something that night all those years ago and I've been searching for it ever since. I'll let you know how it goes.

The reality is this doesn't get to be over for me. I don't get to know who I would be today had this not happened to me, and I mourn for that person. She seemed like she was on her way to being great.

There are two people who know the truth about that night and one of us has thought about it every single day since; about what happened to me in that alley and the fear I felt all the while it was happening. I wonder, in years to come if he has a family, if he'll feel that same fear when his children go out for the first time; whether he'll warn them about people who prey on and hurt others. Perhaps, then, maybe he'll understand.

I don't wish harm or upset on anyone. I don't want anyone to suffer, that would never bring me joy. All I've wanted since that night was to hear the words: 'I was wrong' and 'I'm sorry'. An apology for what was done to me is all I was ever after.

As horrible as the details of what happened to Saxon Mullins in an alleyway out the back of a nightclub in Sydney's Kings Cross were, they lasted for only a few minutes.

Saxon's legal case lasted five years. Her case raised serious questions about what consent to sex actually is. Her story, as told to our program, led to changes in the law. But the criminal process was, for Saxon, deeply unsatisfying. It provided no finality.

'The criminal law is a blunt and brutal method of social education,' the-then head of the NSW Criminal Bar Association, Stephen Odgers SC, would tell me about the sticky notion of using criminal proceedings to educate about consent. 'Yes, we want to educate our community to engage and to behave in a civilised way, but you shouldn't rely on the criminal law as the key mechanism for doing that.'

Seven years down the track, I ask Saxon to reflect on her own experience of the criminal justice system.

'My experience of the criminal justice system from the view of the survivor was so awful,' Saxon says. 'People have asked me if I'd recommend going to trial or not, I don't know the answer. I have no idea of the answer. Because it's such a horrible event.'

She adds that when 'someone says it has to be blunt and brutal, I kind of laugh with tears in my eyes.

'Because I think to myself, "You really don't know what blunt and brutal is."'

* * *

Sydney's rape trials are held in a once-glamorous, now-shabby ex-department store, then called Mark Foy's, now known as the Downing Centre.

It's a strange sort of place, an awkward antipodean nod to Le Bon Marché in Paris. Ground-floor windows peopled with the ghosts of Mark Foy's mannequins. Interwar white brick architecture, trimmed with buttercup yellow faience sills, square turrets, and, inside, dirty seats you flinch before sitting on.

'The Downing Centre is a grub of a courthouse,' one criminal barrister who has many sex cases there tells me. 'It's a horrible fucking place.'

In my days as a young newspaper reporter in Sydney, my courts-round 'work husband' – a TV reporter who adopted pitch-perfect sonorous judicial tones and insisted on being addressed at all times as 'M'Lord' – would let out a groan with me whenever we had to make our way down from the uptown Supreme Court to what we termed, eyes rolling, 'the lower jurisdictions'.

We'd scarper down the road, elbow our way through the teeming masses, and I'd try not to think too hard on the human misery, taken down in my scrappy Pitman's shorthand. We'd dictate our notes back to each other, lest we missed a vital word.

I still have a mental image of an act of sexual abuse upon a child described in a particularly grim incest case, which I have never been quite able to scrub from my brain. I won't have thought of it in years and then I'll drive past the Downing Centre and there it is again, flashing through my brain like a grainy silent film.

The steps outside the Downing Centre were peopled with angry dads and toothless smokers, barristers in crumpled gowns, paralegals in synthetic suits and bored camera operators pacing for hours like caged lions, waiting for women with blonde hair and red jackets and men wearing lurid ties and a thin film of MAC pressed powder to send the text: 'dark hair, goatee, blue shirt, mid-thirties, coming out NOW!'.

Then, the chase. It lasted sometimes a block or two down the street, the fugitive's eyes darting as he looked for somewhere, anywhere, to get away. 'Do you owe your victim an apology?' 'What do you say to all of the people you have hurt?' 'Are you *ashamed*?'

On other days, out would file the victim. Crews would feign dignified patience, pretending not to scramble as, for instance, a wizened woman with sad eyes and thin lips creased around the memory of a thousand cigarettes, would say, flatly, 'He got ten years, I got life. There is no justice, none at all.'

The women with the blonde hair and red jackets would nod sagely, lip-gloss glinting.

Then they'd wait. Give her time to disappear around the block. Now, RUN! Back to the office to tap, tap, tap.

Cue, next morning, shock jock: 'Now I don't know about you, but I think that what happened yesterday in the District Court of New South Wales was a *bloody disgrace*!'

It was at this wretched carnival that nineteen-year-old Saxon Mullins found herself on Wednesday, 28 January 2015. Saxon was jet-lagged, having just arrived home from Ireland, to where she'd run away to escape her trauma. She had travelled by train to the Downing Centre with her mother, sister, brother-in-law, and two friends who were to give evidence.

They were ushered into a room full of other witnesses who were to be sliced and diced by defence barristers.

'It's kind of like a dentist's office,' Saxon would later tell me.

She and her family found dark mirth in the fact that the distraction provided to ease witnesses' boredom was the murder mystery board game Cluedo.

'That was a moment of absurd hilarity,' she says. 'And then we kept getting updates from the court, and more updates, and more updates. And the more updates we heard, the less funny Cluedo seemed to be. It became a lot more sombre.

'We just waited and waited there. For hours and hours. I think it's the most anxious waiting area in the world.'

As it happened, they waited all day. The legal argument stalled, and the court wouldn't be ready for Saxon until the following day.

She arrived on the Thursday wearing a pinkish red polka dot dress with a sash around the middle.

'I bought that new dress for court and, as soon as I put it on, I thought, "Fuck, it's going to happen,"' she remembers.

The trial was heard before Judge Sarah Huggett.

Like all complainants of sexual offences, Saxon Mullins was described as a 'witness'. That meant that, like any other witnesses in a criminal proceeding, she was required to stay out of the court when she was not giving evidence. Unlike the accused, she did not have legal representation in court. She did not have the right to remain silent.

Saxon later tells me that she thinks 'witness' is a ridiculous description of what she was.

'I wasn't a witness. I didn't just hover over my own body while this was happening.

'I was definitely there.'

* * *

Saxon was cross-examined that Thursday by Ian Lloyd QC – a loquacious veteran of the Sydney criminal bar known to everyone as 'Lloydy'. Like many of his comrades at Sydney's criminal bar, he could regularly be found at the nearby Courthouse Hotel.

Outside the court, Lloydy was enormously good fun and could be very kind. Inside it, too, he was charming and favoured the 'you get more with sugar than vinegar' style of advocacy.

But he could also, by his own admission, be, when he deemed it necessary, an 'aggressive advocate'.

'He was really smug, that's how it seemed to me,' Saxon says.

'When he thought I wasn't upset, or I wasn't taking it seriously, he would then switch to being very serious.'

Despite her tender years, Lloyd addressed Saxon as 'Madam' twenty-eight times during the cross-examination.

'*Madam*, I suggest to you, you will say whatever you think helps your story, whether it's true or untrue.'

'*Madam*, the truth is you consented to intercourse that night, didn't you?'

'You may laugh, *Madam*. Do you understand that this is a very serious situation for my client?'

'What the hell was *that*?' Saxon muses, years later, of the 'Madam' trope.

'What other reason would you do that, other than to paint me as something I was not – an adult woman totally aware of all the things that she's creating with this man?'

Ian Lloyd is not permitted to discuss this individual case, but he is completely upfront about his reasoning when referring to any young complainant as 'Madam': it's not a case of chivalry or antiquated deference.

'As a defence barrister in a sex trial, the last thing you want the complainant to come across as is some sort of young, naïve girl,' Lloyd tells me. 'You want to neutralise her as a human being. So you call her "Madam". You want to put age on her. That's a tactic we barristers adopt. If we call her by her name, that would be humanising her for the jury. We don't want that.'

* * *

Saxon Mullins had been dehumanised before.

'You have your trauma in this box where you keep it,' Saxon says. 'Mine is May 12, 2013.'

I've known Saxon for three years now, but the 12 May box is one I've only asked her to open once.

The twelfth of May was a continuation of the eleventh of May, the night when Saxon and her best friend, Brittany Watts, set off on a train from their home town on the New South Wales Central Coast for Saxon's first big night out in Sydney. Saxon had just turned eighteen.

They snapped a 'selfie' that night. Their skin glows in the way it does when life's all still a big adventure, their teenage brows yet to be furrowed by complications and disappointments.

'We were still living at home with our parents,' Brittany Watts remembers. 'We were quite young-minded, to be honest, looking back at it – we were very sheltered. Growing up where we did – our coastal town was very small, and everyone knew everybody. So I don't think we were very mature eighteen-year-olds.'

'Just super-carefree, and kind of getting started,' Saxon recalls. 'Didn't have any worries in the world and this was kind of like the beginning of "awesome".'

Brittany had experience with boys, but says Saxon was less worldly. She was a bright but mostly unsophisticated teenager who hadn't had her first kiss until she was seventeen. She'd had the same group of friends since she was fourteen, had only been out a handful of times. She'd never had sex.

'Saxon, she never really had any boyfriend-type of figure at that point in her life, and definitely no sexual contact with anybody,' Brittany says.

'I was very young,' Saxon remembers, 'I didn't think I was at the time. At eighteen, I thought, "God, I'm so old to be a virgin, this is ridiculous – borderline embarrassing." But when I look back on it now, the biggest thing that stands out was I was just so *young*.

'I feel like [that person] – she was a very different person, then. I feel like she was really let down by a system that wasn't supportive, by people who knew that system and were even less supportive.'

Before she got to that system, she first had to go through that night.

Saxon's story began before state government lockout laws killed Sydney's red-light strip of Kings Cross.

In the Cross that night, Saxon and Brittany walked a well-trodden path of many a newly minted young adult before them.

Past the giant Coca-Cola sign that lit up the district, past the strip club hawkers, past glistening, rotating kebab lamb and unspeakable crimson sausages languishing in *bains-marie*, the fat bubbling out of them long since hardened to an inedible outer shell. Past massage parlours, skanky brothels, junkies and pimps. Past the flash, flash, flash of the cars and the streetlights, and the beckoning neon signs.

The girls were going with friends to a nightclub called Soho, which was at that time one of the most popular clubs in the Cross.

On their way, Saxon and Brittany stopped at McDonald's to meet their friends. To save money, they had decided to 'preload' their booze – a bottle of American Honey bourbon – the sort of liquor adolescent girls think dreadfully sophisticated, but after a bad night or two, never, ever, imbibe again. Thinking of them, I recalled a song my girlfriends and I would sing, knowing we weren't terribly classy, in our final year of high school. *'There's a party in a ditch, would you like to come? Then bring a bottle of Bacardi Rum.'*

Saxon and Brittany had decanted the bourbon into two plastic cola bottles. They can be seen on CCTV from the night, hunched over the white laminex McDonald's table, in the sort of furious teenage conversation that's usually punctuated with 'like', 'LOL' and 'no way!' and 'get OUT!'. They're sipping from the cola bottles on the table. Saxon is wearing a sleeveless white polka dot top tucked into a flippy black skater skirt, with tights and boots. The obligatory straightening irons have tamed her curls. Another girl comes bounding up behind her and gives her a massive hug. She looks like she's having a lot of fun.

By the time they left McDonald's and went to a place called World Bar, the girls had shared about three-quarters of the bottle of bourbon – meaning Saxon had consumed approximately seven standard drinks. At World Bar, they shared two so-called teapot cocktails – a sweet concoction poured out of teapots into two little shot glasses. They shuttled between World Bar and Soho, drinking a couple of extra vodkas as they went. They finally chose Soho to settle in. By that time Saxon's standard drink tally had climbed to ten.

'I had been eighteen for just shy of two months,' Saxon says. 'I had been out a handful of times. I had a *lot* to drink. I was merry, but I was drunk. Doing drunk things. [Brittany] and I were talking in an English accent all night. A terrible English accent – you know, we were being silly. We were doing what drunk people do.'

'Oh yeah, we were having heaps of fun,' says Brittany. '[There are] just little snippets that I can remember. We were laughing, and we were talking to people, socialising. We were just taking it all in. Because we had never seen, kind of like, a nightclub scene like that before.'

The girls can be seen, again, on grainy CCTV, heading up the stairs past security guards and into Soho.

Inside, the night was known as Woodstock, themed after the 1969 music festival. Girls wore garlands in their hair and flared hipster trousers, baring belly buttons pierced with diamond studs and spray-tanned abs, toned at gym classes. Boys wore peace sign necklaces and round, blue Lennon glasses. Each week, the dancefloor was a heaving mass of pumping arms, dilated pupils and grinding teeth. The air cut with laser beams and doof-doof. By all accounts, for the private school graduates from Sydney's wealthy suburbs who went there, Woodstock 'went off'.

Soho's licensee was Andrew Lazarus, a hard-working, smooth, Greek-Australian pub baron, who enjoyed loyalty from his staff and his community.

Lazarus lived with his wife and three kids in a five-bedroom wedding cake of a pile in Vaucluse, on Sydney's south head peninsula.

Vaucluse is one of Australia's most exclusive suburbs, all trophy homes and giant, gnarled Moreton Bay figs, tennis courts and infinity pools, parquet floors and Pilates classes, Lexus SUVs and faces plumped with filler and views back to the city across the glittering, glittering harbour.

Lazarus' son Luke, then twenty-one, was a business graduate and a constant fixture at Soho. He worked part-time at the club.

Soho marketed itself to its patrons with an official Facebook page. The page told a story about the values of the place and how it was happy to paint itself to the world. In one 2013 post, a meme showed a picture of a busty, heavily made-up woman taking a selfie, with the words 'Only God can judge me'. Beneath it is a picture of God, with the caption: 'You're a Whore'.

The same year, the page shared a post where the user said, 'both my dogs are retarded ... when you get 2 metres near them they just roll over and open their legs waiting for you to give them attention ... it reminds me of half the girls in Sydney'. 'Oh Sydney ...' the Soho page admin wrote.

A third post, posted eight days after Saxon met Luke at Soho, captioned 'Evolution of Dance', showed four images of dance styles – from demure in 1970, to rock 'n' roll in 1980, to bump and grind in 1990, to an image in 2011, where the man appeared to be penetrating the woman from behind. The Soho page admin posted 'ahhhhh'.

Luke Lazarus had dark, close-cropped hair, large and round brown eyes, a Mediterranean complexion. He was the sort of boy that anyone who has spent time around nightclubs knows – stocked with free drink cards, pumped up. Talks a good game, and has 'friends' in high places.

A psychiatrist's report presented to the court would say that he had 'an inflated sense of power, and a sense of entitlement'.

'At the Soho Club, he did feel a sense of power and authority as this was a family-owned business,' the report said. '... This sense of entitlement may have given him a false sense of superiority and feeling of invincibility.'

Luke also worked at the brewing giant Lion Nathan.

'I essentially had the world at my feet,' he would later say. 'I had what I perceived to be, and what many others perceived to be at the time, the best graduate position for what I wanted to do in Australia.

'I could have been a CEO.'

Luke was an alumnus of the prestigious Bellevue Hill boys' school Cranbrook, alma mater of the likes of James Packer and his media magnate father, Kerry, before him. The school's motto was *esse quam videri* – 'To be, rather than to seem to be'.

'Luke, throughout his school career, had been of small stature and had been subject to quite a bit of abuse himself in terms of being teased and bullied,' Dr Christopher Rikard-Bell would later tell the court. 'And even though it may have been subtle, I think it had a significant impact on him.

'Now he found himself in an environment where he was empowered, and he was of high status, and he wasn't under threat of being bullied by others. In fact, he was in a position of privilege where he actually was able to feel a sense of superiority. And so, I think that this may have contributed to how he was able to convince himself that whatever he was doing was in his and others' best interests.'

The night Saxon and Brittany found themselves at his father's club, Luke had been at a twenty-first celebration and was arguing with his parents, who had pressured him to split up with his American girlfriend because she was not, like them, Greek Orthodox.

'We were incredibly in love with each other,' Luke would later say. 'We both said to each other we were obsessed with each other.'

Andrew Lazarus would later tell the District Court that the pair had broken up a few weeks before because Luke 'chose his mother', who was particularly upset about the relationship.

'He had always been a terrific kid and has always done what he was told, but at that time we were fighting as a result of the break-up,' Mr Lazarus would say. 'That night, he wasn't himself. [His mother and I] pleaded with him, "Please, you are not in the right frame of mind, you are not in the right state, please come home with us," and he ignored us and jumped on the bus and went with the other kids to the Cross.'

And that's where Luke Lazarus met Saxon Mullins. By the time Saxon and Brittany got to Soho just before 4 am on 12 May, the dancefloor had thinned right out. But not enough for two eighteen-year-olds, still excited about their first big night out, to care.

'This guy started dancing with me, so I just danced with him,' Saxon said.

Luke Lazarus had seen Saxon across the dancefloor and 'thought she was attractive'.

'He said that he was the part-owner of Soho or something, showed me a card and I was like, "Yeah, all right,"' she said.

Luke would say he was 'moderately intoxicated, but well within my limits'.

Brittany Watts beats herself up that she allowed herself to lose sight of Saxon, even if it was only for minutes. 'I was dancing with a guy. And instantly after, I realised that I couldn't see her. I was panicking, because I didn't expect the worst, I just didn't know where she went,' she said. She began texting her friend asking where she was.

Saxon says Luke told her he was going to take her to a VIP area. Although Luke would tell the court that after they went to a VIP area behind a DJ booth, he told her he wanted to go 'somewhere private'.

'I just kind of followed him through a corridor, I think, and we didn't really say anything,' Saxon says.

Saxon, seeming to be unsteady on her feet, can be seen on CCTV in the cloakroom at the back of the club. Saxon is gesturing back up the stairs in the direction they had come from.

'I pointed up to be like, "Oh, aren't we going to the VIP area?"'

She turns around and balances herself as Lazarus walks towards a door.

'I've kind of seen him open this door to outside and that didn't seem really right ... And he says, "Oh it's this way," so I said, "Okay, sure, I believe you."' Unfortunately for Saxon, she would never be asked about this at trial and the Crown's submission that that's what she was saying was later questioned by a judge.

Luke reaches out to pull Saxon towards the door. She can then be seen outside the door. The CCTV is time-stamped just four minutes after the CCTV showing Saxon enter Soho.

She can be seen turning and motioning back up the stairs. She wasn't in a VIP area. She was in Hourigan Lane – a place out the back of the club that satisfied all the clichés around 'dark alleyway': roaches climbing the walls, graffiti, gravel carpeted with dirty fallen autumn leaves, lit only by the blue of the moon. At one end, in the moonlight, the outline of the CBD gleamed, with Centrepoint Tower reaching up into the night sky.

The CCTV ended at Soho's back door. Although there were two cameras pointing into Hourigan Lane, the footage from the Golden Apple Brothel camera next door was, investigating police were told, 'not available' and the one at the end of the lane was broken. Outside, Luke and Saxon got to the end of the lane, where they kissed.

'That's when I realised, "Oh, this isn't the VIP area," and so I kind of made, I said I had to go back to my friend. And he said,

"No, no, stay with me, stay here," and I said, "No, no, I'd really like to go back to my friend now."'

Saxon says she repeatedly told Luke that she wanted to go back to Brittany. 'And he was like, "No, it's fine," and I went to move away and he kind of pulled me back and pulled my stockings and my underwear down. So, I pulled them back up and I said, "No, I really have to go now." And I went to turn, and he pulled me back and he said – um,' Saxon looks off to the side and shakes her head, swallowing.

'He said, something … "Put your fucking hands on the wall." And … so I did.'

While Lazarus mostly agrees with this account, he denies swearing and says he did pull Saxon's stockings and underwear down, but that she didn't protest.

Saxon has been asked many times since why she acquiesced and it's hard for her to explain – she says she just froze.

'I didn't know him. And, you know, the few things he said to me before we went outside were just nice, calm, normal things and then all of a sudden, after I tried to leave it was, "Put your fucking hands on the wall," it wasn't, "No, please, stay with me,"' she says.

'There wasn't any request. It was a demand. From someone I had never met before. In a dark alleyway. Alone. And I was scared.' She nods.

Lazarus tried to penetrate her vaginally, but he had difficulty.

'He said something like, "Oh shit, you're tight."'

Saxon replied: 'What do you expect? I'm a fucking virgin.'

'So he said, "Oh, shit, really?"'

But it wasn't over. Saxon says Lazarus then told her to get on her hands and knees and arch her back. And in the gravel, in the dark, having never had a sexual experience before, that's what Saxon did.

'I just did it. At that point I was just kind of in autopilot a little bit. I just wanted to go. And this was kind of the quickest way I thought I could leave. I just thought, "Just do what he says and then you can go,"' she says.

Saxon pauses and swallows. She speaks slowly. 'And that's kind of when … he, ah …' she shakes her head. 'I don't know how to say that bit.' She screws up her face. 'He had anal sex with me,' she whispers, spitting out the words.

'It was pretty painful. And I was just trying to like, I know it doesn't make sense, but block it out. Like, just wait till it was over.'

She would later testify that she told Lazarus to 'stop' – something he has always vehemently denied.

I asked her what he did when she asked him to stop. 'Nothing.'

'I mean, I didn't even get kissed until I was seventeen years old. I had this grandiose, romantic, "it'll be by candlelight, on a bed of roses, with someone who loves me ..."' She laughs sourly. 'And you know,' her eyes harden, 'no one dreams of their first time being in an alleyway, with someone whose name I can't even remember.' She shakes her head. 'No one wants that.'

Her first sexual encounter lasted a few short minutes.

'I got up and I went to walk away, and he said, "Oh wait, put your name in my phone." And I just, autopilot. I just did it. To leave. I didn't want him to follow me. I didn't want him to ask me any more questions. I just wanted to leave. So I just put my name in his phone. And I ran.'

Luke Lazarus would say he wanted Saxon's name as part of a 'trophy list' of women's names in his phone. And this trophy list would come back to haunt Saxon in court.

'I just ran. And I don't even remember how I got to my friend. And I just started crying. *Hysterically* crying.'

Saxon called Brittany.

'She was crying, and she never cried – I'm the crier,' Brittany says. 'I've never really seen her cry, to be honest. So she was in hysterics, which was very shocking. So I knew something had happened.

'She was up the street, near the crossing. And I just ran to her, I guess,' Brittany remembers. 'I ran towards her and she actually collapsed in my arms, which she's never done. She's just so strong and ... emotion – she doesn't show it like that. So it was just, instantly, I kind of knew something had happened.

'And it was from that moment that everything in her ... changed. It was like, that's when I saw it. Seeing her, fall apart. It was almost like she just crumbled. And I will never forget that moment.' Brittany whispers 'sorry' as she puts her head in her hands and messily wipes her tears away.

'She fell into my arms, she was basically hyperventilating and trying to tell me what had happened. And very, you know, she wasn't able to actually explain, you know, "This is what happened." It was just between breaths, trying to tell what had happened. And I was just in such shock. I didn't even know what to do or what to say. So I just kind of held her. And I thought, "Okay, I need to get you home."'

'I thought that once I left the alleyway, all the pain would go away,' Saxon would later say in her victim impact statement, 'but it didn't leave me for weeks.

'I know a part of me died that day. The part that trusted others. The part that saw the good in everyone. The part that held my innocence.'

The girls had no money to catch a taxi home. So they stumbled to Kings Cross station to wait for the first train.

'Looking back on that now, I kind of regret that,' Brittany says. 'I wish I'd gotten her home earlier.'

As the girls waited in the small hours of that May morning for the station doors to open, Saxon sobbed.

'I remember someone came past ... [and] said, "Oh what's wrong, honey? Did a man do this?" Just expecting it to be some sort of boyfriend–girlfriend drama. And the worst thing someone could have said to her.

'And everyone kept asking her if she was okay. And it was awful, because she was just trying to keep herself together to get home, and you know, break down.'

When they finally got on the train, it hurt Saxon to sit down.

'There were quite a few people on the train at that time, and even moving risked someone talking to us,' Brittany remembers. 'We didn't want to move, because she was in pain. So there was just ...' she trails off at the awful memory. 'Yeah, it was just a horrible situation. And it went *forever*. It just felt like we were on that train for *years*. To get back home.'

When they did finally get to Saxon's sister Arnica's house, Saxon was bleeding.

'She couldn't sit down, we had to ... she was lying down, rather than sitting, because the physical pain was just too much. And yeah, I mean, to be honest, looking back on it, I didn't really know what to do. I didn't know how to react or how to even help because it was just so shocking that it happened.'

The girls had organised to stay at Arnica's house. Just after 10 am that morning, Arnica's phone sounded with a text message alert. The little blue thought bubble on her smartphone screen showed a message from 'The Chosen One', a reference to Buffy the Vampire Slayer. That was her name for Saxon.

'Okay I have the story to tell you. It's actually really heavy. Okay so. We went to the world bar and soho ... At about 4.30 Brittany and I went back to soho and this boy started dancing with me and he was the co-owner of soho (like for serious, he actually was) he took me out this back door we went down this alley and then he was aggressively hooking up with me and ... then I was trying to get away and then he just went "no, put your fucking hands on the ground and arch your back" and I didn't know how to leave so I just did. And how do I put this delicately? Anal. Yep. And then I ran away and called Brittany and waited for her and cried. The end. Yeah.'

Arnica is ten years older than Saxon. She's a litigator at a large law firm. She has long dark hair and a brown-eyed, clear gaze.

'Immediately my heart was in my throat,' Arnica says.

Arnica insisted they go to the police. Saxon agreed. She went through the grim ritual of not showering even though it was all she wanted to do. Keeping her underwear and clothes to be placed in an exhibit bag. They headed for the cop shop and then to get a medical examination.

Dr Ellie Freedman was the director of the Northern Sydney Sexual Assault Service who examined Saxon when she presented to hospital about lunchtime on 12 May.

'She'd been up all night, so she seemed pretty tired, pretty subdued,' Dr Freedman told me.

'My memory of her is that she was quiet, composed, a little withdrawn, but able to give us a coherent story about what had happened to her.

'Saxon had a number of minor injuries, but most noticeably, she had grazing on both knees where she'd been kneeling on the gravel, and when I did a genital examination, she had a number of painful grazes around the entrance to the anus,' Dr Freedman says.

'She was in pain, and it was extremely difficult for me to examine her because it was very painful.'

That day, Luke Lazarus tapped out some text messages to a friend: '*I honestly have zero recollection of calling you, was a sick night. Took a chick's virginity, lol,*' he wrote.

'*Bahahaha. Nice popping [those] cherries. Tight?*' the friend replied.

'*So tight … It's a pretty gross story. Tell ya later,*' Lazarus wrote.

He would later be overheard on police telephone intercepts, having a conversation with someone from the club. He was relieved to discover that the CCTV found at the club at that point was of him leaving through the back door of the club with another young woman, who said they only went out to get 'some air'.

'This is the great twist,' Luke said, 'because literally the last two days I've been fucking contemplating my suicide.'

'Why would you be contemplating suicide if you're an innocent man?' he was asked.

'I was just incredibly nervous and having been terrified at having been a person potentially accused of committing sexual assault.'

He expressed his relief to his friend.

'I'm going to cancel this lawyer because there's no point spending a thousand fucking dollars.'

Saxon took the next week off work.

'I sat in the bath. I didn't want to see anyone. I was,' she trembles, 'I was so humiliated. I didn't want to do anything. I just wanted to sleep.'

THE TRIAL

It is not necessary to accept everything as true,
one must only accept it as necessary.
FRANZ KAFKA, *THE TRIAL*

For students of jurisprudence, Kafka's plight of an innocent man being tried and convicted for a crime he did not commit is rightly accepted as tyranny. 'It is better that ten guilty persons escape than that one innocent suffers,' is what's known as Blackstone's ratio – as expressed by English jurist William Blackstone in the eighteenth century. 'Blackstone's ratio' is oft-repeated by many of the barristers I have spoken to for this book – including Ian Lloyd QC, who represented Luke Lazarus when Lazarus was charged and tried for the rape of Saxon Mullins.

'The numbers of false complaints may be low in sexual assault cases,' Lloyd told me, 'but that's not much comfort when you are the poor accused, languishing in prison because of a false complaint.'

But the inverse of this Kafkaesque notion is the futility that many victims of crime are faced with as soon as they throw their hat in the jurisprudential ring. Is there an equally disturbing quality to the notion that a person who is a victim of crime should be so thwarted by the slings and arrows of the criminal justice process that it simply isn't worth the hassle to come forward? Or that, at the end of it, they are left with little but more trauma?

Certainly, for the countless survivors of sexual crimes I have spoken to over the past few years, there is one commonality that stands out perhaps more than any other: to be disbelieved and disrespected in a courtroom when you are reliving a terrible event from when you were a child, or a vulnerable young woman, cuts people to the bone. I've spoken to people who have abandoned the process because the undermining that inevitably occurs is just too much. And to people whose loved ones killed themselves before the process of assassinating their characters was over.

Since we featured Saxon Mullins in a *Four Corners* program, 'I am that girl', in May 2018, she, too, has spoken to many other survivors of sexual assault who have been bitterly disappointed by what they faced when they came forward to tell their story.

'They call it the second rape, it's this awful event,' Saxon says. 'And I think, for me, it's bundled up lots of memories into one horrible circle. So not only was I having flashbacks while on the stand with that memory moulded into this memory, I now have being called a liar moulded into all these memories – it's all sort of amplified.'

Lloyd was doing his job – providing what he saw as the best possible defence for his client. The discussion of what follows should be clearly prefaced with the caveat that his conduct in this case is not at all unusual and would be considered by many of his colleagues as completely permissible, honourable and business as usual. So, none of this is a personal swipe at him. It also seemed to me that he has respect, and, yes, some measure of sympathy, for the young women who come before him. Saxon, too, is now philosophical about his role and holds no personal rancour. But inevitably, for Saxon, as she says, what happened in court amplified her trauma significantly. It's instructive to peer behind the curtains of cases like this to see how that transpired.

Saxon's flashbacks of what originally had happened to her at Kings Cross are now bitterly entangled into her experience in the witness box and what would end up being a five-year legal ordeal.

She stopped being able to watch courtroom dramas on television. She shuddered when she passed the Downing Centre.

Like every criminal defence lawyer, Lloyd and his team had to construct a different version of the narrative to the one Saxon was claiming took place. It was a question of subtleties. Both Saxon and Luke agreed on most of the facts. There were granular points of difference though and it was a case, for the defence, of exploiting those in all their scarifying detail.

Luke Lazarus' basic contention is that he did not know Saxon wasn't consenting to the sex. He denied that he swore at her when he asked her to turn around and put her hands on the fence (which was sometimes referred to as the 'wall').

'I did not raise my voice, or [sic] I wasn't demanding anything – I just said it as I had been talking to her,' Luke said. Lloyd asked if Saxon had said 'no' or 'stop' or tried to pull away from him. Luke answered firmly in the negative.

When Luke tried to penetrate her vagina, he said she moved back towards him with her body and he believed that meant 'she was encouraging me, and ... sex'. But when, as he put it, 'it wouldn't go in', and he said, 'Fuck, you're tight,' and she replied, 'What do you expect? I'm a fucking virgin,' for reasons known only to him, he then said, 'Okay, well, get on your hands and knees and arch your back.' He did this so he could anally penetrate her.

The defence case was that Luke Lazarus thought Saxon Mullins would have then consented to anal sex, in circumstances where Luke knew she was a virgin. Four time-stamped minutes after entering the club, having consumed ten standard drinks, alone with him in a dark alleyway she'd never been to when she thought she was going to a VIP area. On her hands and knees, in the gravel.

Dr Ellie Freedman, given the grim task of taking Saxon's anal swabs the following morning, could see that it was an experience that Saxon would have found demeaning and humiliating.

'If you read her account of what happened ... there is no way that anything that happened to her [gave] her sexual pleasure,' Freedman says.

In his evidence, Luke seemed to try to indicate that Saxon was getting something approaching pleasure out of it. He seemed to put a lot of stock in the fact that Saxon's body moved back towards him.

'I ... put my penis in her anus and, as I did so, she ... pushed back towards me, slowly,' he told the court.

'Did she say "no" at any stage?' Lloyd asked him.

'No.'

'... [And] when you moved to her anus?'

'No. She did not say the word "no". Then, as I moved forward slowly, she moved back slowly and then I moved back and forwards slowly and she did the exact same thing. Her body – throughout – her whole body, she was moving back towards me. And then we finished and then I stood up, pulled my clothing back on and she did the same.'

Luke would later apologise for how he treated Saxon. But not before she had to go through the legal ordeal she endured that day at the Downing Centre.

Saxon, of course, maintained in her evidence that she did tell him to 'stop'.

When she told him she was a virgin, Saxon told the court that Lazarus responded, '"Oh shit, really?" and I just kept saying, "I need to go back to my friend."'

'You have told us that you said "Ow"?' the Crown prosecutor asked her.

'Yeah,' she replied.

Lloyd pounced on what he saw as an inconsistency between this evidence and Saxon's original police statement. As very often happens when a complainant tells their story over and over, there are discrepancies in how they express it at different times.

'You say here, "I think at one point I told him to stop,"' Lloyd asked her.

'That's correct,' Saxon replied.

'Well, you weren't certain, were you?'

'I was, yes.'

'Well, you don't say, "I told him to stop," do you?'

'That's correct.'

'You say, "I think at one point I told him to stop."'

'That's correct.'

'They're very different meanings in English, those phrases, aren't they?'

'I suppose so, yes.'

'Are they?'

'I didn't think they're that different.'

'Did you finish the HSC?'

'Yes, I did.'

The Crown objected. Lloyd pressed on.

'You studied English through to the HSC?'

'That's correct.'

I remember reading this line for the first time, back in 2018, and gasping at how patronising and disrespectful it sounded. I thought of the funny, friendly barrister I'd talked to on the phone and imagined the cognitive dissonance Lloyd would have had to employ to treat someone like this.

'You know the difference between "I told him to stop" as opposed to "I think at one point I told him to stop"?'

'That's correct.'

'... And I suggest to you, Madam, you were expressing uncertainty in your choice of words?'

'I disagree.'

Associate Professor Annie Cossins from the Faculty of Law at the University of New South Wales is perhaps Australia's most prolific academic writer on and contributor to legal reform in the area of sexual assault. Dr Cossins founded the National Child Sexual Assault Reform Committee – a body comprising all State Directors of Public Prosecutions, various District Court judges, academics, and Children's Commissioners. She was also a member of the taskforce that led to reforms of New South Wales' consent laws before Saxon's case. Saxon's case made it clear to her that those reforms had not gone far enough.

I spoke to her for *Four Corners* and early in our discussion she pointed out that the granular inconsistencies in Saxon's evidence – from the police statement made just a matter of hours after the incident in the laneway to her evidence at trial – were far from unusual in cases involving a complaint of sexual assault. In fact, she argued, they were typical.

'It's actually probably not advisable for someone to be giving evidence in that traumatised state,' Dr Cossins said, in relation to Saxon's first police statement given later on the day that the incident occurred.

'But, nonetheless, she had to make a report, and she did. She made a quick complaint to the police. Which was great. But it's entirely normal,' she cautioned, 'for evidence to be inconsistent from one period of time to another, because of the effects of trauma.

'The other thing that most laypeople don't realise is that inconsistent evidence is actually no measure of veracity. We think that it is – we think that if someone's inconsistent on one day, and says another thing on another day, it's a measure of their truthfulness. The brain doesn't work like a video recorder – and what interferes with the brain's ability to remember events with clarity are emotional states. So if you are in a highly traumatised emotional state – that will interfere with your memory recall ability.'

When you are a defence counsel like Lloyd, looking to raise reasonable doubt in the minds of jurors, inconsistencies are your stock in trade.

But the sexual assault trial is not a place of nuance. As Stephen Odgers said, it is a blunt and brutal instrument. The types of answers it favours – affirmative/negative – rarely allow for nuance. Like most sexual assault complainants, or witnesses of any kind, Saxon had been instructed by the Crown to keep her answers simple and just to answer the question. And like many to whom I have spoken about the experience, it rendered her feeling powerless.

'I felt like, even though I had hours on the stand, I felt like I didn't actually get to say what I wanted to say,' Saxon says. 'I was so scared, getting asked the same question in different ways, I just couldn't recall, "am I right, am I not right?"

'It made me less sure of myself. I guess the point was to make the jury less sure of me, but it made me less sure of myself.'

Then there was the question of the alcohol. Saxon estimated to the police that she had consumed sixteen standard drinks that night. She worked this out by the fact that a bottle of American Honey had twenty standard drinks in it, she and Brittany had used most of it to split between themselves and decant into their Cokes. Her memory was that she'd finished her Coke bottle by the time she left McDonald's. She then had two teapot cocktails with Brittany, which seemed to contain a lot more alcohol than they actually did as the girls repeatedly filled the little shot glasses from the teapot. She had also had a vodka and cranberry juice and a vodka and orange.

As it happened, the CCTV showed there was still some liquid left in Saxon's Coke bottle. Each teapot cocktail was a comparatively weak concoction and had only two standard drinks per pot. The CCTV from the night is grainy, but it doesn't appear that Saxon is stumbling as she walks into Soho.

'You see, *Madam*, I suggest to you, you have exaggerated your consumption of alcohol to try and lend a degree of credibility to your story?' Lloyd put to Saxon. 'That's what I'm suggesting to you.'

She did not reply.

'... You exaggerated your consumption of alcohol. Do you agree or disagree?'

'I disagree.'

Later, he took exception to the fact that when Luke Lazarus asked her to type her name into his phone, she had spelled her full name with initial capital letters.

'... [Y]ou typed your name in, correct?'

'That's correct.'

'And you would have the jury accept that you were very drunk?'

'That's correct.'

'You typed in Saxon Mullins?'

'That's correct.'

'You put in at least the second capital "M", didn't you?'

'That's correct.'

'You would have had to touch a particular key to do that?'

'That's correct.'

'You were obviously keen to get it grammatically correct and the spelling exact?'

'No.'

At this point the Crown prosecutor objected.

'I withdraw that, perhaps that's a matter of comment ... You see, Madam, I want to suggest to you that you weren't so drunk that you couldn't type your name properly, type texts to your sister properly, correct?'

'That's correct.'

'You found your way around the streets of Kings Cross, you navigated distances, didn't you, that evening?'

'That's correct.'

'However drunk you were didn't interfere with that process?'

'That's correct.'

'You had no trouble navigating?'

'That's correct.'

'Within the club you were dancing?'

'That's correct.'

'... You had no trouble going down those stairs, did you?'

'That's correct.'

That's correct. That's correct. That's correct. That's correct.

All correct. Saxon, like countless women before and since, was able to walk convincingly well, blagged her way past bouncers, probably spoke clearly when she did (that little rehearsal you do, 'speak clearly, walk tall'), knew how to spell her *own* name, bothered to use capital letters when she did, used a full-stop in a text and finished another sentence with a question mark. How many women have done all of this, and yet when they actually stand still, or manage to get home, find themselves staring at the ceiling, the room spinning? How many of them can't remember little details of the night until a memory jag and then it comes flooding back in humiliating detail? 'Oh god, why did I say that?' 'Why did I talk to him?' 'How exactly did I get home?'

Whichever way you cut it, Saxon Mullins had just turned eighteen years old. She'd been out drinking just a handful of times before. She'd had about ten standard drinks. Her defences were down.

But the defence argued that 'Madam' was terribly good at handling her liquor, that she took her alcohol 'quite well', she didn't 'get drunk easily'.

Put some age on her. The last thing you want is for her to come across as some sort of young, naïve girl. You want to neutralise her as a human being.

So you employ whatever it takes. As you're going through the evidence, you take out your highlighter pen. Hang on a minute, the text to her sister, sent the next morning. '... [T]*his boy started dancing with me and he was the co-owner of soho (like for serious, he actually was) ...*'

Not exactly what she said in her evidence. He didn't dance in her police statement. She was dancing next to Brittany '... *when a male came up to me. The male took my hand and said, 'Have you met the DJ?'* Bingo.

'Madam, you sent this text message on the morning, didn't you? ['That's correct.'] At, well, it's got to be after 10.16? ['That's correct.'] And would you agree with me that, as a matter of logic, your memory of events would have been better then, than it is now, almost two years later?'

Saxon didn't know what to say. Lloyd assured her he wasn't trying to trick her. So she replied that she agreed.

'So you *were* dancing with the boy?'

'No ... I wasn't.'

'So why did you put it in the text that you were dancing with the boy?'

'I was just sending her a condensed story, I wasn't giving her every detail. It was just easier.'

'Madam, if you were giving a condensed version this is a detail that never occurred?'

'That's correct.'

'Why would you add something that simply didn't occur?'

'I ...'

'If you're giving a condensed version?'

'It's just easier.'

'What, it's easier to tell a lie, is it? To tell an untruth?'

'I just said he was dancing with me because it was just easier.'

'What, first thing that came into your mind, is it?'

'Yes, that's correct.'

'Do you often commit lies to paper?'

At this point Saxon laughed nervously, in the way a teenager often might when they find themselves in a situation like that.

'You may laugh, Madam. Do you understand this is a very serious situation for my client?'

Saxon understood. She says she felt ill-prepared for her evidence. The standard instruction from the Crown prosecutor – to keep her answers short and not elaborate – wasn't, she says, suitable for every question and she felt it left her sounding less articulate, confused, at times overly blunt, and mostly, not herself.

'I think my desire to just answer in as few words as possible sort of changed how I would normally talk. And it made me ... it made me more on edge,' she says.

'There were just some times when I should have said more, I don't know ...' she trails off.

I ask her whether she knew, before she stepped into the witness box that day, that the defence barrister's role was to completely discredit her.

'I didn't,' she quickly replies, 'and it was really *jarring*, I guess, is the word, once I realised where he had actually been going with it the whole time.'

The defence's intended destination became most apparent to her when the so-called 'trophy list' emerged from nowhere in her cross-examination. After Luke Lazarus had finished with her that night, and she'd pulled up her stockings, he'd asked her to put her name in his phone. But she says she just put it in, mechanically, and that was that.

On the screen in the courtroom, she was shown a list of women's names – at the end of it was hers. It was a screenshot from Luke Lazarus' phone. Saxon says she had never seen that list on the night. She began to cry.

'You see your name there?' Lloyd asked her.

'Yes,' she managed to say, tearfully.

'It upsets you to see your name on that list?'

'Yes.'

As she cried, Saxon realised so many things at once. First, that she was just one of many – that Luke Lazarus had a *list* of women.

'[I was] thinking, "Not only do I feel crap, but do they feel crap? Those women, do they feel crap?"' she tells me.

'I believe I've been assaulted, you know? Who are these other women on this list that I have put my name onto and in what context did they put their names onto it?'

It's a sobering thing to contemplate, that in this day and age, fifty years of second-wave feminism down the track, a young man would keep a list of the names of his sexual conquests on his smartphone.

'I was a bit horrified,' Dr Annie Cossins told me. 'I thought, "Wow, why does he have to do that? Why does any man need a trophy list of women? Is that what young women are there for?" I find that quite sad.

'I put myself in Saxon's shoes and I thought, "Oh god, imagine finding out that – that's all you meant? You were just to be added to a trophy list ... That's your value as a human being."'

As Lloyd peppered Saxon with questions about it, and she wept, she was reeling and lost for words.

'... [You] saw the other names?'

'I don't recall.'

'You *may* have seen the other names?'

'I don't recall.'

'You couldn't have missed the other names.'

'I don't recall.'

'And you've put your name at the bottom of a list of girls' names.'

'That's correct.'

'... You typed your name in – correct?'

'That's correct.'

You can almost feel the dissociating as you read the clipped replies. Drift off to escape what's before you. Saxon would later clarify to the court and to police that she saw nothing on the phone when, in autopilot, just to get away from Lazarus, she put her name in his phone. The Crown prosecutor would make the point that the question of whether she had seen the other names depended on where the cursor was.

But also skittling through her mind, as Lloyd grilled her, was the realisation that the jury was effectively being told that the trophy list was the true reason why she was going through this ordeal – that she was some sort of vengeful woman hell-bent on bringing down this man with the notches on his digital bedpost. That her tears were of anger and hot shame, rather than trauma. Hell hath no fury, and all that. And she says she just couldn't imagine what sort of person would do that.

'The kind of woman who will consent to sex and then decide to ruin someone's life because you put her name at the bottom of the list of other names ...

'That's what they thought I did,' she says, incredulous at the thought of someone actually doing that. 'Now they were implying I didn't just lie about what he did to me. They were saying I did something so horrible I couldn't ever imagine someone doing.

'I can't even understand how that would even be an argument.'

Luke Lazarus would later give evidence to the court to back up this theory.

'I couldn't recall her name and I said to her, "Can you put your number – put your name in my phone?" And handed her my phone, I gave her, with the note up, and the screen was alight. At that point she took it, looked at – clearly looked at the names and wrote her name at the bottom … Her demeanour clearly changed.'

'In what way?' Lloyd asked him.

'She no longer had a smile on her face that she had before, she was disgruntled. She looked – yeah …' Lazarus trailed off.

'Rather than your conclusions what did you observe? So, she no longer had a smile on her face?' Judge Huggett asked him.

'A stern look on her face,' Lazarus answered. 'Yeah, she wasn't smiling sweetly anymore and she was – there was a serious look on her face. I realised that, at that point, that it was clearly a very, very rude thing for me to have done. She gave me the phone back and she just – and she walked away.'

He realised *at that point* that it was a very, very rude thing to do.

Saxon finds it hard to wrap her head around the sort of diabolical person who would go to the trouble and heartache of going through a criminal justice process – putting her underwear in a plastic bag, getting the hospital anal swabs, doing the police interviews, enduring the years of waiting, the defence counsel grilling, the embarrassment, the undermining – just to get revenge on a guy because he had her name on a trophy list after a sexual encounter.

I asked her if there was any incentive for someone who feels a little bit demeaned that their first sexual experience wasn't the romantic thing they thought it was going to be, to go through this, if they don't think it's rape.

'No. No,' she answers, firmly. 'I have gained nothing from this. I didn't … The only reason you would go through this is so that no one else has to.

'There was no personal benefit for me to do this.

'I have no idea why anyone would go through a trial, or a police investigation, or another trial, if they didn't have to.

'If I was just embarrassed, or I was just upset, I wouldn't have gone through all of this just to prove a point.

'There's nothing in this for me. It's just …' she trails off and pauses. 'For them to even say that shows that they have no idea.'

Her sister Arnica agrees. 'Why would she want to pursue this and put herself through that again and again?' Arnica says. 'You know, we did talk about things – like, I would say, "If you don't want to go through with it, we, your family, support you. We will do whatever you want to do."

'But Saxon had been wronged and she wanted to see that through ...'

It is no small exaggeration to say that Saxon paid an enormous price for seeing it through.

When Lloyd asked Saxon about her medical examination at the Northern Sydney Sexual Assault Service by Dr Ellie Freedman, later on the day of the incident, he was careful to point out that Dr Freedman 'describes your emotional presentation as quiet and composed'.

'That's correct,' Saxon was again bound to say.

Dr Freedman would later say that Saxon's 'withdrawn' demeanour was not unusual – she had seen it many times in women who were victims of rape.

'I've been working, responding to recent complaints of sexual assault for over ten years and I couldn't tell you what a typical presentation is,' Dr Freedman told me.

'Some people are very distressed. Often people are really in a state of shock.

'We see people very soon after these events and people can't really process what's happened to them – there's no "normal" or "right" way for a victim to present.'

Lloyd then took Saxon to Dr Freedman's description of the incident in her medical notes, which said that the man [Lazarus] 'pushed her down on all fours'. It is conceivable to see how, in the blur of something like this, that sort of thing could happen – the doctor could misinterpret or mishear what was said as she's jotting down bits of this experience – concentrating on listening to a young woman who is traumatised (as is her job as a medical professional) rather than providing a note that is word-perfect for a court of law.

'Well, if the doctor recorded that from you, it would be wrong, wouldn't it?' Lloyd asked Saxon.

'Yes.'

'Because you say that didn't happen.'

'That did not happen.'

'Madam, again, I suggest to you that's what you told the doctor?'

'That did not happen.'

'And you were again embellishing your account to make it more believable.'

The Crown prosecutor objected, and the judge pointed out that Saxon didn't recall telling the doctor that.

'Madam, the truth is you consented to intercourse that night, didn't you?'

* * *

It's difficult for any witness being doubted and undermined, but for a teenage complainant who is alleging sexual assault, it also involves rehashing the frequently uncomfortable sexual details to a room full of strangers.

'For an eighteen- or nineteen-year-old to be able to do that,' Annie Cossins says, 'is extraordinarily difficult.

'I remember someone at a conference once saying to people in the room, men in the room, "Okay, could you please, first, all draw your penis and then describe it,"' she recalls. 'And everyone was incredibly embarrassed – it was a room full of judges and lawyers. And yet that's, essentially, what women and men who are sexually assaulted have to do.

'None of us have to do that, every day of the week, do we?'

Over and over, reliving the ordeal. Over and over, not believed.

'And he took – pulled your stockings down and your underwear?' Lloyd asked.

'That's correct.'

'And you didn't resist?'

'That's correct.'

'And he tried to enter your vagina from behind?'

'I don't recall.'

'But he may have?'

'He may have.'

'And he said words to the effect, "Fuck you're tight"?'

'After I was on the ground.'

'He's been trying to enter your vagina, you've just accepted he may have done that?'

'Right.'

'He said to you, "Fuck you're tight"?'

'No.' [Saxon's evidence was that he said 'You're so tight.']

'And you said, "What do you fucking expect, I'm a virgin"?'

'Right.'

'You said that, didn't you?'

'I did say that, yes.'

'And then he entered you?'

'Yeah.'

'What, anally?' the judge cut in.

'While I was on the ground, yes.'

'And he did ask you if you could put your hands and knees on the ground?' Lloyd continued.

'Yes. That was before that conversation, yeah.'

'... He tried to enter your vagina and then he entered your anus?'

'That's correct.'

'And as he was entering your anus you pushed back towards him?'

'I don't recall.'

'But you may have?'

'I may have.'

'And then he finished, and you put your clothes back on?'

'That's correct.'

'And he then asked you, as you said, yes? Today? To put your name in his phone and you did so?'

'That's correct.'

'You then saw the names of other females and you became emotional?'

'Today?'

'Well, did you see the names of other females?'

'That night, no, I don't recall that.'

'... Madam, I'm suggesting to you in concluding my cross-examination, that once you put your name at the end of that list of girls' names on that phone, your attitude changed?'

'I disagree.'

'You then became upset and you left the lane?'

'I disagree.'

'That you felt that you'd been used and were just a trophy.'

'I disagree.'

'And I suggest to you that you have lied in this courtroom about what took place in that lane?'

'I disagree.'

After the grilling was complete, Saxon walked, exhausted, down the grubby Downing Centre steps.

In the years since, she's thought many times about how she was treated.

'Of course you have to put up the defence for your client and I don't think anyone who is on my side or his side of this argument, thinks that shouldn't happen,' she says of Lloyd's cross-examination. 'But giving the best defence of your client, where does that end?

'And where does your best duty to the court start again? Like, where, in destroying my character, is that the best defence for your client? Is that the best way to do it, is that the only way to do it?'

* * *

Ian Lloyd QC, like every other barrister, cannot discuss individual cases. But I asked Lloyd how he felt about this process more generally – discrediting witnesses who are young girls reliving the worst ordeal of their lives. Did he ever feel guilty? His answer was one I'd hear again and again throughout this process.

'I think the short answer is no,' Lloyd says, evenly.

'I don't feel guilty about it, because my job is to defend my client to the best of my ability, and if that involves highlighting deficiencies in a witness' account, as unsavoury as that process may be, I feel no guilt or shame in doing so.'

But, I point out, he knows more than anyone how malleable this stuff can be – because of the fallibility of memory when it comes to the little details. Where were you standing in the room? What colour was his shirt? Did you have four drinks or five?

As I ask him this, I recall an exercise I was required to do when I was at university and working part-time in a retail store. All the shop assistants were gathered together for a meeting and a faux shoplifter came through and 'stole' some garments. Immediately afterwards, we were asked to write down a detailed description of the thief's appearance. I had an accurate description of the hair and skin colour, where in the store the thief had been and how they had gone about their theft. But inexplicably, I had the thief in a shell tracksuit with three stripes down the side. The thief wasn't wearing anything remotely similar. Where did the shell tracksuit come from? A cliché about what a shoplifter looks like?

This was only moments after the 'crime'. Now, to be fair, I wasn't raped by the shoplifter, the scarifying details to be forever etched on my brain. But I know from years examining these cases, and speaking to the victims of these crimes and the lawyers involved, that people are often hazy on the extraneous details. Their mind, looking to be accurate and precise, invents a three-stripe shell suit where in fact there were jeans and a hoodie.

What this means is the more time that transpires between the crime and the trial, the better it is for a defence counsel. It is not difficult to create a reasonable doubt when it is one person's word against another's and the crime is carried out in private.

'I think that's a fair comment,' Lloyd says. 'The reality is, that the whole search for evidence to establish a reasonable doubt is effectively a delving into the grey area of anybody's credibility and reliability. It goes back to what a defence counsel does. I am paid, fundamentally, to create a reasonable doubt.

'And if you can't take the heat, as defence counsel,' he says, referring to how this might play on the conscience, 'get out of the kitchen.'

But the more I talk to him and other defence counsel, the more I think that many *can't* take the heat. And I don't mean that in a pejorative sense. They are very skilled at what they do. Their role is vital and requires a keen intellect. But it's not really reasonable for us to expect them to 'take the heat' without also giving them more tools to deal with it. That the cognitive dissonance they must employ, day in, day out, just to do the basics of the job, can't help but be corrosive. And the standard lines they all give aren't reflective of what they truly feel about the process.

From our discussions, I can see Ian Lloyd wants me to know that he has a heart. And he does. He empathises with these women and children who come before him with their awful stories. It is, by his own admission, 'a very difficult process defending these guys'.

Despite Ian Lloyd's best efforts, Luke Lazarus was found guilty by the jury in that first trial.

A parade of witnesses lined up to give character evidence for Lazarus, including his local mayor, the chairman of the South Sydney Rabbitohs, a Greek diplomat and the parish priest from Lazarus' local Greek Orthodox church.

Character evidence is routinely used in sex trials to mitigate against sentence. He may have raped this woman or child, the argument goes, but he was a nice guy in the rest of his life.

The priest went beyond saying simply that Lazarus was a good guy, to say that he had suffered an 'injustice'.

The references prompted the then Minister for the Prevention of Domestic Violence and Sexual Assault, Pru Goward, to say she was 'appalled'.

'Not only does this diminish their standing, it can shatter the confidence of the victim and often discourages them from seeking justice,' Goward said at the time.

Saxon was perplexed at why they would do this.

'A murderer could walk past twenty people on the street and not kill them. That doesn't mean that they haven't killed other people,' she says. 'He could be a fantastic employee. That doesn't mean he didn't rape me. He could be a great friend. That doesn't mean he didn't rape me. None of these things have anything to do with what happened to me.'

The other thing that struck me about this, as witness after witness told the court what an exceptional young man Lazarus was, was that Saxon had none of that.

'You don't have an expensive lawyer to represent you, you don't have witnesses who can say how great you are. You simply have your character dissected. How did that feel?' I asked her.

'I could have had all my friends testify about how I act, and what I usually do and how great of a person I am. Maybe that would have made a difference. But I don't get that opportunity.

'His witnesses' statements make him look reliable – apparently I don't look reliable.'

Saxon believes that therein lay the power imbalance.

'Someone who has personal connections with important people who are prepared to give evidence as to what a fantastic guy he is. There's more weight in their stories, apparently, because of who they are and their standing.

'It's hard, because I get that he's their friend, or their family member, or their co-worker,' she says. 'But … I'm a real person. I'm sitting in front of them, and they're basically saying, "We don't believe you."

'And it comes back to, what am I gaining from this? Why would I do this?'

Saxon comes from a nice family and she has lovely friends. They support her and it was clear to me just how much they love her.

'But you go to court and these people are just outright calling you a liar. It's something you cannot forget.'

The legal profession hit back at Pru Goward for criticising the character references, arguing that it might constitute a contempt of court.

'No member of the community should be deterred from providing evidence in a criminal matter,' the Junior Vice-president of the NSW Bar Association, Arthur Moses, told *The Sydney Morning Herald* at the time.

'Ministers of the Crown should be mindful that their positions come with both privileges but also obligations to not make comments which may have the tendency to interfere with the proper administration of justice.'

Goward was undeterred, but it was another example of just how alone a complainant is in a sexual assault trial, and how the people who work in this legal sphere will baulk at anyone who tries to rock their status quo.

Saxon did have her verdict. Which, like most complainants I've spoken to, was, all at once, something … and nothing.

'It didn't change anything, you know?' Brittany Watts says of the impact of Luke's guilty verdict on her best friend. 'It still happened to her, regardless. It was still brought up again for her in her memory and I don't think it even helped her that much to see him guilty, in a way.

'Because it still happened. That's not going to change it. Does that make sense?'

Whatever small, cathartic closure she may have got from the decision that day in the Downing Centre, the legal system wasn't done with Saxon Mullins yet. She didn't realise it then, but she was only halfway through.

HORNSWOGGLE

About nine hundred kilometres from Sydney's Downing Centre is William Street in Melbourne's legal district. At its centre, in the shadow of the Supreme Court of Victoria's neoclassical dome, is the home to many barristers who appear before the court – Owen Dixon Chambers. Named after Australia's most venerated High Court justice, the chambers mark the original home of the Victorian Bar.

In the foyer of Owen Dixon's west wing is a portrait gallery.

The paintings hang on walls the colour of a battleship. Their subjects wear yellowing horsehair wigs, lace cuffs, scarlet gowns, stern eyebrows and sceptical gazes. Among their ranks is a prime minister, three governors-general and seven justices of the High Court. In the better ones, the eyes burn with savage intellect. Some have a playfulness and even a kindness about them. Some have ruddy noses. And so many are men. Yes, mostly men, old and white. The paintings of the women are judiciously spaced, because there are so few of them. They shine like beacons, because women tend to wear colour. Whereas the men, with the exception of the judges in red robes, are generally in muted greys, navy and black.

Some of them look like they'd be excellent dinner company, some of them are pale and dead-eyed and look like they'd have you for lunch, washing you down with a glass of Hill of Grace.

Think of those images of High Court Justice Dyson Heydon (whom the High Court has acknowledged sexually harassed six women at the Court) peering down his nose at the viewer, and you'll get the picture.

A portrait of the gallery's namesake was added in October 2017. The painting shows a portly man of Celtic persuasion. He has snowy hair, deep-set large eyes, more than one chin. His mouth is pressed together in the sort of smile that approaches a grimace. He looks bemused and faintly embarrassed to be sitting there. Like an elderly uncle who has been roped in to sitting for the family snap, he'll endure it if he must. His hands are clasped together. On one arm, a gold wristwatch. He wears a dark suit with a pale shirt and a blue tie. He was, at time of painting, Victoria's most senior barrister, having signed the Bar Roll in 1961.

Several weeks after his portrait was added to the gallery, a document would be tabled in the Australian Parliament which was of special interest to the painting's subject. It was the final report of the Royal Commission into Institutional Responses to Child Sexual Abuse. The commissioners had heard many days of evidence and read countless pages of submissions, which concerned this elderly gentleman, many of them written by him.

His name was Peter O'Callaghan QC.

O'Callaghan was a silk of Irish descent brought up in humble circumstances in Horsham in the western districts of Victoria's Ballarat diocese. Once a motor mechanic, he went back to school and did so well, he won a scholarship to study law at the University of Melbourne.

An old friend, former High Court Justice Susan Crennan, said at the opening of the gallery that he was known 'not only for his wit, but also for his court craft'. He was the sort of advocate who littered his submissions with words like 'hornswoggle'. Which, to those less accustomed to the quainter reaches of the English language, means to get the better of someone. To swindle, cheat, hoodwink or hoax. '[He is] a person who has shown so many of us how it should be done,' Justice Crennan said of her friend. She quoted Yeats. 'Think where man's glory most begins and ends, and say my glory was I had such friends.'

Yes, Peter O'Callaghan was a friend to the Bar, a much-loved mentor, a member of a luncheon club for forty years, who gently shuffled off this mortal coil, aged eighty-eight, in March 2020. His life was celebrated with a requiem mass overseen by the former

Archbishop of Melbourne, Denis Hart. He was carried out of St Bede's, Balwyn, to the strains of 'Danny Boy'.

'He was a great raconteur,' said the Victorian Bar's official obituary. 'He was the epitome of the good man. He spoke no ill of anyone and took unfounded criticism with a shrug of his shoulders. He relished life.'

The victims of O'Callaghan's church take great issue with the phrase 'unfounded criticism'. These are people who were sexually abused as children by priests of the Melbourne Archdiocese and came to Peter O'Callaghan to manage their complaint. Dark shadows fall over the faces of these survivors when his name is spoken.

For twenty years, Peter O'Callaghan was on a retainer for the Catholic Church as Independent Commissioner of the notorious Melbourne Response. He was appointed under Catholic Church canon law. The scheme was set up by George Pell when he was Archbishop of Melbourne to deal with the clergy abuse cancer, to use his word, spreading through his archdiocese.

When looking for a barrister to run the show, O'Callaghan, a committed Catholic who was, like Pell, a Ballarat diocese boy, seemed the perfect choice.

When critics publicly took issue with the barrister's methods, they were not met with a mere shrug of O'Callaghan's shoulders. O'Callaghan fired off fifteen replies to submissions or evidence to the Victorian Parliamentary Inquiry into the Handling of Child Abuse by Religious and Other Organisations which in any way questioned his work. The replies spanned more than 350 pages. He made more submissions in reply than any other person or organisation. He called the claims of people – including police officers, advocates, priests, politicians and parents – 'scurrilous', 'baseless', 'nonsense', 'false and malicious' and, in some cases, attacked their credibility.

Catholic priest Father Kevin Dillon supported many survivors who went through the Melbourne Response and who had found it traumatic and intimidating. When Father Dillon questioned the scheme in an interview with a newspaper journalist, O'Callaghan responded by writing to the priest in an email marked 'confidential', asking him to identify the complainants so he could contact them and ask which parts of the Melbourne Response they found so intimidating.

'I was incredulous that the "Independent Commissioner" would ask me to identify people who were coming to me for pastoral support,' Father Dillon wrote to the inquiry. When Father Dillon ignored the email, O'Callaghan then sent the 'confidential' email to the newspaper's letters editor.

'Mr O'Callaghan publicly chastised me for "ignoring" his email (which I had), clearly annoyed that I had not immediately jumped according to his instructions!' Father Dillon wrote.

Some who came up against O'Callaghan were met with threatening legal letters.

Dr Judy Courtin is a lawyer who represents numerous victims who have been through the scheme. Her advocacy over many years helped bring about the Victorian Parliamentary Inquiry, and, later, the Royal Commission into Institutional Responses to Child Sexual Abuse.

Courtin received a legal letter from O'Callaghan for an opinion piece she wrote in *The Sydney Morning Herald* in November 2016, which was savagely critical of the Melbourne Response. The piece did not even mention O'Callaghan's name, nor refer to him even in oblique terms.

The timing of the naming of the O'Callaghan gallery is interesting, although the Bar is adamant that it's coincidental. The Royal Commission heard its evidence about the Melbourne Response in August 2014. The Bar named the gallery in Peter O'Callaghan's honour that October.

Chrissie Foster, one of the people who blew the whistle about the Melbourne Response to the Royal Commission, was floored when I told her the gallery was named after O'Callaghan.

'*Why?* Why *him?*' Chrissie said, forcing the words out of her mouth like it hurt to form them.

O'Callaghan convinced Chrissie's family not to go to the police, saying he'd have to discontinue the Melbourne Response compensatory process if her family reported their two daughters' abuse by paedophile priest Kevin O'Donnell.

O'Callaghan told the Royal Commission he had a 'complete anathema for clerical sexual abuses' and 'would welcome people taking those miscreants to court'.

But Chrissie's family's experience wasn't an isolated communication breakdown or a one-off error.

Judy Courtin did a doctoral thesis into the Catholic Church and whether its victims found justice – completed in 2015 – during the Royal Commission. She says O'Callaghan had a 'marked impact on these victims'.

'The interviewees,' Judy told me, 'said they felt very "uncomfortable", "intimidated", "victimised", "demoralised", "daunted", "caged-in", "confronted", "distressed", "deeply disempowered", and "frightened" by the Independent Commissioner.

'For many,' Courtin continues, 'having an experienced and elderly QC in that position meant victims were out of their comfort zone and on guard.

'One female victim likened her experience with the Independent Commissioner with that of her confessor when she was a child. She said: "I felt I was a little girl again having to confess my sins to the priest. Now the priest is a QC, but he wanted to know everything ... [and] asked some really probing questions."'

Courtin continues, 'One female interviewee concluded that the Church was "trying to close it all down, keep it quiet". [He] caged me in every way he possibly could ... every angle I tried to come from ... where I could get some sort of acknowledgement from the Church, some understanding, he was able to put a lid on ... He discouraged me in every way possible ... I [c]ame out of there thinking there was no point me doing anything as there is no way I can get any resolution."'

Despite O'Callaghan's best efforts to convince it to the contrary, the Royal Commission was not kind to his legacy. It found that while he upheld 97 per cent of the 351 complaints he had heard, he discouraged victims from making police reports and that was 'not appropriate'. It found he told them if they did go to the police, their attempts to get compensation from the Church would be terminated. He helpfully reminded victims their cases were weak, referred to the 'haziness of [their] recollections', doubted their predators would see further jail terms.

The Victorian Parliament's Inquiry into the Handling of Child Abuse by Religious and Other Institutions also found in its

Betrayal of Trust report that of the 154 files it reviewed, there was no evidence that O'Callaghan had encouraged victims to go to police in ninety-three of them. 'Thirty-six were identified as those where there was no seemingly justifiable reason for the Independent Commissioner not recommending a referral to police.'

While victims had the right to have the Church pay their legal costs for the Melbourne Response, O'Callaghan didn't inform many of them of that because he 'didn't feel it necessary'.

One of those victims was Julie Stewart.

Julie remembers O'Callaghan coming to her home in a working-class suburb of outer Melbourne.

'He was concerned about his car parked out the front of the house.'

'What, because someone might steal it?' I ask.

'Yep,' Julie shoots back, 'I know, right?'

O'Callaghan didn't inform Julie that the Church could pay her legal fees for her contested hearing in the Melbourne Response.

In that contested hearing, she was vigorously cross-examined by her abuser's lawyer, with the abuser who still terrified her sitting just metres away along the table. She remembers O'Callaghan presiding over the hearing, for what it was, sitting across from them.

'I thought about the victims in a murder trial,' she tells me. 'The person's dead. They don't have to relive being killed, but we do. Over and over. I remember thinking that a murder trial's easier than this.

'I was twenty-two at the time – it was horrific. It's like you are alive, and you're having an autopsy done on you.'

O'Callaghan did believe Julie. And she, like many victims I have spoken to, found him superficially pleasant enough. But once he upheld her claim, he referred it to a compensation panel administered by the scheme. For her lifetime of pain, the panel awarded Julie the princely sum of $25,000. Once she received it, she then gave $3500 to her lawyer and used $1800 to repay her psychologist. She was required to sign a deed of release that she took to mean she was not allowed to speak of it to anyone, and which prevented her from suing the Church. The Victorian Government would, many years later, in 2019, legislate to overturn these unfair deeds.

Between its inception in 1996 and 2014, the Melbourne Response paid almost $7.8 million to Peter O'Callaghan. The entire sum it paid to all of the victims of paedophile priests it compensated was $9.7 million. The average sum received by the survivors was $32,000. And, to put it into focus, what O'Callaghan earned in one year from the scheme was fourteen times more than Julie was compensated for her ruined life.

Julie Stewart's situation was not atypical. The scheme set up by the church with O'Callaghan at the helm, and a solicitor from the firm Corrs Chambers Westgarth, was not financially generous. Its compensation was capped at $50,000, for say, anal rape by a creepy priest in a draughty presbytery at the age of eight and the ensuing misery it caused.

'People were urging the Archbishop ... that parishioners did not "put money in the plate" each Sunday in order to pay for the criminal acts of priests,' O'Callaghan told the Royal Commission.

'As an institution, I don't understand how you can accept that a person behaved like that,' Glenn Davies, the former head of the Victorian Sexual Crimes Squad, told me. 'I don't understand it.'

Davies had crossed swords with O'Callaghan in the Victorian Parliament's Inquiry into the Handling of Child Abuse by Religious and Other Institutions.

'He knew that these people [the paedophile clergy] had committed these offences. He knew they were guilty, and he didn't even encourage reporting and he didn't go to police,' Davies says.

'For him to be held up as some sort of champion or some sort of role model for barristers or for the judiciary, it's disgraceful.'

Chrissie Foster's daughter Emma suicided because of the abuse. Her other daughter, Katie, is permanently disabled after she ran into the path of an oncoming car as she self-medicated to deal with the pain of what happened to her. Chrissie and her late husband, Anthony, campaigned tirelessly to expose the Church's appalling response.

Chrissie's voice is scratchy and weary on the phone when we discuss the Peter O'Callaghan QC Gallery.

'As the parent of victims, it's highly insulting,' she says. 'I don't like it, but what can I do? It's their little club. I'm nobody.

'The Victorian Bar, they're right up "there" and I'm nothing. So what can I say about it?

'But personally,' her voice breaks, 'I think it's outrageous. Why was it done? Why? Why glorify Peter O'Callaghan?'

* * *

Allan Myers QC is another Victorian Western District Catholic boy made good. Myers represented O'Callaghan and Cardinal George Pell in the Royal Commission.

Writing an obituary for O'Callaghan in the *Victorian Bar News* Winter 2020 edition, Myers said of his 'decent, compassionate, wise and just' friend that, 'Peter was subjected to entirely unfounded and unfair criticism for the work he undertook as the independent commissioner. This criticism was very hurtful to him.' Myers had donated the money for the Bar to commission celebrated artist Rick Amor to paint O'Callaghan. The news of the donation was announced in the *Victorian Bar News'* Winter 2017 edition, released on 30 June.

The O'Callaghan portrait was completed just in time for the release of the Royal Commission's final report.

The Victorian Bar's president at the time was Matt Collins QC – he gave a speech at the unveiling of the portrait, as he did with every other painting hung in the gallery. But he has no special memory of it.

'If there was a coincidence of timing between the unveiling of the portrait, which occurred while I was president of the Bar, and the Royal Commission, I was oblivious to it,' Collins says. 'I can understand why it may make for a good story, but it is no more than a coincidence.

'The reason for having a portrait in the gallery was no more than that Peter was a venerated, senior member of the Bar, so much so that the gallery had been named after him, and there was a desire to honour him by commissioning and unveiling his portrait while he was still alive.'

I actually discovered the gallery's existence because Collins – who is young, ferociously talented and urbane – was talking to me about diversity.

Collins' passion while president was encouraging more women, people of colour and LGBTIQ lawyers to the ranks of the Bar. He wanted to champion these people and, in order to do so, commissioned a series of black and white photographs of barristers which showed just how much things are changing.

When he said it was in the Peter O'Callaghan gallery, I did a little double take. I thought I'd heard incorrectly, or that perhaps there was some other Peter O'Callaghan I didn't know about. But, sure enough, it was him.

For victims of sexual crimes, the unquestioning decision to use O'Callaghan's name for their gallery speaks volumes about the Victorian Bar's attitude to victims of sexual crimes.

As one prosecutor, who is not permitted to put his name to comments on the record, said to me, 'You walk into chambers, and you see these portraits of these men on the walls and there is this heroic perception of these men.

'And I just don't really accept that they are heroes. But it's a received wisdom at the Bar.'

Barrister Kathleen Foley says most women advocates she knows hate walking through the gallery. In May 2018, when she was on the Diversity and Inclusion Working Group of the Victorian Bar, she objected to an email from the Peter O'Callaghan Gallery Foundation, which noted that it had unveiled three new portraits in the past year. All three on the list were men.

The email said in that past year the Foundation had commissioned four portraits and a group photography piece of 700 barristers. The five subjects of the four portraits were men. The Foundation had been donated eight portraits – all except one were men.

'I've received a mini-barrage of emails already this morning,' Foley wrote, 'about the email below – mostly making the obvious point that the Foundation has commissioned eight portraits of men and not a single one of a woman.

'Given the sea of male faces one sees when one walks into the Peter O'Callaghan Gallery, I would have thought commissioning portraits of women to even up the balance would be a priority for the Foundation.'

In a later email she wrote, 'For my part, and for many women I know, the gender bias is more than apparent from walking through the gallery.'

The Bar has said that it has difficulty raising the funds for the portraits, that men are more forthcoming in offering portraits of themselves, that it plans to commission more portraits of women. Walking through the place, you can see why Foley and other women barristers feel as they do.

But it's an even more profound feeling for survivors of sexual crimes. I ask current Victorian Bar president Wendy Harris QC about how the gallery's name makes survivors feel.

'I feel sad for them for all sorts of reasons ... that I can't even begin to describe,' Harris says of the survivors. 'But I don't see a connection.

'The gallery wasn't named for Peter either because or in spite of his brief for the Catholic Church. And it would be quite wrong of us to do that, I think, to make judgements – because of the cab rank rule.'

The cab rank rule means barristers must take a brief as if they were a taxi on a rank, not inquiring into who they are driving or where they are going, as it were, before they accept the fare.

'We are taxicabs,' Wendy Harris says. 'For barristers, a brief is a brief, if we have the capacity to do it and the client's willing to pay our brief, we do it. Many people think that banks are evil. But I have no hesitation in working for banks because I'm obliged to.

'I'm a taxicab waiting for someone to hop in the back seat. And it would be terrible if the same logic were applied because I had acted for banks, many of whom were lambasted in the Royal Commission, that that somehow tarnished my legacy, that wouldn't be fair.'

'Everyone I've ever cross-examined presumably hates me and would think it grotesque for my portrait to be hung in a gallery,' Matt Collins says.

'That kind of goes with the territory. A well-rounded person can't be defined by the people they have represented.'

Collins is not defending the Melbourne Response *per se*.

'It may well be an appalling scheme, I assume it is,' he says. 'But to say that the barrister engaged by the Church is therefore the evil architect of the whole thing, and to be equated with the Church itself, is a big leap that cannot be taken.'

Whatever way O'Callaghan's behaviour over that twenty years is viewed by history, Collins also doesn't support rewriting history every time society changes its values.

'Personally, I am not in favour of pulling down statues or renaming institutions because of shifting societal values. The cab rank rule is one of our most important principles at the Bar, and that is one of the reasons why I am sensitive to these kinds of criticisms,' Collins says. 'I've acted for cigarette companies and coal mines and lots of unfashionable and unpopular people and companies. None of that says anything about my personal values, except that I honour the cab rank rule – I believe that everyone, no matter how diabolical, has the right to proper representation.

'To try and equate someone's personal values to those of a client that they have represented is terribly unfair to the individual. What would I have done if [sacked homophobic rugby player] Israel Folau had asked me to act for him – someone who apparently believes I am destined to burn in eternal damnation?'

Collins is a gay man.

'The answer is I would have acted for him.'

I remember how the cab rank rule was drummed into us when I was at law school. It seemed an utterly noble and honourable thing that, no matter how vile a client might seem or be, they were entitled to a proper defence because the presumption of innocence was golden.

But from a non-lawyer's perspective, to equate O'Callaghan's role in the Melbourne Response to the cab rank rule seems artificial. It's like a cab driver picked up a passenger and ferried that same passenger around the same city for twenty years.

And the Royal Commission made specific findings about the 'cab driver' himself – about his own conduct, not just that of his client, the Melbourne Archdiocese. It's a bit different from Wendy Harris turning up to court to diligently do her job, only to be unfairly associated with greedy banks, or Matt Collins spinning an argument on behalf of a cigarette company and being blamed for health hazards caused by smoking.

As a barrister, O'Callaghan was, like all legal practitioners, an officer of the court. What that term practically means was enunciated by Lord Reid in the British House of Lords in the famous *Rondel v Worsley* case in 1969: '[A]s an officer of the court concerned in the administration of justice, [a legal practitioner] has an overriding duty to the court, to the standards of his profession, and to the public, which may and often does lead to a conflict with his client's wishes.'

In 2009, then Victorian Supreme Court Chief Justice Marilyn Warren spoke of the duty of an officer of the court in a speech to the Judicial Conference of Australia Colloquium. 'The practitioner's role is not merely to push his or her client's interests in the adversarial process, rather the practitioner has a duty to "assist the court in the doing of justice according to law". The duty requires that lawyers act with honesty, candour and competence, exercise independent judgment in the conduct of the case, and not engage in conduct that is an abuse of process ...

'The lawyer's duty to the administration of justice goes to ensure the integrity of the rule of law. It is incumbent upon lawyers to bear in mind their role in the legal process and how the role might further the ultimate public interest in that process, that is, the proper administration of justice.'

For me at least, discouraging complainants of child sexual abuse perpetrated by clergy from going to the police rests somewhat uneasily with the duty to the proper administration of justice.

The late Justice Philip Cummins in his 2012 Report of the Protecting Victoria's Vulnerable Children Inquiry also looked at the Melbourne Response and O'Callaghan's role. While Justice Cummins did not make any adverse findings about whether the scheme acted faithfully according to its own criteria, he said, 'the fundamental issue is that the processing of crimes against children should be the subject of state process'.

O'Callaghan told the Cummins Inquiry that the imposition of an obligation to refer a crime against a child to police would be 'draconian' and it was 'the victim's right to complain to the police and to have a say as to whether or not a complaint should be made'.

'The Inquiry considers that, in the long term, the potential discomfort or distress to an individual victim caused by the mandatory reporting of the alleged abuse will be outweighed by public interest in triggering a criminal justice response that holds the perpetrator publicly responsible and aims at deterring potential abusers from using the cover of large organisations and positions of authority or influence over children to commit abuse. The public criminal process would also have a significant public educative effect ...'

And later: 'A private system of investigation and compensation, no matter how faithfully conducted, by definition cannot fulfil the responsibility of the State to investigate and prosecute crime. Crime is a public, not a private, matter. The substantial number of established complaints of clerical sexual abuse found by Mr O'Callaghan (many of which are likely to relate to offences committed against children), reveal a profound harm and any private process that attempts to address that harm should be publicly assessed.'

When discussing the Melbourne Response, Cummins recommended an amendment to the *Crimes Act* to 'create a separate reporting duty where there is a reasonable suspicion a child or young person who is under 18 is being, or has been, physically or sexually abused by an individual within a religious or spiritual organisation'. The duty would have specifically covered O'Callaghan as it referred to '[a] person who holds an office within, is employed, is a member of, or a volunteer of a religious or spiritual organisation'.

These recommendations and those by the later *Betrayal of Trust* report by the Victorian Parliament led to a change in the law in 2014. That legislative reform required mandatory reporting to police in circumstances including those O'Callaghan would have been in when he received information from children about living priests.

Barrister Patrick Noonan, who appeared for an institution accused of covering up child abuse in the Royal Commission, thinks there is a 'very valid argument' that O'Callaghan's behaviour was not consistent with his duty as an officer of the court.

'And the Peter O'Callaghan Gallery occupies the main public entrance to Victorian Bar premises,' Noonan says. 'It ought to be the place to showcase the best of the Bar and Peter O'Callaghan is an odd choice on any view; others to have premises prominently named after them are eminent jurists or legal pioneers.'

Noonan is sure that the Victorian Bar would not have been aware of all the findings of the Royal Commission (crucially, Matt Collins as president was not – and the decision to name the gallery was made by his predecessor, the decision to add the painting was made by a committee), but, of those who did, Noonan says, 'You'd think it would have been a red flag that O'Callaghan presided over a system that became so notorious it was a factor in governments calling a state inquiry and a Royal Commission; and resulted in settlement outcomes considered so unjust that the state has since legislated to allow them to be overturned.'

Noonan thinks there are plenty of other worthy people in the Bar's history after whom the gallery could have been named instead of O'Callaghan.

'There must have at least been *one* person in the history of the Bar whose efforts didn't result in a Royal Commission and legislation to overturn the unjust consequences of their work,' he says.

Judy Courtin quotes the gallery's aim to 'act as a source of inspiration for future generations of barristers'.

'If future generations of barristers were to speak with victims of clergy child sex crimes who had relied on Mr O'Callaghan's investigations and finding,' Courtin begins, 'they may well question why such a prestigious gallery is named in this man's honour.'

The fact that many criminal barristers I have interviewed for this book haven't read the final report of the Royal Commission, despite its very careful analysis of how the criminal justice system affected the complainants they find themselves cross-examining, says something. Shouldn't these people be the most invested in what is being proposed to change the system in which they operate every day? Wouldn't they be curious? For a profession that is notoriously gossipy, it seems strange to me that so many I have called didn't know that the Royal Commission found O'Callaghan discouraged victims from going to police.

To me, the fact that it never even occurred to the Bar that naming their gallery after O'Callaghan might offend anyone speaks volumes. While far from an unreconstructed villain, and a man who was loved by many and in other ways someone who had left a positive legacy, he was someone who had also caused distress, and who profited richly from a system that professed to help victims, but really retraumatised and silenced them.

It says things about how the Bar sees victims. Or how it *doesn't* see them. When it comes to talking about victims, I've often found barristers switch off. They go silent. There's a feeling that they don't want to know, but they don't want to show that they don't want to know. They listen patiently, then they change the subject.

Their responses often range from clearly pained and empathetic but not quite knowing what to say, to stiff and cold and legalistic, to paternalistic and heartless. Victims seem to be a problem for barristers. They don't quite know where to put them. They know their system doesn't treat them well and they don't know quite what to do with that.

I often come away from conversations with barristers feeling that they see victims as people whose unwieldy expectations have to be managed. In their genuinely noble commitment to the presumption of innocence, there is often a sense that protection of the rights of the accused is a higher pursuit. Protection of the rights of victims is associated with the low-brow – the stuff of tabloid sentimentality. It's *expected*. It lacks nuance and substance.

They frequently make comments like, 'Look, they may well feel that way, but that's certainly not the intention.' 'Look, the decision [to acquit their perpetrator] is a sign of the system working as it should.' 'Look, they should take comfort in the fact that just because it wasn't found beyond reasonable doubt doesn't mean it didn't happen.' 'Look, no one is saying the system is perfect, but it's the best one we've got.'

Perhaps it can't ever be perfect, but it seems to me that it can be better.

* * *

I tell this story because it is emblematic of a problem that the Bar is facing across the country – that it is dominated by older white men and what that means for the women and children who face them in the criminal justice system. It's a problem also exemplified by the stories of systemic harassment of women lawyers by Dyson Heydon while he was a High Court justice, as acknowledged by

an independent investigation commissioned by the High Court –
perhaps the most compelling so far of the Australian #MeToo cases.
That Heydon, who was at the NSW Bar, could get away with what he
did for so long, and rise to the very pinnacle of the legal profession,
hiding in plain sight, says a lot about the power structures in the law.
About what is taken seriously. About whose voices are valued.

An independent High Court investigation found Heydon
sexually harassed six former staff members, and the fearless
journalism of *The Sydney Morning Herald*'s Kate McClymont and
Jacqueline Maley has uncovered many more complaints against
him. He has denied the allegations.

Former President of the NSW Bar Association Jane Needham
SC says she has heard many stories of sexual harassment about
male barristers and judges from women members of the profession.
She told *Guardian Australia* that when she began encouraging
barristers' chambers to implement sexual harassment complaints
procedures, she 'was phoned by one indignant head of chambers
who said: "We don't need that, we're all gentlemen here."'

'"Why don't women complain?" has an answer,' Needham
wrote in an opinion piece in *The Sydney Morning Herald* the week
the Heydon scandal broke in June 2020. 'It lies in the imbalance
of power. Most judges, senior partners and senior counsel are
men who generally have no experience of the impact of sexual
harassment or abuse in women's lives.'

In the two weeks after the High Court investigation findings
about Heydon were exposed, Needham tells me that she received
fifteen sexual harassment complaints from women lawyers about
New South Wales barristers or judges – an average of one every
day. The feedback she received from some of the older male
members of the Bar? 'We're going to have to protect ourselves
against false complaints.'

She tells one anecdote about a senior barrister complaining to
her that he wouldn't be able to tell jokes anymore. When she asked
him what sort of jokes he meant, he volunteered jokes like when
his secretary was asking for something, he would make her ask on
her knees.

When Needham suggested he not tell that joke anymore, the
barrister insisted, 'She thinks it's funny!'

'Yes, and she's dependent on you for a job and an income,' Needham was forced to remind him.

Needham agrees that this sort of attitude can't help but inform how some of these men treat the women, children and male complainants of historical crimes whom they cross-examine in sex trials.

'I do think there is a real lack of comprehension of the kinds of trauma that people have suffered,' Needham tells me. 'It doesn't surprise me that the difficulties that I've observed men at the Bar in reacting sensitively, and with care and empathy, to allegations of sexual harassment then feeds into those people having a disrespectful attitude to complainants in the witness box,' she says.

Like all barristers, she appreciates that there is a need for defence counsel to demonstrate that a witness in a criminal trial is not believable beyond reasonable doubt, but, she says, 'You have to unpick the difference between doing that job and treating the complainant with a degree of negativity and derision.'

It's instructive, then, to look at the statistics on what sort of people make up the Bar.

Fifty-one per cent of the legal profession is made up of women, and law schools are turning out bright young things at a rate of knots, but still, at the Bar, gender and age diversity is very much wanting.

Of all the barristers working in our two most populous states – New South Wales and Victoria – one in four are men who have already reached their sixtieth birthday.

'When I was president of the Bar,' Matt Collins says, 'I thought of it, over-simplistically, as having two halves. About 50 per cent of the barristers were fifty years old and younger, with close to a 50–50 gender split, and overwhelmingly, though not entirely, progressive.

'For many in that cohort, change cannot happen fast enough. Many of them would tell me that they found any focus on the traditions of the Bar a bit cloying.

'The other 50 per cent of the Bar are aged over fifty – now what profession in the world has that?'

Collins says the over-fifties set skews 'about 80–20 male'.

'[That's] because of historic male over-representation, women being appointed to judicial office at rates disproportionate to their number, and the fact that there is no retirement age for barristers. There are practising barristers in Melbourne who are in their eighties.'

Now, while this is a great thing for combating ageism, it can't help but affect the thinking of the overall profession.

'Many in that cohort would tell me that anything that the Bar did, anything that I did, that was about diversity and inclusion, was just wrong-headed, that the proper role of the head of the Bar is to get work for barristers and to uphold its traditions,' Collins says.

Collins made it his mission to try to force change.

'Knowledge is power, in my view. I released publicly everything we did, holding nothing back, even when it reflected badly on the Bar. Transparency is important. I thought it was a way of blowing fresh air into the place.'

'That's the only way that you are going to stop things like describing forced oral sex of a child as "plain vanilla sexual penetration"?' I ask him, in reference to the now-infamous phrase used by Robert Richter QC in a sentencing submission when describing the crime of forced oral rape of a teenager, a phrase for which Richter later apologised as being a terrible choice of words.

'Yep,' Collins succinctly replies.

'That just can't happen anymore,' I venture.

'That's right,' says Collins. 'There's a broader societal shift going on. Barristers should be, if anything, finely attuned to that because they are generally intelligent and interested in the world and we see what's going on.

'But it's like everywhere else in society, there are still some – particularly older, white men – who have views that make them cultural dinosaurs.'

He continues, 'I just thought you had to have the policies in place to ensure that it is clear that the Bar has a no-tolerance approach to issues such as discrimination, sexual harassment and bullying. And then try to create a safe space where barristers were empowered to call out bad conduct when they saw it.

'For example, in the sexual discrimination area, I had women barristers say to me that they were on a floor of mostly male barristers who would go to lunch at the Melbourne Club, where only men are allowed. I thought that was just unacceptable in 2018.'

It's not such a huge leap to think that a man who thinks it's okay to exclude the women on his floor when choosing a lunch venue might also have some antiquated views and practices when it comes to how to treat women in general.

'Cultural change is frustratingly glacial,' Collins says, 'but the arc is trending in the right direction.'

He tries to 'not get mired in pessimism'.

'In 1981 there was one woman silk, and there hadn't been any women Supreme Court judges,' he says. 'We're now at, what, about 40 per cent women Supreme Court judges and 50 per cent on the County Court, more than 50 per cent coming into the Bar are women. I mean, that is actually, in the arc of history, remarkable progress.

'But there are legacy issues. Of course there are.'

Victoria's statistics are improving, but still not great. New South Wales is far worse. There, a sexual assault complainant like, say, Saxon Mullins, can expect to be cross-examined by a man and, further, not a young man.

Just 23 per cent of the 2413 barristers in New South Wales are women. To put that in perspective, 48 per cent of the NSW Bar is made up of men aged fifty and above. So there are more than twice as many barristers who are aged fifty-plus than women of *any* age.

'[It's] a culture that is, I think, generally more combative and less collegiate than ours. Progress is commensurately more difficult,' Collins says of the NSW Bar.

'And the thing about that is,' I counter, 'that that can only translate to the court context, the way things play out in court?'

'Of course,' Collins replies.

'Remember too, that judges in superior courts, close to 100 per cent were barristers. More than 90 per cent were silk. And silk in Melbourne, we're still at only 16 per cent women silk.'

'Silks' are more formally known as Queen's Counsel (QC), or the modern iteration, Senior Counsel (SC). These are, in Commonwealth countries including Australia, the most senior and best-paid barristers. Barristers apply to 'take silk' – known as such because of the silk robes with fancy rosettes that they wear once they are appointed.

So the number of women who are appointed as silks, still quite scandalously low, has profound implications for who makes decisions about law in Australia, and, by extension, for the experience of everyone in courts – especially, it could be argued, the women and children who come before them as victims.

Men make up 88 per cent of silks in New South Wales and are the ones who, if you are accusing a high-profile or well-resourced defendant as Saxon Mullins did, you are likely to find yourself facing. Of the 451 New South Wales barristers who say they take on sex crime briefs, fewer than a quarter of them – 109 – are women. And just 1 per cent of those women are silks.

This has implications for law reform as well as for styles of cross-examination.

Politician Trevor Khan is now a member of the New South Wales Legislative Council, but used to be a solicitor advocate in country New South Wales, meaning he appeared for clients in courts as a barrister does. Khan says he has been frustrated by the incredibly conservative nature of the legal profession in his state.

He was on the Family Issues Committee for the Law Society – the peak body for solicitors – for six years before entering parliament, and says he found the position, 'almost without exception', 'was to oppose *any* reform'. Khan says he struggled to convince them that they should be more constructive, that they couldn't just keep saying 'no' all the time.

'But, really, the Law Society and the Bar Association are extraordinarily conservative on law reform,' Khan says.

'When we were pushing through reforms on the law of provocation in regard to domestic violence murders and on homosexual advance defence [this was the old common law precedent that allowed that a person could be acquitted of a crime if they were "provoked" by a person making a homosexual advance], the Bar Association and the Law Society opposed those reforms!

'It was bizarre,' Khan says. 'There was no reason why you should be able to get off with manslaughter to those sorts of crimes and yet, in both of those areas, the Law Society and the Bar Association opposed it.'

The New South Wales women talk about how things are better in Victoria – 30 per cent of Victorian barristers are women, and of those who say they do crime work, 39 per cent are female.

As it happens, Wendy Harris QC points out, Peter O'Callaghan can take some of the thanks for why the barriers to women joining the Victorian Bar were reduced. In the 1950s, some barristers got together and formed a company that bought the building that houses Owen Dixon Chambers. O'Callaghan was, later, the chairman of the committee that bought the building next door – Owen Dixon West – to expand the space. They chose to offer tenancy for barristers on a month to month basis – a system unparalleled in the common law world.

It meant that people taking the great leap into self-employment (barristers are not employed by firms) could take maternity leave without having to worry about paying rent for their chambers. It meant that Victorian barristers didn't need to stump up a large sum of cash to get started – known as 'key money' – which is essentially like a sizeable deposit on a house. For the fancier and most sought-after Sydney chambers, this requires an outlay of about $450,000.

'It is the single greatest foundation upon which our Bar is based. Because it breaks down those barriers to entry,' Harris says. 'It means that I can give up my chambers on thirty days' notice if they become too expensive, if I want to go and have a baby. Or, if I want to go and have a baby, I will get subsidised, by the Bar, while I go off on my maternity leave. Commercial landlords don't offer those kinds of terms.

'And what that has meant, in practical terms, is much greater diversity, much greater ability to support women at the Bar, much greater support of minorities.

'It's not hard to see that if you have a diversity of approaches and not just cookie-cutter table-thumpers – and I'm not talking about anyone specifically here – then almost inevitably, yes, you're going to find different ways home, aren't you?'

But when sorted into seniority, most of the women in Victoria are more junior barristers.

While 10 per cent of the men practising criminal law at the Victorian Bar have taken silk, only 1.3 per cent of women criminal barristers have earned that distinction.

Julie Condon QC is one of the handful of women criminal silks practising.

'I think that old chestnut of not having enough confidence in themselves,' she says, proffering part of the reason her sisterly silken ranks are so thin. 'Oh for the confidence of a middle-aged man!

'I put in my application when I was forty-six. I think there would have been plenty of guys who would have put in for silk at the age of forty-two with the practice I had at that time.

'Look, it's a conservative profession. For so long we've had private school boys who went to Melbourne Grammar, whose dads were judges or barristers and who just felt that this was their destiny. But I do think that things are slowly shifting from those days.'

I'm continually told that governments are keen to appoint women to judicial office to combat perceptions of sexism and patriarchy on the bench and that has led, in Victoria in particular, to a dearth of women senior counsel.

'I had an analysis done because I was interested in it,' Matt Collins says, 'what would the composition of the Bar in Victoria be if no one had been appointed to the bench, male or female, since 2000?'

'It would have had the result of roughly doubling the proportion of female silks.'

Condon says she doesn't have children and doesn't know how she would do it if she did. 'If you are a woman and you have kids,' she says, 'it's almost irresistible to take up a judicial appointment. It's a lot less work, fewer hours, salaried, reliable. That's hard to turn down.'

Condon was one of those talented women barristers appointed to the bench, but she didn't enjoy it, and asked to leave after nineteen months.

She, like Matt Collins and Wendy Harris, likes to be optimistic about the future.

'I can feel evolution,' Condon says, with a smile. 'I have a very strong sense that times are changing. I am very confident that in twenty years' time, the make-up of the criminal Bar will be very, very different from what it is now and, hopefully, some of those women will be declining judicial appointments and sticking around to take silk.'

I really want to believe her. For women coming to court as witnesses and accused. And for the excellent women I know who are at the Bar. But there are still good reasons why it is difficult for women to go to the Bar in the first place, or to stay there.

Because women barristers get no maternity leave, time out of a notoriously clubby workforce means missing out on briefs. When you are trying to build up your practice, taking a year or six months out can have a chilling effect on your ability to get briefs and make money when you return.

One female silk in Sydney said while women might work part-time after their first baby, to do it after their second, too, is incredibly difficult at the very time they are trying to make a name for themselves. 'They often just decide they want a guaranteed income after baby number two,' the silk says, 'and so they go to work for a law firm as a solicitor in a salaried position.'

And what does this male skewing of an extremely privileged and powerful workforce mean? It means a male culture that has been loath to make meaningful changes.

It means Dyson Heydon – not to mention all the other barristers Jane Needham has been hearing about – getting away with what's alleged by so many women for so many years. And those women feeling powerless to make accusations.

It means Dyson Heydon saying in a textbook about the law of evidence used by generations of law students, of children and sexual offending: 'Children sometimes behave in a way evil beyond their years. They may consent to sexual offences against themselves and then deny consent. They may completely invent sexual offences.

'Some children know that the adult world regards such matters in a serious and particular way, and they enjoy investigating this mystery or revenging themselves by making false accusations.'

Yes, he wrote it in 1984, but it still speaks absolute volumes. I find it hard to imagine a female judge saying the same.

It means Dyson Heydon dissented on a 2012 judgement in the High Court which upheld a conviction of rape in marriage. The reasons of the other six judges of the court went for sixty-five paragraphs. Heydon's long-winded reasons for excusing the man for raping his wife because, in his view, the law could not be retrospectively applied, went for 183 paragraphs.

It means younger me at the Supreme Court Library, climbing a ladder to find an old law report, only to look down and catch two older barristers shamelessly peering up my skirt. Or, during the same stint at a law firm, men referring to the 'sexetaries' at the Christmas party and me being warned to keep myself nice. Jane Needham has similar memories of sexist behaviour of her young days at the Bar – she was shocked, in the aftermath of the Heydon revelations, that this stuff was still happening to young women.

It means that when the subject of a well-known female criminal barrister comes up in the company of one of her colleagues, he says, 'she's been very, very successful and she is a very hard worker', but, he adds, unable to help himself, 'I just wish she'd brush her hair every now and then'.

He knows he's being sexist – in fact, he volunteers that fact with a chortle, but he just can't help throwing it in there for good measure.

It means forced oral rape of a teenager being described as 'plain vanilla sexual penetration'.

Or Court of Appeal Justice Mark Weinberg thinking an allegation of a person, with other people nearby, grabbing a boy by the genitals in an open corridor was taking 'brazenness to new heights' in a way that was 'implausible'. Ask the women in your life, Your Honour, how often men do this sort of thing to women. It is no surprise that those so inclined might also do it to boys.

It means a barrister asking me, mid-phone interview, 'Tell me now, are you a good-looking woman?' I'm at a loss for words, so I tell him to ask a mutual acquaintance. He replies, sometime later, with a thumbs-up emoji.

It means teenage Saxon Mullins being repeatedly referred to in the witness box as 'Madam'.

It means Peter O'Callaghan has a gallery named after him and no one gave it a second thought.

THE RAT

'It's being ground to bits in a slow mill; it's being roasted
at a slow fire; it's being stung to death by single bees; it's
being drowned by drops; it's going mad by grains.'
TOM JARNDYCE ON THE COURT OF CHANCERY, *BLEAK HOUSE*, CHARLES DICKENS

Some of the steeliest advocates I have met in my twenty years as a journalist covering legal cases have been women. And some of the kindest people I have spoken to in my research for this book are older male lawyers. Women are not always, by definition, warm and empathetic. Older men are not necessarily sexist, pompous or cruel.

That said, there is an inner circle of older blokes that prompt the more reasonable barristers to roll their eyes.

'The old thumpers of the bar table, yelling and screaming at the witnesses, that style has gone out of fashion,' says Ian Lloyd QC, who cross-examined Saxon Mullins.

Lloyd, like most barristers, will tell you that the table-thumpers are now few and far between.

'As the questioner, you want to be the ringmaster, but if you yell and scream at the witness, jurors get their backs up,' Lloyd says. 'And if they don't like the advocate, they don't like the cause.'

But it seems to me that if, as a barrister, you cut your teeth at a time when retraumatising witnesses and going on the offensive is what got you results, it will be harder to change your ways.

The women, children and grown-up boys who come to tell their grim stories of sexual crimes may well find themselves meeting a man – particularly if the accused is well-resourced – who learned his craft at a time when what was acceptable in terms of cross-examining victims of sexual crimes was vastly different.

Philip Dunn QC is a Melbourne barrister of a 'certain age' and he remembers being a 'table-thumper' in the past. He's now known for his skills of gently coaxing a witness into making admissions against their own interest.

'In a sex case what you're looking for is the RAT,' Dunn tells me, 'the Rival Alternative Theory,' he says. 'And the RAT is another explanation for the facts. Not necessarily that black is white, but that black may not be black.'

'Could be charcoal?' I offer.

'It could be pale black,' he shoots back.

The Dunn school of thought is that it's much better to achieve your aims through gentle nuance than with a blunt instrument. Get the witness to like you and coax admissions from her accordingly. Catch her off guard. Bedazzle the jury. Far from thumping the table or bullying the witness, Dunn is the sort of super-smooth, gentlemanly advocate who charms the birds out of the trees, who, in the words of an old political press secretary I once knew, could 'make you eat shit and think that it's strawberry jam'. When barristers are suggesting someone I should talk to who knows how to do it 'right' – that is, without unnecessarily traumatising a witness – they often tell me I should call Phil Dunn.

He is, of course, immortalised in the O'Callaghan gallery, in one of the better portraits in the collection, by Melbourne artist Martin Tighe. It's of Dunn and Robert Richter QC, and styled after Rembrandt. The two men are pools of light in a sea of black chiaroscuro. Caught in a courtroom moment, they look back at the viewer, the use of light and shade 'isolating the advocates', in the words of the artist, 'in the darkness of the trial'.

Richter is perched, like an owl, peering down through his glasses in disapproval, the way he might at an impertinent witness. Dunn, caught in a momentary glance, is an altogether softer presence in the painting. He's ever so slightly shambolic.

Phil Dunn tells a good yarn.

He's defended, he tells me, 'look, hundreds' of sex cases. Cases of men accused of sexual crimes – dodgy religious brothers, sleazy stepfathers, date rapists and creeps.

And in the old days, he readily admits, counsel like him would have a field day with the victims.

'You could cross-examine people about their sexual history,' Dunn says of his formative years at the Bar. 'The junior Bar used to say, how many bibles have you had thrown at you?'

Bibles are, of course, used in court proceedings when a witness swears an oath to God to tell the truth, the whole truth and nothing but the truth. Bibles flung across the courtroom were seen as badges of honour.

'Because the odd complainant would heave the bible at you in cross-examination, particularly at committals,' Dunn remembers. He explains that things often got down and dirty at committal, as they still do, because there was no jury to upset. You were trying to knock the whole thing out before it got to trial, and the mantra was 'whatever it takes'.

Nowadays, Victoria, like all Australian jurisdictions, has prohibited questions about 'the general reputation of the victim with respect to chastity' and, indeed, any questions about the victim's sexual history can only be asked with the permission of the judge – who has to weigh up the potential distress, humiliation and embarrassment to the victim and the possibility of discriminatory hostility in the jury.

But not back in the bible-throwing days of yore, when advocates like Dunn could go to town.

'This was in the days when you could ask questions like, "When did you last have intercourse?"' Dunn remembers.

If it did get to trial, and it was for a rape, Dunn says he would always try to get a largely female jury, skewing past middle age, because, in his experience, middle-aged and older women did a good line in moral judgement.

'The female jury [was] much harder on the complainants – much harder than the men,' Dunn says. 'And you'd always take them through the acts of intercourse – "and then you lay down, and then you opened your legs, and then you did this and then that, et cetera" ... So, in a sense, we blamed the victim.'

These barristers came through in an era of mandatory corroboration – that is, an era when the witness' testimony was not enough. It's not widely known outside the criminal legal fraternity that, in the 1990s, the requirement for mandatory corroboration – which used to form part of a judge's directions to the jury – was abolished.

Former Victorian Chief Crown Prosecutor, now defence barrister, Gavin Silbert SC, a friend of Dunn's, says the rule requiring mandatory corroboration 'was abolished for obvious reasons, because everyone was being acquitted'. He continues, 'Because there might not have been corroboration. Often there wasn't corroboration.'

Sex offenders – against adults or children – rarely commit their crimes with an audience present that might later come along to court and testify to the fact that the offence took place.

Now, courts have realised, and instruct juries on the basis that paedophiles and rapists don't tend to advertise their crimes.

But back before it changed, it was incredibly difficult to secure a conviction for a sex offence – especially when the defendant had the money to spend on a silk.

Sally Flynn QC does both defence and prosecution work – although much of her work on sexual matters has been on the prosecution side. She says many older male barristers 'grew up in the system when it was stacked against complainants and you can see that affects some of their thinking'.

'My dad was a police officer,' Flynn says, 'and he would say that back then, if a child was a complainant and the guy denied it, the brief wouldn't be authorised.'

'If you are a male barrister in your sixties or seventies, you have come through in an era where there were much longer cross-examinations of complainants, where you could not convict on the evidence of a child or on uncorroborated claims.

'I think it would be hard to change from that mindset to where we are now.'

'I'm very old and I've operated under both systems,' Gavin Silbert tells me over *raciones* and fashionably orange wine around the corner from the Supreme Court. 'And the way I used to do it in the early nineties wouldn't be the way I'd be doing it now.'

Silbert, who really isn't that old and has a hint of a smile even when he's being deadly serious, was a defence counsel for many years before he went to the Office of Public Prosecutions. He remembers well the days in the seventies, eighties, nineties, and even beyond, when skewering a complainant of a sexual offence – be it a savage rape, a ghastly act of paedophilia, a date gone wrong or otherwise – was thought to be the only way to go. It was thought to be not just effective, but completely acceptable.

'One has to be a lot more sensitive and a lot more empathetic and sympathetic and touchy-touchy, feely-feely now, rather than simply going in like a bulldog and trying to tear someone apart – there's no question about that,' he says. 'I mean, there was a time when you'd just try and eviscerate. And I don't think juries are impressed by that now.'

'So apart from juries not being impressed by it,' I venture, 'is that a purely sort of professional technical thing?'

I'm thinking this man who has always been helpful and decent, this man who has recently been running a campaign on welfare recipients ripped off by a government Robodebt scheme, a man who has, as prosecutor, had to mop up the trauma and the disappointment of complainants who have had a terrible time in the courts, this man will say 'no'. But he doesn't. He says, 'Yes, yes.'

So it's not about him having a road to Damascus conversion about treating people more nicely?

'No-no-no-no!' he replies, emphatically. 'If you are appearing for someone, you're trying to do the best you can for them. Come what may. I mean, we live in a different age. I just think you've got to judge the way juries react to things, and I don't think they react well to what they perceive as bullying of a vulnerable witness.'

I appreciate his honesty. I wonder whether he'd ever had a moment when, back in the bad old days when bullying vulnerable witnesses was de rigueur, when such behaviour was allowable and encouraged, did he ever go home and feel a teensy bit bad about what he'd done?

'I don't think I ever took it beyond doing a good job for the client,' Silbert replies, clear-eyed.

'Really?' I say, biting my lip, a little bit incredulous that this genial fellow could not feel bad about retraumatising victims.

It reminds me of a very decent man I know who is in the armed forces. 'How did you feel being behind those guns,' I once asked him, 'knowing that people on the other side of them would be killed?'

'I didn't think about it,' he replied with a shrug of his shoulders. 'We're trained not to think about it.'

I didn't believe him. 'Come *on*,' I needled. 'You can't be serious – you must have thought about it once or twice?'

But he really hadn't. He slept very soundly.

Silbert will allow me this: he doesn't think the complainants he was cross-examining were making it up.

'I mean, look, look, sometimes ... There are a number of occasions where I think juries have got it wrong,' he says. 'There's no question about that. And I must say the majority of cases would be when they've acquitted instead of convicted. I'm not conscious of wrongful convictions. Yeah. I'm just not conscious of that.'

Peter Morrissey SC has done some of the most bruising defence work at the Bar – including the trial of Robert Farquharson, the father who drove his boys into a dam and was found guilty of murder. Morrissey is a very decent guy and, for reasons many find hard to understand, he genuinely believes Farquharson was innocent and, in his words, 'that Robbie Farquharson trial *got* me'. He's also done a number of sex trials, including paedophile clergy.

Like Silbert, and, indeed, most barristers I interviewed for this book, Morrissey tells me that going in too hard these days on a complainant in a sex case is absolute folly.

'In today's world, bullying is an extraordinarily risky approach,' he says. 'Because the sympathies of the fact-finder, whether it's a magistrate or a jury, are very much with victims and with normal people.'

Morrissey is, like many barristers, a character. He loves a chat. His chambers, on the same floor as Phil Dunn's and Robert Richter's, are typically messy. I like him for that, as mine would be too. He is all but a teetotaller, yet because he seems like the kind of guy with whom you could enjoy a glass of red, his shelves are lined with unopened bottles from grateful clients. On a summer day when I go in to see him, pre-COVID isolation, he's wearing ratty tracksuit pants and sneakers. This is despite him readily admitting that barristers 'earn too much'.

He has a big heart, acting pro bono with a group of other barristers, led by Julian McMahon SC, for the reformed Bali 9 drug smugglers Andrew Chan and Myuran Sukumaran. That's how I first got to know Peter Morrissey, when I reported a series of stories for the ABC TV 7.30 program on the fight to try to save Chan and Sukumaran from execution.

During that awfully bleak time, I warmed to Morrissey immediately. He calls you 'comrade' and answers the phone 'Hallo pal!'. He's kind and smart and, most of all, trustworthy. Not slick, nor patronising, nor sexist. Not an egomaniac who spends his time finding 101 ways to tell you just how superlative he is at his job.

He's a social justice Catholic, which I had been brought up to be, although I had long since left. He'd sometimes sign off on our phone calls 'God bless' – whether that was to tease me or because he actually meant it, I'd roll my eyes, but I didn't really mind.

When I'm interviewing another lawyer for this book, I start waxing lyrical about what a good egg Peter Morrissey is. The lawyer I'm speaking to cuts in and interrupts me.

'You wouldn't want to be cross-examined by Peter Morrissey,' the lawyer says. He purses his lips and shakes his head. 'I'm telling you, you would not like it at all. Just so you know.'

* * *

There is a man whose name often comes up when lawyers are talking table-thumpers.

His name is John Desmond, and, at the time of writing, he has been at the Bar for thirty-five years.

'I think a table-thump during a closing address can be quite useful,' Desmond tells me.

'So you literally thump the table?' I ask him.

'Bloody oath, yep.'

Desmond is unabashedly 'old school'. Which doesn't mean that he is a villainous caricature. He is a character – calls you 'mate' as soon as he meets you, has a good sense of humour and has some fairly progressive views about how courts should be structured to better accommodate victims. He's up for a conversation, doesn't blanch at criticism, believes in what he does. And when he goes to court to represent a client accused of these crimes, he's not afraid to admit he goes to war.

'Yeah, stand 'em up, knock 'em down,' he says. 'That's the job!

'It's a trial – the guy's saying, "I'm not guilty, I didn't do it", so if it's child sex, nothing's happened. If it's adult sex, it either means, it was by consent, or nothing happened.

'And they're pretty significant allegations to be made against a bloke – I mean, gut-wrenching, for an innocent bloke, an innocent man. Stomach churns.

'So it's a confrontation.'

Desmond says what 'the punters' – his clients, the accused sex offenders – love, is 'the sound of their barrister having a go'.

'If they're gonna go down, this is them speaking, then they wanna go down with a fight. They don't wanna go down thinking that their barrister pussy-footed around, and didn't ask the hard questions.'

What if, I counter, the punter is someone like a priest who has anally raped an eight-year-old?

If, Desmond tells me, the accused is a recidivist offender (as many of the priests and brothers who have come before the courts have been), but is insisting that *this time*, he didn't do it, then Desmond needs 'to go in harder' on the complainant – accusing them of just being on the bandwagon. He adopts a menacing nasal tone to demonstrate the technique he adopts.

'You've heard what so and so said – heard he was found guilty two years ago,' he says. 'Made a victims of crime [compensation application] *have you, Mr Jones*?'

Desmond's published views at times recall Phil Dunn's words about trying to get an older female jury. In *The Age* newspaper in December 2019, Desmond was quoted in an article about whether there was a bias in favour of male jurors in Victoria.

'I would say, anecdotally, *"au contraire,"*' Desmond told the newspaper. 'There's nothing better than having a good grandmother on a jury. She knows what little missy gets up to and how she behaves. She's got the experience of life to know that there are young girls out there that say and do things that aren't quite according to Hoyle, so I'm happy with mature women.'

It wasn't the first time Desmond's comments about jury composition hit the press. In July 2008, *The Age* reported that Desmond had tried to exclude Greeks from a jury in a sex trial in the Victorian County Court in which the complainant was Greek.

'I don't want a Greek juror empathising with a Greek complainant, Your Honour,' Desmond was reported to have said. When the judge responded that he was 'not going to have a jury selected on the basis of race, nationality', Desmond's argument took a more bizarre turn.

'See, the allegation here, this is a Greek complainant and her nationality will be established on the evidence, your Honour, it's part of the narrative and there are allegations here of anal penetration and there's a common misunderstanding in the community that Greeks like anal sex and she might readily then be seen to be compliant and in fact wanting it,' Desmond was reported as replying. 'That would be doing her a disservice, it wouldn't be fair to either party.'

Asked by Judge Roy Punshon what he meant by not being fair to either party, the newspaper reported that Desmond replied, 'Well, there's a misconception in the community that Greeks readily engage in anal sex.'

Desmond first came to my attention because of a rather extraordinary appearance in February 2018 on an SBS *Insight* program on the way sexual assault victims are treated in the legal system.

He appeared via video link from Melbourne. When host Jenny Brockie raised his 'reputation for being tough in cross-examination', Desmond replied that he had heard that said of him.

'I would say I'm robust,' Desmond told the program. 'Having said that, the caveat over all of this, of course, is at a trial it's presided over by an experienced criminal lawyer, i.e., the judge.

'The judges do not allow brutal cross-examinations. If you're asking me would a complainant feel it's a brutal cross-examination, she may well do, but the objective measure, the umpire, will not allow a brutal cross-examination.'

During the appearance, Desmond looked exhausted. He had large, purple circles under his eyes. Towards the end of the show, Jenny Brockie asked him what he would do if a woman he loved 'a daughter, a partner, was sexually assaulted'.

'Would you want her to go to court,' Brockie asked as the camera panned to Desmond, who was looking down and off to the side, his brow furrowed, 'knowing what you know?'

'I've wrestled with that question many times, Jenny,' Desmond started as his voice began to falter.

'I-I don't know the answer to it. I hope I would support, if it was my daughter, in whatever decision she made.' As he said this, he gulped and grimaced, looking to the ceiling instead of the camera.

'I would inform her as to the way the system operates. But,' he said, trembling, 'if it were her decision not to proceed, I feel I wouldn't encourage her to participate.'

'And why is that?' Brockie probed, cocking her head to the side. 'What is it about the process that makes you say that?'

Desmond looked off to the side, his eyes reddened with tears, gesturing with his hand as if to pull the words from the air. 'Umm, I suppose it's the role I play.'

He shook his head then vigorously wiped his eyes. He then returned his gaze to the camera, somewhat sheepishly, and managed 'Pardon me. It's difficult, that question.' He looked away, pained.

When I began researching this book, I looked back at the *Insight* program and I thought, 'I must look into this guy.'

Desmond tells me now that Brockie blindsided him when she personalised the question, and it was thinking of his daughter in that position, not the impact of his work on complainants in general, that upset him. He has no regrets about that. His style, is, he says, robust. He prepares for his cases very, very carefully, so he knows the case better than the complainant does. He says he thinks anyone thinking about complaining to police needs to know this.

'Over a dinner party, if someone said [to me], "A bloke raped me," and there's no eyewitnesses and no injuries and it happened ten years ago – I'd explain to her the process,' he says when I ask him what advice he would give to anyone who thought about becoming a complainant in a rape trial.

'And I'd say, "I think you are going to find some difficulty going through all of this. It's your choice, but she's not going to be easy. You know, you are going to be confronted with blokes like me, who are saying, 'This is all bullshit.'"'

'[His] approach is designed to rattle you, mess with your head, invoke a fight or flight response and therefore destroy your credibility,' one barrister tells me of Desmond's style.

I decided to look at some of the transcripts of his cases to get a better understanding of what that meant.

In March 2020, Desmond featured in the victim impact statement of the mother of a woman raped by a man called Nicholas Weston when she was staying in Melbourne at his Airbnb apartment.

I'll call the mother 'Jenny' and the daughter 'Sophie'. They live in a small community in a remote part of Australia.

Jenny had also been a victim of sexual assault – first as a small child in care, between the ages of four and eight – and then as a teenager when a stranger broke into her home. She had also, for many years, been a social worker in the sexual assault field.

'I had done everything to make sure this would never happen to my own child and now it had happened, and there was nothing I could do,' Jenny wrote in her victim impact statement.

'It feels heartbreaking to watch my child go from being such a confident young woman to now being fearful of the world and knowing that she has little power or control over what happens to her, if someone else chooses to hurt her.

'Her world view, her emotional/psychological state has completely changed and with it, her capacity to pursue her hopes and dreams ...

'[She] used to love going out, playing sport and being surrounded by her friends. [She] had a great sense of humour and boundless energy. Today she mostly locks herself away in her bedroom for hours and sometimes days, without speaking to another person.'

Victim impact statements are usually reserved for talking about how the crime impacted the family, how the accused made them feel, but Jenny was so incensed about defence barrister John Desmond's behaviour in court that she singled him out in the statement.

'I felt ashamed that, in my lifetime, the way victims of sexual assault are questioned in these trials and the way they are portrayed to the jury hasn't really changed or improved,' she wrote. 'Mr Desmond's behaviour was a disgrace.

'There are more humane and sensible ways to represent your client without resorting to a performance of degrading and absurd statements against the victim.

'Despite this, I am proud of my daughter for seeking justice, as I know that if she had not done so now, this would have left her with regrets later in life and of even greater feelings of powerlessness.'

Jenny later told me she couldn't believe the way that Desmond acted.

'It was like something so out of the past and quite shocking. Something out of last century. Easily. It was like, this is a really bad performance … It was actually bordering on ludicrous … If I hadn't seen it, I wouldn't have believed that it was still possible. That someone like him could be operating and still behaving that way.

'And he was given the floor and he was allowed to go on and on and on and on with the same thing and coming back to it all the time and reiterating it over and over to the jury and being so theatrical.

'… He was dipping down and jumping up and doing all the facial expressions. It was like out of a Shakespearean play in a sense. … [A]nything he could draw on to make her look … Basically the word was "slut" underneath it all, which he was getting to.'

'*In fact, I suggest to you that you were having your way with him. Your sexual way.*'

'*I'd suggest, what you achieved is you've preserved your reputation of not having jumped into the cot, with if not the first, the second opportunity with the bloke who's twice your age. What do you say to that?*'

'*You're a binge drinker, weren't you?*'

'*Whilst flirting with my client, you said words to this effect, "How fitting is it I worked at FCUK because all I want to do is FCUK." Now did you say that or something very close to it, [Sophie]?*'

'*No.*'

'*Have you worked in FCUK?*'

'*I've worked in French Connection.*'

'He never spoke to me kindly at all,' Sophie says. 'I think he thought he would be able to trip me up, that it would be easy – I think he thought I am pretty stupid.'

But when that didn't work, Sophie says he changed tactics, and became 'meaner and meaner and more rude'.

Sophie and Jenny remember the judge often rolling his eyes at Desmond, but they believe he did not pull him up on his behaviour enough.

'I think he didn't want to be accused of not giving the defence enough of a fair trial,' Jenny says.

'So, I think the judge, in my view, was holding back so that there could be no possible chance of anything coming back on him as being unfair to the defence.'

Jenny says Sophie and the friend who was staying with her at the Airbnb when the sexual assault happened were incredibly distressed while giving their evidence – with Sophie's friend coming out of the court at one point and collapsing onto Jenny's husband after Desmond's cross-examination.

'She was collapsing under the pressure of him and [Sophie] was just in tears,' she says. 'They were both very upset and very distressed and everything they said he was twisting and turning into this whole theme of "You girls wanted this right from the beginning. This is what you set out to do. Blah, blah, blah."'

'I'm so proud of [Sophie] and I'm so amazed she was so strong and so tough, but it's really taken a hell of a toll on her,' Jenny says.

Sophie says that in the lead-up to the case, she was told that the trial wouldn't be like 'in the movies, where they yell and slam their hands down on the table'.

'And I went in there and that's exactly what it was like! I thought, "This is exactly like a TV show!"'

She says it was all so absurd and theatrical that she would frequently turn to the judge and look at him as if to say, 'Is he seriously allowed to behave like this?', but he was. It continued.

'I would look around and say, "No one's going to say anything?" This can't be legal. This cannot be legitimate that I am sitting in a room full of lawyers and yet they are all like, "No, this is good, answer the question."'

And it wasn't as if Sophie had unrealistic expectations. She had already been through a committal proceeding, in which she says she had had the opposite experience. She says the defence counsel, while still trying to mine her evidence for reasonable doubts and trying to trip her up, did so with a measure of decorum and civility.

'It wasn't a pleasant experience,' Sophie says, 'but I did not come out going, "I hate that guy." I can honestly say that I would meet for a coffee with that defence barrister,' she says. It's not something she would ever say about Desmond.

Jenny decided to mention Desmond in her victim impact statement because she wanted both him and the judge to know the impact his behaviour had.

'Did we really have to go through all of that?' Jenny wonders.

'We still could have followed natural justice and seen that this person was innocent until proven guilty. We could have done all of that without the denigration of my daughter in the process.

'I think I was trying to almost say to [the judge], it was really directed at him and Desmond really, that you two men here allowed this to go on and you didn't stop it.

'In this day and age, it was a disgrace. I said it was a disgrace that you're allowed to do that, and you are still doing it.'

She's sure the judge had his reasons for not pulling up Desmond more, but it was 'allowing a naughty boy to be a naughty boy'.

She agrees that the process caused secondary trauma for Sophie.

'So, she's got to wear that. She's got to wear that for the sake of the system. That's what we're saying, isn't it? In the end? She's got to wear it.'

I ask Sophie what she would do if she met Desmond now – what would she say to him? She doesn't really want to give him the satisfaction of thinking she cares.

'Honestly, I think I would just laugh at him,' she says. 'But it's not funny that he's still allowed to be in the courtroom ... I don't hold him as much accountable as the system ... He's being allowed to practise, and he shouldn't be, Sophie says, adding that she felt that the techniques employed were from 'the Stone Age'.

'But the worst part is that people are standing by and letting this stuff happen and being silent.'

Desmond himself made a formal objection to the part of Jenny's victim impact statement that criticised him being read out in court because, he argued, it was not relevant to the sentencing of his client. Judge Frank Gucciardo allowed the objection and instructed

Crown Prosecutor Charlotte Duckett to tell Jenny she could not read that part aloud.

Desmond tells me now that the implication of Jenny's complaint about him in the victim impact statement was that Judge Gucciardo didn't sufficiently do his job by intervening to stop improper questions. That wasn't true, Desmond says.

'The Gooch,' he says, referring to the judge's nickname in court circles, 'he's reasonably proactive in sex cases. He doesn't hesitate to stop barristers doing what he thinks is inappropriate ... He's very up to speed in ensuring there's not a demeaning or overbearing cross-examination.'

I wonder why it has to be up to the judge to intervene – why can't Desmond check his own behaviour?

'What, tone it down?' he asks. 'Dial it back? I'm trying to get the guy off!'

Trying to get the guy off, Desmond believes, is doing whatever he can, within the rules, as robust as that may be.

'Now if ... that's how she felt,' Desmond says of Jenny's complaint, 'yeah, that's how she felt. Big deal, I feel Collingwood should win the premiership – not relevant to the process!'

I gasp at him, incredulous that he's just said this to me in all seriousness.

'Yeah, but come on!' I say. 'Collingwood winning the prem – her daughter was raped! And the thought of your daughter being raped and cross-examined made you cry on TV.'

'Yeah, but she's not my daughter!' he says.

'Yeah, I know, but you said, "So what, Collingwood ..." You can't say that!' I say, exasperated at the almost comical lack of empathy he's showing in that moment.

'What do you mean?' he asks. 'All I'm saying, it's an irrelevant comment to this process. If that's her opinion, fine, it can't be expressed in a victim impact statement.'

Michele Williams QC, a retired senior Crown prosecutor who was the first head of the Specialist Sex Offences Unit at Victoria's Office of Public Prosecutions, won't comment on this particular case or Desmond, but she says she thinks a victim or family member making a comment about the style of a barrister in a victim impact statement is fair and should be allowed.

'Well, I think it is actually a purpose of sentencing because, as a matter of law, it's the way a trial is conducted and hence, also, the way a complainant is cross-examined, so it can be taken into account. It can be,' Williams tells me.

But Williams concedes that it rarely happens as defence counsel are generally protected from that sort of criticism.

I speak to a number of prosecutors who agree that Desmond's style is often effective, that somehow juries seem to enjoy the theatre of it and he often wins trials. So the myth circulated by barristers that 'juries hate this stuff' is not, in those prosecutors' experience, necessarily borne out in the results.

Desmond, not surprisingly, agrees.

Nonetheless, his antics did not win over the jury in the Weston trial. Nicholas Weston was found guilty on four of the five charges and sentenced to eight years in prison, with a minimum non-parole period of five years and three months.

Another transcript from a Desmond defence I obtained was from a rape case called *R v Artiga* in 2015. The transcript related to a committal proceeding in the Melbourne Magistrates' Court.

In that case, a young woman was raped by a stranger, Victor Artiga, who entered her share house after she and her friends had a party. Someone had accidentally left the back door unlocked. The young woman had been drinking that night and had vomited and gone to bed. She woke up in horror to what she thought was a dream of a man penetrating her, only to realise that a man actually *was* penetrating her, a man she'd never met before.

Desmond's cross-examination thesis was that she had drunkenly met this guy and let him in.

'Did you have sex that night, having initially thought, "No. I'm not looking to get laid"?' Desmond quizzed her.

'No,' she replied.

'Are you sure, given the alcohol?' he pressed.

'No.'

'You're not sure, are you?'

'I'm sure.'

'You are sure?'

'Yeah.'

'How do you know, if you were that drunk that you are actually feeling – I will just give you a description of the words that you say in your statement – you had the spins and you wanted to throw up and then you actually did throw up?'

'Yes, but I was fully conscious the entire time and in command.'

'It would have been very embarrassing,' Desmond later pushed, 'for you to accept this, if one of your friends had walked into that room and discovered you in bed with a man none of them had ever seen before? That would have been terribly embarrassing for you, wouldn't it?'

'Yes,' the victim managed.

Except that didn't happen. One of her friends *didn't* come in and discover them. She *wasn't* embarrassed. She was scared. Frozen in fear, she let the man out of the house. He stole her mobile phone.

Artiga had a string of prior offences going back to when he was still a child. A victim himself of sexual assault, he had been in state care from his teens. He had nothing in common with this student or her friends.

After she let Artiga out of the house the victim immediately went to her friend, woke her up and told her what had happened. Their flatmate then called the police. In the bathroom, her friend told the court, the victim cried and told her she'd been raped. That was in the February. She went immediately to police. She had persevered with an investigation and then, seven months later, this horrible process. She was prepared to go to trial to get justice.

What RAT, as Phil Dunn might have said, what rival alternative theory, was there, for a woman doing all of this? Victor Artiga would later concede there was none.

The committal was in September 2015. The following June, while still on remand, Artiga would tell a psychologist that he had watched a television program on sexual assault which made him regret his behaviour and he decided to enter a plea of guilty.

But, nine months earlier, he had no such remorse.

'What were you wearing to bed that night?' Desmond asked the victim.

'Um, I was wearing a dress, ah, but took it off when I went to bed, so I was just wearing my underwear,' the victim said.

'A bra as well as panties, or just panties?' Desmond pressed.

'Just panties,' she replied.

'Again, I'm not trying to inquire into too much detail, but are they the skinny ones – skimpy ones – or are they sort of full-length sort of things, the pants?'

'Um, no, they were just briefs, like ... yeah,' she replied.

And if they were 'skimpy ones', what then? Does a woman who wears skimpy undies impliedly consent to sex with a stranger? What possible relevance does this hold beyond another rape myth?

It calls to mind a famous Irish case, which led to massive protests in the streets and women tweeting their underwear with the hashtag, #thisisnotconsent.

During the trial, in Cork in the south of Ireland, defence counsel Elizabeth O'Connell pointed to the fact that the seventeen-year-old victim had worn thong underwear on the night she went out nightclubbing with her friends and was, she alleged, sexually assaulted by a 27-year-old man she met that night.

'Does the evidence out-rule the possibility that she was attracted to the defendant and was open to meeting someone and being with someone?' O'Connell was reported as telling the jury.

'You have to look at the way she was dressed,' she said. 'She was wearing a thong with a lace front.'

The defendant was acquitted. In the Irish case, the skimpy undies trope actually worked.

These rape myths were once common in sexual assault cases. Journalist Michael Magazanik reported in *The Age* newspaper that in the infamous Heros Hakopian trial in 1991, barrister George Traczyk likened the rape of a sex worker to, 'the rape of a woman wandering through a Housing Commission car park, wearing make-up, mascara, and a seductive mini-skirt'. Mr Traczyk said the community standard would be 'what did she expect?'

The judge presiding over the case, David Jones, said Mr Traczyk's questioning had been 'beyond reproach'. Magazanik, who is now a solicitor who specialises in this sort of work, reported that the Victorian Bar released a statement arguing that 'barristers are obliged to make every reasonable argument on behalf of their client'. Magazanik tells me the Bar sent a delegation to meet with his editor and complain about his journalism in an analysis piece on the case. George Traczyk is still a practising barrister. Traczyk said, through the Bar Council at the time, that he 'found all rape repugnant'.

In Victor Artiga's trial, Desmond's questions about the actual rape were equally problematic. The victim described having a dream and waking up from it to 'the sensation of being penetrated'.

'Again,' Desmond continued, 'I'm not trying to be acute about this, but you're the one that used the word "dream". You have not stated "nightmare".'

'I guess I hadn't chosen to use the word nightmare,' the victim answered.

'Because it wasn't an answer,' Desmond shot back. 'It was, if truth be said, you were fantasising. Isn't that the position?'

'No. That's not the position,' the victim replied.

No, the young student was not fantasising about this creepy opportunist who had discovered an unlocked back door, let himself into a house, crept into a bedroom, and vaginally penetrated a sleeping woman. No, that was not a 'fantasy'.

When later sentencing Artiga in the County Court, Judge Paul Grant would single out this word as something which had distressed the victim.

'Your barrister took issue with the victim's account and suggested that what happened to her was not a nightmare, but a fantasy,' Judge Grant said.

But back at the committal, Desmond pressed on. Moving on to the fact that, just like Saxon Mullins, in the fear of the moment, the victim did not scream out, or hit her rapist or do all the things that women are expected to do when they are raped. She just got him out of there.

'You become aware of a sensation of a penis in your vagina and you feel that hand on the waist and it's the combination that stirs you awake, so that you then turn around to see the face of a man you don't know, right?'

'Yes.'

The victim said, when asked, that she didn't know what had actually stopped the sex. This is where Desmond got into the myths about what a woman should do when she is paralysed with fear and finds a stranger in her bed, with his penis inside her.

'How about "Get out of my bed, I haven't ... what the hell do you think you're doing to me?" That didn't stop it, did it?' he asked.

'No,' was all she said.

'No, because you knew in your mind that you'd invited this man, maybe you'd never met him before, in a drunken state, into your bed. Isn't that the position?'

'No.'

Desmond asked the victim to confirm that, in her normal life, when not drinking, she would never put herself in 'this position'. The Crown prosecutor objected. And you have to ask, really, *what* position? Going to sleep in your own bed after a party? Exactly what 'position' was that?

After the rape was interrupted by the victim waking, the victim asked Artiga if he had ejaculated or if he had worn a condom. In another creepy move, Artiga started to comfort her in her distress.

'Not the act of a rapist, do you agree with that?' Desmond said. Again, the prosecutor objected. Again, what is the act of a rapist? It's conceivable a rapist might try to cover his tracks by comforting someone. It's conceivable a rapist might feel bad for what they had just done. Especially one who, as it later emerged, had repeatedly been a victim of sexual assault himself. And in fact, I have seen evidence in so many of these cases where a rapist – either of an adult woman, or of a child – 'comforts' their victim in a very creepy way after sexually assaulting them.

The young woman would say in her victim impact statement that she had been unable to escape the reality of having been raped in her own bed by a complete stranger.

'Victor's actions have instilled a level of fear that I have yet to overcome,' she wrote. 'Albeit having moved out of the house where it happened, I still experience nightmares of waking to him there.

'Shadows in my room turn into figures lurking in the dark, while a rustle outside or a knock on the door remains enough to raise my heartbeat.

'I can hardly bear to be alone at night and must sleep with the lights on to settle my fears.'

She was on anti-depressants and receiving counselling.

'Victor may have left a deep scar on my life, but he has not destroyed it,' she said. Nonetheless, the rape is not something she wishes to speak about. I did speak to her friend, who was also cross-examined by Desmond, and who was the first person the victim woke.

As Desmond pressed the friend during her evidence, his questions were peppered with phrases like 'it's a pretty simple question' and the magistrate had to intervene on several occasions during the friend's evidence because she was so distressed. The young woman cried as she was forced to say the words she remembered the victim telling her, words she felt uncomfortable speaking in court.

Fortunately, she had a kind magistrate.

'I'm really sorry you're finding this difficult,' Magistrate Hawkins said. 'I think we all understand how difficult it is for you, but it's really important ... Now, take a few deep breaths and, say, in and out five times, slowly. Then draw on all your strength to tell us.'

'Um, from my memory, um, she blurted out through tears, um, "Some guy's dick was inside me."'

Desmond didn't let up. 'Do you agree she didn't say, or she didn't use the word, "rape"? She didn't say, "A man's raped me" or "A stranger's raped me" if you prefer? Do you agree? That's not a word she used.'

The friend didn't want to agree with that because the victim had told her that – just not immediately. 'She said that in the bathroom,' the friend replied.

'She-she went against the wall and, like, crumbled into a ball ... As she was trying to process it, I think that she said, I think twice, she repeated, sort of whispering, "I can't believe I was just raped."'

But Desmond wanted to fixate on the first conversation the friends had had after the incident, not something later in the night. Magistrate Hawkins acknowledged that it was 'stressful' and that she probably wanted to get it over with, but she must listen carefully to the questions.

'She didn't use the word rape in the first conversation?' Desmond asked.

'No.'

'You've told us. Nor did she say to you whether he had, I'll say, was having sex with her or to use your phrase, "had his dick inside her" without her consent. She didn't use the word "consent" at all?'

'It was pretty obvious that it wasn't consensual,' the friend began.

'No,' Desmond cut in, *'listen to the question*. You're being asked what the girl said.'

'Okay,' the friend returned.

She became frustrated as he repeatedly tried to tell her that the victim hadn't used the word 'consent', nor used the word 'rape'.

The friend said she agreed that the victim didn't use the word 'rape' at that point.

'Or consent, or non-consent, or any word that addresses that subject or topic, agreed?' Desmond pushed.

'I still don't agree,' the friend replied.

'No,' he cut in. 'Concentrate on the words,' he continued, 'she didn't use the ...'

'Look,' the friend maintained, 'I disagree.'

'What word, then?'

The friend was infuriated by his tone now. 'My answer I'm giving you is "disagreed".'

Desmond didn't give up. 'Yes, well, listen to the question, because I'm putting to you, your answer, with respect, is non-responsive.'

At this point the magistrate got involved. 'No, she *is* responding,' Magistrate Hawkins said to Desmond.

'Your Honour, the witness is being asked to address the words that are used, not her attitude,' Desmond replied.

'Mr Desmond, she responded to that ... and she's disagreed with the proposition that you put, which she is entitled to ...'

'Which is what?' Desmond shot back, before the magistrate could finish her sentence. 'What proposition did I put?'

'I can't, precisely, the words ...' Magistrate Hawkins began.

'Well exactly,' Desmond said, again finishing Magistrate Hawkins' sentence. 'And I daresay the prosecutor can't even remember.'

'... Please don't argue with me, Mr Desmond.'

'Well, that's my job, with respect, Your Honour.'

'No,' the magistrate replied, 'it's to be respectful.'

Desmond retorted a couple of times that he *was* being respectful before being urged by the magistrate to 'Now, move on'.

Back on the *Insight* program, Jenny Brockie wondered whether judges pulled him up very often for his cross-examinations, and Desmond replied, 'Occasionally, yes.'

'I've actually seen a transcript of one of the trials that you appeared in,' Brockie said, 'where you were interrupting the witness and you were pulled up by the judge for interrupting the witness numbers of times. Does that happen often?'

'Look, unfortunately that does happen from time to time. I do my best to allow the witness to complete the answer but, yes, I am guilty of that from time to time of interrupting the witness.' Brockie said that this led to an argument with the judge.

'At one stage the woman's lawyer says that you are interrupting her client and the judge says you do it all the time,' she said.

'You have the advantage over me, Jenny, of a particular transcript of a particular case, I am not challenging you … If you have read the transcript,' Desmond replied.

'Do you do it all the time?' Brockie asked.

'No, I don't do it all the time. I am not permitted to do it all the time.'

Nonetheless, he doesn't mind giving it a red-hot go.

I'M NOT THAT GUY

The blood-dimmed tide is loosed, and everywhere
The ceremony of innocence is drowned;
The best lack all conviction, while the worst
Are full of passionate intensity.

WB YEATS, 'THE SECOND COMING'

John Desmond may not fight with judges 'all the time', but he's had the odd spectacular doozy.

Desmond got into a very heated argument with another female judicial officer – Elizabeth Hollingworth, a tough and no-nonsense justice of the Supreme Court of Victoria – in December 2017. This particular exchange became so toxic that it led to Justice Hollingworth accusing Desmond of lying to the court and, as a result, the jury had to be dismissed. The reason it caught my attention is that the sequence of events led to a very significant delay in the complainant achieving justice.

The pair had started sparring on the very first day of the trial, when Justice Hollingworth had indicated she might rule against Desmond on a matter and he had replied that 'it may or may not be a ground of appeal'. Hollingworth was clearly angry with him even back then.

The trial concerned a truly awful sexual assault where an ice-addicted man had broken into a woman's home, blindfolded her, gagged her mouth with duct tape, secured her wrists with cable ties, hit her on the side of the face with a table leg and stood on her throat until she lost consciousness.

Desmond says he had convinced Legal Aid to run a test case about a new DNA technology which had been adopted in Victoria by forensic scientists but had not been universally accepted overseas. There had been, Justice Hollingworth would later reveal, no fewer than thirty mentions and directions hearings in the case. There had been an appeal to the Court of Appeal on the DNA evidence.

The trial ran for seven weeks before it was aborted, the judge said, because of Desmond's conduct. At that stage, it had been five and a half years since the accused had been arrested. It is hard to imagine how the victim must have felt. Justice Hollingworth made little attempt to contain her immense frustration.

Despite the relentlessly adversarial nature of the criminal justice system, prosecutors and defence barristers often come to agreements about how they might proceed – those agreements are then put to the court. John Desmond's insistence that there had been an agreement of that kind in this case is what led to this trial being aborted. Desmond told the court that the junior counsel for the Crown had muttered to him in court, 'sotto voce' that the prosecution would not be relying on some crucial scientific evidence in the case, leading Desmond to say 'pardon me' to the doctor who was giving evidence and to then indicate that his cross-examination would conclude.

'It may be picked up on the tape [recording of the trial] if there is a tape still in existence, I don't know that yet,' Desmond told Justice Hollingworth.

When Justice Hollingworth repeated the words and the scene back to him, Desmond repeated to her that 'I would be seen on the video, if there is a video.'

Her Honour was clearly immediately sceptical and irritated. She quizzed Desmond again as to whether it was the junior prosecutor to whom he had spoken, and when he said that it may have been his instructing solicitor, she replied 'what a stupid remark to make'.

'Honestly, Mr Desmond, the time you waste on irrelevant material is breathtaking,' Justice Hollingworth said.

'Why didn't you get this put on the transcript or recorded? This is a pretty important matter, if the Crown were not going to rely on [the evidence].

'Why didn't you then turn to [me] and say, "I'm told that the Crown isn't going to be relying on this?" There are so many ways that experienced Counsel would get something so important put on the record.'

Desmond replied that if Counsel said something to him, he 'accept[ed] it in good faith'.

'That's a pretty stupid thing to do with something as important as this, Mr Desmond,' the judge replied.

Desmond then offered that he had had a further conversation with the junior Crown prosecutor when the parties left court in which he reiterated they would not rely on the evidence and that 'I know from past experience on occasions the tape or audio still continues'.

The judge turned to the Crown prosecutor and asked her if that was true.

'I spoke with [the junior prosecutor] yesterday,' the Crown prosecutor replied, '[and he] said that he did not give such an undertaking ... [H]e says that he has no recollection of Mr Desmond asking that particular question.' She added that the junior prosecutor would not give such an undertaking in her absence.

When Justice Hollingworth got the relevant video footage and played it, the judge said, 'It show[ed] at no stage did Mr Desmond lean over and speak to [the junior prosecutor].'

Desmond did say, 'Just pardon me, doctor,' but, instead of leaning over and speaking to the prosecutor, he looked down at his notes and said nothing. This clearly incensed the judge. 'Now, having seen this video, Mr Desmond, what do you say in relation to any alleged agreement with the Crown?' Justice Hollingworth asked.

Desmond replied that there was a conversation 'at some point that day', but he conceded that the recording showed that he was mistaken that it was in court.

'But you said to me this morning that the reason you finished your cross-examination was in reliance upon [the prosecutor's] assurance just given to you,' Justice Hollingworth replied. 'That's palpably untrue; palpably untrue.'

'Your Honour has just accused me of lying,' Desmond replied.

'Yes, I have, Mr Desmond.'

'Then I'm out of this case.'

'All right, that's a matter for you, Mr Desmond.'

Desmond then said this was the 'third time' Justice Hollingworth had 'effectively accused [him] of lying'. He did not, at this point, give up on arguing with the judge – pointing out that the expert witness had done his own re-analysis of the DNA evidence.

'That is utterly, utterly, irrelevant, Mr Desmond, like so much of what you have said,' Justice Hollingworth said, barely concealing her exasperation.

Justice Hollingworth told the jury it was with 'great regret', that she was forced to dismiss them and to discontinue the trial. It would take a new trial, a new jury, a new defence counsel and another fifteen months for the victim in that case to receive justice.

'The end result, the way that it all panned out for me, that I had to pull out of it,' Desmond tells me now, 'I mean, it's the most disappointing result of my career, to have invested so much time in the case,' he says.

Almost astonishingly, the new barrister for the offender argued in his plea before he was sentenced that a mitigating factor in taking time off the sentence should be 'delay' in the length of the proceedings.

'[D]elay might become relevant ... in relation to a question of fairness and the impact the delay ... on the accused, in terms of having a serious matter hanging over his head for a lengthy period and the anxiety and difficulties associated with that,' the new defence counsel submitted.

The accused was arguing delay because his lawyers chose to engage in a protracted test case over DNA which was billed back at great cost to the state via Legal Aid. What about his victim? What about the impact on her of the delay?

Justice Hollingworth pointed out that it was 'not a matter of blaming [the offender], but he chose to retain someone who ran every conceivable point' and 'this isn't one of those cases, it seems to me, where the prosecution or the court bear any blame for this'.

Justice Hollingworth acknowledged the stress of the delay for the victim, during 'frustrating and difficult' court processes and commended the victim for behaving 'with great courage and dignity throughout'.

I'll call the victim 'Lucia'. She was a migrant woman from South-east Asia. I've never met her. Lucia's victim impact statement showed just what a crime like this can do to a person. She was 'very afraid' of the dark because it happened at night. She said it felt 'like someone was watching me'. So she had to sleep with the lights on. She had to move in with her sister because she was afraid to live alone.

'I had to wear sunglasses all the time, because I didn't want people to see my bruised face and ask me what happened,' Lucia said as she read the statement to the court.

She used all her sick leave, had to change jobs and sell the house where the rape happened. Her relationship suffered, and she lost friends. She was diagnosed with PTSD.

Then, Lucia had to arrange leave from work every time hearings were repeatedly adjourned.

'I had to prepare myself emotionally each time and it just keeps stopping and starting. I don't know how many times I was told it was happening and then it was postponed again.' This, again, was because of the strategy employed by the defence. 'I find that court process really emotionally draining. The first trial, I had the energy for it, but the second time around I felt so drained. I struggled to find the energy to tell the story over and over again.'

Nonetheless, she threw herself into her job, did voluntary work, and, as a committed Christian, her church kept her going.

'When this first happened, I was angry with God,' Lucia told the court. 'It was hard for me at first to understand why this would happen. At the same time, I feel like God protected me during the incident and after. I could have died, or the police could have never found the person. So I felt that God helped me, even as I felt angry with him.

'Each time I went to court, I went by myself, because I don't want my friends or relatives to be impacted by the trauma that I have been through. It's bad enough that it happened to me.'

Her statement is so gracious, considering what she has been dragged through. She thanked the Crown team and Justice Hollingworth, saying they had been 'lovely'. 'It is very important for me to come to court and [see the] sentencing [of] him as part of my healing,' Lucia said.

Justice Hollingworth finally sentenced the offender to ten years and two months imprisonment, in March 2019 – almost seven years after he was first arrested and nearly six years after he was charged.

'Your first trial, in late 2017, had to be aborted after seven weeks, due to your previous counsel's conduct,' Justice Hollingworth told the offender.

At the time of writing, the offender's new lawyers have again appealed the case to the Victorian Court of Appeal.

John Desmond's actions in the case became the subject of a complaint to the Victorian Legal Services Commission (LSC). Neither he nor I know who made the complaint.

Desmond was frustrated at the delay it took for the complaint to be processed and finalised by the LSC. He got barrister Robert Richter QC to assist him with drafting a twenty-page response to the LSC and he waited, and waited.

'Oh, it was extraordinary, the delay,' Desmond tells me. He says Richter told him he'd also had a delay in similar circumstances and, 'These bastards, they take forever.'

'I've got to take this seriously, because depending upon the outcome,' Desmond tells me, 'this could affect my career. They are blaming me for the discharge of a jury, now, what had it been? Three or four months with [the jury]? They've said I've lied to a Supreme Court judge. So if they find against me, are they going to make me apologise? I suppose I could live with that. Are they going to suspend me? Or are they going to take my ticket away? I mean, you think worst-case scenario.'

It took twelve months to finalise the complaint – which ultimately saw the LSC electing not to make a finding against Desmond.

I say to him that he must have been very relieved.

'I was, very relieved,' Desmond says.

It occurs to me that it must have been strange for Desmond to have the tables turned in this way. To be the subject of scrutiny, rather than the scrutineer.

'As you know, as a barrister, truth is a very malleable concept,' I say to him. 'There are ways of making things seem true or untrue, when it's the opposite.'

And, I add, that for someone like him, it's hard to believe that he would deliberately lie to a court about something that he believed to be captured on CCTV, when the CCTV could so easily prove him wrong.

'There's no way you're going to do that, because you're going to look like an idiot if it turns out to be the opposite of that, right?' I ask him, and he agrees. 'And yet, that's what happened. And yet, somehow, somewhere along the line, some sort of miscommunication happened, right? So it's exactly like those people who give you inconsistent statements. It's like, you are now in that position like those people, right?'

'Yep,' he replies.

'And that feels shit.'

'Tell me about it, yeah,' Desmond says.

'Does that not give you pause to make you think, when you're going really hard with these people, maybe dial it down a bit, because they could be someone like you, where there's been some sort of brain snap, there's been some sort of miscommunication?'

But Desmond deadpans in return that 'No, it doesn't.'

'Why?' I'm incredulous again.

'Because my job is to be effective and competent,' he replies.

Complaints to the Legal Services Commissioner against barristers are extremely rare. And even when they do occur, the legislation preventing the Commissioner from making public comment about whether she is 'investigating' provides a serious impediment to transparency.

Commissioner Fiona McLeay believes part of the problem until now has been that people just weren't aware that they could complain, and she is now working to try to increase the commission's visibility and improve its website. In the eleven years to December 2019, there were only thirty-one complaints made against criminal barristers that involved allegations of being abusive or rude, putting clients under duress or using undue pressure, intimidation or breach of the rules or legislation.

Of the thirty-one complaints, the LSC informs me in a statement, 'there were no cases where the barrister was found to have breached their ethical or professional obligations'. Fiona McLeay tells me not to imagine that the fact not a single case has been proven means that there aren't discussions between her office and barristers.

'And, you know, lawyers don't like getting that sort of letter,' she insists.

But not a single case upheld? Not one over eleven years? It seems extraordinary.

'Yeah, look, I don't know what to say to you,' McLeay says.

She says 'to be frank', she gets frustrated by lawyers moaning with each other about the appalling things that might have been said or done by this barrister or that, then doing nothing about it.

'They never actually contact me about it,' McLeay says, 'So I can't do anything about it if I don't know about it. So, I've been pushing back a bit on that sort of stuff when I get the opportunity. Because if they genuinely know that there is something they think is inappropriate, then they should tell me.'

* * *

In my hundreds of conversations with survivors over the past few years, I don't think any of them have ever mentioned going through any sort of complaints processes about what they endured in court. I get the feeling most of them would have no idea that the mechanism exists. And even if they did, they're generally just too spent to go there.

Jenny's daughter Sophie, the young victim of the Airbnb rape by Nicholas Weston, defended by Desmond, spoke of the exhaustion caused by the process.

'I am tired of this,' Sophie wrote in her victim impact statement, 'and I just don't have anything to give anymore. I have spent the last two and a half years trying to move on, instead my life has been disrupted consistently on a course to prove that, yes, in fact he did do what I said he did.'

While she understood that it was rare for victims to get the outcome she did, like so many of the victims I have spoken to, she felt 'no victory, no justice'.

The feeling she was left with, in the pit of her stomach, was 'I am raging'.

'After the trial and everything leading up to this point, I hoped I would feel some relief and justice. However, I have not felt any of that. I am grateful, and I do acknowledge all the hard work and time that has gone into this case by the police and the justice system.'

But the same system that secured the outcome against her attacker also brought her the rage.

'I feel there are significant issues and flaws with the system that has made this experience traumatise me all over again,' she wrote. 'I hope these aspects of the system can evolve so that the experience of attempting to get justice isn't so painful ... Knowing what I know now and how worn I feel, I honestly don't even know within myself if I would advise another victim to go through this process.'

It's a common refrain and a depressing insight into the system.

The barristers still tell themselves that young women as bruised by the courtroom experience as Sophie says she was are the outliers. Most of them think the dog days are over, courtroom bullying is unwise, and the pendulum has swung dramatically in favour of accusers and away from the accused. They give the impression that, even if they were once that sort of advocate, they've realised now that, in 2020, that style of advocacy is 'folly'.

They think there is a rump of older barristers who give the rest of them a bad name. Who huff and puff and blow the house down. They all think, 'I'm not that guy.'

Emma Henderson and Kirsty Duncanson, from Melbourne's La Trobe University, have been conducting long-term research with barristers which has revealed, they tell me, that what barristers think they do versus what they really do are two quite distinct things. Many of them *are* that guy. They just don't realise they're that guy.

Henderson and Duncanson say a central theme to emerge in their interviews with the barristers was that so-called 'rape myths' no longer played a role in trials because legislative changes, judicial attitudes and societal shifts 'mean that juries will no longer accept such arguments'.

'Rape myths are,' Henderson and Duncanson wrote in a paper on this subject in 2014, 'pre-existing social narratives and understandings about sex and rape that have consistently re-written rape as sex, situated responsibility for sexual violence with complainants, and cast rape as a charge easily made but difficult to disprove ...

'These myths include that a woman's sexual history and what she was wearing at the time of an alleged rape is relevant to the assessment of the accused's culpability; that a "real" rape involves a dangerous stranger, a public space, and the use of physical force which leaves physical injuries; that a woman who voluntarily goes home with a friend with whom she has been drinking and then claims to have been raped is likely to be lying. These myths exist as familiar and taken for granted narratives throughout Australian and other common law cultures.'

In lay terms, rape myths are basically the idea that a rape looks a certain way. They ignore things like, as happened in the Saxon Mullins case, that a victim often freezes when in sheer terror instead of calling out. They ignore the fact rape victims often don't kick up a fuss at the time of the assault because they are afraid of their attacker (like in the *Artiga* case – the victim quietly let the intruding rapist out of her house, and then went to see her friend and crumbled).

They ignore the reality of people who are on the wrong side of a power imbalance – say, children, vulnerable people with cognitive disabilities, or even women in employment contexts where there is a power imbalance, such as the Harvey Weinstein cases that sparked the #MeToo movement. Rape myths point the finger at why these people may often see their attackers again, are victimised by them again, and do not appear to demonstrate their feelings of revulsion, because they do not have the power to do so.

I will never forget preparing a story as a journalist, and a senior male colleague asking of an eight-year-old boy making an allegation of abuse in a public swimming pool, 'But why did he go back to the pool?'

'Why did he go back to the pool?' I asked, exasperated. 'He went back to the pool because he was *eight*.' Then in his forties, the victim still wept to speak of it. But not just eight-year-olds go back to their abusers. Women in complicated power dynamics do too.

Rape myths aren't just some sort of feminist academic buzzword, they are the reason that ordinary people who come to tell their stories about the worst thing that ever happened to them – being raped or sexually abused – have such a hard time in court.

Henderson and her other academic colleagues Nicola Henry, Asher Flynn and Anastasia Powell analysed ten rape trials for the *Griffith Law Review*. The academics consistently found examples of rape myths being exploited by defence counsel.

So, in a rape of a co-worker in an aged care home, where the accused pushed the complainant onto a bed and forced his penis into her mouth, the complainant was repeatedly questioned about her behaviour with him – as if workplace flirting was an indication of consent.

'*What I'm suggesting to you is that there was a flirting, a mischievous relationship going on between you. What I'm suggesting is that you were physically, and by gestures, flirting with him.*'

In another case where, like the *Artiga* case, the woman awoke to find the accused raping her, she had been dancing at a party at the flat with nine other people including the accused man.

Henderson and her colleagues noted that the accused became 'fixated' with the dancing, suggesting that a level of consent for the sexual act somehow followed naturally from this 'flirtatious' behaviour in dancing 'near' the accused.

In a third trial, where a woman was camping, 'retired to her swag' and the accused came and, ignoring her protests, sexually penetrated her, the authors noted the defence barrister resorting to the notion of the 'ideal rape victim'.

Q: How hard did you push him?
A: As hard as I could.
Q: Did it have any effect?
A: No.
Q: You were trying to physically resist him?
A: Yes.
Q: Did you yell out a single word?
A: No.
Q: Why not?
A: I was scared.
Q: What were you scared of?
A: Scared that he would do something else.
Q: Effectively, you lay there on your back?
A: Yes.

Q: You didn't put your legs up?

A: No.

Q: Once again, you didn't say anything?

A: No.

Q: But you didn't scream?

A: No, I froze.

Q: Would you say now that freezing in those circumstances was an irrational thing to do? … You didn't have any injuries?

A: Not that I can remember.

In Victoria, where Henderson and Duncanson have been conducting their research, there have been numerous legislative reforms introduced to try to excise rape myths from playing out in jury trials.

For instance, they point out Jury Directions on Consent introduced in 2006 require that a judge must address the jury in directions to expressly explain that certain actions do *not* amount to consent. They include: that the person didn't say or do anything to indicate a free agreement; that she or he did not protest or physically resist; that she or he did not sustain physical injury; and that on another occasion, she or he freely had sex with the person (or any other person).

And guiding principles added to the Victorian *Crimes Act* require that courts have regard to the fact that there is a high incidence of sexual violence within society, sexual offences are 'significantly under-reported', a significant number are committed against women, children and vulnerable people who have a cognitive impairment or mental illness.

The principles also address the 'stranger' rape myth by saying offenders are 'commonly known to their victims' and that sexual offences 'often occur in circumstances where there is unlikely to be any physical signs of an offence having occurred'. And, as mentioned earlier, they do away with the concept of mandatory corroboration.

There are also legislative prohibitions in Victoria and all Australian states on questions about 'the general reputation of the victim with respect to chastity' – they can only be allowed in limited circumstances where they are substantially relevant to a fact in issue or are in the interests of justice.

Henderson and Duncanson argue that, unfortunately, the liberalising of judicial directions to try to dismantle rape myths in court has not led to a rise in the conviction rate, nor, indeed, a rise in convictions for rapes like, say the victim in the Weston case, which don't pander to the stranger rape myth stereotypes.

'Empirical evidence indicates that in the main, the jury directions have made little difference to the outcome of rape trials and that juries have not felt impelled by the directions to convict where evidence of consent has been absent,' Henderson and Duncanson write.

They note that 'while reporting rates have stayed roughly the same, both the number of cases proceeding to trial, and conviction rates, have fallen steadily'. They say that it's sometimes argued that this is because there are more 'non-traditional' rape cases coming to trial – that is, those that involve stickier notions around consent and when it started and finished. But, they say, that argument doesn't necessarily wash. 'With no correlative drop in the proportion of traditionally accepted "real rape" complaints, [it is argued] that the testing of the stories of sexual violence has actually become more conservative post-reform.'

Associate Professor Michael Salter is a criminologist from the University of New South Wales whose research is primarily on violence against women and child abuse. He says that the premise of, for instance, legislation requiring judges to make judicial directions after defence barristers have already done the damage is 'naïve'.

'So it kind of rests on people's ability to be in possession of information but to not allow themselves to be tainted, or not allow themselves to include that in their linear chain of reasoning,' Salter says.

'It's got this very naïve nineteenth-century kind of cognitive bias. It really speaks to the nature of the emotional architecture of the criminal justice system.'

And he says in his own discussions with defence barristers, there is a 'normalisation process' when it comes to believing in this stuff.

'In order to defend their clients, they are not objective,' he says. 'I think they do ultimately have to come to believe that false allegations are common, that women are malicious, that children are seductive, in order to rationalise the way that they earn a living.'

Henderson and Duncanson's candid interviews with barristers over the past year give some clues as to why these rape myths persist at trial, despite the jury directions.

Of course, in their formal interviews with Henderson and Duncanson, just like in their discussions with me, the barristers began by asserting that they did not exploit rape myths and that was a feature of the old days, of the table-thumpers.

One barrister said to them in an interview, 'in terms of exploiting rape myths, I don't believe anyone does that anymore. I've not seen anybody do that in cases I've been involved in. If anybody did, I would deal with it and say it's not appropriate. I would expect a judge to correct it.'

They also said that juries were 'smarter than that'.

'There's something about having twelve people up there on the jury with different experiences that actually, three or four people, you might be able to play on some rape myths, but someone in that group is going to be able to talk some sense into the others about any rape myths so, personally, I don't do that,' another said.

This reflects what barristers told me – Peter Morrissey SC, for instance, said that Melbourne juries were particularly sophisticated, and you could not get away with things you might in less cosmopolitan parts of the country.

But like many of the barristers who spoke to me for this book, the barristers who spoke to the La Trobe researchers thought that the pendulum had swung too far in favour of complainants.

'It does sometimes … make a trial feel really imbalanced for someone who is acting for the accused person,' one barrister told the researchers. 'So that we have, it seems, this huge support of witness advice services, [a] support person in the room … bring your dog, bring your toy, alternate [sic] measures … it seems really imbalanced.

'Sometimes all of those supports that are legitimately put in place convey an impression to the jury that, without them knowing what the evidence is, that … this man must be dangerous. She needs to be protected. She needs to be elsewhere.'

They even expressed dissatisfaction with the broader legislative definitions of what rape or sexual assault can be.

'The problem [is that the definition of rape trivialises] – and I don't mean to say it's nothing if someone goes a bit further than was expected – I'm not saying that's nothing, but to equate that to … rape, it doesn't help anyone. Because now, people go "I was raped" and you know what? What does that mean? What does that even mean anymore?'

Well, it means that someone had sexual relations with someone else without their consent. That's what it has always meant.

John Desmond says the reforms have meant that while he used to win 80 to 90 per cent of his cases, now it feels more like 50–50.

'I tell clients it's changed from ten or fifteen years ago, where [it was] "This is a walk up start, we're gonna win,"' Desmond says, adding that these are now 'difficult cases' for the defence.

I point out that it's highly unlikely that 80 to 90 per cent of his clients, while having been found not guilty by the very onerous criminal burden of proof – beyond reasonable doubt – were completely innocent of the crimes of which they were accused.

'Yep,' Desmond says. 'That's the process. It's not my job to think about whether any of them were guilty or not.

'But unless you want to change the system to a lower burden of proof, which, as I said on that crazy *Insight* show, the day that they do that will be the day that I stop doing my job. If we have a burden of proof beyond reasonable doubt, inherently what that means is that you're accepting that so long as no innocent person goes to jail, we're acknowledging that a lot of guilty people are going to walk.'

Desmond says one of the changes he's 'not a fan of at all' is the judicial direction that witnesses who make prior inconsistent statements are not necessarily lying.

'I mean, for fuck's sake!' Desmond says, 'it's the last bastion of the defence lawyer! Prior inconsistent statements! And they're trying to take that one away.' He concedes that defence counsel still have ample opportunity to rebut this, but having a person with 'the weight of the judicial office' making this direction makes it very difficult.

Ian Lloyd QC also says, 'As a defence counsel, it's getting harder and harder,' because of the reforms brought in by the Royal

Commission into Institutional Responses to Child Sexual Abuse and various law reform recommendations.

'It's becoming, I won't say impossible, but very difficult, to get an acquittal,' Lloyd says. 'And now the Attorney-General here in New South Wales has introduced legislation that requires judges to give a direction, basically telling the jury that any remote connection between an accused's prior convictions for any sexual crime and current charges should be allowed.

'We are no longer looking for striking similarities. If he's got a conviction for anything to do with sex, more or less, it goes in,' Lloyd says.

The new New South Wales law takes up the recommendation to stop evidence about the accused's prior offending against children from being kept out of the case. This sort of information was previously excluded because it was thought that it might unfairly prejudice the accused person's right to a fair trial.

The legislation, which came into effect in July 2020, ushers in a presumption that evidence of the defendant having a tendency to have a sexual interest in a child or children will have 'significant probative value' to the case and it also limits what the courts can consider in rebutting that presumption and not allowing the evidence.

New South Wales Attorney-General Mark Speakman said of the law, 'these reforms will help to ensure that offenders don't evade justice through the exclusion of relevant evidence'.

'We can't undo the horrors of the past, but we can make sure that our legal system offers a fairer and more effective response for victims and survivors.'

Lloyd really struggles with these sorts of legislative reforms.

'As a human being, do I care about perpetrators getting tougher laws against them? Of course I don't!' he says. 'As an objective lawyer, though, the law is going too far towards complainants. It's getting to the stage where we are going to get people convicted on the basis of very little evidence. It's getting harder to win these cases.'

Speakman, who ordered the inquiry into consent laws after our *Four Corners* story on Saxon Mullins, has been a reformist attorney-general in this area. For example, a new law was introduced in 2018 to allow judges to inform juries in sexual offence trials that people may not remember all the details of a sexual offence, or may not describe a sexual offence the same way each time. The judge can also explain that trauma can affect different people differently, including how they recall events, that it's common for there to be differences in accounts and that this applies to both truthful and untruthful accounts.

It's up to the jury to decide whether all of this affects the complainant's reliability and it's also discretionary for the judge, but it is, nonetheless, an important nod to the difficulty of capturing computer-like memories of these incidents.

Another new reform introduced by New South Wales means the judge must warn the jury that a delay to report doesn't mean the complaint is false, that there might be good reason for that delay.

The argument by barristers that the pendulum has swung too far in favour of complainants is not borne out in statistics. An analysis by *The Age* and *The Sydney Morning Herald* newspapers of sexual assault statistics published in September 2019 found that of the 52,396 sexual assaults reported to NSW Police between 2009 and 2018, charges were only laid in 12,894 cases.

Of the 12,894, 7629 went to court. Of those, 2308 were dropped at trial, 1494 found not guilty. The remaining 3827, or roughly 50 per cent of the total that went to court, were found guilty. That's just 7 per cent of the cases that originally went to police.

The Royal Commission into Institutional Responses to Child Sexual Abuse's Criminal Justice Consultation Paper quoted Australian Bureau of Statistics research from 2014–15 saying while 55 per cent of physical assault victims and 39 per cent of victims of threatened assaults reported to police, only 25 per cent of sexual assault victims took that step. It said between 8 and 15 per cent of all matters reported to police ended with a conviction.

* * *

In the barristers' interviews with Henderson and Duncanson, only two senior prosecutors, who happened to be women, would admit that the rape myths which help to enable those low conviction rates to exist, continued to circulate.

'They [defence counsel] do it in a way that they can go far enough but they don't overstep the mark so that the judge then doesn't have to intervene,' one of the prosecutors told the researchers.

'The example I gave you ... where the girl [sat in the front seat of] the taxi ... defence counsel made a huge thing of that in his closing address, to the extent that the judge actually intervened and said, "Look, just because someone does that doesn't mean that they are consenting to the sex", but it had already poisoned [the jurors'] minds.'

Front seats of taxis, wearing 'skimpy underwear to bed, drunk', 'put yourself in the position'.

'[One] judge said that "a man's not made of steel" when a security guard slept with an underage girl after he knew she was underage, and stated that she was very worldly,' the prosecutor told the researchers.

'There are comments like that all the time and ... people who are well-educated, like [this judge who] used to work as the Crown prosecutor in the sex offences section at the OPP ... come out with some appalling comments.'

Michele Williams QC, the retired senior Crown prosecutor who headed up the Specialist Sex Offences Unit at the Office of Public Prosecutions, says the 'old-school type of barrister, where the idea is you bash the witness up as much as what you can, from start to finish and, if you can, inject sarcasm and incredulity ... where you just denigrate, you ridicule' is supposed to have gone out of vogue.

'We've moved into a ... Well, we are *meant to have*, moved into a far more sophisticated way that we cross-examine witnesses,' Williams says.

But she's doubtful that they really have. And she says there remains a decent number of mostly male barristers working in sexual offences who still behave like this.

'Well, see, if you go back to all the reforms that were mooted and brought in, that was meant to change the whole world, the way we did all this.

'Has it? Has it changed anything?

'It hasn't changed some of these guys at all. For the newer ones coming through, yes perhaps they're ... a bit more sophisticated. They know that they're not meant to speak like that.

'But there are still a lot who do. I mean the whole point about the legislation and the, if you like, changing the way that we conducted sex offences, was it recognised that complainants were retraumatised, that a lot basically said, "Look, the experience in the courtroom is far worse in many respects than the offence itself, or [the pattern of] offending."'

She would put the percentage of defence counsel who act in sex cases and who still behave in this way at times as high as 30 per cent.

'Some of these famously bullying barristers, as well, of course they don't really give a damn what the judge says or whatever, and in a way they're able to bully or intimidate the judicial officer as well.'

When Henderson and Duncanson were doing their interviews with the defence barristers, once the researchers actually explained to them what rape myths were, they conceded that they were used in trials.

Henderson and Duncanson say that one other very interesting part of their research was the impact of doing this work on the barristers' mental health, or, as Henderson says, 'a really extraordinary degree of what we are calling vicarious trauma'.

'So a large number of them used to do a lot of this work because if you wanted to, if you are a barrister, the only work you would do would be sexual assault work because there's so much of it,' Henderson says.

'But we found a large number of them don't want to do it anymore because they can't cope because it's so difficult,' she says.

As a matter of coincidence, I spoke to one of the barristers who volunteered that he'd been interviewed by Henderson and Duncanson and who fell into that category. He did not want to be named.

'I stopped doing sex trials about a decade ago because I just could not hack it,' the barrister told me. 'It's not a pleasant experience for anyone, cross-examining complainants in these cases, and then to have to go home to your kids.'

'It really did take a toll on me. It was the worst part of the job.'

The barrister admitted that's why he moved from sex trials to intellectual property.

'It's very hygienic and antiseptic and you don't have to deal with vaginas,' he said, referring to the protracted cross-examinations dissecting who did what to which body part.

'The criminal Bar is pretty Bolshevik about defending an accused person's right to a fair trial. And often, if that means eviscerating a witness, so be it.

'On the complainant's side and on the defendant's side, there's a lot of attendant emotion and it's hard to find a way that's going to work that avoids trauma.

'The whole purpose of running a criminal trial is to win. And that involves a fundamental and often brutal attack on the complainant's credibility. We are often crafting ways to catch witnesses out – that's what we are paid to do. When it comes to the trial, it can be ugly.'

Ian Lloyd QC says, 'It's one of the tools in our toolkit – to try to shake the reliability of the witness. It's an adversarial process, with defence on one side, prosecution on the other, the judge as the umpire and with the jury sitting on the sideline.'

It is adversarial, it is robust, but does Lloyd ever go home and feel a bit sick about what he's done to some poor girl who is coming forward to complain about the worst thing that ever happened in her life?

'I think any lawyer would say that,' Lloyd says. 'And they would look at their job and say it's not an easy job to do because you are dealing with human emotions, but that's the job we have to do.'

As he's told me, it's difficult to defend men like this – the paedophiles, the rapists, the opportunists and the groomers. Men, almost all men, who are much less likely to plead guilty because of the hot shame of being tagged with this label – sex offender – and what it means for the rest of their lives.

You can get over being accused of being someone who once stole cars to support a drug habit, who got into a punch-up at a nightclub, who embezzled money to pay gambling debts; but how do you get over the stigma of sexually abusing a child or raping a woman?

So they want to defend at all costs.

'Most barristers can only handle doing a certain number of these cases,' Phil Dunn QC says.

He has, for instance, done 'at least twenty' paedophile priest and religious Brothers child sex cases.

'They're very wearing because every hand is turned against you,' Dunn says. 'And you feel it – I can tell you anecdotally what it's like acting for these guys. Some of them are quite creepy and some of them are like bewildered rabbits in the headlights.'

He says that the Brothers he represented were often poorly educated, coerced by their families into joining, worked 'like dogs', and shuffled into boarding schools for boys from the age of twenty-one, where they went on to rape those boys.

'I just think they were damaged human beings who had no idea how to deal with their fellow human beings, had no idea how to deal with their sexuality,' Dunn says. He has fights with his wife over this when he exhibits sympathy for them.

'If I had a brief for someone like [one of Australia's worst serial paedophiles] Father [Gerald] Ridsdale, I'd be first of all delighted to be doing a big case,' he says, 'but then I'd think, "Aw cripes, this is gonna be hard," because I know this from my own life experience, doing what I do, what these cases are like …

'You know … you've got half-a-dozen blokes who are all now in their sixties and seventies saying, "He's a ripper bloke, [Brother or Father So and So] is the best man ever", and then you've got some bloke saying, "He used to take me into his room and masturbate me." You know, or "make me masturbate him".

'And you don't know where the truth lies, and you don't have to know where it lies but you've got a question mark in your mind. And then you can't find evidence because the boarding house was bulldozed twenty years ago. Nobody knows who slept in what bed anymore.'

I cut in, saying that the files were burned by a now-deceased bishop.

'Yeah, exactly!' he says. 'But you're left with this looming sense of doom because if the complaint had been made at the time, you could have established it one way or the other. But now you can't.'

It can't but mess with a barrister's head. And, although these people say they are okay with it all – they're just accepting a brief, proving a case beyond reasonable doubt, not ever getting emotionally involved – scratch the surface and it's hard not to arrive at the conclusion that they're really not okay with it after all.

Politician Trevor Khan says of his time doing sex trials as a solicitor advocate in country New South Wales that 'my general feeling is that I wouldn't want to do that law again'.

'Looking back,' I ask him, 'as an advocate, hand on heart, were there ever any moments where you think, "I really shouldn't have done that"?'

'Yes. Yes. Absolutely. Yep. Yes,' Khan replies.

'There's now a Supreme Court justice, a very good Supreme Court justice,' he says, 'who used to be counsel for me. I can remember in one trial that was a sexual assault matter, he was vomiting out the back.

'And this was on the day that he was going to have to cross-examine the victim. He was vomiting out the back. In the car park. It impacts quite seriously on many people's core.'

When you dig a bit deeper with these guys about this process, they open up.

'I've spent forty-three years in this misery – both defending and prosecuting,' Lloyd tells me. 'It's tough, it is tough, it's as simple as that.

'You can't say much to the contrary really – anyone that says it's easy is an idiot.'

I think of John Desmond's appearance on *Insight*. The purple circles under his tear-filled eyes, the dramatic gestures, the words: 'I suppose it's the role I play.' He insists that that was just because of his daughter.

'I don't find the work stressful,' Desmond tells me. 'That's just me.'

I ask Sally Flynn QC, whose work in sex cases has mostly been on the prosecution side even though she is at the private Bar, how she deals with the secondary trauma of constantly hearing about these terrible things.

'I probably don't, and I probably should,' Flynn replies.

'I don't think that we've talked about vicarious trauma enough or recognised it enough. I tend not to get as many sex trials now that I'm silk, because the Crown don't tend to brief silk for County Court sex trials,' she says.

'I don't know how barristers do back-to-back sex trials. Because I think it's unhealthy and I think you just couldn't keep it up.

'Probably the hardest thing I [find] is if a child complainant is the same age as one of my children. Because you automatically put yourself in that position or put your child in that position. Looking at child pornography is harder.'

Flynn has never bought merchandise from the Japanese *Hello Kitty* brand for her kids, because of a case she did which was particularly upsetting, one of the very few she's had overturned on appeal, where the child victim was wearing, in the forensic pictures, *Hello Kitty* pyjama bottoms. That child and those pyjamas never quite went away.

'So it definitely changes you, I think,' Flynn says. 'But you've just got to put up the barriers. What else do we do?

'We all talk. You go to your friend and you go have a glass of wine and you debrief. Not any non-lawyer friends. Only barrister friends you do that to. We all probably drink too much. Because it's an escape.'

At the time we're speaking, the ABC TV documentary *Revelation* about sexual abuse in the Catholic Church is about to come on TV.

'No way on earth that I'm going to watch that!' Flynn tells me. 'I'd *run*. I'd run from that kind of stuff.

'Because I just deal with enough and I don't think I can deal with any more. I watch crappy [TV], like MAFS [*Married at First Sight*] and *MasterChef* and just fun, with people smiling and laughing. And I don't want to deal with anything else.'

After years of covering these sorts of cases myself, I relate to what she's saying. We share anecdotes about how we wince when our husbands happen to put on the television and there is a scene with violence against children or women. I get almost angry with mine if he persists. My secondary trauma cup is too full.

My brain is like one of those slide carousels from the 1970s, and every now and then a trigger places a card into a slot and the projector lights it up and, 'click'. There is that image of that awful thing that happened to the victim. Lit with that slightly sickly orange filter those seventies pictures always had, flickering in my mind.

Chatting to Flynn on the phone one night after my kids have gone to bed reminds me of a conversation I once had with an older journalist, when I was a young cadet. I was trying to convince him to watch some arthouse film that was depressingly traumatic but brilliantly received. I was being a typically annoying young person, who had not yet seen real trauma, teasing him about his saccharine taste in films.

His flash of anger reminds me of what I am now like when my husband accidentally leaves the TV on a violent scene on Netflix. 'No,' he said finally and firmly.

'Can I ask why?' I ventured.

He then proceeded to tell me about when he was in Rwanda during the civil war between the Hutus and Tutsis in 1994. He was walking through a field and he felt this squelching underfoot and wondered what it was.

'I was walking through a field of severed heads,' the journalist said. 'And ever since that, I don't watch depressing movies anymore.'

'It has a toll, you know?' Phil Dunn says. Like Flynn, he says he is 'absolutely convinced' there is vicarious trauma in it.

'I always say to my wife and my secretary, "When this case is over, I'm having a few weeks off, I'm going to mow the lawn or ride the bike around the block or something."'

'But then something else happens which catches your eye and away you go. You pay a price and it wears you out,' he says, adding that work–life balance is 'a bit pie in the sky'.

'I mean, there are plenty of my colleagues whose marriages don't survive,' he says.

Flynn says that it's difficult to get barristers to talk about vicarious trauma – and if the Bar was to put on a seminar about it, the concern is that barristers might not attend.

'I don't know,' Flynn sighs. 'People get – people get so worried, that people are going to judge them and think there's something wrong with them if they go to those kinds of sessions. Which is wrong. But people like to think that we're bulletproof, and we don't want to admit that we're vulnerable in any way.

'Because, you've got to remember, we're self-employed. And we're only going to get briefed if people think that we're in control.

And, all of a sudden, we're admitting that we're not, you're thinking, "Am I going to get briefed?"

'Are solicitors going to think, "Ooh, Sally Flynn's gone a bit around the twist, might give her a miss for a while"?

'And all of a sudden, your practice falls over. So, you've got to be careful. We've got to protect ourselves as self-employed barristers. But, at the same time, you know, function. It's not easy.'

She says she hopes the stigma attached to seeking help changes and barristers do get counselling or guidance for dealing with extremely traumatic and stressful cases.

Phil Dunn has done more of these trials than most, but over the years, to protect his own mental wellbeing, he's had to refuse to do some categories of cases.

'I refuse to handle child pornography, I just say I'm not interested … it wears you out, it degrades you,' he says, wearily.

Like with Flynn, I'm curious when I speak to Dunn about what being in that frame of mind – not really processing or dealing with the secondary trauma you are wading through, pushing it down and pretending it doesn't exist and that you are just a taxicab, dispassionately picking up the next customer, working crazy hours, always moving on to the next case – does to a person.

He cuts me off.

'Why do you think [he inserts the name of a famous barrister] drinks half a bottle of Scotch a day?'

'He does drink Scotch, and my understanding is he drinks it of a morning,' says Michele Williams QC.

'He does that to get him to the space. Whereas others maybe would do it after, you know, to de-stress afterwards, but not to get them there. Do you know what I mean?

'I think it's well known that barristers drink too much, and you know, that's what gets us through. Yeah. It's been a way that we … You know, what we do after we've finished the trial, we de-stress.'

I tell her that journalists, also dealing with distressing material, are often exactly the same.

When I'm talking to one barrister I speak to off the record, he says to me, candidly and, of his own admission, several wines down, that he is a drunk. That all the best criminal barristers are drunks. 'That's the only way that we can do what we do,' he says. He then thinks better of it and asks me not to quote him.

I will never forget going to a Christmas function at Sir Owen Dixon Chambers in Sydney in 2017 – they had awarded me their annual Law Reporter of the Year award for my first book, *Cardinal*.

I said to a barrister that I didn't know how they could do the work they did – watching child rapists go free, seeing complainants smashed by the onerous burden of proof, constantly processing distressing material.

'Look around you,' he said, gesturing around the busy room. 'Can you see anyone not drinking?'

'Many of us defence counsel like a drink,' says Ian Lloyd QC. 'It's our way of processing the stress that we live with, in every serious case that we do.'

He finds the recommendations of mindfulness techniques offered to barristers to try to cope with the vicarious trauma somewhat amusing. 'The Bar Association has told us that we should de-stress by doing yoga or knitting,' he says, drolly.

I can no more imagine Ian Lloyd doing yoga or settling down to a night of clacking away at a homespun Aran jumper than I can imagine him mounting a broomstick and flying to the moon. He's with me on that one.

'Perhaps understandably, for most of us, those suggestions were binned,' he says. 'For many of us, a drink or two enables us to live with the stress of what we do.'

If you've built a fortress around yourself, where you can't even speak about the trauma, can't admit it lest you lose your practice, and you pretend everything is okay, it's almost like you are negating that people *can* feel trauma, or at least belittling the effect of it. I wonder what that does to the defence barrister's ability to feel empathy for the person they are savaging? Does it knock the edges off their empathy?

'Yeah, that's a really interesting way to think about it,' Flynn says.

'Oh I think it's even more than that,' Michele Williams says.

'I think there's a total disregard because they don't want to face that. If they face that, then they fear they can't do their job.

'Or they fear that, they don't want to stop to think, other than those who are truly callous and laugh about it later.

'But I think there's an element of, you know, it might be unconscious, to be fair, that you don't want to really face the fact that you're bashing up a thirteen-year-old kid, and then go home to your own children. You know?

'So there's a complete separation of self, if you like.

'They've removed their personal self from it. They're putting on another guise, they're putting on, "This is my barrister self. This is me doing my job. So I'm not going to face or acknowledge, I'm going to totally disregard that I'm treating this thirteen-year-old child with disrespect, because if I did face up to that, I couldn't go home to my own thirteen-year-old child."

'So I think there's a separation, which in the long run is not good for their own mental health.'

Phil Dunn QC admits that sometimes the difficulty of these cases leads to a 'siege mentality' in defence counsel.

'The courts are turned against you, the juries are turned against you, so it's all difficult. And the only other people you can talk to about it are fellow barristers,' Dunn says.

I say to him that feeling under siege at the same time when you are constantly faced with very confronting material which most people would never have to think about in their entire lives must be difficult.

'I think the battle experience tends to make you think the victim is potentially a liar,' Dunn admits. 'You have to be careful to approach it in a more nuanced way.

'I know plenty of colleagues, who in sex cases will say, "Got 'em, bloody *bitch*," [or] "It's just another fucking made-up complaint."

'And they are battle-scarred. And their battle experience, and their sense [is] that the system is being gamed by the prosecution and the victim – to the disadvantage of justice and their client.'

I say that that's a distorted view, given the low statistics on sexual assault convictions.

'Not to them, not to them,' Dunn replies. 'Experience tells every barrister there's a false complaint somewhere, and the system is being gamed by a lack of disclosure by the prosecution or the judge is against them or the police [are against them].'

One thing that strikes me in speaking to many of these barristers, mostly men, is that the thing that keeps them going is the idea that somewhere, out there, is the elusive false complaint. Most will say that these are rare and far outstripped by cases in which there simply wasn't enough evidence to convict beyond reasonable doubt. They'll tell you things like 'tell the boy that he did well' in relation to an historical clergy abuse case where it fell over on expensive appeal, or 'no one is saying she's making it up' …

The spectre of the false complaint, however rare most of them will tell you that it is, is what allows them to continue to do what they do.

And still, what they do, despite their protestations that the table-thumpers are gone, is awful.

SURVIVAL

Georgie Burg, a survivor of a serial Anglican paedophile, John Aitchison, had no idea how bruising it would be to make her way through the system when she finally came forward to disclose her abuse to Canberra police in January 2015, after decades of keeping it to herself.

'We're the sort of family who really respect justice and the justice system, and I've always felt that survivors should come forward if they're at all able to and I felt like a hypocrite if I didn't,' Georgie says.

'I felt like if I didn't, I'd be betraying my own children, I'd be betraying our marriage and what we've always taught the children about the police. If you are in trouble, you go to a policeman and they will help you.'

The police did help Georgie, but she will never forget what it was like to go to court.

Georgie's mother was British and so Georgie speaks the Queen's English in rather proper tones. She's very bright, very articulate, and very, very traumatised. She's a mother who clearly adores her own children, but sometimes they seem to remind her of who she might have been.

Two bleak memories of her court experience stand out in her mind – she thinks they speak volumes about how the men (and they were, in her experience, all men) see the people who come before their courts.

When she was to give her evidence, she remembers being brought to the remote witness room – so as not to be in the same room as her abuser.

'In the remote witness rooms you have a detached little, almost like a kitchenette sort of arrangement,' Georgie says.

'I was taken into that by two of the sheriffs and my witness liaison manager and in the corner was a little, really battered-looking, ancient-looking teddy bear. And other than that it was completely bare.

'This was a remote witness room in the ACT that is used for the most traumatised and youngest victims – I was very specifically told that – so it really jumped out to me that this was the only human indication that a child had ever been in those rooms.

'And I said, "I'm so glad that these kids at least can take a teddy bear in with them when they testify."

'And the sheriff said, "Oh no, no, no, no, that teddy bear has been here for about fifteen years. Last week it was named by an eleven-year-old who just testified against a family member, but kids aren't allowed to take those into the remote witness rooms."

'And I said, "Why?"'

'Why?' I venture, not sure if I want to know the answer.

Georgie couldn't work it out. It made no sense.

'And the sheriff said, "Look, it's absolutely terrible, but they are not allowed to because it can be considered as prejudicial to the jury."

'And I said,' she continues, '"These are kids, that is a teddy bear and it's a little teddy bear and [they] have to sit behind the desk anyway. What on earth?"'

Georgie asked the court officials if anyone had tried to change that rule.

'And the sheriff shook her head and said, "We've tried."'

Right on cue, as I hear Georgie weeping on the other end of the phone about the teddy bear, my nine-year-old bursts into the room. We've all just started lockdown during the coronavirus pandemic and she's feeling a bit anxious. She just wants a cuddle. She's always done a good line in cuddling, that one. Ever since she was born.

She has a menagerie of plush toys out on the landing outside the room where I'm speaking to Georgie. The thought of her being that child, in that room, one of her teddies or bunnies taken from her arms, in case it might remind the jury that she is a child, slays me.

I give her a cuddle, promise I won't be too long and tell her she needs to go because Mummy is having an adult conversation.

As Georgie and I start talking again, her second story is even worse. During her evidence, she tells me, she became so distressed that she had a nosebleed.

'Sometimes, when you are testifying, as a survivor, there's so much energy involved,' she says. 'Because you're so focused on the fact that you're testifying, it's like you don't actually think of yourself as a person anymore.

'You don't think … of the fact that your nose is bleeding, or that you're crying, or whatever, you're just so caught up in reliving this horrible thing.'

She says the stern but kindly sheriffs who were attending to her noticed her streaming nose and asked the judge for a break.

'So the recess had been called and they were sort of mopping me up,' she remembers. 'I've never forgotten it because it just was horrific. The sheriff said, "Oh, don't worry about it. We had a little girl in here a while back and I've never forgotten her. She was about eight and she was wearing a white dress that had red cherries on it."

'And she said, "This little girl, she's testifying against someone, like her father," I think the sheriff said. And she said, "Her nose started to bleed, and no one asks for a recess and this little girl didn't stop talking, she just talked and talked, and, in the end, her white dress wasn't white anymore."'

Georgie weeps as she contemplates the blood cherries on the little girl's white frock.

'Oh my god,' is all I can manage.

'And I just thought, that little thing, eight years old,' she says.

'You just picture your own little ones.'

Georgie's a talker. Talking helps her and heals her. She's a person who, now that she's finally come forward with her story, wants to be heard, and that's what seems to keep her going. Those two memories are the things that Georgie Burg would have to talk about to debrief with her husband more than anything else. They'd go for a drive in the countryside near their home outside of Melbourne and talk about the teddy bear and the cherries.

'We'd just drive through Mount Dandenong and out past Healesville and the Black Spur and things and I just talked about those two things over and over because I couldn't ... you know that kind of thing where you can't believe it happened, that it's real, that the justice system that I had believed in so much ... It needs to change.

'These are not,' she says, '"Witness X" or "Number 75" or anything else, these are children.

'And if the justice system is going to take away their entire identity, refer to them as an alias or a number or a set of initials or whatever else, they can at least treat them as human beings when they are doing these incredibly, almost *inhumanly* brave things.

'I don't know how to change it. I don't know if I can change it.

'I'm not someone people listen to, but if I can be involved somehow and just be one little voice saying, "I've done it, and this is what happened," at least maybe somehow it might change one day.'

* * *

'Many survivors told us that they felt that they were the ones on trial,' the Royal Commission into Institutional Responses to Child Sexual Abuse stated in its *Criminal Justice Consultation Paper*.

'Some survivors told us that the cross-examination process was as bad as the child sexual abuse they suffered,' it said.

'Many survivors told us that they found the process retraumatising and offensive.'

In order to protect the accused at all costs, so he or she is presumed innocent until proven guilty, it often feels like the system narrows its eyes in suspicion at the complainant until the bitter end. The inverse of innocent until proven guilty is suspect until proven otherwise. That's a damaging psychological process for a person who has already been betrayed, for whom trust issues are common, to have to go through.

'When we think about victims of sexual crimes,' says Victoria's Victims of Crimes Commissioner, Fiona McCormack, 'and you think about what has happened to them, this degradation, betrayal, violation – when they come to court, they have expectations, not unreasonably, that they are going to be treated with respect, that there's going to be a process but it's going to be fair.

'And they're seeking some sort of acknowledgement of what's happened to them – particularly from their community.'

But often, that's not what they get.

McCormack says it was interesting to read the Victorian Law Reform Commission's 2016 review of the role of victims in the criminal trial process and to compare the submissions of professionals working in justice services, speaking of all of the reforms that have been introduced to the system over the past thirty years, and then to compare those submissions with what survivors say.

'The submissions from the victims very much reflect what I've heard over the years and what, sadly, I'm still hearing today,' McCormack says, 'and they are just *scathing*. Absolutely scathing.

'Many victim survivors have felt completely betrayed, they've felt violated.

'So many people say that it was worse than the sexual assault, the trauma they experienced going through the criminal trial process was worse than the sexual assault.

'And when I hear of people harming themselves, attempting to take their life, I think, "What does that say about us as a society?" I appreciate that we have to interrogate whether somebody is in fact telling the truth, but I think that we've got a long way to go in terms of not retraumatising a victim survivor.'

Often, it's subtler than the thumping of tables, or raising of voices.

The key themes told to the Victorian Law Reform's Victims of Crime Report from victims who were witnesses were that cross-examination was disrespectful of their dignity as human beings.

The list of adjectives used by victims interviewed for the report about their cross-examination tends to suggest that the 'table-thumpers' – literally or metaphorically – might be more common than the Bar likes to think: 'Humiliating'; 'distressing'; 'brutal, abrupt and traumatising'; 'intense, offensive, ruthless and terrible'; 'aggressive and insensitive'; 'repetitive'; 'confusing'; 'damaging and gruelling'; 'horrid and intimidating'; 'bullying'.

'Persistent, distracting, patronising, hectoring and badgering'; 'stressful'; 'awful, attacking, and designed to unravel [the victim]'; 'harassing'; 'bad, frustrating, inappropriate and embarrassing'.

And, of course, 'like being on trial'.

The report presented anecdote after anecdote of victims 'whose feelings, needs and interests were disregarded or overlooked in the criminal trial process' – be they adults or children.

One Centre Against Sexual Assault referred in a submission to the inquiry about a nine-year-old victim of sexual offences, who was 'unlikely to have received such cold and offensive treatment as she experienced from the defence lawyer, at any other time in her life, apart from during the child sexual offences'.

Writing in the *UNSW Law Journal* in December 2019, Professor of Law and Criminology Annie Cossins says, 'A criminal trial is a public spectacle, a place where we can see justice at work.

'[But in] Australia, we have limited ways of preventing a sexual assault trial from turning into a stone-throwing exercise by defence counsel while complainants, with no legal representation, have no control over the trial process.'

Criminologist Michael Salter says that both in Australia and also in comparable common law jurisdictions overseas, the statistics are telling.

'In sexual assault matters, both adult and child, really for the last fifteen years, we've seen increased reports and flat, or decreasing, rates of prosecution,' Salter says.

'And certainly one of those explanations is that there is increased willingness in the community to report and then there is more pressure on police and prosecutors to progress matters that arguably previously wouldn't have been taken seriously. But essentially, once they're getting to the court, actually the culture of the court is not shifting.

'You've got a significant history of law reform in Australia. What we're not seeing shift at the same rate is ultimately the outcomes for victims and survivors are not changing.

'I would suggest that this is not simply about procedural matters and procedural reform, but the emotional architecture of the court is more important and for the players in the criminal justice system, whether they're barristers or they're judges or whomever, they're very familiar with that emotional architecture. So even where there is a procedural reform that's supposed to deliver a different outcome, you have barristers that are able to use implicit strategies to reassert the old status quo.'

So you can have rules and legislation around how the barristers are supposed to behave, but they don't necessarily change things.

'I do think that the concept of humiliation here is really, really crucial, because it is psychologically an incredibly powerful emotion,' Salter says. 'It is one that is felt deeply by the person who's targeted, but it's also one that is very observable for judges and for juries in the general kind of fact-finding endeavour.

'So ultimately, how do we change not just the procedural obstacles for justice survivors, but how do we shift the emotional obstacles?

'Because I think in the context of the criminal system, we are talking about a very lucrative psycho-politics of humiliation.

'What you're paying the big bucks for when you're paying for a barrister who's got a very good track record and word of mouth in getting acquittals in cases like this, you are paying for the implicit strategies that he has developed in order to flout the spirit of recent law reform.'

And that means, using tone and subtle techniques, like, for instance, he says, 'addressing a nineteen-year-old as "Madam"'.

* * *

Saxon Mullins' trauma was about far more than the style of cross-examination employed in her trial. For Saxon, it was what she had to go through after Luke Lazarus was convicted and she thought her involvement in the criminal justice system was over.

Lazarus appealed. And he was successful in the Court of Criminal Appeal on the basis that the trial judge had misdirected the jury as to Lazarus' state of mind. Even the lawyers I have spoken to about this concede it is 'complicated'.

Luke Lazarus' conviction was quashed.

Because Lazarus was by this stage so well-known in New South Wales, the courts have the option to order a judge-only trial, so the jury will not be tainted by media discussion about the case.

The new trial was set down before Judge Robyn Tupman.

Saxon again put on the pinkish red polka dot dress she'd worn to the first trial, and attended the New South Wales District Court for Round Two. When I ask her what she did with the dress afterwards, Saxon says, quickly and definitely, 'I threw it in the bin.'

'I think we always expected that Lazarus would appeal,' Saxon's sister Arnica Mullins tells me. 'Just given the amount of resources that he has.

'I actually didn't think it would be successful. I believed that my sister had been raped and that to go through a retrial would just be another traumatic experience for her … that Saxon would have to relive that experience again, was heartbreaking.'

I ask Saxon what she thinks about judge-alone trials, given her experience. She laughs fatalistically.

'I don't think they're awesome,' she says. 'I just don't think you can substitute twelve peers with one person.'

The trial before Judge Tupman took a radically different course.

'Basically she didn't believe my account,' Saxon says. 'She didn't believe my timeline. She didn't believe me.'

Judge Tupman arrived at an alternative interpretation of the evidence before her. On the critical point of what Lazarus himself believed, essentially, she preferred Luke Lazarus' version of events. She didn't accept Saxon was so drunk that she couldn't have consented to the sex. And she accepted Luke Lazarus' account that Saxon had not told him to 'stop', because, in her first police statement, Saxon had said that she thought at one point she had asked him to stop.

'She pushed back towards him and then back and forwards as the anal intercourse took place …' Judge Tupman said in her judgement, which acquitted Luke Lazarus.

'She did not say "stop" or "no",' she said, applying the logic that because Saxon had first said, 'I *think* [emphasis mine] at one point that I had asked him to stop' and then later asserted that she did then ask him to stop.

'She did not take any physical action to move away from the intercourse or attempted intercourse.'

It is arguable that there are several issues with these statements by Judge Tupman and some of them are nuanced.

The first is one which courts often wrestle with and is extremely difficult in the case of a 'beyond reasonable doubt' standard of proof. And that is the reality that victims of sexual crimes, as discussed earlier, routinely make inconsistent statements along the way because they are affected by trauma.

Dr Ellie Freedman, the doctor who physically examined Saxon on the day of her police statement, sees it in a practical sense – how inconsistencies appear in the accounts of the rape victims she sees at the height of their trauma, when people are typically not thinking straight. In a way, it's actually the worst time, if you think about it, for someone to give evidence to police.

'Immediately following a sexual assault, most people are so confused, they're trying to make sense of what happened to them,' Dr Freedman says.

'And the thought of going and describing a really intimate sexual experience to a complete stranger at a police station is really difficult for most people to do.'

Victoria's Victims of Crimes Commissioner, Fiona McCormack, says the impact of trauma on memory in relation to sequence of events, or particular details, 'can be borne out in these kinds of processes and can be pounced upon'.

'Some would argue that identifying prior inconsistent statements is a key strategy for the defence, for discrediting a witness,' McCormack says. 'Skilful cross-examination often involves "tripping up" a witness in an attempt to prove inconsistencies between earlier tellings of their stories.'

Glenn Davies, the former head of Victoria Police's Sexual Crimes Squad who has since worked in survivor advocacy, says inconsistencies were something police constantly had to manage.

'And an inconsistency doesn't automatically mean that someone is lying,' Davies says. 'An inconsistency can be a failure of someone's memory – someone who was traumatised and doesn't have consistent recollection.

'Someone who was traumatised and got things out of sequence because their brain function actually shuts down in the process of being traumatised.'

That's why, Davies says, he moved towards a practice of getting statements made over several days – because 'you've got someone who has not yet been able to process the whole thing'.

'It's entirely natural for a traumatised person to have different recollections at different times,' Davies says.

'The new way of doing this [as police] is to take our time, allow people to process, not committing a person to a fine grain detail until they've been able to piece it back together as to what occurred.'

But then there is the whole point that, in this case, it was simply 'I *think* I told him to stop' versus 'I told him to stop'. A fairly subtle difference in the heat of the moment.

'"I think", in the process of recollection and recovery from an intensely traumatic incident, it wasn't uncommon in my experience for the victim to be sorting out the event, what happened next and piecing it together, trying to remember, it being very difficult to remember because of the trauma, having difficulty processing – yes, "I think" is a phrase that's not uncommon,' Davies says.

Davies is not commenting on Saxon's specific case, as he is not familiar with the details of it, but says that in his experience of interviewing many victims of sexual assault over many years, this is 'a processing thing that people do when they are going through the activity of recalling what happened. If something is a bit hazy – you are replaying it in your head – you are confirming to yourself – we don't have automatic recall of every single thing that happened to us.'

He says that this is compounded when the interview takes place very shortly after the event, when a person has had 'little or no sleep, where they are still in shock, maybe, and they are still coming to terms with the enormity of all of that'.

'You've drunk the most that you have in your life and had the most traumatic thing that's happened to you in life.

'And then to be quizzed and to have every single word examined and "we are going to put that to the court in the fine grain detail that you have just given us", it doesn't seem fair.'

He says while, in his experience, police have much more training in the impact of trauma, 'people in court – defence barristers and judges – don't have any expertise in this at all'.

For Professor Annie Cossins, it's also important to consider that the fact that Saxon froze in the moment and did not fight back is not a sign she was consenting.

'That could just mean that [she had entered] into what's known as a "freeze response",' Cossins says. '[A person's] ability to have conscious control over their body disappears and they do what they are told to do, usually out of fear – and Saxon did say in her evidence that she responded the way she did out of fear,' she says.

'I think lawyers and judges and fact-finders generally need to know about this phenomenon known as "the freeze response". It's well known by psychologists and psychiatrists that there are actually three responses to fear,' Cossins says, adding that this is 'well researched in the literature'.

'There's fight, flight and freeze.' Cossins adds that 'the average layperson and the average lawyer' thinks that a person faced with Saxon's dilemma will 'run out of there, or will fight their attacker'.

'But we need a bit more education, I think, as a community, [because] the third response is "freeze" and a freeze response usually occurs when the person can see that "fight" and "flight" aren't options for them.

'There's no evidence in her very long reasons … no evidence at all, that [Judge Tupman] was aware of the freeze response,' Cossins says.

Cossins argues in her December 2019 piece for the *UNSW Law Journal* that Judge Tupman also focused on Saxon's behaviour, and failed to look 'for any steps taken by [Lazarus] to ascertain whether Mullins had consented'.

'There was a great focus on her lack of resistance and her apparent … failure to have said "stop" or "no",' Cossins told me. 'I don't think that we can judge a sexual assault complainant's behaviour based on how we think we might act in that situation or how we see other people act in that situation, or how we see other people react in that situation on TV, for example.'

Judge Tupman thought it was immaterial whether Luke Lazarus swore at Saxon Mullins when he told her to, as Saxon had asserted, and Lazarus had rejected, put her 'fucking' hands on the wall.

Her Honour accepted the evidence of defence witnesses who said Luke Lazarus had a good character. The judge also relied on the evidence of a female friend of Luke Lazarus, who told the court she had had anal sex on first dates.

'This piece of evidence was given in cross-examination by the Crown, did not go to character, but provides in my view some objective insight into contemporary morality,' Judge Tupman said in her decision.

'I do not accept ... [the Crown's argument about the unlikelihood of a virgin consenting to anal intercourse as her first sexual experience] ... when looking at the event together with the evidence of the young people who gave character evidence [for Lazarus] and especially the young woman to whose evidence I have just recently referred,' Judge Tupman said.

'Their evidence allowed some insight into the contemporary morality of that group of young people.'

This part of Her Honour's judgement provoked much outrage.

Stephen Odgers SC, who is chair of the NSW Bar Association's Criminal Law Committee, spoke to me for the *Four Corners* program and he tried to explain what the judge was getting at.

'So it was really, the judge was responding to that proposition that it could not have been a belief [by Luke Lazarus] in consent [by Saxon] by saying, "Well, there's some evidence before me of a contemporary morality, at least in some people, in some circumstances, in some parts of our community, where it was conceivable that somebody might consent even in those circumstances,"' Odgers said.

'And she referred to one witness who gave evidence, which tended to support that.

'And so, Her Honour was rejecting an argument that it was inevitable that there was a lack of belief in consent, or no reasonable basis, by saying, "Well in fact, there is some evidence to the contrary,"' Odgers said.

Odgers did not see this as a problem and pointed out that the case wasn't decided on that basis alone. But the thing I find difficult to not keep returning to is that it was the evidence of one person. Judge Tupman does not refer to others giving evidence about anal sex on first dates.

'She used Saxon's lack of resistance and this term "contemporary morality" to come to the conclusion that Lazarus had formed a belief based on reasonable grounds,' Cossins says.

As Cossins wrote in her journal article: '[H]ow is one woman's sexual experiences representative of eighteen-year-old virgins?

'Was this young woman an expert in contemporary sexual mores? Had she carried out a survey of her age group? Are there no other "contemporary moralities"?'

But also, it's hard not to question conflating the actions of a teenage virgin who had had *no* sex of any kind with the actions of a more sexually experienced young woman who, at that stage in her sexual life, had come to the point where anal sex was something she had become comfortable enough to do with someone she barely knew. Not to mention anal sex, short minutes after meeting a stranger, on her hands and knees, in a dark alleyway she'd never been in before.

As Cossins writes, 'by justifying sexual intercourse with a non-consenting woman, the term "contemporary morality" could be used to excuse any sexual act in any circumstances'. As long as, presumably, you can find someone to say that they had done that thing.

'Thinking about contemporary morality and the fact that one person's view was taken to be *the* view,' Saxon's sister Arnica says, 'especially someone who was a friend of Lazarus, wasn't there on the night, doesn't know Saxon, doesn't know her moral compass, is a little disturbing.

'The fact that this friend had more say or had more influence over the outcome, rather than Saxon, who was, first night out in Kings Cross, she was a virgin, she'd barely even kissed a boy before and all of a sudden to put this in a basket of someone who might be happy to go and have anal sex in the back alley in Kings Cross, is upsetting and it makes me angry.

'Because that's not my sister.

'Even if that *is* the gauge that the judge took, and that's the view that she had, I don't think that should be cast across everyone. That shouldn't be the paintbrush that we determine the outcome of this.'

But it was. It was the paintbrush. Saxon is now, seven years later, able to say the words that used to be too hard to utter. She says she's 'yet to meet anyone' who agrees that this is something they'd do as their first sexual experience. In fact, she says, 'it absolutely is a violent act'.

'Strictly, in my own case, an unaided, unlubricated penetration is absolutely a violent act,' Saxon says.

Judge Tupman did, like the police, the prosecutors and the jury, accept that Saxon Mullins did not consent to sex that night.

But the critical point became whether Luke Lazarus knew she wasn't consenting.

'I stress that I do not accept that the complainant, by her actions, herself meant to consent to sexual intercourse and in her own mind was not consenting to sexual intercourse,' Judge Tupman found.

'Whether or not she consented is but one matter. Whether or not the accused knew that she was not consenting is another.'

Essentially, Judge Tupman found that, although Saxon was not consenting, the prosecution could not prove beyond reasonable doubt that Luke Lazarus had no reasonable basis for believing that she *was* consenting.

'I accept that this … amounts to reasonable grounds, in the circumstances for the accused to have formed the … genuine belief, that in fact the complainant was consenting … even though it was quick, unromantic … and … may not [have] occurred if each had been sober,' Judge Tupman said.

'It's really hard to reconcile that kind of verdict,' Arnica Mullins says. 'That a judge can say, "Well, yes, the victim, or the complainant, she believed that she had been raped, but then the person who had perpetrated the act for them, well they didn't think it was rape." I don't know how you can reconcile that kind of verdict … or, I don't know how that gives any clarity for anyone else in the future. It just creates even more of a grey area.'

Odgers did not have a problem with the reasoning.

'Most people,' I pressed him, 'who we've spoken to have been shocked by this case. Why are you not shocked?'

'Because I understand that criminal trials are complex things where there are difficult issues of law and factual determinations,' Odgers replied, evenly.

'People have different perspectives, but I'm concerned that the process is a fair one and I think the process was a fair one in this case.

'It's true that, in our culture now, it's desirable that people take steps to ensure that there's consent. We all desire that in a socially advanced society.

'But to make somebody guilty of a serious criminal offence, where they're liable to go to jail for many years, we do require that they have that necessary guilty mind and the test for proving that is, in this case, proving beyond reasonable doubt that there was no reasonable basis for the belief that she was consenting.

'And the judge was not satisfied that that was proved by the prosecution in this case.'

Robyn Tupman set Luke Lazarus free.

That night, there was a celebration at the Lazarus family home in Vaucluse. Tabloid photographers snapped pictures of guests spilling out on the Vaucluse nature strip the next morning.

In them, one young blond man with fashionably side-swept hair and dark glasses, saunters, barefoot, wearing a navy suit jacket and shirt, unbuttoned to the tanned navel, and swimming shorts. He is following a dishevelled-looking man who had earlier been seen accompanying Lazarus to court. He still appears to be in the previous day's creased clothes.

'What are you all celebrating?' The *Daily Mail*'s headline said.

'Luke Lazarus threw a "huge party" at his family's eastern suburbs home hours after being cleared of raping an 18-year-old virgin behind his father's nightclub in Sydney's inner-city Kings Cross,' the online tabloid told its readers.

'Mr Lazarus, who sighed and hugged his weeping mother when acquitted on Thursday afternoon, appeared worse for wear on Friday morning after the rave at his parents' $8 million Vaucluse home.' Lazarus would later say in a radio interview that the event was hardly "a party".

'Neighbours told *Daily Mail Australia* dozens of young people dressed in suits arrived at the Lazarus mansion on Thursday at 6pm, less than two hours after the 25-year-old was cleared of rape.'

'That's just poor form,' Saxon told me, in 2017, about the Vaucluse event, whatever it may have been.

'I don't really have anything good to say about that. I don't understand why they would do that. If you think he's innocent, then that's fantastic, but again, you know why he was in a trial.

'You know I'm a real person. You know the ramifications of what happened, but you don't care, clearly. I think it's just disgusting.'

Her sister Arnica pointed out that there was no such celebration in the Mullins home after the jury's guilty verdict in the first trial.

'Something that Saxon always says to me is that you have to have compassion for people, no matter what,' Arnica said. 'And Saxon is deeply compassionate, even for her abuser.

'And the fact that they had a party celebrating this triumph was very upsetting because it showed that they had little regard for Saxon's welfare, or any care at all for what she went through.'

I asked Saxon what she did on the night of the Tupman decision.

'I sat on the couch with my mum and my sister,' she told me, 'and cried. And went to bed.'

The Crown appealed the Tupman decision to acquit Luke Lazarus in the New South Wales Court of Criminal Appeal (CCA).

The court found, that, for the second time, a second trial judge in this case had made an error.

This time, the CCA found that the law required Judge Robyn Tupman to look at what steps Luke Lazarus took in forming his reasonable belief that Saxon had consented, and as she did not say that she had done that, she had erred.

'Whether she did [look at what steps Lazarus took] or not, we don't know,' Odgers explained. 'She may have, but because she hadn't said that she had regard to it [*sic*], the court had to conclude that there had been a breach of the statutory requirement. That meant that the verdict had to be quashed.'

But while it could be said that the verdict was, technically, quashed, the Crown's appeal was dismissed and there was no retrial of Luke Lazarus. The court took into account the fact that it would be at least five years after the incident itself.

'Another factor was that there had already been two trials, the accused had been put through two trials, not just the accused, of course, the complainant [Saxon] as well,' Odgers said.

'And then a third factor was that he'd actually served ten months in prison,' he said.

I asked Stephen Odgers SC what his 'visceral reaction' was to the way this case played out.

'I don't have a reaction to this case,' Odgers replied. 'I look at the law and the decisions of the courts, and I couldn't see any clear errors in the reasoning of the courts of criminal appeal in either decision. I can understand why they made a decision not to order a new trial. So I don't have an emotional reaction to it.'

Arnica Mullins did.

'The Court of Criminal Appeal judgement left us with nothing,' Arnica told me. 'It's not like there was opportunity, I think, for either side to have any resolution. We're both now left with, there's nothing. You know?

'[It was] "Yeah, we think something has gone wrong, but too much time has passed, let's just leave it."

'I don't think that's the outcome that Saxon wanted, either way. A final resolution would have been better than nothing.'

For Saxon herself, the end to her legal battle that day in December 2017, almost five years down the track from her night out in Kings Cross, was not dramatic.

'It was kind of strange,' Saxon tells me. 'We were waiting around for a while, and then you're just in this room with, like, three judges, and there's all these other lawyers and stuff, all these other appeals, and they basically just say, "Case dismissed".'

'And how does that feel?' I ask.

'I was kind of in a bit of shock.' She sighs. 'I don't know what I was expecting, but I guess I just wasn't ready, and I guess it's this kind of instant feeling of being deflated. Like, that was it. That was all we had. And then, in two seconds, it went. They went, "No. It's over." Five years, done.

'I just didn't know what to do. Yeah.'

It's hard to imagine a bigger anti-climax. A conviction, a jail sentence, an appeal, an acquittal, an appeal, the acquittal quashed, the judge has erred, but then, appeal dismissed, limbo.

'I guess the first feeling after the appeal was just kind of aimless, directionless,' she says. 'This is what I had been working towards for five years. And it was almost like I had the world wide open to me, except I was still hurting.

'Like, it got to be over for everyone else.

'There's no other avenues. Everyone's done. Everyone goes home and then it's just me and I'm still here and I'm still doing it, even though it's not happening anymore. I'm still living it. It was weird and lonely.'

'It's very hard, because, Saxon told me not to cry,' Arnica says, her eyes shining nonetheless. 'But when someone's your younger sibling, I see it as my job to look after her. And I feel like I failed her. Because, "What if?" You know, all these "What ifs"?

'"What if I'd gone out with her that night?" Because we go out together all the time. We're so close ... I play through these scenarios in my mind – "What if, what if, what if?"

'I guess the fact that Saxon came forward, there's been two trials and still no real outcome – I don't know what comfort that gives to anyone else ...

'What comfort does that give to [someone] in the future if they want to come forward?'

Those words, those questions, about why someone might come forward in future, return to me again and again during my research for this book.

And if victims don't come forward, what then?

Back in 2018, Saxon's friend Brittany Watts looked at the ceiling, tears rolling down her young cheeks, as I asked her what had 'changed' in Saxon.

'It's hard to talk about because I actually don't talk to her about this because I wouldn't want to tell her that she's different,' Brittany said. 'There was, like, a light in her. She was so bright, she was so happy.

'Everyone loves Saxon, like, everyone loves her. And this light has just ... it's just not there anymore. The hope you have when you're young, that your future is gonna be bright and happy and you're gonna do what you need to do to have the best life that you can? That hope? I just don't see it in her anymore.

'And that's hard. Because she has to fight for it now, you know? But she just had it. She just had that happy brightness about her and so much trust in people, you know? And that's gone. And it's destroyed.

'You know, she's still fun now – she's still happy, and we still have fun and everything. But there just, still, is something just there that you see sometimes that's missing. And I just always wonder what she would have been like if this never happened. I just think she would have been a completely different person.'

While I first interviewed Saxon Mullins in 2017, the final appeal in her case delayed any telling of her story. And strangely, while all complainants of sexual assault are already entitled to anonymity at law, the court had placed an extra suppression order on naming Saxon. It meant that, incredibly, she – and we – had to make an application in order for Saxon to tell her own story. That meant advising Luke Lazarus' lawyers and giving them an opportunity to oppose. Thankfully, they didn't.

Saxon's name became public for the first time on our *Four Corners* documentary, *I Am That Girl*, on 7 May 2018. The response to the story was astonishing. Our program was flooded with well-wishes from people across the country. Parents sat down with their daughters, and, importantly, sons, to watch the story and to discuss the issues about consent it raised.

The program ended with the following words from Saxon Mullins, as she walked through the now-deserted streets of Kings Cross. 'On a social level, I think we need to teach people about making sure that the person you are with wants to be with you.

'Enthusiastic consent is really easy to determine.

'And I think if you don't have that, then you're not good to go.

'All you need to say is, "Do you want to be here?" and very clearly, "Do you want to have sex with me? Do you want to be doing what we're doing?"

'And if it's not an enthusiastic yes, then it's not enough.

'If it's not an enthusiastic "yes", it's a "no".

'That's it.

'And then, you're committing a crime.

'Simple as that.'

I was sent messages of support for Saxon from high-profile people – actors, writers, business leaders, high-profile lawyers, politicians from across the spectrum.

'I find it hard to believe these are all real people,' Saxon bashfully told me. 'Talking about me and my story. It's insane. I can't believe how lucky I am.'

The day after the story, New South Wales Attorney-General Mark Speakman described Saxon's story as 'harrowing' when he referred the state's rape laws – particularly Section 61HA of the *Crimes Act*, which examined the meaning of consent and the reasonableness of the accused's belief – to the New South Wales Law Reform Commission for an inquiry.

'Look, if you put yourself in [Saxon's] shoes, she's been humiliated in an alleyway at the age of eighteen,' Speakman told me. 'She's had to tell her traumatic story in court. She's had to face two trials, two appeals, and still no final outcome.

'From her viewpoint, the whole process has been, I imagine, just a huge disappointment. Just shaking your head in disbelief and frustration.

'Look, it's not a satisfactory outcome for a complainant to go through four hearings, two trials, two appeals, and in the end the accused has to be let go because we've had the judicial process going on too long.

'What this shows is that there's a real question about whether our law in New South Wales is clear enough, is certain enough, is fair enough.'

Luke Lazarus and his family would never agree to interviews with our program, despite numerous conversations and emails with the family and his lawyers. I had envisioned a scenario where Luke might say what he had learned from all of this. I went into the process holding Luke no malice and aware that this had ruined his young life.

But the communication with the Lazarus family suddenly stopped. We never quite worked out why.

Instead, Luke Lazarus elected, ten days after our program aired, to do an 'exclusive' interview with Sydney commercial radio broadcaster Ben Fordham. I discovered this when Fordham, whom I had known socially some years before, called me, anxious to get in touch with Saxon and tell her that Luke was being interviewed. I told him that Saxon had told me she had said her piece and had nothing more to say. He called back again later, saying his bosses were 'offering Saxon the chance to hear the interview before it goes to air'. I had the impression that perhaps there was concern about what they were putting to air and, at the very least, the effect it would have on Saxon. Saxon passed on that she didn't want to hear the thing before broadcast 'or at all'.

'I feel an enormous amount of sympathy for Saxon Mullins,' Fordham told his listeners at the outset. 'I thought how Luke Lazarus treated Saxon Mullins was despicable.'

'My impression of you, from a distance, is that you are a rich kid, you're spoilt, you're powerful, you're someone who took advantage of a young eighteen-year-old girl who was drunk, who was a virgin, who didn't want to lose her virginity by having anal sex with a stranger in an alleyway,' Fordham said to Lazarus.

'I get the impression, Luke Lazarus, that you pushed this on her, you knew you were doing the wrong thing, and while you may have been acquitted by the courts, the court of public opinion views you as scum.'

Lazarus replied that he wasn't surprised that people thought that because they were getting their information from 'media publications that are just trying their best to get clicks'. He said that he had nothing to hide. Lazarus gave the impression that he was simply acquitted, and that was that, when in fact the Court of Appeal criticised the judge's reasoning for the acquittal and found that she had erred in law.

He accused our program of getting things wrong, which he didn't spell out. We didn't. Each sentence in the story was fact-checked by three members of our team by reference to the court documents. We said nothing that could not be substantiated by evidence. It was then subjected to an exhaustive two-week production process, which involved lawyers raking over every part of the script and senior producers again poring over it, querying each line. But this was not a special case. That's what we do for every *Four Corners* story. I have never worked for another media outlet that does this for all stories.

Lazarus also made much of the fact that he actually had, in that brief four-minute window between meeting Saxon and anally penetrating her, taken her to a VIP area of some sort.

He reiterated what he said in his evidence, including that he did not swear when he told Saxon to put her hands up against the fence and that she didn't tell him she wanted to go and that her words at trial were not 'no' but 'stop'.

'She told you that she was a virgin,' Fordham began. 'Your response was to ask her to get on her hands and knees and to try and have anal sex with her.'

Lazarus remained silent for a moment. 'Um, well, sorry, is there a question in there?'

'It's a statement,' Fordham replied.

'Okay, well, um, my response to this has always been very clear,' Lazarus replied.

'Um, ah, her physical actions told me that she was consenting,' he continued, adding that a 'very experienced judge' had agreed that his belief was reasonable.

'Nowhere in this is her saying, "I don't want to do this, don't do this, stop."'

But Fordham pressed on. 'Why would you do that when she's just told you that she's a virgin ... Luke, I'm asking about your thought process when this girl told you she was a virgin, why was your thought to have anal sex with her?'

Lazarus replied that it was her 'physical body language' that told him she was 'participating in sex'.

'So, if I'm a man assessing the situation,' Lazarus continued, 'and I'm watching a woman, not only consent but participate, as she has admitted, then I'd ask you, "How is a man to know that a woman is not consenting when she is participating?"'

How is a man to know?

'Do you feel that you took advantage of her?' Fordham later asked.

'Took advantage? Aaahh, no.'

He hasn't learned, I thought as I listened to the broadcast. He hasn't learned at all.

He did say that he felt really remorseful 'for the pain that she's had to endure. It's terrible for ... to hear that she's in that pain, is, really upsetting.' He was 'sorry' for causing her that pain. But nonetheless, he was willing to continue to undermine Saxon's credibility by, throughout this interview, implying that she was lying, and he didn't seem to have thought about what his actions really meant.

On the 'popping those cherries' text message exchange with his friend, where he had texted *'It's a pretty gross story. Tell ya later*', Lazarus said, 'It was anal sex in a lane, it's certainly not conventional.' Fordham said it was 'horrifying and sickening and most people would be reacting in the same way'. But Lazarus was unrepentant.

'Um, first of all, I'll just say that that comment about being horrified and sickened, I don't think is fair. Again, I've been found innocent.'

First, the question wasn't about his guilt or innocence, it was about how morally questionable it was for him to do what he did. And second, he hadn't been 'found innocent'. His jury conviction had been quashed by a judge – meaning that, in the second trial, he'd been found not guilty – that is, the prosecution had not proven its case beyond reasonable doubt. But that judge had then been found in error by an appeals court.

At the time the interview was broadcast, Lazarus was actually in a strange legal no-man's land which, as Stephen Odgers SC would explain to me, meant 'the real problem here is, we don't have a determination ... And so, at the end of the day, we don't have a proper determination of the factual issues in this case, and that's regrettable. But we don't always get perfect justice.'

Fordham asked Lazarus if he had ever written a letter to Saxon Mullins.

'I actually did write one, once, but I was told that I should not do that,' Lazarus admitted.

'Why not?' Fordham asked.

'My lawyers told me that was not something I should do.'

I had so hoped that Luke Lazarus would talk about how, on reflection, his decision to persevere with anal sex with an eighteen-year-old virgin who had had too much to drink, in a dark and filthy alleyway, on her hands and knees in the gravel, well, perhaps that decision wasn't right. How he wouldn't treat a girl like that now. How the decision to proceed with the anal sex knowing that she was a virgin, in those horrible circumstances, was strange and, consent or otherwise, callous. But there was none of that. He did the old 'I'm sorry she was hurt' without acknowledging why exactly he had hurt her so badly. He just didn't seem to get it. Still. After all that time. This was his moment to redeem himself. He didn't.

Of the inquiry set up by Attorney-General Mark Speakman, Lazarus cautioned that whoever oversaw it would 'need to be very careful' because often there would be sex between two people without words spoken and 'it might be hard to delineate what is consent and what is enthusiastic consent'.

'So, I think a bit of care needs to be taken if the laws do change,' Lazarus advised the law-makers.

I think a bit of care needs to be taken.

It's not clear what the law-makers thought of that exchange, if, indeed, they ever bothered to switch on 2GB that afternoon. But nonetheless, sweeping changes to the law were recommended as a result of Saxon coming forward.

The Law Reform Commission inquiry's draft report into Consent in Relation to Sexual Offences in October 2019 proposed that the law should contain specific inclusions such as that 'a lack of physical or verbal resistance does not, of itself, mean there is consent to any other sexual activity'. It also said the law should state circumstances in which a person does not consent – and they included if the person 'does not do or say anything to communicate consent'.

Where, before, the law convicted a person if there were 'no reasonable grounds' for his belief in consent, that was to change to the belief 'is not reasonable in the circumstances'.

And, crucially, the consideration of any 'steps' taken by the accused to ascertain consent (a consideration which Judge Tupman did not spell out and led to the quashing of her decision) would be replaced with 'whether the accused person said or did anything to ascertain if the complainant consented' and 'if so, what the accused person said or did'.

This is important, because it requires a judge or jury to look, in a more proactive way, at exactly what was done by someone like Lazarus to see if the person he was having sex with wanted to do it.

At the time of writing, the Attorney-General and his department are still considering those, and many other changes discussed in the draft report.

In December 2018, Saxon Mullins was awarded a Young People's Human Rights Medal by the Australian Human Rights Commission.

'I'm so glad that we live in a society where we are willing to listen to women,' Saxon told the crowd in her acceptance speech. 'But with that, I can't forget,' she said, her voice faltering a little, 'the reason that I am up here.

'And I think the root cause of that is something that we can all change …

'So, I'm not doing anything later,' she said with a small giggle. 'Do you want to change the world?'

Saxon is now working with a group of criminologists and advocates from Rape and Sexual Assault Research and Advocacy on an initiative developing minimum standards in rape laws across the country to far more strictly define notions of consent. She is truly an amazing young woman.

Arnica told me her little sister was walking tall.

'I am so proud of Saxon and the strength and the courage that she has shown,' Arnica said. 'She may be my baby sister, but I look up to her more than anyone else.

'The strength that she has given me. If that was me, I don't know that I would've been as strong as she has been.

'I hope that she provides strength to other people [to know] that, despite the outcome, the right thing is to come forward.

'And to persevere. And to tell your story. Because people shouldn't get away with what happened to Saxon.'

THE WITNESS OF FIRST COMPLAINT

As I put together the story about Saxon Mullins, her case had special resonance. Because six weeks before, I, too, had been a witness in a sexual assault hearing. I had experienced what it was like to be vigorously cross-examined, to be doubted, to feel under siege even though you are not the person accused of a crime.

That committal hearing preceded the trial of Catholic Cardinal George Pell.

The Pell case was a five-year ordeal for all concerned – the complainants, the cardinal and even, at times, the counsel on either side of the Bar table.

After a jury found Pell guilty of abusing two teenage choirboys at St Patrick's Cathedral when he was Archbishop of Melbourne in 1996–97, Pell appealed and lost in a majority decision in the Victorian Court of Appeal. But when he appealed again, his convictions were quashed in a unanimous decision of the seven judges of the High Court of Australia.

Unlike Saxon, of course, I wasn't the complainant and I hadn't been through a sexual trauma and all the awful things that that entails. I was what's known as 'the witness of first complaint'. As a journalist, I was the first person that one of the men who had made accusations against Pell had ever told about what he said Pell did to him when he was a little boy.

The High Court proceeded on the assumption that the jury had assessed the evidence of the living choirboy as 'thoroughly

credible and reliable' (an opinion shared by the majority of the
Court of Appeal), but in April 2020 it found that because of
the 'compounding probabilities' of opportunity witnesses at the
cathedral, the jury, acting reasonably, ought to have entertained a
reasonable doubt that Pell was guilty. Essentially, the finding meant
that because no one else saw it and there wasn't, according to other
witnesses, whose evidence was unchallenged, the opportunity for
the crime to take place, the jury must have had a reasonable doubt.

That tortuous process is now over.

A month after the High Court threw out the cardinal's
convictions, the full, unredacted final report of the Royal
Commission into Institutional Responses to Child Sexual Abuse
was released. The commissioners (whose terms of reference were
focused solely on whether Pell knew of allegations of child abuse
by paedophile clergy) were scathing about Pell. They found that
he knew of allegations in the Ballarat diocese where he grew up
and started his career from 1973, through the late 1970s and
early 1980s when he worked as a consultor to the local bishop
who moved a notorious paedophile priest around, and that his
knowledge extended right into the 1990s when he was auxiliary
bishop in Melbourne.

But this is not a book about Pell. This is a book about the
experiences of witnesses. And through my experiences with the
complainants against Pell, I found myself becoming a witness too.

My interlocutor in the Pell committal proceeding was to be
Robert Richter QC. At this point I want to be clear that the story
that follows of my encounter with Richter as a witness isn't about
him as an individual. It's about him as an advocate in court for his
client, employed to provide the best defence he believes possible.
But in doing so, he adopted 'old-school' tactics that I find deeply
troubling. The question throughout this book remains as to where
the balance is to be struck between the rights of defendants and
the rights of witnesses – and of complainants in particular.

* * *

The first time I met Robert Richter was about five years before
our encounter in court. It was February 2013 and I had just

started working for the ABC TV *7.30* program. I had been asked to go to Richter's chambers to do a 'pick-up' – that is, going along to interview a person to send back the 'grabs' to an interstate colleague.

Richter's chambers are on the seventh floor of 530 Lonsdale Street. Crockett Chambers, set up by Richter and some other silks, was a place with which I would later become very familiar. It would be where I would regularly meet with Peter Morrissey SC, one of the barristers who would represent me in the Pell case. The floor is home to some of the most famous names at the criminal Bar. It looks just like you'd expect such a place to look. The women on the front desk are friendly and apologetic about their eccentric charges. It's a place of scratched Chesterfields and desks piled up with documents and shelves laden with bottles of Scotch and shiraz sent from grateful clients.

Once known as 'The Red Baron' for the shock of ginger hair on his head and beard, Richter was, in 2013, a man in his late sixties. The red had now faded to a shade of melting sleet, his eyes were framed with owlish statement glasses. He wasn't tall, but what he lacked in height, he famously, in the courtroom, made up for in determination. He was perhaps Australia's best-known criminal barrister – counsel to the wealthy and the notorious. At that point, before George Pell, his most high-profile client had been Mick Gatto during Melbourne's underworld wars. Richter had managed to secure Gatto an acquittal for the alleged murder of gangland rival Andrew 'Benji' Veniamin at an Italian restaurant in Carlton. Gatto shot Veniamin dead, but Richter had successfully argued that it was in self-defence.

A year after my meeting with Richter, I interviewed Gatto about his role in boxing and he showed me a tattoo of Richter he had had done after his release from prison to show his thanks to the Red Baron. I wanted to film it, but Gatto was having none of that. In his memoir, *I, Mick Gatto*, Gatto reported that Richter said he hoped he didn't regret the tattoo.

'How would I regret it?' Gatto wrote that he replied to Richter. 'You're a beautiful man and I love you.'

When I went to interview Richter that February, he delivered the 'grabs' with customary aplomb, and we discussed, off the record, some other stories I was investigating at the time. That the discussion was off the record stayed with me, because he would later try, as defence counsel, to get me to betray confidences given by other sources. I don't remember much about our conversation beyond the impression that, while pleasant, he had the air of a man accustomed to people acting deferentially around him – a quality he shared with many other men in the law and politics and business whom I had interviewed over the years.

Another thing that stayed with me was that, as the crew was packing up the gear in those stuffy chambers and we chatted off the record, Robert Richter smoked.

Granted, it was his space, not mine. But this was many years after smoking in offices had been outlawed. It was many years after the normal etiquette, even in a social context, even outdoors, was to ask someone if they minded if you smoked. But Richter didn't ask. He just lit it up and smoked.

As a journalist with a potential source, I just smiled, I hoped not too stiffly, and nodded. But I remember coming out of that office, smelling the acrid stench that had by then permeated my clothes and my hair, and rolling my eyes. I remember remarking to the cameraman about it. I remember that the smell made me feel, for the rest of the day, ever so slightly nauseous.

Sometimes little things say a lot about a person. I'm sure Robert Richter, someone used to making assessments about people all the time, and using those assessments as a forensic tool, would say the same.

* * *

I was asked to give a witness statement to Victoria Police in July 2017. *Cardinal* had come out in May of that year. As a journalist accustomed to being the writer of the stories rather than the subject, it had been a strange and exhausting time. The weekend before, *The Age* and *The Sydney Morning Herald* newspapers ran extracts of my book. There were news pieces about the 'headline stories' – namely, the 1990s St Patrick's Cathedral allegations against George Pell that would later be the subject of his trial and acquittal.

The notion, much later imbued with what the High Court determined must be subject to reasonable doubt, that the Archbishop of Melbourne could have abused two teenage choirboys in the 1990s was, to use a journalistic cliché, explosive stuff.

On Monday, 15 May 2017, Victoria Police had been investigating the allegations for just short of two years.

The then Victoria Police Commissioner, Graham Ashton, reiterated in the nine months since our *7.30* story on the Ballarat allegations that a decision on whether to charge Pell was 'imminent'. I had no idea of when that might happen while I was busy writing *Cardinal*. If Pell was charged before our publication date, the publishers had agreed the book would simply have to sit on the shelf until his legal process was over.

On the night of Tuesday, 16 May, that is, the night after publication, and after several days of news stories about the Pell allegations about which I had written, a story landed in the *Herald Sun* newspaper.

Someone sent me a picture of the paper's front-page splash.

'*D-DAY ON PELL.*

'*FINAL ADVICE FROM PROSECUTORS ON PROBE. POLICE SET TO DECIDE FATE OF CARDINAL GEORGE PELL.*

'*The Herald Sun understands that the DPP has advised police that based on its assessment of the evidence, they can charge the cardinal. But the DPP advice makes it clear that ultimately it is up to police whether to act.*'

Gavin Silbert SC, then the Senior Crown Prosecutor, sent the Pell brief back to the police, to tell them they could charge if they wished.

'The allegations of the complainant, if accepted by a jury, were sufficient,' Silbert much later told me in an interview for this book. 'I didn't have to form a judgement on whether it would be accepted by a jury – just, taking it at its highest, and assuming they were accepted, they were sufficient.'

Silbert also believed that 'Witness J', the choirboy complainant against Pell, was a very compelling witness.

'I thought so,' he said. 'I mean, the jury accepted him at the end of the day.'

On 28 June 2017, Pell was charged with historical crimes against children.

Very soon after, Victoria Police contacted me to ask me to give a witness statement. It was strange to go to their offices in Spencer Street, to meet members of the taskforce that I had for so long been unsuccessfully chasing, in the hope that they might collaborate with me on the story I had dug up. They had always been assiduously polite, but gave me nothing. Now I was their witness.

I willingly gave the statement because I wanted to do the right thing by a man who had told me about things he'd never told anyone else, a man who in every single dealing I have had with him has been nothing but decent and courteous.

'I don't think the defence will be interested in you at all,' one of the cops told me when I asked if I was likely to be called to be cross-examined. 'You're just too much trouble for them.'

The reality would turn out to be quite the opposite.

Some time after that, as I was wandering with my husband and kids on a Saturday morning through the cheese section of a fresh food market, I ran into a source. The source had recently been in Richter's company. He told me he didn't want to alarm me, but that Richter had told him that the key to the case was discrediting Milligan.

That's when the sick feeling started. A feeling that lasted for months.

* * *

The first warning shots were fired in September 2017. They came from Richter's instructing solicitors, Galbally and O'Bryan.

Two subpoenas arrived – to my publisher and shortly afterwards to the ABC. Each one was astonishingly broad.

The solicitors wanted every single piece of correspondence I had exchanged with anyone in preparing the book and in response to the book. All footage, audio and visual material. And all documents including statements, notes, photographs, recordings and plans provided by any person.

An equally broad subpoena of the ABC asked for similar material about the *7.30* episode on the Eureka Pool allegations about Pell.

It made sense that the defence would be interested in the raw footage, correspondence and any documents associated with the complainants who had gone to police. But to comply with this summons, I would have to send a comical amount of material which was completely irrelevant to criminal proceedings against Pell.

I'd be sending them details of conversations with seminarians who had been through Corpus Christi seminary with Pell about how the young trainee priest was rough on the footy field. Or material on Vatican finances. Or research on canon law. Or former priests gossiping about how their hearts sank when they found out on the priestly grapevine that Pell was the new Archbishop of Melbourne.

Not to mention publishing correspondence about whether, for instance, we had copyright permission to publish an extract from a song in the book, editorial discussions about style and phrasing that had no bearing on the case, marketing and publicity communications about the type of font to be used. Or broadcasting decisions about which 7.30 producer we'd send out to cover a follow-up press conference on the Pell story – would it be Gus or Andy?

It was utter nonsense, had no bearing on the case whatsoever, and would have caused me countless hours of wasted time. It seemed to me onerous, pointless, oppressively wide.

It was decided that I would need a QC. Around this time, I was working on a story with Dassi Erlich, who had been awarded the highest ever damages payment to a survivor of child sexual abuse in her case against the Adass Israel community. The tiny orthodox Jewish community had employed, and protected, a woman called Malka Leifer as principal of the school. The court found that they had also enabled her to flee from justice. Leifer had, with the assistance of members of the community, fled to Israel in the middle of the night and is, at the time of writing, still in a protracted legal battle to fight extradition to Australia to face multiple charges over Dassi and her sisters' allegations.

The Supreme Court judge who had awarded the damages to Dassi was Justice Jack Rush, who did not enjoy his brief time on the bench and had gone back to the Bar.

When I read Rush's comments about Dassi's case, I thought, 'This is the guy for the job.' Rush awarded exemplary damages to Dassi and his judgment was, I thought, excellent. He spoke in a blistering and unvarnished way about institutional betrayal of a child sexual abuse survivor. He was rightly condemnatory of the people who had let Dassi down.

'The conduct of the Board is deserving of the Court's disapprobation and denunciation. I have no doubt that the conduct was deliberate ... The conduct amounts to disgraceful and contumelious behaviour demonstrating a complete disregard for Leifer's victims, of which the plaintiff was one. The conduct demonstrates a disdain for due process of criminal investigation in this State.'

'Go, Justice Jack Rush,' I remember thinking as I read through the judgment. Rush was also famous as the fiercely smart and uncompromising Counsel Assisting the Bushfires Royal Commission into Victoria's devastating Black Saturday fires and the defence counsel who acted for smoker Rolah McCabe in her landmark case against British American Tobacco, and for unions and victims against asbestos manufacturer James Hardie. As *The Sydney Morning Herald* said of him some years ago, 'His story has mostly been one of representing the aggrieved Davids against corporate Goliaths.' I liked everything about that CV.

He is also a really decent bloke. I remember one time, when it was all getting to me, and I burst into tears, Jack Rush told me about the last time he had cried. I won't betray his confidence by saying when it was, but I thought it was so kind of him to volunteer it when I was perched on the end of a seat in his chambers at Owen Dixon West, feeling like a cry-baby.

In November, Jack Rush wrote to Galbally, describing the 'width and lack of any form of specificity as to required documents' as 'oppressive and objectionable', that it had no bearing on the criminal charges against Pell, and committed me to a large amount of time and resources for 'what at best may be described as a fishing expedition'.

'The breadth and generality of the schedule is such as to make defective, as an abuse of process, the whole summons.'

Rush offered to meet with Galbally 'and thus avoid a court dispute' which he did, and Galbally said he would narrow the scope. We were now at the end of November 2017.

The next letter refined the scope of the request, sensibly excluding editorial and production issues, and those where we were corresponding with our lawyers and claimed legal professional privilege.

However, the scope was still strangely wide. They wanted correspondence with people who knew nothing about the details of the allegations against Pell. They were still seeking all footage filmed for the program – which would include exterior shots of St Patrick's Cathedral, or town 'pretties' as we call evocative shots, of Ballarat. They were still seeking all notes in preparation for the *7.30* episode, but I couldn't see how they would possibly be relevant. And they wanted documents that I felt sure would inevitably have no bearing on the proceedings.

By the time, on 29 November, I accepted the Walkley Book Award for *Cardinal* in Brisbane, I could barely speak due to a throat infection. Two days later, I was to fly to the Philippines for a *Four Corners* shoot. In between all of this, constantly, I was sifting through hundreds of pages of documents and constantly corresponding with lawyers and colleagues about the Pell summons. It took up all my spare time.

I tell the story of this interlocutory saga not to compare what I went through to that of deeply traumatised people who are complainants in sexual cases, but rather, to illustrate the 'whatever it takes' mentality lawyers adopt in these cases. And the unfairness that places upon witnesses, whomever they may be, who find themselves swept up in the maelstrom of a sex trial, where it is determined, for whatever reason, that this process will bear fruit for the accused's case. In the case of a well-resourced defendant, which Pell undoubtedly was, all of this is magnified considerably by legal teams who will give anything a college try.

* * *

As this was all happening that November, a desperate mother got in touch.

Her name was Caroline Redmond. In one of those weird twists of fate, Caroline was a maternal health nurse who had, years before, looked after my youngest child. I became very ill after my baby daughter was born and had to go back to hospital for a spell.

Caroline remembered me, remembered my daughter, remembered my son. Caroline has a flinty memory for details. She's a record-keeper.

Caroline was, in November 2017, still reeling from what happened to her son.

But in November 2017, I was in another fog. The fog of preparing to be a witness. Apart from the incessant dealings with the lawyers, I had been utterly bombarded with information about Catholic abusers across the country. My inbox pinged incessantly with anger at concealment, with suicidal ideation, with conspiracy theories, with overseas journalists wanting appearances, with news tips, with thanks – so often, thanks, from victims who had never told a soul. Or had finally found the courage to come forward. Or just wanted someone to listen and thought I might. I tried to reply to everyone, knowing how vulnerable so many of them were, but it was futile. I felt like I was letting them down.

And in the midst of all that, I let Caroline down. She left a message for me:

'I would like to know if Louise is at all interested in my son's story and his experience at St Kevin's College. I can understand that Louise has moved on to other issues of public interest as being immersed in the Cardinal and the responses would be taking up much of her energy. My son is very close to finishing his VCE exams and feels ready to make a media report and needs a good contact. The anachronistic approach towards him and the fact that this has been occurring alongside the [Royal Commission] has been ... words can't describe how the institutional response is continuing in a school that has been offered assistance to make it right.'

Caroline's initial message had been about St Kevin's College, the Catholic school attended by the choirboys whose allegations were at the centre of the Pell case. The boys had been granted choral scholarships. At that time, knowing, as I did, that neither choirboy had disclosed to the school, I felt somewhat sorry for St Kevin's to be caught up in a scandal that was not of its own making. It had, I thought, been connected to the Pell case only by, it seemed, unfortunate coincidence.

So, to have a mother contacting me about that school at that time didn't raise my interest any more than any other school would. I do recall thinking that I would, upon returning from the assignment in Manila, call this woman. But in the maelstrom of the endless task of complying with the Pell subpoena, I never got to it. So, I'm afraid to say that I forgot about Caroline Redmond. The information about her son simply crammed to the back of the overstuffed filing cabinet that was my brain, falling away to nothingness.

But it hadn't fallen away for Caroline and, crucially, it hadn't fallen away for her son. The boy's name was Paris Street. He was twenty. Inside him, souring his soul, was a quiet, corrosive anger.

Paris was a child victim of a sex crime. Paris, too, would have a bruising encounter with the legal system and a determined QC focused on winning his case.

* * *

As the spring of 2017 turned to summer, it became clear to me that Pell's team, as is common legal practice, were trying to 'knock out' the case at the committal proceeding – that is, before trial.

I told Jack Rush I had 'serious concerns' about the summons as it stood. He made further suggestions to narrow the scope. By this stage it was 12 December 2017. I was in Sydney at the time, working brutal hours filming and still researching a story. In between all of that, the emails flung back and forth from Jack Rush, to the ABC lawyers, to my colleagues, to my publishers; trying to comply with the wretched summons.

One of the real difficulties we had was that there were suppression orders in place in relation to Pell's charges. When the police had charged Pell back on 28 June, they had not announced the nature and quantum of the charges, the total number of complainants, and what each of them were alleging. Incredibly, this information was never made public and still hasn't been. In my twenty years in journalism, I have never seen concessions like this made for any defendant, no matter how high profile.

We asked that this information be provided to our lawyers on the basis that we could meaningfully answer the summons.

At this time, we also engaged Peter Morrissey SC.

Morrissey's chambers are on the same floor as Robert Richter's and he had known Richter's junior in the case, Ruth Shann, for years. He had a meeting with the defence and managed to convince them to whittle it down significantly.

The defence team wrote to us four days before Christmas. I was supposed to be on leave. We had been having legal meetings that went all day.

Meanwhile, I spent countless hours, all my free time, sifting through and collating hundreds of documents, reading each one carefully so I would not, accidentally, break a confidence. As a journalist, you make promises to all sorts of people and my best guess is that the legal team for Cardinal George Pell was the last group of people to which the sources who had spoken to me might want to have their private information delivered.

On 3 January 2018 our ABC lawyer flew to Melbourne for a legal meeting with Jack Rush and my colleagues to determine whether each document was relevant to the summons.

We sent all of the agreed material by the end of January. We heard nothing for some time.

Then, on Thursday, 8 February, all of a sudden, the lawyers began asking for transcriptions of my shorthand notes. 'Such transcriptions are covered by the summons and we had understood from public statements made by Ms Milligan about her process that she would type out a transcription soon after interviewing a witness.'

But many of the notes they sought were not at all the sort of things that I would immediately transcribe because they were hastily taken notes relating to countless conversations with various people who would later be interviewed formally on camera anyway.

For the first time, they also raised social media and Twitter 'interactions'.

They also became obsessed with a checklist of choirboys that I referred to in my book, when I was trying to find the relevant choirboy who had made allegations about Cardinal Pell. But this was not a formal 'checklist', it was simply that we asked each person we spoke to whether they had spoken to other journalists and whether they had spoken to police.

I was in Sydney finessing the final script and news stories for *Four Corners*, and was to fly back home to Melbourne on the weekend before the Monday broadcast.

I was to provide all of the information they sought, including doing their work for them translating my shorthand, by Tuesday 13 February.

During that time, I was already working after hours, after finishing my day's work, after putting my children to bed, compiling and sorting documents about which we were claiming the journalist's privilege or legal professional privilege and sending them to Jack Rush.

I assumed the defence team of a man accused of multiple offences against children might give up on the unbelievable request to get me in my own time to translate all my notes. They did not.

On the morning of 17 February, I trundled down the driveway to pick up the newspaper. After the usual fiddle to find the edge of the plastic wrap, I opened it up. There, on the cover of the *Good Weekend* magazine, against a black studio backdrop, was Robert Richter. He was wearing a barrister's silken robes. He held his owlish glasses in his hand. He looked caught in a moment, surprised, benign.

'Here we go,' I thought.

I saw it as another episode in a fairly obvious publicity campaign for the cardinal.

'The cardinal has been set up to fall by people who know nothing about the actual charges,' writer Tim Elliott said Richter told him, 'indignantly'.

'He's innocent, and he needs help.

'... You're not going to have a taskforce set up and millions of dollars spent, and nothing comes out of it.

'... I just wanted it known, straight off, that this is not one of those cases where he is going to lie down,' Richter was quoted as saying, adding that he had 'voluminous' evidence that what was alleged against Pell was 'impossible'.

Richter's words seemed dismissive of the complainants: 'The whole anger around the abuse in the Catholic Church has been focused on [Pell],' the piece quoted him saying.

'It makes it much harder to reach the truth. People who come out of the woodwork after 40 years or whatnot are usually damaged. The question is, "Who damaged them?".'

The feature charted Robert Richter's progress from birth in the former Soviet state of the Kirghiz Republic, to German refugee camp, to Israel, to, when he was thirteen, moving to Melbourne.

As the vice-president of the Victorian Council of Civil Liberties, in 1993, Richter spoke out against the introduction of a law that would have people convicted of child sex offences banned from loitering near schools and parks.

He had argued that there ought to be a statute of limitations for sex offenders that stopped people being charged thirty years after the event because 'they are not the same person'.

Their victims are not the same person either. They are fundamentally broken by someone who thought it was okay to rape them as a child.

'It's tempting … to imagine there's a certain psychic toll associated with defending the apparently indefensible,' Elliott wrote.

The comments Richter made in the piece about his client Pell's case caused a serious stir in the legal profession.

It wasn't something on my radar at the time, but it's something some of the lawyers I have spoken to for this book have been very surprised about. It has often been raised with me that they cannot believe that the Victorian Bar didn't make a public statement about it at the time.

Under the Legal Profession's Uniform Conduct Rules for barristers, section 76 governs media comment.

Section 76 of this code prohibits a barrister from 'taking any step towards the publication of any material' which 'appears to or does express the opinion of the barrister on the merits of a current or potential proceeding or on any issue arising in such a proceeding, other than in the course of genuine educational or academic discussion on matters of law'. Essentially, this means that barristers are not allowed to talk to the media about current cases in which they are acting.

Section 77 spells out that, in relation to current proceedings, barristers can really only speak about the nature of the proceedings, the identity of the parties, the nature of the orders in the case, the orders or judgement and the client's 'intentions as to any further steps'. By February 2018, Pell had been charged and there had been several preliminary hearings in the Magistrates' Court pending the upcoming committal proceeding so there is no argument that Richter wasn't referring to a 'current proceeding'.

'*He's innocent, and he needs help*' goes to merits of a current criminal proceeding of Pell, as does '*What was alleged was impossible*'.

'*You're not going to have a taskforce set up and millions of dollars spent and nothing comes out of it*' is a comment on the lack of merit of current criminal proceedings by suggesting that Pell's charges were a fait accompli because the police had spent so much money on the taskforce. It also questions the integrity of the police – implying that the amount of resources devoted to a case is what motivates them, rather than criminal justice.

'*The whole anger around the abuse in the Catholic Church has been focussed on [Pell]… People who come out of the woodwork after 40 years or whatnot are usually damaged. The question is, "Who damaged them?"*' questions the merits of the current case by questioning the credibility of the complainants.

The final comments are also offensive to complainants and the phrase '*Who damaged them?*' suggests that because they came '*out of the woodwork*' after so long, they have the wrong guy. And he also implies their complaints are based on broader '*anger around the abuse in the Catholic Church*' which has been '*focussed on [Pell]*', rather than genuine complaints of sexual crimes.

It is extremely problematic to use delay in a witness coming forward to give evidence as a way of discrediting them. The child abuse Royal Commission found there was an average of thirty-three years before men disclosed their child abuse by Catholic clergy. But more significantly, law-makers have spent many years refining legislation to combat the misnomer that delayed complaint meant false complaint or unreliable witness.

Since 2015, the *Jury Directions Act* has prohibited defence counsel, prosecutors and judges from saying or in any way suggesting to the jury that 'complainants who delay in making a complaint or do not make a complaint are, as a class, less credible or require more careful scrutiny than other complainants'.

The judge is prohibited from saying or in any way suggesting that because the complainant delayed, it would be 'dangerous or unsafe to convict the accused' or even that 'the complainant's evidence should be scrutinised with great care'.

The Act also requires judges to direct the jury before evidence is led that if there is a delay in disclosure, that delay in making a complaint in sexual offences is 'a common occurrence', there is 'no typical, proper or normal response to a sexual offence'.

And yet, here is Richter, ventilating these notions in a national news magazine cover story, while appearing to breach the rules that govern his profession.

I could not see how this was an academic or educational discussion about the law. It was a newspaper magazine feature, with Richter jauntily posing on the cover in his barrister's robes.

So, if someone may have breached these Bar rules, what happens?

Very little, it would seem.

The matter can be referred to the Legal Services Commissioner, but that process is not transparent. Legal Services Commissioner Fiona McLeay is not permitted to discuss whether or not Richter was the subject of a complaint, but tells me, more broadly, never to assume that there hasn't been one and that the barrister wasn't expected to give, for instance, an undertaking that it wouldn't happen again.

Which sounds, for a warrior like Richter, simply terrifying. A warning, a non-penalty, delivered behind closed doors, with no public scrutiny. Awful.

Making a complaint is not an easy thing to do in this notoriously clubby world. Who would risk it? They'll bitch about it behind the scenes, but, as McLeay says to me when speaking more generally about the difficulty of getting complaints about barristers, if asked to speak up, they'll shuffle their feet and say, 'Well, I wouldn't want him to lose his ticket.'

The messages to complainants and potential witnesses in the *Good Weekend* piece were pretty clear. And the article appeared only fifteen days before the start of the committal proceeding.

Meanwhile, back at the ABC, the document war with Pell's solicitors continued apace. On 13 March, after receiving the latest bundle of documents to comply with their subpoena, they said that they were 'unable to decipher Louise Milligan's notes'. They wanted them dictated or transcribed by me – or, failing that, to read them in evidence – something they knew would displease the court and set the judicial officer against me.

They wanted me to sit and read pages and pages of material which, while technically complying with the summons, was largely irrelevant to the case – by 19 March, which was six days later.

I was now furiously working on Saxon Mullins' story for *Four Corners*. We wrote to Galbally complaining about the onerous task of complying with this in the time they had allotted. I was, after all, not a party to the proceedings. I was simply a witness. I had been given no assistance and was not compensated for my time.

Galbally was undeterred – saying they were 'happy for her to dictate the notes and we will transcribe'. At this stage, the 27 March deadline, when I was due to give my evidence, was looming. My sense of dread was escalating. I had no idea what preparation for court would entail. I was incredibly busy, with a full-time job-and-a-half at *Four Corners* and with my young children. I had zero downtime. My inbox was filled with hundreds of emails, all about the subpoena. Every spare minute of my energy had gone into complying with their summons.

The Crown is of no assistance in these situations and largely leaves the witness to their devices, checking in occasionally and being terribly apologetic at what you're going through. If you stand up for yourself and express frustration, you feel like a whinger. They nod sympathetically, and if they're on the phone you can imagine their pained expressions. They've heard it all before. You know they've heard it all before. You apologise even though what's being asked of you is completely ridiculous.

All the while, I just kept thinking of what complainants in sex trials go through. Having to manage this minefield and these demands on their time when they are about to relive the most awful things that ever happened to them. It must be horrendous.

In the end, Pell's team refused to back down. Richter appeared before the magistrate overseeing the Pell case, Belinda Wallington, and claimed that my notes in 'her own style of shorthand' could not be translated by the defence team.

The day of my evidence on 27 March was a Tuesday. The Thursday night before that, in my hotel room in Sydney after working long hours that day, I sat up making recordings of the shorthand notes.

After I was already a fair way into the dictation, I received an email which said I had to dictate in a particular way, referring to page numbers in the brief as I went.

I began to feel that they were wearing me down, so that when I did come before Richter on the Tuesday for my evidence, I would be completely exhausted.

The numbered documents were hard copies that were in Melbourne – rather than sending them electronically, they had dropped them in to Jack Rush's chambers. Given that I was in Sydney, I would need to fly back, get them, and start again.

On the Friday, as I was arriving at Sydney airport to fly home to Melbourne, I got wind of an upcoming story in *The Australian*.

A mother of a choirboy who, it was being alleged, was a victim of Pell had given evidence and was cross-examined by Richter.

The woman, with whom I had an excellent relationship but was not at that point allowed to speak to because we were both witnesses, had also had a difficult time in cross-examination, preventing her from feeling she was able to give her evidence clearly, making it sound like I had written her account without her consent.

Nothing could have been further from the truth. I had told her verbally I was planning to write the book and wondered if she minded if I told the story, using pseudonyms for her family's identities. The woman, who is an easy-going sort of person, despite the pain she has gone through, was fine about that.

I had friendly text messages from her from both before and after the book was published.

The story asserted that I did not have consent to tell the boy's story in my book. I scrambled, as I prepared to board the plane, wondering who to call. I eventually got in touch with a lovely colleague on Facebook Messenger with whom I had worked at *The Australian* at the start of my journalistic career. I told him what had been said in court wasn't the full story; I did have consent and the family accepted that too. I had text messages to prove it, they couldn't run material (which, it had to be said, other court reporters had not run) which was in error.

He told me that he'd sort it out. He went to see the senior journalists on the 'backbench' of the paper – the people who make the decisions about what's in and what's out.

He contacted me very soon after. 'Mate, I'm so sorry, all I can get for you is they are going to put the headline in quotes,' he said. I understood they wanted to report what was said in court but I was telling them it was incorrect.

It was an enormous kick in the teeth from the newspaper I had loved. Where I had started my career and, as a determined young court reporter, produced work they consistently celebrated. A place where, when I left, the editor had made an incredibly glowing speech and had, in following years, often said I'd be welcome back. A place full of people I had considered my friends. People with whom I'd socialised over many years. We had laughed at endless dinner parties, brought our kids to play dates, joked with each other on Facebook, ended our text messages 'xxx'.

I felt at that point that the paper was running a pro-Pell line. And its pages had featured speculation about our alleged collusion with Victoria Police (which never happened) or that, after our 7.30 story, the DPP had advised not to charge (he didn't). But this felt new and pointed. This was them refusing to listen to the friend I had called – one of their most trusted and loyal soldiers – who was passing on from me that they were making a mistake.

This was a national broadsheet carrying something that smeared my reputation and did the handiwork of a defence team for an accused when I'd told them it wasn't correct. On this particular day, at this particular juncture, I felt like it was the final straw. But there were so many other final straws to come.

I spent the weekend before my appearance, when I should have been trying to compose myself ahead of an incredibly stressful experience, again dictating my shorthand into my phone, complying with the wretched number system.

I will never forget that night, reading this desperately sad material. Somehow, reading that stuff aloud is more brutal.

Actually saying the words and describing the scenarios that no one ever talks about in normal life.

Listening back to those tapes now, you can hear the exhaustion as I try to make out scratchy notes which were never intended to be used for that purpose. There are lots of long pauses and halting sighs as I try to interpret shorthand from almost two years before.

At one point, I read back some notes from a complainant from Ballarat who had had an incredibly unfortunate life. His brother and his wife had been abused, though by other people in the town. His brother and wife had both suicided. I choked a little as I stumbled upon, from nowhere, a couple of lines I'd jotted down when he was telling me about the last night of his brother's life.

'[My sister] found him. Laid his suit out on his bed.' It didn't say much more. I suspect that, at that point, when I was sitting with this man face to face, I would have stopped taking notes and listened to his pain for his brother. I do remember how overcome he was as he told me.

Perhaps the worst section was from Ballarat survivor Rob Walsh, only tangentially connected to the Pell trial because he had a brief conversation with a complainant at the footy, but they made me read everything he told me anyway.

The shorthand told a truncated, brutal story of what it was like to be at St Alipius, in the eye of the child abuse storm involving notorious priests such as Gerald Risdale and Edward (Ted) Dowlan. Of how Rob's two brothers and his cousin had all died by their own hand. How he'd left school semi-literate and had to catch up by doing classes when he was twenty-five.

How he would never reach his potential, was a carpenter–builder but couldn't work normal hours or run a company. The fact that he spent fifteen years trying to bring his two abusers to justice.

'I am desolate. I am behind in the rent and divorced,' I mouthed into my voice recorder slowly. 'Some days I just shake my head and go, "Why me, why did I go to that school?"'

You could hear my voice breaking as I read out how Rob described the suicides. And listening to it, even now, in 2020, the sadness overwhelms me again.

'Martin. He put a shotgun in his mouth in the bath. The policeman lifted him out of the bath. His. Brain. Fell. Out. That policeman resigned that day ...'

'... Noel was taught by Dowlan. Also died in single car accident. Eureka Street. Put his car into a lamp post at speed. Single car accident ... I was not in Ballarat when Noel died. He was nineteen. It was devastating.'

And later, I hear my breath catching again: 'Greg Graham gassed himself in his thirties. Little Greggy. I know twelve suicide victims. Little Greggy. He was from ... ethnic background. No father. Lived in small miner's cottage in Ballarat East. Five kids, single mum, easy target. Anybody who went to St Alipius then was abused. Anyone in my class was abused ...

'We are left penniless, broken. And then you see what [Bishop] Mulkearns [of Ballarat, who moved Rob's abuser, Gerald Ridsdale, from parish to parish for years] was living in. Just destroy life after life after life. And he's living his life in luxury. Ridsdale will outlive me.'

At this point, on the recording, I let out a long sigh because it was just becoming too much, again thinking about the tragedy of this man's life. This man who, at my book launch for *Cardinal*, just stood at the back during the speeches, and cried non-stop. I could see him back there as I spoke at the launch about what motivated me to do this work. It was people like Rob who kept me up all night, writing. People who had to do literacy classes at age twenty-five because they dropped out of school so young.

'Show me a child of seven and I will show you the man,' I dictated from Rob's joyless notes for Galbally and Richter, for no forensic legal purpose that I could discern. 'Slow learners. Poor families. Single parent families.'

I was still sending the eleven recordings on the Monday morning. That is, the morning of the day before I was to be grilled in court.

I went to see Jack Rush at midday to prepare. I was completely spent.

Rush, however, had an extraordinary capacity for calming a witness. He went through everything and reassured me, not coaching about what to say, but gently guiding how to manage what I did say.

He told me that I was 'a crier' and that was okay, that if I did cry, it was not a problem. Just to take a break, compose myself and carry on.

I, too, fully expected that I would cry. As it happened, I did not.

He reminded me that it was the magistrate's court, not Richter's, and that accordingly, if I had an issue with Richter's questions, address it to the magistrate, not to Richter.

Keep the answers simple, was his message. But don't be pigeonholed into giving a wrongful answer for the sake of the brevity defence counsel is demanding. If you disagree with what he's saying, hold your line without being argumentative. You know your stuff better than anyone.

Rush told me Richter would repeatedly try to corner me into giving 'yes or no' answers. He said if I thought that the question really couldn't be answered by a yes or a no, there was nothing wrong with politely turning to the magistrate and telling her that. And calmly explaining that if Mr Richter would like to rephrase his question, then I could attempt to answer it.

It would show the court that I was attempting to accurately answer the questions, that I was attempting to give my best evidence.

I had arrived at Jack Rush's chambers that day feeling anxious about the task ahead. But I left with a lightness in my step I had not felt for some time.

Nonetheless, the night before was surreal and deeply distressing. I felt suspended from the corner of the ceiling, looking down on my body as I tossed and turned like sheets in a front loader, unable to relax, unable to sleep, dreading, dreading, dreading.

And all the while thinking, thinking, thinking: 'Don't let those guys down.'

THE COMMITTAL

You make your way to the event that you have been dreading encased in a sort of Perspex bubble. Head pressed against the cold glass of a taxi window, eyes gazing out at the grey city zooming past. The leaves are starting to turn. Your husband grips your hand, his eyes keep darting across at you, trying to make small talk. He says 'Sweetie' a lot. You smile weakly. You feel like you've swallowed a battery.

You've gone over your notes so many times you just can't bear to look at them anymore. You've thought about every single thing that might be asked. You have little scripts worked out in your mind. Don't be argumentative. Don't elaborate unnecessarily. Don't cry.

You try not to think too much about the men who went out on a limb for you and the crimes they allege. Because then you will cry.

As the taxi arrives at your barrister's chambers, there is a group there to support you. Your journalistic bestie, your irrepressible publisher, your loyal former boss. The conversation, even at the time, is a blur. There is a lot of 'oh darling' and hand-clutching and arm-squeezing and trying to lighten the mood with discussion about shoes.

You're so grateful they are there, but you find it hard to focus on anything they say. Conversation sort of floats above your heads like thought bubbles in a comic book. You nod. But you know that at this point, there is nothing else for it. You just have to get in there and do this thing.

* * *

The scene of the interrogation was the Melbourne Magistrates' Court – a charmless, mid-nineties temple of the same sort of misery that Saxon Mullins found at Sydney's Downing Centre.

Outside, in the long queue that formed in the morning, were the same chain-smoking petty crims and lawyers in rumpled suits. The same bank of bored television camera operators and hair-sprayed reporters with jewel-toned jackets and microphones, their necks craning as they watched down the street, bracing for action.

But on this day, like every other of that historic committal proceeding, the atmosphere was significantly heightened. Beyond the usual suspects, there were international reporters and crews who had come to see this man who had wielded so much power appear before the criminal courts. There was a huge bank of police in high-vis gear, who would surround Pell each time he came to court. There was a small huddle of women who were there as his supporters.

The televisual and photographic capture of the march of witnesses and perpetrators into and out of court buildings is known among the reporters as 'court walkies'. It was a very familiar process for me, as a court reporter for *The Australian* in Sydney who had, in the early 2000s, covered all of the big trials of the day. At times, during really huge cases, the frenzy around the person would become decidedly intense. During the trial of disgraced, flamboyant stockbroker Rene Rivkin, the media scrum following the late Rivkin outside the New South Wales Supreme Court became so febrile that I, who had long locks at the time, was actually dragged to the ground by my hair as my colleagues scurried after him.

Newspaper reporters like me needed to hear what the person was saying, lest you missed a good line, but nonetheless, we would generally hang back a little. But our friends, 'The TVs', would shadow the person down the street, microphones thrust at them, branding themselves for their evening o'clock bulletins as the man or woman on the spot. The person you could trust to be in among the action. *First at Five. The One to Watch. See the Full Story.*

My job was more about analysing the nuanced complexities of the grim human theatre we attended every day. That said, I participated – encouraging snappers to get 'the shot' and texting back and forth to alert them that 'he's coming!'. As it became clear the person was going to stay schtum, I would retreat back into the court and try to act cool and speak the language of the court to the lawyers, in the hope that they might put me in touch with their client.

The people doing the 'court walkies' often looked the same. They would adopt fixed, neutral expressions – not smiling (inappropriate), not angry (guilty), not sad (giving the reporters what they wanted – a piece of their private emotions).

Sometimes they would lose it and get aggressive with cameramen (perfect, keep filming), or play a paranoid game of cat and mouse, hanging around until court cleaners started vacuuming the floor, in the hope that the journalists would fear missing their deadline and skedaddle, *sans* shot. The sex offenders were notorious for that one.

The journalists had nicknames for the strange cavalcade of crims. 'Barry the Catt', 'The Granny Killers', 'The Playboy Rapist', 'The Vampire Gigolo', 'The Bunny Fucker'.

Occasionally, the court gods would sprinkle fairy dust on the whole thing and a witness or an accused would do something altogether batshit crazy and give the bulletins something to really go with that night.

Apart from the crazier crims, the crews would follow and snap ashen-faced victims or grieving family members in huddles. They'd question corporate high-fliers facing the music and bureaucrats who had been dumped in it. And last but not least, they would chase defamed celebrities whose sartorial take on 'courtroom demure' was always keenly anticipated and much-discussed. Those were always three-city-block chases. Perfect for, as the digital era became entrenched, those *Daily Mail*–style long news reads, with lots of sub-headings and 'Snap', 'Snap', 'Snap'. Paragraph, paragraph. Sub-head. 'Snap'.

So, on that March morning, here I was, contemplating court walkies. My ears rang as I tried to fix my mouth into something that seemed the appropriate neutral position as the cameras flashed. It was mortifying. As journalists, it's always drummed into us that you are *not the story*. Never become the story. It's the weirdest thing, when you have no interest in becoming the story, but you have no choice.

I was there because the story of these men was important and in the public interest and because, on the other side of it, were people who had taken a huge gamble and, in that process, had taken me into their confidence. They weren't there that day, but I couldn't get them out of my mind.

It was strange to be later shown the photos. I actually look incredibly serene. Climbing the steps to walk through security, I realised I had lost my husband, Nick, and the rest. I suddenly felt alone and exposed. But, turning around to find them, someone must have, in a split second said something nice, or slightly amusing, because I smiled. And a photographer snapped. Rookie error, Milligan. Don't smile.

That last picture depicts a woman who is confident and relaxed and rested. The complete opposite of everything that she was. She was a woman who hadn't slept a wink, nor eaten a morsel. Who had spent the entire night before vomiting. Who seemed to have lost sensation in her fingers and toes. Who just kept thinking of how awful it must be for the men she wasn't allowed to speak to, who must have felt so incredibly alone.

To this day, walking past the Melbourne Magistrates' Court makes me shudder.

* * *

The committal proceeding was before Magistrate Belinda Wallington, the Supervising Magistrate for Sexual Offences.

Wallington is a striking woman with shoulder-length dark hair, who has that indefinably proper judicial air, speaks in rounded vowels, and, when she breaks into a smile, radiates a warmth that puts you instantly at ease. She is what used to be described as 'a lady'. In court, she was fair, firm and kind. Having watched judges and magistrates over many years in courts, the really good ones have this ability to, with a very subtle turn of phrase, or a kindly glance, make the witness realise that they are in steady hands. Wallington gave off that air.

By some coincidence, Magistrate Wallington had made my acquaintance the previous year – on the day that my book was first published. I was to be interviewed about *Cardinal* by former ABC

Melbourne *Mornings* radio host Jon Faine in his *Conversation Hour*. Faine and his producers were pleased the conversation would slot right in to their Law Week discussion with, I would discover when I got there, Wallington and another magistrate, Pauline Spencer.

At that time, there was no sense that Wallington might be the judicial officer presiding over the committal proceeding because there was no proceeding, nor charges afoot.

It's doubtful Wallington knew either that I was going to be there until she arrived at the studio. I certainly didn't know that she would be – not that it would have had any special significance at any rate.

The producers asked if we would all be happy to stay the full hour, and we said we would. I had the briefest exchange of pleasantries with Wallington and Spencer before we went into the studio. We did not discuss the allegations against Pell either then or during the recorded interview. During the interview, I spoke largely about the wider historical and legal issues with the Catholic Church and Pell's response as a bishop and archbishop to the sexual abuse issue within the church.

'We're not going through [the details of the allegations about Pell] on radio,' Faine told listeners. 'This book has been so carefully legalled. The content has been so carefully checked. As have the television broadcasts.

'We're not prepared to, live-to-air-unchecked, go through the actual specific details, because the slightest inconsistency would be seized upon by the Church's lawyers ...'

Faine also twice reminded listeners that the two magistrates had nothing to do with the discussion he had had with me.

Several times during the program Faine stated that Pell vigorously denied any allegations of abuse, which the cardinal described as a smear campaign by the ABC.

The only time I engaged with Wallington during her part of the broadcast was to ask her about how difficult it was for victims of sexual assault enduring the criminal justice process – similar themes to what I am exploring, as it happens, in this book. She replied by discussing a range of initiatives the court had taken to improve victims' experience.

I then said, much later in the program, that I thought it was 'really lovely to see two judicial officers engaging like this'.

Despite this entirely innocuous exchange, both Wallington and I would later be unfairly targeted.

* * *

Before proceedings began on 27 March 2018 at the Melbourne Magistrates' Court, I was introduced to senior Crown prosecutor, Mark Gibson SC, for the first time. Until then, Ailsa McVean, a polite and patient Crown solicitor, had made all of the contact. While Richter cut a distinctive figure, Gibson was an altogether subtler presence. He looked like someone who, if not a Crown prosecutor, might have been a senior mandarin in the Treasury department. I had been told by a defence barrister that he was a subtle but surprisingly fearsome opponent who convinced juries almost by stealth. Which is exactly what he would end up doing in this case.

We were ushered into a fluorescently lit meeting room and Gibson ran through how it would proceed. He was courteous and mild-mannered and asked if I had any questions. I felt as well-prepared as I could be. But it did occur to me that I was privileged and that complainants wouldn't be anywhere near as prepared as I had been. They wouldn't have lawyers coming with them to court, who could spring to their feet if anything inappropriate happened. Because their evidence was given in a closed court, they wouldn't have a gallery of journalists reporting anything inappropriate that the defence might try on.

I just wanted to get this over with. I thought it might last a few hours. It would last an entire day.

I made my way into the witness box and sat down. I elected to take the affirmation, not the oath on the bible. George Pell was sitting in my line of sight, wearing the same black shirt with clerical collar and beige jacket he would wear every day to court. He took notes. I didn't make eye contact with him, lest it threw me off my game. He didn't try to make eye contact with me.

'Would you state to Her Honour your full name, please?' the court tipstaff asked.

'Louise Elizabeth Milligan.'

'And your current occupation?'

'Ah, journalist.'

Gibson asked if I'd re-read my police statement and if it was 'true and correct'.

'Absolutely,' I replied.

Gibson tabled Exhibit 76, Exhibit of Louise Milligan, dated 11/07/17. He then thanked me and sat down.

Robert Richter QC stood up. I retained a neutral, pleasant, calm face. Just like in the court walkies. I straightened my back.

Richter made it clear from the absolute outset that he intended to smash me. He never deviated from that course.

Demolishing me and my evidence would be helpful because some of the complainants in the case had told their story to me and if he could find inconsistencies in those stories and create doubt – that I had 'poisoned the well' in some way – then he might have a chance of having the case knocked out before trial. Criminal barristers have repeatedly told me in research for this book that defence counsel often go harder in committals than trials for this purpose – to try to avoid ever having to come before a jury. They also don't have to worry about upsetting jurors by seeming aggressive with the witnesses, because there is only a magistrate presiding.

One of Richter's first lines of questioning was about the date on which I had first spoken to the man who disclosed a complaint to me. He was obsessed with getting the exact date on which the man had contacted the ABC, and suspicious I didn't have one, even though I could narrow it down to a reasonably tight time frame. He repeatedly cut me off when I tried to explain that I knew it was within a fairly narrow time frame, but I just could not pinpoint the precise date.

'I do remember that –' I would begin to say, but he would just cut me off again.

'No, no! Just the date, please?'

'It was in August 2016.'

'August covers a whole month. Can you tell us the date?'

'I can't tell you the exact date.'

'Why?'

'I can tell you that it was –' I began.

'No, no,' he cut me off again, like a cantankerous schoolmaster reprimanding a disobedient girl, '*Why?*'

'Well, I'm attempting to answer why.'

Wallington intervened for the first of many times that day.

'Isn't she answering that question?' Her Honour asked.

'No,' Richter shot back.

'I think she is,' Wallington replied.

He was playing a game of setting me up as if I wasn't cooperating with him when I was simply trying to explain my answer, something which, simultaneously, he wasn't going to allow. He turned to me.

'Yes?'

'It was several days after 27 July 2016,' I replied. That had been the date of the *7.30* program about Pell.

'Right. Why can't you tell us the date?'

'Because I don't remember the exact date.'

In all my experience of interviewing survivors of sexual crimes, reading their transcripts, seeing evidence tendered to the Royal Commission, over and over again, the strategy used to 'catch' them is dates.

It's an easy play, because people don't – surprise, surprise – remember the exact date on which they did something.

I felt this was also an attempt to smear my reputation – something that would become a constant theme of the evidence – because Richter considered it sloppy for a journalist not to record the date of a conversation with a source.

'Is that because your original notes did not have a date on them?'

'Yes.'

'Yes, and your original notes were in a form of your own form of shorthand?'

'A form of Pitman's,' I replied, referring to the traditional method of shorthand I had been taught as a cadet journalist.

'Yes, a varied form of Pitman's.'

'Pitman's combined with longhand,' I replied.

'The words that are written down in Pitman's are not the words, the precise words, that you then reproduce in written form when you've done that?'

I remembered what Jack Rush had said about not being dragooned into answering simply in the affirmative or negative just because Richter said I had to. I turned to the magistrate and addressed her in the most proper tones.

'Your Honour, if I may, this is not a question that I can answer with a "yes" or a "no",' I said.

'Ah, I, when I have a conversation with someone, like anyone else, there is memory involved. And so straight after that conversation, I can remember the details of that conversation. Two years down the track, it's more difficult for me to remember the details of that conversation, and therefore, looking at the shorthand is harder to understand exactly what the shorthand says.'

'Yes, but you didn't always transcribe things straight away, did you?' Richter pressed.

'I transcribed things straight away when I knew that they were potentially going to be used for my book,' I answered.

'Yes?' He would draw this word out in a way that indicated boredom and irritation.

'Or when I knew that I wasn't going to be able to interview someone straight after.'

'Yes?'

'So in [the case of another of the Pell complainants] I was interviewing him that day, so there was no need for me to transcribe my shorthand –'

'Well, can I ask this –' he started.

'– I had a [television] camera,' I finished.

His tone oscillated between boredom, irritation, scepticism and anger. He used patronising phrases like 'You follow?' and tried to pigeonhole me into admitting things that weren't true – for instance, that I had amended a document to somehow distort a complainant's evidence. When I told him that was 'totally and utterly untrue', he asked whether if he were to examine my hard drive or my metadata it would reflect that.

This was, I would later find out, one of his tried and true methods. He would use it on a fifteen-year-old complainant of a sexual crime whom he cross-examined in the same uncompromising manner he questioned me. It seemed like a way of trying to rattle the witness and get them to doubt themselves and perhaps make an admission against themselves.

It's like that feeling when you drive up to a random breath test and even though you haven't imbibed a drop, you feel sort of nervous.

He then tried to tell me that this was the 'first lengthy conversation you had' with the complainant. Which was absurd, because I had interviewed the complainant for *7.30* on camera about nine weeks before. He had copies of the unedited interview. Interviews require careful negotiations and discussions to convince someone to go on camera, speaking about an extremely sensitive subject. People don't just jump in front of the lens at the drop of a hat. I couldn't see how anyone would think that that could happen.

The first lengthy conversation I had had with the complainant, I said, was in May 2016, 'when I met him with his sister and his solicitor and his solicitor's husband'.

He asked if I had transcribed my contemporaneous shorthand notes of that meeting.

'No,' I replied, 'because I recorded an interview immediately after.' That is, a television interview, which, from the perspective of a television reporter, was all I would ever use. But Richter cut me off again – he didn't want context, or nuance, or best evidence, he just wanted my words to suit the narrative he had already constructed in defence of his client. A narrative which in this case, was wrong.

'Don't worry about the reasons,' he quipped.

He drilled for inconsistencies between the notes I had taken before the interview and the interview itself. That assumed that I was preparing all of this for a court proceeding, rather than, as was my job, a television program. And also, I tried to say I didn't recall any changes in the complainant's evidence, but again, he cut me off. The whole thing was a nonsense. I didn't write my shorthand for him.

He then started quizzing me on the detail of the notes about what the complainant had told me in the meeting with the man's sister and his lawyer and her husband.

'You would know, would you not, that if you're interviewing or speaking to a potential witness –' he began. (I wasn't, I was speaking to a potential interview subject in a nightly current affairs program on the ABC.)

'– you shouldn't be doing it in conjunction with other people, should you? … You shouldn't be talking to four people at the same time.

'You should be talking just to the person that you want to interview …'

'I don't accept that,' I replied. In fact, when I was seeking to interview a vulnerable person, as any complainant of sexual crimes is, it was good to know, if I could, that that person had a good support network, that they were giving informed consent, that others who cared about them might ask questions that they didn't think of – which in this case, they did.

He wanted to know 'why' I didn't accept it.

'Because this, in particular, this was a meeting, it wasn't an interview,' I said. 'We were discussing the possibility of whether … he did an interview with me.

'And it was about, talking about, the ramifications of that. It wasn't about going through a blow by blow account of what happened to him.'

He wanted to know what the complainant said, and I gave some detail about where the alleged offences had taken place.

'I have words like "The Pope", he described Pell in Ballarat as being like the Pope,' I added.

'What, [he] described Father Pell as being like the Pope?' he asked with much laboured incredulity.

'He was considered this, you know, sort of God-like figure in Ballarat. Like the Pope,' I answered. 'It's a common thing that people have said to me, from the time.'

'It may be a common thing,' he continued, 'but Father Pell was not well known to these people at [the complainant's school] St Alipius, was he, to the children?'

'Absolutely untrue,' I replied. 'He was very well known to all of the children at St Alipius. Every child that I have spoken to, now an adult, who was at St Alipius at the time, said they knew Father Pell.'

I found some of his lines of questioning quite problematic, such as his assertion that 'children's memories can be fickle, obviously?', to which I immediately replied, 'Everyone's can be.'

He was ignoring, here, the findings of the Royal Commission into Institutional Responses to Child Sexual Abuse. By March

2018, we had been talking for years about the fallacies around children not being reliable. This also ignored how far the law has come in relation to its treatment of the accounts of children. The Judicial College of Victoria makes specific reference to the *Jury Directions Act 2015*, which says this about the accounts of children:

> The trial judge, prosecution and defence counsel ... must not say, or suggest in any way, to the jury that:
>
> (a)   children as a class are unreliable witnesses; or
> (b)   the evidence of children as a class is inherently less credible or reliable, or requires more careful scrutiny, than the evidence of adults; or
> (c)   a particular child's evidence is unreliable solely on the account of the age of the child; or
> (d)   it would be dangerous to convict on the uncorroborated evidence of a witness because that witness is a child.

The other thing Richter was missing was that these people were no longer children. They were adults who had been living with this history for, in some cases, nearly forty years.

I wondered how much he employed this technique when speaking to the complainants themselves. And whether he was pulled up on it by the magistrate or the prosecution. There was no jury to mislead, here, but he was perpetrating a false myth which judges themselves are told not to allow.

'I'm not interested in what's been told by children who may or may not be making things up,' he said, again returning to that 'children are not reliable' trope.

He asked me what other checks I had made. I said I had referred to the Royal Commission's evidence, which had been very substantial on Pell's role at St Alipius and other places in Ballarat.

'You checked that with St Alipius, didn't you?'

'I didn't check it with St Alipius.'

'Why on earth not?' he asked.

'Because so many said it to me that I didn't dispute it. People who didn't make allegations against Cardinal Pell.'

'But the people who said it to you were children at the time, all right?' Again with the unreliable children. I was getting really irritated now with his dismissive attitude towards children.

'I remember my childhood pretty clearly, Mr Richter.'

He then asked me to start naming some of the people who had told me this. I remembered that some had asked to be off the record, and I did not want to betray their confidence in such a public forum.

'I can't give you an exhaustive list of those ... because I am a journalist and I claim the journalist privilege under section 126K of the *Evidence Act*,' I said. It was a sentence I would say many, many times that day.

The section allows that if a journalist has promised a source not to disclose a person's identity, neither the journalist nor her employer are compellable to give evidence that would disclose that identity or enable people to work it out. It's not an absolute privilege because it is up to the judicial officer's discretion to determine whether the public interest in disclosure of the source's identity outweighs the adverse effect on the source and the public interest in 'the communication of facts and opinion to the public by the news media'.

I knew that this would become a large theme of the day's evidence. It would also lead to a further court proceeding later that year.

Richter wanted to know if I had asked the sources whether they would waive confidentiality for me.

'I haven't asked them if they would waive confidentiality. I have made it known to them that I would be – I would be sticking by the agreement that was made ... because I don't feel it's appropriate for me to put pressure on them, given that I am giving evidence in a criminal proceeding.'

He pressed me several times on the question of adults and cut me off when I tried to answer, repeating his question and wanting a simple 'yes or no'.

Again, I used Jack Rush's strategy and turned to Wallington. 'Ah, Your Honour, I don't think this is best answered by a yes or no.

'Many of the adults who were parents of the children at the time were not supportive of the children if they were making complaints about Cardinal Pell because they were from very Catholic families ... There was difficulty.'

Gibson intervened for the second time that day. 'I object to the question, Your Honour, on the grounds of what relevance that has to the statement that, or the evidence, that this witness has made in terms of first complaint from [another complainant], and in terms of the issues that Your Honour has to decide in this committal.' Read, he's wasting time, Your Honour.

'Well, with the greatest of respect,' Richter said, employing what I saw as his sarcastic tone again, 'I don't think my learned friend has read the section 32 permission that we got to question this witness ...'

The section 32 application concerned, it seemed, whether 'conduct' had 'influenced and contaminated witness accounts'. Bear in mind here that the men I spoke to had gone to the police and given statements the year before I met them. I had nothing to do with that process. And yet that's what was being ventilated here.

The only exception to that was the man for whom I was the witness of first complaint. And Richter wasn't asking me about him. But he made it sound like I had spoken to a number of people prior to going to police. And that he was fairly examining 'the extent to which she has operated as a conduit of information between persons has influenced evidence in her desire to obtain a story'.

I was, it seemed, a diabolical Svengali, manipulating and contaminating witnesses up hill and down dale.

He referred to one man I had interviewed, who had made comments about the confessional. That man had been a complainant to the police (and, again, long before I met him) but had, sadly, died about two months before the committal hearing.

'All right,' Wallington interjected, '[that complainant] is no longer, as we know, a witness.'

Richter said, 'That's as it may be,' but emphasised the man's relevance given his relationship to another complainant. 'He may no longer be a complainant because he died of cancer,' he began.

I could feel the anger and sadness rising in me. Yes, technically, the man died from complications related to leukaemia. But not before drinking all day, every day, for years. His friend had told me he was 'drinking himself to death'. I told myself not to get upset.

Richter moved on to a line of questioning that suggested that because another complainant's lawyer had put in an application to the Victims of Crime Assistance Tribunal, the complainant was somehow just after money. That money is largely for counselling and medical expenses. In this particular case, the complainant's lawyer had told me she was doing this because he was hoping to get some treatment to ready him for the court process. There is a very modest special financial assistance award that can be granted to victims on top of funding of counselling. The maximum award – for murder or rape – is $10,000. The maximum for the category of offences the crime this complainant was alleging is $3250. Hardly the princely sum that would justify going through the years of hell that is a criminal justice proceeding.

'He said that [his lawyer] had put it in for him, that he didn't really give a shit,' I said. 'She just told him, you know, that he should do this,' I told Richter.

He then implied that the complainant had approached the lawyer because she was a 'compensation lawyer'. In fact, he had been referred to her because his sister, a senior social worker, thought it was appropriate to see a lawyer given that he was making an allegation about such a high-profile person. I said I wasn't aware that the lawyer was a 'compensation lawyer'. And certainly, there had been no compensation claim mentioned.

Then he tried to pull a swifty on me, which was kind of amusing because it was so wrong.

'You were referred to [the lawyer] by police at some stage, were you?' He put the question as a statement, hoping the witness (me) would agree.

'Absolutely not,' I replied. In fact, I had been referred to her by another survivor.

There was not a single question that he asked in an open way. Every single question was accusatory in tone and phrasing. I was to be painted as a liar.

I remember a barrister explaining to me that, very often, in committals, the defence really hasn't yet worked out its case. It's on a fishing expedition, scratching around for leads, sometimes scratching in the dark.

I got that, but it seemed a bit ridiculous when what he was alleging, with such confidence, was patently wrong. I can imagine that you could still achieve the same outcome without treating the witness with such disdain. It didn't seem to do his case any favours.

Some of the inconsistencies Richter would cross-examine me endlessly about turned on granular distinctions between a type of alleged abuse that involved the anus. And the discussion about it went on, and on, and on.

Gibson intervened a few times, because Richter was moving beyond me recounting what I had asked the complainant and what he had alleged about the abuse, to my opinion of what a certain form of words meant. Whatever they did mean, none of it was pleasant given that it was alleged to have happened to an eight-year-old boy, almost forty years before.

This part of my cross-examination went to the inevitable inconsistent statements that people make in telling and re-telling their story. And how they are such easy fodder for defence counsel. And if this section, dwelling as it did on the anal cavity, was horrible for me, I can't imagine what it was like for the man who made the allegations himself, recalling his boyhood, forced to repeatedly go into scarifying anatomical detail.

By this stage in my evidence, I was starting to tire, having had almost no sleep the night before. My energy was sagging. I was trying to keep my back ramrod straight, to appear alert. But I could hear the flat tones in my voice as he raked over the vile details of the allegations. I could feel myself losing focus.

Nick gave me encouraging nods from the public gallery.

'Sorry, can you recall ... repeat that question?' I asked at one point. Snap out of it, Milligan.

He began quizzing me on the specifics of what the complainant had told me, dwelling constantly on the terminology. Was it the anal cavity?

I felt sick. 'I remember it was a very embarrassing conversation,' I managed. 'And I remember talking about it immediately afterwards to my manager.' I explained that the complainant didn't remember the fine anatomical detail of what had happened. And he didn't know the difference because the events had taken place so long ago, when he was a little boy.

But Richter was undeterred. He kept on, asking whether the man knew the difference between the anus and the rectum.

I said he didn't, and that the complainant 'wouldn't be capable of that' because he was talking about something that had happened a really long time ago.

He again asked about the anus and the rectum and I again replied that the complainant couldn't remember the difference.

'Couldn't,' he said, sarcastically. 'All right. And this was a man on whose reliability you relied?'

'Yes,' I replied.

He wanted to know whether I had asked this 'clearly troubled soul' what he had told psychiatrists, whether I'd asked for his psych reports, and, when I said I hadn't asked for those things, he wondered why I had 'no interest' in them.

'I wouldn't say that it was of no interest to me. It wasn't something …'

He cut me off again. 'Then why didn't you ask him?'

'It wasn't something that came up,' I replied.

'But if it was of interest to you, it should've?'

'That's your opinion, Mr Richter, I disagree with it,' I replied.

He accused me of 'trying to gloss over' inconsistency in the man's account in the 7.30 story.

'That's your assessment of it, Mr Richter. That's not my assessment.'

My assessment was that the alleged abuse of an eight-year-old child may not be remembered in the fine anatomical detail he required.

He even tried to get me to comment on the complainant's evidence to that committal proceeding – something which the law permitted me to know nothing about.

'Obviously, I'm not aware of the contents of [the complainant's] evidence, as I am a witness in this matter and have not heard about it, because it was behind closed doors,' I replied.

I was really, really tiring. The sleeplessness and having to focus intently on every single question was wearing me down. He was so determined to show me up, trip me up, make me look like a lying tabloid hack.

My body temperature was sky high. I rarely visibly sweat, but I could feel perspiration running down my back, underneath my tweed jacket. I was thankful that I had left it on. The overheating left my mouth like coarse sandpaper. I repeatedly sipped from the water they provided.

I turned to Wallington, 'Um, I just need a convenience break, if that's okay?'

'Yes, we probably all do,' Wallington said. 'Ten minutes?'

I remember going to that bathroom, staring at the fifty shades of beige around me and trying to pull myself together. It was a place I would go on to spend an awful lot of time in that day. The air was buzzing, all around me. My cheeks felt hot. I couldn't really feel my feet. I knew I just needed to get my shit together and concentrate.

I came back feeling determined to keep going again.

And what did he do? He went back to the anus, the sphincter and the rectum. He knew exactly what he was doing.

He referred to the complainant's use of the word 'hole'.

'So he's saying, "there's a hole in your bottom". Yeah? We know about the hole?'

'And in between the cheeks,' I replied.

'He's not talking about the cheeks, is he?'

'Well, the entrance to the hole is in between the cheeks.'

'Well,' he said, dripping with sarcasm again. 'We all know the anatomy.'

'Yeah,' I replied.

'But he's not talking about the cheeks, there, is he?'

'That's what I took him to mean.'

'Is he talking about the cheeks?'

'No, that's what I took him to mean.'

He was angry now. 'No, no, no! You asked him that?'

I had become deathly calm. I was feeling good again. I was not going to let this man verbal me into a response that suited him and his client.

'You, you can say what you think I said, or what you think I thought but that's what I took him to mean,' I said, calmly.

'Well, it's the problem of other minds,' he replied, irritated.

Raising his voice repeatedly, he described an allegation in the complainant's police statement which, he said, referred to 'my anus'.

I corrected him, because I knew this stuff in detail. '"Anus *area*",' I pointed out.

'Were you aware of what he said in the police statement?'

'At the time when I had this conversation?' I asked. 'Yes, and that's why I had this conversation.'

'That's right,' Richter continued. 'Because you felt he was giving a completely inconsistent account, right?'

'I felt that there were differences in his account,' I replied.

I do understand that Richter was well within his rights to prosecute potential inconsistencies in the complainant's account. That's what defence barristers do. The Crown had to prove the allegation beyond reasonable doubt, and if there was a doubt prompted by inconsistency, then he was entitled to exploit it. However, I did not agree with the way he was characterising the differences in the way the man had expressed the allegations.

My other issue was that, as he went about this, he treated me with such unnecessary disdain, and he went on about these anatomical differences for a good ninety minutes (bearing in mind that's longer than the duration of many witnesses' entire evidence).

Back and forth we went, over and over, the distinction between the 'anus' (him) and the 'anus area' (the police statement and me). The anus, the rectum, the sphincter.

'Now, the distinction between the anus and the rectum, right?' he started.

'Yes,' I managed.

'And the distinction is that the anus is the sphincter, yes?'

I replied, 'Yes,' although, to be honest, I had never in my life turned my mind to that particular definition. I doubt I have ever given any thought to a sphincter. In truth, my answer was somewhat mechanical.

'And the rectum is the channel?'

'Yes.' Mechanical answer again.

He asked more detailed questions about what was alleged to have happened to the sphincter, versus what happened to the rectum, trying to disprove my belief that the complainant simply had a different definition of what was anal penetration from what I had. I flatly told Richter I disagreed with him, which angered him.

'Well it's not a different definition,' his voice was loud and insistent now, 'because ... the anal sphincter is ... the anus, isn't it?'

He was trying to, again, dragoon me into saying that the complainant had alleged one crime at one time, to me, and another crime to police. 'That's a strict legal definition, Mr Richter. He was speaking –', but he cut me off, asking, 'What definition are *you* talking about?' I replied that a person speaking in conversational terms may not get the legal definition.

He then pressed that what the complainant was alleging to me was 'in the anal sphincter, right?' Of course I said the man had not used the word 'sphincter'.

'No, he used the word "anus" as distinct from "rectum", yes?' Richter asked.

'He used the word "anus" and he used the words "the hole".'

'Yes, the hole being the anus and the sphincter, and the rectum being the canal, correct?' he said, loudly.

At this stage I was completely confused, completely grossed out, just trying to keep it together. I'm sure I have never used the words 'anal sphincter' in a sentence in my life. I was thinking that the complainant would have had no idea what the differences Richter was banging on about were, or why it should have mattered to his eight-year-old self.

'Ah, well, he used those words. I'm –' I started to say, but he cut me off again.

'You used those words?'

'Sorry, I used the word "rectum". (Yes?) He used the word "anus" and "the hole".'

He then went back and forth about what part of the hole. In the hole? I repeated 'at the entrance to the hole'. He went back and forth about the canal and the sphincter and 'higher up the rectum'.

'My, what I took from this conversation –' I tried to say.

He interrupted me again.

'Is that what he's saying to you?'

'– is that he was [talking about] in his bottom.'

'In his bottom, yes, and to say, "in his bottom" when one is talking about the anus, is the anal sphincter, is it not?'

I was sick of this disgusting, wearying conversation. These are the sorts of disgusting, wearying conversations that complainants are forced to have in Australian courts every day. These are the sorts of disgusting, wearying conversations that defence lawyers use to catch them out on seeming inconsistencies in scarifying anatomical details.

When he commenced another definitional spiel about the definition of 'anal' and 'anal sphincter', I decided I'd had enough.

'I have to say, Mr Richter, I haven't put a lot of thought into anal penetration in my life. It's something I don't like thinking about very much …'

But he wasn't finished. He asked yet another question about the sphincter. 'Yes?' he prodded.

'The sphincter,' I managed, 'it's not really a word I ever use.'

Finally, finally, someone spoke up for me.

'I think it's time to move on,' Wallington told Richter.

But he was in his weird anus-sphincter-rectum zone, and it seemed he still didn't want to leave.

'Well, I don't know about that,' he returned, miffed at the suggestion. 'That's an important issue, Your Honour.' And so he ignored what she had just said, and turned again, to me, to his anus and his sphincter and his rectum.

'You understand, don't you,' he began, in that patronising tone.

Her Honour now cut him off. And made a blindingly obvious point:

'In terms of any inconsistencies, I'll be able to judge that from what's in the material and [the complainant's evidence]. I'm not being further –' she tried to finish but he even cut her off – the judicial officer.

'Well,' he started.

'– assisted,' she tried to continue.

'I'm testing this,' he pressed.

'– by this,' she finally managed.

'I'm testing the witness' credibility in terms of what she's reporting,' he continued. He turned to me and said that what I was trying to do was reconcile things by omitting from the 7.30 story and my book things that would damage the credibility of the complainant.

'I reject that,' I replied.

'You reject that. Okay,' he replied, sarcastically.

I told him that we were advised by Queen's Counsel and management that 'the appropriate way to run the story was how we ran it'.

'Was how?'

'How we ran it, what you saw,' I replied.

I was conscious now that I was getting into dicey territory, because I did not want to disclose the confidential advice given to me.

He said my job as a journalist was to give a truthful representation of the witness' credibility to the public, to which I replied, 'That's your opinion.' It wasn't my best answer, but I was mentally scrambling about what to do in regard to what I had been legally advised.

'Oh,' he said, smirking, 'it's not your opinion as a journalist that that's what you do?'

'My opinion is that we did a responsible job of that story,' I replied. The story had been raked over by a QC and ABC legal for weeks, not to mention two producers, an executive producer, the head of current affairs. It had been referred up to the highest levels of management in the organisation for a review. All had agreed that it was appropriate.

'I asked you a question,' he was getting really fired up now. 'Is it your opinion as a journalist that you [should] give to the public, blemishes and all in terms of credibility of someone making serious allegations, and you didn't do that?'

I rejected that. I had given a story to the public which had been unvarnished in its descriptions of the complainant's 'blemishes'. The man had led a very hard life – having to cope with the suicides of his brother and wife. He knew many other people from his school and town who had been abused and had suicided. He said he had been abused by two people. His life had gone off the rails. He'd turned to drugs and alcohol and had been convicted of assault. He'd been in prison. This was disclosed in the story. He volunteered it freely and was ashamed of it. And none of it was remotely unusual for victims of child abuse. In fact, it was, as I discussed at length by reference to evidence tendered to the Royal Commission in my last book, a very typical trajectory.

'I did give a story to the public, which included [the complainant] blemishes and all,' I said. '... I can only tell you what I was advised to do.'

'No, no,' he continued, clearly agitated, refusing to back down, again pointing out that I should have disclosed the 'inconsistencies' in what the complainant told me, versus what he told police.

'I stand by our story,' I said, unflinching.

'You didn't answer my question. 'What –' he started.

I cut him off this time. 'That's my answer.'

I had reached a stage in my evidence where I refused to be hectored by this man any longer. The anus/sphincter/rectum nonsense had set a fire in me. I resolved not to let myself feel bullied by him again.

'Okay. That is your concept of giving credibility to a public audience in relation to a witness making allegations.'

'That's my answer,' I repeated.

'Thank you?'

'I stand by our story.'

'All right. You stand by the story, and indeed, in your book you have a whole chapter about credibility, don't you?'

'Mm-hmm.' I nodded.

'And what you do say is that [the complainant and his best friend, also a complainant, who had died] had full credibility, yeah?'

I tried to answer. 'The –'

'That's what ...' he continued, but I decided to answer anyway.

'You're taking that out of context, Mr Richter.'

'Yes? Yes? ... Were you?'

'You're taking that completely out of context.'

'Were you, in your book, conveying that [the two complainants], you believed that they had full credibility? That's what you're saying,' he said, now trying to verbal me.

He left that one wide open.

'I [wrote] a chapter about credibility –' I began.

'Yes?' he ventured, in a snide tone.

I was really fired up now. 'And I [wrote] a chapter about the process in which someone's credibility is torn apart in this sort of forum, because they have a criminal past.' (He tried to interrupt here, but I continued.) 'And that – that is what the chapter of the book was about.' I kept powering on as I could see he wanted to cut in again.

'And I was looking at evidence to the Royal Commission that people who have a criminal trajectory of drug abuse and alcoholism and other ways of going off the rails – that that was precisely the trajectory of many people who were abused as little children.'

'I see?' he responded, somewhat surprisingly, because he, doing this work every day, surely would know more than most people in the community that that was true.

'And so, when they came to this process that we're in now, they had a disadvantage.

'And they could be torn apart. By people like you.'

I glanced up at the courtroom. I could see the court reporters furiously scribbling. '*By people like you.*' I caught Nick's eye. He nodded his head and widened his eyes, as if to say, 'Go, Sweetie!' My publisher Louise Adler was also nodding vigorously.

At some point for the first time, I glanced at George Pell. I had been studiously avoiding looking at him. But at that moment I noticed that, rather than looking at me with malice, or anger, he was looking in a sort of quizzical way, as you might study a new and exotic animal at the zoo. His face, usually so impassive and hard, had what I can only describe as a softness about it. He was looking at me as if to say, 'Who *is* this creature? What is this woman all about?'

Richter, a QC, backed up by a junior and a team from Galbally and O'Bryan, while the complainants had no lawyer, did not seem to see the irony in what he said next.

'You did not think that someone facing an allegation after forty years has a disadvantage,' he began. The subtext to this seemed to be chiding the child victims for not coming forward earlier to complain about this powerful man.

'Because they also need to look for witnesses who may be dead? They also need to remember precisely what happened forty years ago? They don't have that disadvantage?'

But accused people do not have their childhoods destroyed. Accused people did not have their sense of trust detonated at a fundamental age. They had an opportunity to live a life. Accused people didn't pluck up the courage, after decades, to finally come forward and tell what happened to them, only to be met with accusatory and disbelieving defence counsel, who think it is in their job description to treat them and any witness who stands up for them as road kill in their quest to secure an acquittal. Defence counsel who then maintain their reputation as the go-to men for wealthy men accused of crimes.

At this point, I felt that Richter seemed to have jumped the shark. Wallington made, again, the obvious point: that this case wasn't about the *7.30* program, or my book. It was a criminal process.

'I haven't read the book,' Wallington said. 'I am looking at the hand-up brief,' she said, referring to the evidence tendered to the court.

That's right. This wasn't a defamation proceeding, try as Richter might to seem to treat it as one by zeroing in on me in this way.

'So unless there's something in this process where there's cross-contamination of evidence, it's not really relevant to these proceedings.'

Richter decided to change direction slightly and to refer to the *7.30* program's depiction of this complainant – that we hadn't, in his view, presented the complainant with the lack of credibility that he thought was warranted.

I actually couldn't believe he was saying this, given how, both in the show and in my book, I had gone to great lengths to explain how the man and his friend had gone off the rails.

'We very deliberately mentioned [the complainant's] criminal past for that very reason,' I returned.

'Not concerned about the criminal past.'

Gibson, who for the first time seemed quite irritated by Richter, intervened. 'No, the question is directed to blemishes, Your Honour, and the witness is answering that question. And I ask that she be permitted to answer it.'

But Richter rode on.

'I'm not concerned about his criminal past because of the spin you put –' he started to say to me.

Wallington cut him off again. 'All right, but I think we've done to death the –' she said.

Richter began, 'No –'

'– inconsistencies.'

It is a testament to his sheer tenacity that no matter what was thrown at him, no matter how little good his endless haranguing about issues the magistrate had already suggested she had heard enough about, he would not back down or give up. There is no other way to say it, but the whole thing just reeked of older white male privilege – don't tell me what to do. I know better. He tried to keep going.

'No,' Wallington said, firmly, 'I think you've covered it.'

He ignored her.

'Your Honour, this witness went on to try and win *prizes* with these things,' he said, raising his voice. 'And won prizes with these things. That's what's gone to the public!'

'All right,' Wallington wearily answered, 'but we're not having an investigation into –' She wasn't allowed to finish her sentence, but what she was clearly saying is that this court, and its time and its resources, were not devoted to an investigation into me. This wasn't a defamation proceeding. It was his client who was accused of crimes.

'Oh, we *are* having,' Richter cut her off, 'in one sense, because she distorted what went to the public.'

'I did not distort –' I began to say.

'And I'm going to put to her that she distorted it even more in her book, so as to poison the public's mind against Cardinal Pell!' he returned.

'I completely and utterly reject that, Mr Richter,' I said.

'Course you do,' he said. 'Yes, you *would* say that.'

'And so would you,' I fired back. 'You're representing a man who is charged –'

Wallington intervened. 'All right, now …' I could see she was trying to stop us from descending into a slanging match. But it is a maddening part of being a witness that the person who is questioning you is permitted to make all sorts of untrue and offensive comments about you, questioning your every motive, but when you try to point out the elephant in the room – his motive, his narrative, his objective – you're cut off.

'Just a minute, just a – who'd been charged and is presumed innocent, correct?'

Yes. So you can treat witnesses in whatever way you choose.

'All right,' Wallington said, again.

Gibson at this point finally intervened in a way which, I would say, felt long, long overdue.

'Yes, I object under section 41 of the *Evidence Act*, Your Honour, in terms of improper questions, tenor, tone, and the like.'

Section 41 of the *Evidence Act* is something I have thought about a lot in my research for this book. As Gibson implied, it refers to improper questions. A court is required to disallow improper questions put to a witness or inform them that they need not be answered.

An improper question is defined as a question or sequence of questions that:

(a) is misleading or confusing; or

(b) is unduly annoying, harassing, intimidating, offensive, oppressive, humiliating or repetitive; or

(c) is put to the witness in a manner or tone that is belittling, insulting, or otherwise inappropriate; or

(d) has no basis other than a stereotype (for example, a stereotype based on the witness's sex, race, culture, ethnicity, age or mental, intellectual or physical disability).

It's not improper simply because it's challenging the witness' truthfulness, or because it's distasteful or private.

Nonetheless, I struggle to think of a single question asked by Mr Richter that day that wasn't said in a manner or tone that I felt was belittling or insulting. I don't think he veered from that sneering, sarcastic, and, I would argue, bullying, tone the entire day.

And while, yes, you could argue that the anus/sphincter/rectum business was 'distasteful', I found the tone also unduly harassing, offensive, oppressive and repetitive. He could clearly see that I was not responding to his definitions around those parts of the body and what had been done to them, but he carried on with it for about ninety minutes.

I struggle to think of a minute of that day in which I didn't feel belittled, harassed, annoyed, insulted. It seemed to me, like a two-for-one job – destroy me and try to knock the case out at committal.

Wallington seemed to agree with Gibson's call at that point.

'Yes, I think the words "respect" and "dignity" come to mind in terms of how we should approach the –'

Richter cut her off, seeming to agree. 'Precisely.'

'Thank you,' Wallington replied, seeming to think she had got through to him. She hadn't.

'Respect and dignity for the cardinal's presumption of innocence would've required you to present to the public a full and proper picture of the credibility of [the complainant's] account of what happened. Correct?'

Respect and dignity for the presumption of innocence are incredibly important. They do not, nor should not, give anyone carte blanche to treat people who come forward to give evidence in good faith in a court of law with such derision. There is no need for it. It's the sort of thing that would not be sanctioned in any other professional place of work or business (except, perhaps, Parliament, another place where men outnumber women and where they throw their weight around). As a law graduate, I passionately support the presumption of innocence. As a journalist, I passionately support robust debate and argument. But if I or any of my colleagues treated an interview subject the way Richter treated me, we would rightly be the subject of howling complaints.

'I stand by the story we presented,' I drily replied.

Later, when he was questioning me about a complainant who was under extreme stress about the upcoming show and his family's reaction to his decision to do an interview, with me giving evidence that he was having a 'complete meltdown' when he was speaking to me, he just wouldn't let me finish answering the question.

'You disagree with it?'

'All I can tell you –' I tried to answer.

'Do you disagree with it?'

'All I can tell you is –'

'Do. You. Disagree. With. It?'

'All I can tell you –'

'Do you disagree?'

Wallington again cut in. 'She's trying to answer the question.'

But Richter didn't want my honest answer to the question. He wanted to frame the question to suit his narrative. The truth of the situation was, it seemed, beside the point. We don't, in any other human context, expect that a person answer with a simple 'yes' or 'no'. We give context and nuance. We explain. A yes or a no doesn't give you the truth. It gives you a superficial answer, but it's not, in my view, best evidence. A witness should be allowed to, within reason, give context to an answer. Not to waffle or to spin, but, where the answer is not a yes or a no, to honestly address that.

The other thing that really got to me was the way he kept speaking to Wallington, as if she didn't know what she was talking about. Only he knew. He didn't show her the respect, I thought, that she deserved.

'No! No!' he shouted. 'It's a simple question!' and then he added that courtroom faux courtesy so often used when someone is being anything but courteous, 'If Your Honour pleases.'

And then, to me: 'Do you disagree with it?'

'I don't recall him saying that he was having a meltdown. That's the answer to my question,' I replied. 'I do not recall him saying that.'

He just would not give up – asking the same question about the alleged meltdown repeatedly, as I tried to answer that the complainant was under 'great duress at the time'.

'Not interested in that!'

Gibson intervened. 'This isn't helpful, in my submission, Your Honour.'

Richter: '*Oh.*'

'If the witness can't remember something, that's the state of her memory,' Gibson calmly continued. I stood my ground.

He also tried to paint the complainant as mentally ill. This really irritated me. He knew, as well as anyone, that people can go through extreme trauma in their lives, but that does not mean they are mentally ill.

'[He was] someone who had had crises in his life and had sought psychiatric help for those crises, as many people have, Mr Richter ... Many, many people ... He'd [much earlier] had a meltdown, but it was in relation to the loss, suicide loss, of his brother and the suicide loss of his wife, that he had a serious – he suffered great turmoil after that. He was grieving, and his life was very difficult, and that he could not cope with that grief, as many people can't.'

When pressing me about information I'd been advised, by Queen's Counsel, to leave out of the 7.30 program, and why I had also left it out of the book, I repeatedly said I thought it was 'prudent' to go with that same advice.

'Okay, so you chose not to put it in, correct?'

I tried to tell him that I did what I did on the advice of Queen's Counsel and management, but he cut me off again.

'I didn't ask you that!

'I didn't ask you for your reasons. You see, you can be re-examined about all your reasons.'

I didn't feel at all confident that I would be re-examined by the Crown prosecutor about my reasons. I was right to think that. Gibson would barely re-examine me at all. He had barely asked me any questions in the first place. I felt like I was the only person who could stand my ground.

Richter tried to cast doubt on the evidence – there was one man who told me he hadn't seen any offending going on when he was friends with the other boys, and it hadn't happened to him. He tried to say this man didn't 'support' the complainants. That wasn't true. I pointed out that that man had sent me a text message to the effect of 'good job' after the story.

When I later tried to give an honest answer, he repeatedly interrupted me and raised his voice.

'Would you listen to the *question*?'

'I am listening, sir.'

Gibson again objected when Richter returned to asking about something he had already covered, at length, earlier in the day.

'Yes, asked and answered,' Wallington said. Here it just felt like section 41 'harassing' again. He then went for the tried and true trick of the defence barrister in a sex crime trial – saying that no one else saw the crime that was being alleged take place. That is, implying that it was uncorroborated.

'Sexual abuse is, as you know, Mr Richter – is something that happens between two people,' I started to say.

'Not usually in public?' he ventured, because some of the crimes alleged happened in a public place – a swimming pool.

'It's often hidden,' I finished.

'Not usually in public,' he asked.

'Well, they allege that it was underneath the water,' I said.

'Well,' he continued, 'their allegations are nonsense and you know that they must be.'

I looked at him patiently, pursing my lips. He wanted to argue that the offences were impossible because they had allegedly happened under water. I had already seen the argument he was now putting forward, ventilated, in the same terms, in an ultra-conservative Catholic journal for which George Pell had in the past frequently written. The writer was disparaging about me. Her arguments precisely reflected Richter's.

And so would commence what would later become the next interminable session – after Chapter 1: Anus/Sphincter/Rectum, was Chapter 2: What could anyone see under the water?

'I disagree with you completely and utterly,' I said. Nick smiled in support from the gallery.

I said it was 'entirely conceivable' that what was alleged could have happened without being observed.

'"Conceivable" is not "did",' Richter said.

'Well, I wasn't there in 1978, '79, and neither was anyone else here,' I replied.

He changed the subject. And moved to the reason I was supposed to be there – as witness of first complaint for another complainant, returning, yet again, to the subject we'd already covered at length – why I hadn't recorded the date of a note with the man, who had telephoned me in the days after the *7.30* story on 27 July 2016.

'I just said to you that it was in the days after [the program],' I answered. When he tried to push me more, I volunteered that there might be a record of it somewhere, as the complainant had telephoned the ABC.

'And that might assist me –' I began.

'No, it won't! No, it won't!' he interrupted.

'– to determine when it was that he actually spoke to me.'

He insisted in very patronising terms that I was supposed to write the date in a diary or notes, 'according to anyone of common sense who might want to recall when those conversations occur'.

I replied that that was his opinion. There was absolutely no journalistic reason why it was necessary for me to record a date on that note. The complainant contacted me very soon after the show, in response to the show. Whether it was the last day or so of July or the first of August was immaterial. I had kept contemporaneous notes of it. And I had transcribed them.

'It *is* [my opinion],' Richter declared. He again raised the date. When I tried to answer, he kept interrupting. When I turned to the magistrate to try to get her assistance, Richter seemed furious. I was only trying to give him an absolutely precise answer to his question. To give an honest answer, based on an honest recollection, and a pretty normal work practice for any of my journalistic colleagues.

'She's not answering the question!' he bellowed.

'I am,' I said. 'I'm trying, endeavouring to answer the question, Your Honour. I've said to Mr Richter, openly and honestly, that [this complainant] contacted us after the *7.30* story went –'

He interrupted me. Again.

'Your Honour, that does not answer the question! Would Your Honour direct the witness to answer the question?'

I turned to Wallington. 'If Your Honour will let me finish?' I refused to be browbeaten into giving wrongful answers, into serving his client's narrative and betraying what I believed to be true, into feeling insulted by Richter.

'All right,' Wallington said. 'Just settle down, everyone.'

Richter looked furious to me.

'All this self-excusing isn't answering the question!' Richter said.

Well it was, it just wasn't giving him the answer he wanted. Which was one that was intended to undermine me, like every other question that day.

'It's not a self-excuse,' I said.

'Oh yes, it is!' Richter exclaimed.

Wallington asked the blindingly obvious question. 'We know … do we need an actual date?'

'Yes,' shot back Richter.

'Is it so vital?' Wallington continued. 'Because it's tied down in the statement to within a few days.'

Richter was really losing it now. I wondered how he thought that causing a spectacle and arguing with the judicial officer he was hoping would throw out the charges was going to play well for him.

And all this over a date which was not, as far as I could see, relevant to anything much at all. Perhaps there was some hidden forensic purpose.

He argued back and forth with me, again and again.

I went for another 'convenience break', this time feeling far more like myself. The detective running the case, Chris Reed, who up until that point had always been fairly business-like, gave me a very encouraging nod. The nods would become more encouraging as the convenience breaks, and the day, wore on.

* * *

Chapter Two in the defence line of questioning – what could be seen under the wretched water in the wretched pool – would now begin in earnest.

'You're assuming that things happened under the water, aren't you?' Richter asked.

'No,' I said, 'I was told that things happened under the water.'

'... And you wanted to believe those accounts?'

'No.'

'No?

'That's untrue, I suggest to you,' Richter said.

It really wasn't. 'That's absolutely untrue,' I said of his accusation that I was simply just wanting to believe those accounts. '... [I]n fact, the day that the story broke in the *Herald Sun*, I was annoyed because it was a Saturday and I was asked to go and do this story and I didn't believe it. So I came at it from a very sceptical point of view,' I told Richter.

I had said this, at length, in my book, which I began to think he hadn't read very carefully. I had recorded that Pell has always maintained his innocence against all charges and complaints, including in relation to the complaints that were the subject of my cross-examination. Pell was acquitted of the 'Cathedral' charges by the High Court, but all charges relating to the 'Swimmers' allegations on which I was being cross-examined were later withdrawn.

He then began his thesis about what could be seen beneath the water from the sides of the public pool, or from the canteen, where the pool manager's wife was working. She had told me and also police that she had seen nothing. Richter's basic argument was that anything untoward happening under the water could not possibly have been missed.

'I don't accept that's necessarily true,' I said. 'Because you could quite easily fleetingly do something without being seen.'

'Fleeting as in accidental?'

'No, not accidental,' I replied.

'No?'

'No.'

He repeatedly quizzed me over what Pell had allegedly done in the water, and how, he asserted, it was 'impossible' that he could have done it.

'That's what [the complainants said],' I said.

We broke for lunch. It was still only one o'clock. How could it only be one o'clock? Nick wanted to know what I wanted to eat. I wasn't hungry. All I wanted was a Coke with no sugar. Everyone told me it was going well, and they were proud of me. I just wanted the whole blasted thing over.

When we went back, Richter read out a long description of what was alleged at the pool and tried to put to me what he thought it meant. When I replied that I wasn't sure, he wouldn't accept my answer.

'You're not sure? Well, that's the immediate interpretation of the passage, isn't it?'

'It's your interpretation, sir.'

'Is that an objective interpretation? Anyone reading this, as I've read out, would assume?'

'It's your interpretation.'

'You're disagreeing with me?'

'No, I'm saying it's your interpretation.'

'Are you disagreeing with my interpretation?' He was angry again. 'Would you answer the question, please?'

I reiterated that I wasn't sure.

'You're not sure. Of *course* you're not.'

At times I was just utterly confused by his circuitous, hectoring questions. But I refused to allow that to distort my evidence. He frequently raised his voice in anger. He was trying to say I had invented a new account, for the court, which would explain why the alleged offending couldn't be seen from the outside of the pool. I had no idea what he was talking about.

'The bottom line is, Mr Richter –'

He cut me off. Again. 'No. No! I asked you a question!'

'But I don't think that there is an adequate answer that I can give that is a yes or a no,' I replied.

'Oh yes, you can! Oh yes, you can!'

'That's your interpretation,' I replied. He started interrupting again.

'I would ask the court … I think I need to explain here,' I said, turning to Wallington.

'No, you don't! Please answer the question!' He pushed me again about my so-called 'new' account.

Gibson objected, explaining that I wasn't accepting the account to be 'new'.

The magistrate thought that was 'fair'. Richter didn't.

He kept going with the idea that it was new and asserting that it would explain why someone outside the pool wouldn't have seen what was alleged. But he said it in what I thought was such a complicated way, it just didn't make sense.

'I really don't understand the question,' I said.

'Yes, you do!'

'I don't.'

He was also adamant that the water was 'crystal clear' and people in the pool would have seen what was happening.

I said I didn't agree with that. 'I think that lots of things can be splashing around and it can be quite difficult to see … under the water.'

'You're not being partisan here, are you?'

'No.'

Over and over, he presented his theory and I said, 'I don't accept that,' and he said, 'Would you just answer my question?' And I just endured it.

'I'm not quibbling,' I said. 'I'm just saying to you that I don't accept that … I don't think that it necessarily follows. That's my honest answer to you.'

'It wouldn't necessarily honestly follow, but logically it would follow?'

'Ah, not necessarily.'

'Not necessarily, but probably?'

'No.'

'You're not even prepared to grant "probably"?'

'No, I can't grant you that, Mr Richter, I'm sorry.'

'You are very, *very* persuasive,' he said.

He then went back, unbelievably, to the anus issue for a while, and then began to pursue another trope – that my book was designed to poison the public's mind against his client in analysing what the Royal Commission heard Pell knew about the clergy abuse issue.

'Are you seriously trying to suggest that you were not trying to paint a picture that he must have known what was going on in his diocese?'

'I find it very hard to believe that he did not know.'

'No, I didn't ask you that.' He repeated the question.

'I wasn't trying to convey a picture. I was going through everything that had been on the public record in the Royal Commission and, at the end of that process, I felt pretty convinced that Cardinal Pell must have known what was going on.'

'And you were trying to give that impression in your book, right?'

'It was a view shared by the Royal Commission.'

'Don't look for excuses not to answer the question.'

'It's not an excuse, Mr Richter.'

He said I had reached that conclusion, and I countered, more than once, that it was 'after looking at all the material. Not before ... As did the Royal Commission, sir.'

'They could have been wrong, too, you know?'

I was just sitting there thinking, 'This man is unbelievable, he has no respect.' I've since heard several defence barristers tut-tut about the Royal Commission, which they believed was too victim-centred. Which, given what had preceded it for the past couple of hundred years since the common law system was established in Australia and the way that victims of sexual crimes had been treated by people like him in courts of law, was quite something.

'... [Y]our book was intended to pervert the course of justice, was it not?'

'Absolutely not,' I replied.

'No?'

'I reject that, entirely.'

'Okay. Well, we'll get to that.'

He then tried to box me into yet another 'yes' or 'no' answer. I turned to Wallington and said I didn't believe the question was best answered by yes or no and 'I will answer it as follows'.

He hated that.

'Only if it's answered yes or – yes and no, Your Honour, and I can pursue my questioning if it is incapable of a yes or a no answer.'

'She should be allowed,' Wallington replied, 'to give a full answer.'

He didn't think so.

Wallington continued that if there was a 'follow on' from 'yes' or 'no' I should be allowed to give it, 'otherwise the evidence becomes a little bit distorted'. To which he answered, irritated, that 'she's the one trying to give speeches, and excuses, and excuse herself'.

Through all of this, I just kept imagining all the vulnerable, traumatised victims of all sexual crimes, who had no law degree, who had never stepped foot into one of these places, who were not legally advised by a top QC as I had been, who did not have a team of lawyers at the ABC to fall back on, who didn't have the support of producers and publishing staff cheering them on and helping them prepare.

I thought of those people, who had spent the past decades burying away their childhood shame, who might have taken to drug or alcohol addiction to make it go away, to dull the throb in their brain, to switch off the disgusting flashbacks of, for instance, a creepy Christian brother who made them do unspeakable things.

I thought of how that made them feel about themselves, how it had shaped their self-esteem, or lack thereof, how it was understandable that, as he'd been dwelling on before, they might at some point have ended up in psychiatric care, or, worse, prison.

How would they manage this kind of questioning? Would they simply acquiesce? Would they allow it to distort their meaning and not give their best evidence? Would they cry? Would they get angry and then do their cause no favours?

How utterly, utterly alone they must have felt.

But in this forum, it seemed that any attempt to empathise with complainants and what they went through was treated as simply giving a platform to liars who had unfairly targeted an innocent man.

Richter told me I was trying to get the public to believe the complainants. 'The answer is very simple.'

'I don't accept that the answer is very simple,' I replied, standing my ground. Which was absolutely true. It was far from simple.

'Okay, don't accept it. But were you trying to?'

I would not back down, just because he wanted me to. He seemed completely perplexed at my impertinence, that I could dare to ask for the ability to give proper answers. He seemed absolutely unable to believe that I could assert my rights in this way.

'I would ask Her Honour if I could answer the question more fully,' I repeated twice, as he interjected.

'Oh, Your Honour!' he said adopting a frustrated tone. 'I'd ask that the witness be directed to answer the question. It is capable of a simple answer!'

But Wallington seemed to get my point.

'She did give an answer and that is – in fact, I had to make a note of it. That is partially the case … Her answer is yes and no, and she was going to elaborate.'

'Your Honour, we don't want a life history of what she's philosophically trying to do with the whole book and this question! The question is very simple.'

So would have been my answer, had he let me give it, instead of wasting the court's time with his absolute refusal to let go of his 'yes or no' dichotomy.

'All right,' Wallington said to him. 'We're never going to get past this unless she's allowed to answer the question.'

'Then I don't want to ask it,' he declared, petulantly. 'I mean, if she can't answer the question with a yes or a no …'

'All right then,' Wallington said, completely unflustered by it all.

'I don't want it answered.'

'Okay,' the magistrate replied.

'Thank you,' he said. At the time, it really did bring to mind a toddler throwing toys out of the pram.

'Put it another way,' Wallington offered, helpfully.

He did, and I answered it. He wondered why it was so hard.

'Because ... the way you were phrasing the question was way too wide,' I replied.

'Oh, *was it*? *Okay*.'

He said I was engaging in a 'blackening and character assassination of Cardinal Pell'.

'I disagree entirely,' I replied.

He then made what in my view appeared to be a weird mistake, which again made me think that he had not fully read the book in his research – by asking why I had made a point of saying that Pell had lived in the presbytery at St Alipius with Gerald Ridsdale – a serial paedophile priest.

In fact, I had made the point in the book that, although everyone assumed Pell must have known about Ridsdale's proclivities because he lived with him, presbyteries were busy places and a lot of people thought it was neither here nor there that they shared the lodging.

'I actually brought it up in fairness to Cardinal Pell,' I said.

I pointed this out several times. But he seemed to have prepared questions on it, and so was going to ask it, even though what I was replying, referring specifically to my book, in no way suited his narrative.

But he kept on with questions about the layout of the presbytery.

'I've just said to you that I said in the book that it didn't follow, that the fact they lived together –' I tried to say.

He wouldn't let me finish and didn't appear to be listening.

'No! No! Just, just –'

'– meant that he knew anything.'

'Tackle my –'

'So I was being fair –'

'Tackle my questions.'

'– to Cardinal Pell.'

'Your concept of fairness and mine differ. Just answer –'

'Quite clearly,' I replied.

He still kept on about how many rooms were in the presbytery.

I had no idea. He brought up that they had separate rooms, separate quarters. Why wasn't he listening? This was taking him nowhere. He seemed so fixated on getting me to answer questions, he didn't appear to me to be listening to what I was saying.

It seemed to take quite some time for him to appear to realise he'd just wasted his time and change course.

He then spent some time trying to paint me as an unethical journalist. One of the people I had spoken to had done a taped interview in person and sent me photos to assist me in describing him in my book. He told me he was fine about me writing about him in the book, he just didn't want to be on television, because he was a shy person. He was talking about things he'd never spoken to his family about.

I said that was understandable – we had a very good rapport. I invited him to my book launch. But when he got a copy of the book, he was horrified to see that he was named. He had never once asked me not to name him. I think he was just confused. He sent me a letter about this saying that he didn't bear me any malice, but he was very upset about it.

Richter pounced on this and tried to cut me off when I spoke about the later conversations we'd had and emails where the man had said he understood it all now and there were no hard feelings at all. I have stayed in contact with this man – he was the reason I was the witness of first complaint. I have a very positive relationship with him and we still to this day correspond and chat from time to time. Sometimes, I feel very guilty that when he said that he just wanted to help the other complainants, that I suggested, because I felt it was the proper thing to do, that he go to the police. And so he had gone to the police, on my suggestion. And he'd been through all this with Richter. And it hadn't been a positive experience at all.

'His questions were just ... how do I put it? You could have said that he was just waiting for me to say the wrong thing,' the man told me recently of his cross-examination by Richter.

The complainant said Richter seemed to have a 'smug look on his face the whole time'.

He got confused. 'I really did not prepare myself properly for that evidence in court,' he told me, 'I just sort of lost it. I was confused. I was blasé about it beforehand.'

He now accepts he was 'a bit naïve' because he thought the process would be relatively quick and straightforward, that he could just tell his story and then have it over.

When he had 'first put his hand up' for this process, he had no idea where it would take him.

'Personally, I would rather just have kept me mouth shut,' he told me recently.

He flew back to his interstate home after his evidence, wondering why he had volunteered for the whole humiliating ordeal.

We came from completely different walks of life. But we had a nice rapport. I always found him a straightforward and gentle presence. He was thoughtful and nuanced about what he says took place and the impact it had had on his life. He certainly had zero to gain from coming forward.

It was talking about my relations with this man that led Richter to deliver what I thought to be his great clanger, alleging that in my emails I was flirting with the man, presumably to get his story. An audible gasp rang through the courtroom from the public gallery.

'You did charm him, didn't you?' (In the background, the prosecutor can be heard, trying to say something.)

'There was a very friendly exchange, sorry, there was a very charming, if not flirtatious, exchange of emails, and, and –' he began.

'I find that absolutely, absolutely, insulting ...' I began to say.

The magistrate looked genuinely angry at this point and swiftly intervened. 'I'm sorry, stop, Ms Milligan, I've not seen anything that fits that description ...'

'No,' he continued, absolutely undeterred. 'Well, Your Honour can look at those –' he began.

'I find that an absolutely sexist assertion, Mr Richter, and I object to it,' I said.

'Yes,' he began, 'I'm not talking about you trying to seduce him, I'm talking about him putting on conversational style and SMSs and the like, which is very familiar.'

'You said that that was flirtatious,' I answered, 'and I think that that is an absolutely sexist –'

The magistrate, seeing the turn that this was taking, pulled him up again. He changed the subject.

The words provoked outrage on Twitter.

'This is what women cop if they write a book about a powerful man.'

'These exchanges between @milliganreports and Robert Richter are phenomenal reading and I want to see the telemovie of this committal already.'

'Did you read the way Richter went after @milliganreports?'

The Twitterverse might have been chowing down this virtual popcorn, but I was genuinely disgusted he would say such a thing.

I have looked back over my emails with the complainant. They range from fairly standard business-like exchanges of information, to pleasantries, to consoling him. They were no different from my correspondence with, for instance, the mother of the choirboy who had died. Or, in another context for my book, someone like Julie Stewart, the clergy abuse victim who went through the Melbourne response. In all of these cases, I was being decent to a person who was vulnerable or needed kindness. I was being human. The tone was no different at all.

I think, again, in an environment where you are treated so deferentially all the time, where you are bulldozing witnesses and most do not know how to manage it, so they just take it. Perhaps it begins to elevate your opinion of yourself. And that little voice in your head that stops you from saying things that are clearly out of line, even in a highly public forum, stops working.

To me, his question flouted section 41 of the *Evidence Act* on improper questions as he had no basis, I would argue, other than a stereotype based on my sex. What else could a female journalist who is exchanging emails with her source in an empathetic way be doing but flirting with them? I would argue it's not the sort of thing he would ever have said to a man.

Having failed at trying to paint me as some sort of journalistic honey pot, he now tried to paint me as a pest. It was curious at best. He berated me for going to 'door knock' a complainant who had made the allegation about Pell to the Church in 2002, describing me going to the man's home and knocking on the door as a 'gross invasion of privacy'.

I was simply doing my job in the most polite and straightforward way.

'And you just landed on his doorstep. Is that right?'

'Well, it's something that journalists do every day, Mr Richter,' I replied.

'It doesn't excuse an invasion of privacy –'

'– I had a very polite conversation with him.'

He peppered me with questions about what I said, whether I announced I was a journalist – of course, complying with my ethics, I did.

The man's face had changed when he realised that I was a journalist and he wasn't happy I was there – he told me I was lucky his wife hadn't opened the door. I politely listened to him.

'So you barge in, unannounced?' was how Richter characterised it. I explained that I didn't barge in, I simply accepted what the man said, and politely left.

We then moved into a stage of the evidence where he tried and failed to get me to identify and name sources and what they had told me. I refused.

'I wish to invoke section 126K of the *Evidence Act*, because it would tend to identify a class of persons about which I claim the journalist's privilege,' I said a couple of times.

He tried to dispute the definition of the legislative protection – that it didn't cover a 'class of persons'.

'So once you identify a class of persons,' Wallington said, intervening, 'that may enable you to identify the confidential source.'

He argued a bit, but Wallington was firm.

When he tried to get me to disclose a meeting with a source and I refused, he wondered why. I said, again, it would identify a class of persons over whom I claimed the journalist's privilege.

'Well, you've been released from that privilege because it's his privilege, it's his confidentiality, and he's given us evidence that he says he had a coffee with you?' he replied.

'I can't answer that question,' I answered.

'Yes, you can, and with respect, Your Honour, I would ask that the witness answer the question.'

I didn't know what to do. I started looking and nodding vigorously at Hugh Bennett, the solicitor for the ABC who had been working on my summons for some months. Hugh, who is a very mild-mannered and unassuming guy, stood up in the public gallery.

'Your Honour, my name is Bennett. I appear for the ABC ... If the defence would like to set aside privilege, then I ask that they formally do so, rather than skirting around the issue as we are doing here.'

Bennett, who had approached Gibson in the recess to try to get the Crown to intervene more on the grounds of relevance, explained that I wasn't in a position to know what evidence the source had given in the court, or the extent to which it had been waived or if I had been released from it.

Wallington was receptive. 'I'm not sure that it matters. The privilege in this case is the journalist's and she's invoking it.'

'No, Your Honour, with respect.'

I turned to Wallington. 'If it assists, Your Honour –'

'Oh,' said Richter, theatrically. I ignored him.

'Of all the people who I have spoken to, who are involved in various ways,' I continued, 'who I claim the journalist's privilege in relation to, none of them have released me and so it's about releasing me from that privilege, and it's something I take incredibly seriously as a journalist.'

Wallington said that she understood that and told Richter that unless he made an actual application to waive it, it couldn't be waived just because someone gave evidence they had a coffee.

Richter was really angry now. Wallington let him go but asked again if the court was going to have the application.

Richter again argued the toss, saying a privilege couldn't exist where a man gives evidence without saying he wanted to keep it confidential.

'No, no, no,' Wallington answered, rightly. 'We don't know what he was – what the conversation was about.'

Precisely. He was trying to snooker me into ratting a source by the mere fact that a person had in some way mentioned me in evidence I hadn't heard or read.

He again tried to get me to nominate who had given me information to identify the dead choirboy's mother.

I again invoked section 126K.

He repeatedly raised his voice, saying, 'No! No!' and refusing to back down.

'I can't go any further than what's in my book, because I claim section 126K of the *Evidence Act* ...' I began.

'The very nature of confidential information [Yes?] as a journalist is that it is ... [Uh-huh?] confidential ... [Yes?] Confidentially given ... [Yes?] And I was given information for my reporting of this by some confidential sources, actually not many – most people put their name to things ...' I said. I was building up a head of steam now and Richter was irritated.

'Yes, but –' he tried to say.

'... But I cannot reveal my sources and I will not reveal my sources, because I claim section 126K of the *Evidence Act*.'

Hugh Bennett from the ABC was forced to stand up twice more to protect me from this attempt to have me betray a source.

Wallington again instructed Richter to move on, he agreed to move on, and she said to Hugh Bennett, 'Get ready to jump to your feet again if you need to.' I felt like Belinda Wallington got it. It was an enormous relief to have her up there.

But Richter wouldn't give up.

Hugh Bennett jumped up again. Richter was undeterred.

'I don't see how, what *"class of person"*? What *class of person*? I don't understand that, Your Honour.'

Wallington admitted that she was trying to follow it too. I got that none of them were journalists. I felt I desperately had to make them understand what it means, as a reporter, to protect your sources.

It was so frustrating. No one had given me the green light to betray their confidence.

'Your Honour, if I may: none of the people who I spoke to as confidential sources have released me as a journalist. And that is the only thing that can release me as a journalist. I-I give an undertaking to people and –'

Wallington tried to speak, but I really wanted to finish – I really wanted this point to be heard.

'... And I'm sure that anyone in this room will understand that. Anyone who has had conversations with journalists off the record would understand the importance,' I said.

And that comment was aimed at Richter. I didn't expect him to remember our own unremarkable, but nonetheless, off-the-record conversation, five years before, but I know for a fact that he had off-the-record conversations with other journalists. And if they started blabbing on him publicly, he'd be livid.

'... Because without that, we might as well take our bat and ball and go home,' I said. 'We might as well stop being journalists.'

Richter was furious again. 'What she says is, with the greatest respect, complete humbug,' he declared.

He then decided to try to undermine my descriptions of a complainant, whom I had described as having 'PTSD eyes'. 'What is "PTSD eyes", please?'

'In my experience,' I began, 'I have dealt with a lot of people who have post-traumatic stress disorder. Their eyes tend to well up with tears very easily. They shine, they look sad, they look like puppy dog eyes. And he had those eyes.'

I could tell that this was the sort of thing that Robert Richter might think was ridiculous psychobabble. Part of his very substantial living was made eviscerating people whom I might describe as having PTSD eyes – calling them liars and fantasists.

'So you make a psychological diagnosis of PTSD on the spot?'

'No, he told me he had PTSD.' That was a mistake. Even though it related to my first chapter, I should never have fallen into the trap of telling him anything I'd spoken about. The whole thing was making me decidedly ill.

He then tried to corner me again and I again invoked section 126K of the *Evidence Act*.

He argued that the source had waived the privilege in his evidence and then, his customary, 'Do you follow?' As if I hadn't been following it in every minute detail, and as if the lawyer for my organisation hadn't been arguing the toss with him for some time now. I looked over at Bennett and widened my eyes.

'No one has waived a privilege,' I repeated.

By this stage Richter was theatrically huffing and puffing.

'I don't make an application, Your Honour, because that's nonsense. I mean, he's given evidence about this!'

Bennett stood up again and reiterated what was true – we did not know the content of the evidence.

There were times when he got me – such as in a line of questioning about an abusive priest. I knew what was coming because I had been mortified to realise some time before that wires had been crossed about two priests sharing the same, very uncommon, first name. When a source started talking about that first name, I said I had recognised it, thinking he was speaking of the other priest with that name.

I don't know what happened, but there was a mix-up. Somehow the other priest's name was settled. And it ended up, to my eternal frustration, in the first edition of my book, later to be corrected.

I couldn't go into any of the contents of any conversation with any source about this, though, because they were confidential, and so I claimed the journalist's privilege.

But Richter knew, in fairness to him, that he had me on this one, and it was incorrect. I admitted as much. He was thrilled with this. But again, he squandered the opportunity somewhat.

'... [W]hat you do is, you kind of try another bit of character assassination by associating Cardinal Pell with a child-abusing priest?'

'Well, he *was* associated with a child-abusing priest,' I replied.

'Cardinal Pell attended ... [the priest's] funeral weeks after [the priest] was charged with multiple counts of offences against children,' I replied.

'What's that got to do with the accuracy of your book?'

'That is an accurate fact. It was reported in the Royal Commission ...'

I had admitted my mistake, but it didn't mean Pell hadn't gone to the funeral of an abuser priest. He had. But Richter was furious with more, 'No, No! Listen to me please!' and 'Do you have trouble with my question?'

The trouble I had was that I couldn't go into why this error had occurred without betraying my source. That it would soon stray into the sort of territory I was professionally bound to avoid.

He then tried again with a bogus theory that because none of the other former choirboys I had spoken to remembered something 'so dramatic', it must not have happened.

'Child abuse is something that happens between the perpetrator and the victim or victims,' I replied. 'It was alleged to have happened in a very quiet place … I don't see how any of those people would have necessarily known … That's why child abuse can occur.'

There were so many typical defence tropes he relied upon – trying to nail a witness down to an exact date, for instance, to trick them into giving the wrong one. I didn't bite.

'Is it your understanding that this happened at – this allegation relates to the end of 1997? Is that your understanding?'

'I-I'm not sure,' I replied.

'You're not *sure*?'

'No.'

'But you write so authoritatively about The Kid [the name I had given to a complainant in the Pell case], and the PTSD eyes, and you express a belief in him?' he asked, sarcastically.

'I did believe him. [Yes. Yes?] He was very believable.'

'Well some people are, in terms of telling lies as well, aren't they, right?'

Wallington intervened. 'You don't have to answer that,' she told me.

He appeared frustrated and angry again. I asked for another convenience break. The cross-examination had been going since first thing that morning and it was now late into the afternoon.

After the convenience break, he tried to get me to agree to the fact that I had written the book without the dead choirboy's mother's permission, as written in that story in *The Australian* I'd tried to have amended.

'[The mother] was confused by the questions,' I began. 'The questions were ambiguous –'

He interrupted me.

'If Your Honour pleases –' I began.

'Your Honour,' he snapped back.

'This is an important point to me, because it is absolutely untrue,' I said.

He then went into a long to and fro about an email which I had never read between publishing staff about 'permissions'. He took it to be about permissions for people telling their stories in the book. But the email had simply related to copyright permissions to reproduce other artists'/authors'/songwriters' work.

I tried to explain that to him, but he cut me off again, repeatedly, as I tried to answer.

'All right, okay, okay ...' he said waving away what I had to say. 'Let's get to the end?'

'Yes,' I replied, wanting that badly.

'And the end is this. You say she never asked you not to publish it?'

'Absolutely, emphatically, she never did,' I replied.

At the end of the evidence, he tried to imply that I knew that Pell would be charged in June and had brought forward the book's publication because of that. I honestly had no idea when Pell might be charged. I knew they had been investigating for a long time and the police commissioner had repeatedly said a decision was 'imminent', but I knew nothing about June. No one gave me that information.

He alleged that I knew in advance that charges were going to be laid against George Pell in June 2017 and rushed the publication of my book to beat them. 'That's your opinion, Mr Richter, and I disagree with it emphatically,' I replied.

'I'm putting it to you and you can disagree.'

'I just did.'

'This was your stab at getting an award, a great investigative work, yes?'

'No.'

No journalist goes into this sort of work seeking awards. You do it because you are passionately committed to a story, because you can't stop, because it's in your bones. You work until 2 am every night and get up the next day and start again. You chip, chip, chip away. When, exhausted, and, in my case, unwell, you accept a journalism award for it, you are just grateful that the ring of fire you have walked through has given voice to the powerless.

At the end of the day, Richter's questions just kind of petered out. I remember some communication with Ruth Shann – he looked as if he was going to ask another question, and she seemed to motion to advise him against it.

The close of his cross-examination, supposed to destroy me, reminded me of a flaccid balloon, slowly deflating. He seemed harried. There was some conversation with the bench about documents to be tendered and that was that.

I couldn't believe it was finally over.

Prosecutor Mark Gibson got up and got some admin stuff out of the way.

And then he allowed me to explain what had happened with the choirboy's mother – how I had obtained her permission, our exchange of text messages and how, despite Mr Richter's accusation that the book had been done without her permission, she and I had exchanged text messages, six weeks after its publication, when Pell was charged:

I wrote: 'I have been thinking of you all day.'

She replied: 'Thank you. You look good on TV.'

'Thanks. I feel like a mess.'

'Nah.'

The Australian had at least two journalists in court that day – perhaps even three. They did not report the new information, nor correct the record. Instead, the original story remains on the paper's website till this day – and the story from the following day made no mention of my clarification.

A later piece of rather purple feature writing said, 'Louise Milligan brought a touch of Hollywood glamour to the committal proceedings, spending a whole day headbutting Richter.'

Hollywood glamour? Seriously? This was a case about allegations of raping children.

'Thank you for coming to court and giving evidence,' Wallington told me at the end.

'Thank you kindly,' I said.

I walked out and had another convenience break.

When I came back, the police detective Chris Reed gave me more encouraging nods and told me I had done really well.

Mark Gibson SC and solicitor Ailsa McVean led me into a room. They told me they were sorry if it was 'lonely up there' and that Gibson didn't intervene more. But that was because he didn't need to. That I had done a great job.

I was completely dazed. But I did feel that Gibson could have done more. I did feel lonely. To be frank, I don't think I have ever felt more alone in my life.

JUST LISTEN TO THE QUESTION, WOULD YOU?

My frustration, my loneliness, my exhaustion did not hold a candle to those who have to go before the courts and tell their story of a terrible childhood trauma.

You could forgive some of them for finding it too hard.

Having been through the experience, and having met other abuse complainants, including one who had since died, the following piece of television was excruciating to watch:

> 'Who's going to believe a little boy from a home, against that conglomerate, mate? You know? Against that bloody Goliath?'

'Goliath' was the third episode of *Revelation*, the brilliant ABC TV series by my former *Four Corners* colleague Sarah Ferguson with producer Nial Fulton. The speaker was Bernie, a Pell complainant who, at the time when the episode was aired in 2020, had never spoken publicly before.

I had long known of Bernie's existence, but had never met him. Bernie started out life at Melbourne's Royal Women's Hospital, where he was abandoned straight after birth by his mother, and he then went to an orphanage at six months old.

He was sent to the Sisters of Nazareth at Ballarat. The austere orphanage would be all he knew of childhood.

Bernie was to be a key complainant witness in the case against Pell. Twenty-two days before I gave evidence, Bernie arrived in Melbourne for his appointed session with Robert Richter in the committal of *DPP v Pell*.

'On March the sixth, 2018,' Sarah Ferguson reported, 'Bernie and his partner arrived in Melbourne for the committal.'

'I started the evening with a full packet of forty cigarettes,' Bernie told Ferguson. 'By the morning, I had two left. And I did not sleep. One wink. Hating the world, hating him, hating myself. Angry. Depressed. Sad. You name it, my whole … all of my emotions just controlled my whole being.'

'Was it fear?' Ferguson asked him. 'What was it?'

'Fear,' Bernie replied. 'Everything. I was scared of going to court.

'I was ashamed, I was embarrassed. I was just hurt, angry.

'And in times of need like that, you turn to your mother, and I didn't have a mother to turn to. "Where's my mum? I want my mum. I don't have a mum. You don't have a mother, Bernard."'

He continued. '"Get out of it, mate, get out of it." And I wanted to die. I'll be honest, I don't care. I wanted to die.'

'At 6 am,' Ferguson reported, 'Bernie rang Chris Reed and told the detective he was suicidal.'

Chris Reed and another police officer immediately arrived to speak to Bernie.

'And court is due to start in a few hours,' Bernie told Ferguson. 'And I'm due to get grilled, like I'm the fuckin' villain. I'm not the villain, mate.'

I'm not the villain. It could almost be another title of this book. It conveys how complainants and witnesses are treated like they are the villains, in order to defend the accused. At the time of course, Pell had been found guilty of other crimes against another complainant, but several days after 'Goliath' aired, the High Court acquitted him.

'You know, and that's why victims don't come forward. They don't, 'cause they don't want to go through the trauma again.'

Bernie pulled out of the committal proceeding and withdrew as a complainant. Bernie told Ferguson he regretted his decision 'immensely', but he 'wasn't ready'.

I wonder how you can *ever* be ready for an experience like this.

Only with the utmost mental discipline. I remember it myself, not being able to allow my mind to drift for a second, lest I be carried along by a tide of questioning and find myself somewhere I didn't want to and should not be. And again, I'm not a victim.

I've never met Bernie and I think he probably just needs to try to heal himself – he doesn't need another journalist raking over his wounds. But he helped me crystallise in my mind why I was writing this book.

It was always going to be Richter's job to do everything he could to discredit the complainant: he was acting in the defence of his client. Rightly or wrongly, that is what our legal system is set up to require defence lawyers to do. This also means family members being dragged into the process because of a horrible new reality about which they were only beginning to come to terms: the possibility that their child or sibling had been abused as a child.

* * *

One man, whom I shall call Charles, is a father who has been through that trial experience. Charles is in his eighties and is a retired public servant who doesn't smoke or drink. He's a nice man and he likes a chat. In the 1970s, Charles and his much-loved wife lived in the far north-west of country Victoria with a large brood of children they affectionately referred to as their 'seven little Australians'. Seven kids with shiny seventies bowl-cut hair, button noses and sunkissed shoulders. The family were good Catholics who attended mass each Sunday and were very much involved in parish life. Charles would help count the money donated by parishioners to the collection plate. The seven little Australians are all grown up now and, in 2015, one of them, a former altar boy the court called 'Timothy', made accusations about George Pell concerning a day of waterskiing that Charles had organised at Lake Boga. Lake Boga is a vast circle of water in the middle of Victoria's dusty Mallee region. A place where locals could get respite from the heat, as they fished Murray cod and pelicans glided overhead. Children could splash about and dads like Charles could launch their speedboats for a spot of waterskiing. One hot summer day in the middle of the seventies, Charles and his family did just that. They invited the assistant priest at the local parish, whose name Charles had long since forgotten. The assistant priest had invited his mate George Pell, who was visiting from Ballarat. Charles had given Pell a tow on his boat. That day, Timothy alleged to Victoria Police, Pell abused him at Lake Boga.

I don't wish to explore what Timothy alleges happened to him and ultimately the Crown never pursued his case to trial. Cardinal Pell vehemently denied the accusations. He remains a free man who strongly asserts he is innocent of any crime, anywhere. What interests me here is what Charles experienced in the courtroom, a person who wasn't making any allegations about anyone. Charles was in his eighties when, in March 2018, he gave sworn evidence in Pell's committal proceeding. Since charges had been laid, Charles had not been permitted to speak to his son about the allegations. His knowledge of them was scant. All he knew was that he loved his boy, and he believed him. To Charles' mind, there was absolutely no reason his son would come forward and endure the process that Timothy did, and to which Charles was also subjected, if it wasn't true. 'As if it was on your bucket list to be cross-examined by Robert Richter,' Charles muses, with a dark laugh. 'The prosecution threw me to the wolves a little bit,' he says on the phone to me from his home in country Victoria. 'We drove all the way up there from home and I was supposed to have some preparation time – I think we had about three minutes. The prosecutor was a bit flustered,' he says. 'I said that I would have liked to have added more to my statement, in hindsight. He said I couldn't bring anything new into the hearing. I casually said I would like to have said this and it threw [the prosecutor] completely.'

Charles now feels great regret about that. He feels his police statement was inadequate, and the defence was able to make much of that. He was in a bind. Charles gave evidence that he had discovered what Timothy had alleged just a week before the police came to take Charles' statement. He said he had been informed of this by another son, who told him Timothy did not want to distress his parents, as his mother had been recently put into a nursing home because she had Alzheimer's. 'I think [Timothy] thought we had enough on our plates,' Charles told the Melbourne Magistrates' Court in his evidence. 'I am happy that I know, and I made [Timothy] aware that I totally supported him,' he said. When he gave his statement to Victoria Police in 2015, Charles was only asked about what happened on the day of the incident, which he had not been aware of. He was not directly asked about whether he knew that his son had made allegations about George Pell. So that was not addressed in his statement. Richter, understandably, made much of this.

'You don't mention that anyone had said to you ever that Father Pell had somehow abused your son, [Timothy], at Lake Boga. You don't say that?' Richter asked Charles.

'I said it to you then –' Charles tried to answer.

'I know you said it to me –'

'– that there was abuse.'

'You said it to me, but that's an invention of yours since July 2015 when you made your statement. You've just –'

It was the style that Richter employed that jumps off the transcript page.

At this point the magistrate intervened. 'Sorry,' Ms Wallington said, 'I don't think he's going to understand what you assert.'

Mr Richter pressed on, interrogating a father who had come to court to support his son. And branding him a liar.

'Yes. You have just made that up after you made your statement, right? At some point after you made your statement between July 2015 and today, you made that up, didn't you?'

Charles was furious. 'That's ... that's ... that is an insult. No,' he replied.

'Yes,' Richter countered. 'It may be an insult, but it's true, is it not?'

'Absolutely not,' Charles replied.

Charles tells me he can't believe now that Richter spoke to him in this way.

'It's grossly insulting inferring that we made it up,' he says.

After it went on for a while, Magistrate Wallington intervened. 'I am sorry,' she began, 'I'm just a little troubled by the line of questioning, because [Charles] speaks of priests in the plural in the statement.'

And he had. 'I am shocked and disgusted that our son was exposed to this abuse,' Charles had told the detectives who took his statement. 'We trusted the priests at the church with the care of our son and all of the altar boys. We were proud to see [Timothy] as an altar boy. The offending priests have abused this trust and have scarred [Timothy] for life.'

But in the court, Mr Richter challenged the magistrate's attempt to intervene to point out that some of the words in Charles' statement could support his evidence in court and it wasn't 'a big stretch' to reach that conclusion.

'Oh, your Honour, it's a huge stretch ...' Richter began.

'Now if that's Your Honour's understanding of "not a great stretch", then I would say that Your Honour has the wrong understanding of what's alleged and how it happened and how it developed.'

After some to and fro, the magistrate said she wasn't going to 'squabble' with Mr Richter.

Richter moved on to another person at Lake Boga that day, whose name had disappeared to the recesses of Charles' mind.

'What was his description?' Richter asked.

'Slightly built – it's in my statement,' Charles replied.

'Yes ...?'

'Something else – something possibly about light complexion.'

'Tell me this,' Richter began.

Charles cut in. 'Their name can be found. You can locate the name of that gentleman.'

In cross-examination, the point is about throwing interference.

'Were you asked to re-read your statement before giving evidence?' Richter asked.

'Yes,' Charles replied. 'And I did not, I did not name the assistant priest in my statement.'

'No, just listen to the question, would you?' Richter cut in.

Charles remembered that Richter was very hostile and frustrated.'

In no other forum would it be acceptable to speak to someone like this. But in our courts it happens all the time.

Richter continued to press Charles on whether he had read the statement recently and also whether there was anything he wanted to add to it prior to coming to court.

'There was nothing you wanted to add, including nothing you wanted to add about being told by [your other son] a week before July that there was an allegation ...?'

'No ...' was all Charles could manage. He was snookered. He'd been told by the Crown not to mention what he wanted to add to the statement.

Charles was frustrated. 'I couldn't elaborate more than what was in the jolly statement,' he says.

'It was the police who told you about an allegation at Lake Boga when they came to speak to you?'

'[My other son] would have told me.'

Witnesses have a habit of saying 'would have' when they mean 'did'. Again, this left it wide open for Richter.

'No. No. No! No "would have". Do you recall him telling you?'

'Yes. Yes.' And then the frustrating bit. 'Did you tell the police that [your other son] had told you about an allegation against Father Pell?'

'They did not ask.'

'They didn't ask. But what, you didn't feel that you should tell them?'

'No, no. I assumed they knew.'

This is the sort of thing that happens with witnesses all the time. Witnesses often only answer what police ask of them. They don't realise that at times it's appropriate to volunteer information, that this is their one chance, that it's going to cost them in court. They trust that the police and the Crown know what they are doing.

'Over the years, you have not been very close to [Timothy] have you?'

The Crown prosecutor objected, on the grounds of relevance. The magistrate went further.

'Yes, I don't think that's an appropriate question, Mr Richter,' Ms Wallington said.

'If Your Honour pleases,' Richter demurred. He tried to change the subject to ask about whether Timothy had suffered flashbacks. But Charles was still livid.

'I really don't understand the question. And that was absolutely insulting. We were a very close family. The whole nine of us. I-I really think that's totally disrespectful to say that to a, to a father.'

Charles now dearly wishes he'd said more. 'I wish I said, "Mr Richter, I have just taken an oath on the bible and I am a Christian. That's an insult." He insulted my family and he insulted me.'

'Why would I lie? I really wish I'd said that,' Charles muses as we chat on the phone. 'I wasn't quite sure why Richter did this to me,' he says. 'He was somehow trying to paint a picture of an unreliable family.

'My wife, if she'd been alive, she'd have been absolutely furious. She would have stood up and interjected. Immediately.'

His poor wife had long since gone to her grave, though. And Richter continued.

'Yes, all right. Let's put it this way. You were never aware that [Timothy] had nightmares?'

'I really don't understand that question. I would say all our children had nightmares.'

Richter tried to put it to Charles that he was not aware that Timothy had had nightmares.

'[He] never displayed any signs of distress or anything like that?'

'No,' Charles replied. 'That's not correct.'

'Not correct … Tell me?'

Charles tells me, 'He was basically attacking me, my character, insinuating that I wasn't telling the truth and endeavouring to unsettle me.'

'It's in my statement where he did show signs of distress, but I didn't say nightmares,' Charles, frustrated, replied in court.

'What sort of signs of distress did he show?' Richter asked. 'From the start … There were many,' Charles replied.

'What sort of signs of distress?'

'From the start – in particular, in secondary school. He was a very unsettled lad. Which puzzled – and I think it's in my statement – his parents – myself and my wife.'

A photograph from the 1970s shows a young blond Timothy perched on the side of a family photo in a cream jumper with beige and brown trim, an oversized seventies shirt collar and brown cords. Timothy's smile seems rehearsed and pensive.

Timothy's father and sister tell me they could never work out why. When he came forward with allegations, it all made sense to them.

Richter gave Charles no more opportunity to discuss what he saw had happened to his son – at the time with no understanding of what the boy was going through.

But he did tell police.

'He was later bullied at secondary school and left as soon as he could. It became usual for [Timothy] to ask [my wife] or me if he was a good boy. This question puzzled us, as he would ask it out of the blue. We would always tell him he was a good boy.'

I read that line several times and it always distresses me to think of this little boy, asking for approval. Was he a good boy? Yes, he was a good boy.

'Even as an adult,' Charles continued, '[Timothy] would not even attend the wedding of his sister, [Michelle] and other siblings. [Timothy] has now told me that he was too ashamed to set foot in a church and was afraid he would break down.

With this information rattling around in the back of his mind, Charles became weary during the cross-examination.

As Richter went over similar ground with Charles again, Wallington eventually cut him off.

'All right, that's been asked and answered.'

Richter gave up. Charles is still furious about it though.

He says he felt like he was being unnecessarily attacked by Australia's leading defence lawyer when he was just telling the truth. 'It was disrespect, total disrespect for the witness, in the way you were cross-examined.

'You left as though you were like a single soldier, fighting a company of soldiers. A single plane, in the Battle of Britain, fighting fifty planes.

'You felt that you were dealing with an immense authoritarian body, on your own.

'You were exposed, totally exposed.'

As Charles wrapped up his evidence, he says the witness support person turned to him and spoke.

'The lady in the video room said, "You did well, you handled yourself well,"' he says.

Charles had stood up to his interlocutor, but he was not a young man. He had lived a solid, law-abiding, god-fearing life. He had a happy family. And the discovery that his son was making these allegations, which he believed, had rocked him to his foundations. So it was distressing to find himself, now, being accused of lying.

Charles goes to mass every week. He takes the notion of swearing on the bible very seriously.

'If I could talk to Robert Richter now, I would say to him, "Why did you try and belittle me and belittle my family as a whole by inferring we were not telling the truth?"' he tells me.

'I can think of nothing worse than being accused of being a liar.

'It's the first time I've been verbally assaulted like this. [My wife would] be just horrified by this,' he says.

'I'm not an aggressive person or a person that wants revenge or confrontation. I suppose up to a point he was doing his job. But what a rotten job to do it to people. By upsetting the person that he's cross-examining. Who would want to be in a job where they belittle people?

Charles came out of the court that day and he says his hands were 'shaking'.

'And the kids said, "Look at your hands, Dad,"' he remembers. He drove home that day with Timothy and his other son. 'That night, I was shaking all night,' he says. 'We tried to relax, but we couldn't because the boys kept seeing things on their mobiles.' Across the world, there were the stories of the parent of a complainant who had a hostile confrontation with Pell's lawyer. 'I thought, My glory,' says Charles. 'What are we involved in now?'

The support, or follow-up, that he says he was promised from the Office of Public Prosecutions, or the police, amounted to nothing.

'I think they were all stressed,' he said of the prosecution team. 'I never had any follow-up. I never heard from them again.'

Charles rings me up every now and then, sometimes just to give me an update on Timothy. He loves his son and he just wants the best for him. He's proud of him and the rest of his seven little Australians. He's a dear man – always an absolute gentleman. And I think he, like so many others, deserved better from our justice system.

* * *

Belinda Wallington would later find there was no evidence of collusion from complainants flowing from my reporting. She found only a hypothetical possibility that I had contaminated the evidence.

At the start of the proceeding, she had played to the Crown and the defence the audio of the Jon Faine *Conversation Hour* piece with me, to ascertain that they were comfortable that it presented no conflict. Both agreed that there was not a problem.

But the day after my evidence, when Richter was cross-examining a senior police officer who had worked on the investigating taskforce, he got into another disagreement with her about evidence.

'Don't shout at me, Mr Richter,' Wallington told him.

Richter responded by calling on Wallington to disqualify herself from the case on the grounds that she had an apprehended bias.

Wallington refused the application.

Nine days later, but before she was to make her ultimate decision to commit Pell to trial (and well before the DPP dropped all charges), an article appeared in the *Herald Sun* newspaper, with the photograph of Wallington and me from Jon Faine's *Conversation Hour*. It quoted an unnamed source describing it as 'gobsmacking'.

'Louise Milligan, the one with the Mona Lisa smile, is key prosecution witness in the case of the cardinal,' it declared.

Mona Lisa smile? Seriously? And I was not a key prosecution witness at all. I was witness of first complaint for just one of these men, and my evidence had been turned into an unnecessary spectacle in what seemed like a headline-grabbing exercise.

But the article, and its source, was far more damning of Wallington, who had been fair and firm during the proceeding, who had not been remotely improper during the *Conversation Hour* and who, frankly, did not deserve it.

I had tried to point all of this out to the journalist in question, who knew better, but he didn't want to hear it. His view was that the moment that I walked into that studio, Belinda Wallington should have just walked out. Even though at that time no charges had been laid and she had not been appointed.

But also, if even the defence counsel who was representing Pell at the time had indicated no problem with it when played the audio, surely that was all that mattered? Of course, by the time that this article appeared, relations between the defence and Wallington had soured.

Wallington was further defamed, along with myself and a McCarthyist list of high-profile women, in an insane conspiracy theory dressed up as an article in the online journal *Quadrant*, a far-right publication.

The piece was headlined 'George Pell and the SJW [social justice warrior] Fembots'.

Fembots. Where do you even go with that? The Fembots were, of course, the pneumatic blonde robots, clad in scanty silver bikinis, in the Austin Powers 1990s comedy film. They had guns concealed in the nipple section of their bikini tops.

The almost comically misogynistic article would also target the 'childless' Chief Justice Anne Ferguson (never making any point about what her parental status had to do with any of this – just leaving it hanging there like it said everything you needed to know), who was one of the Court of Appeal majority judges who would later uphold the jury's guilty verdict in the Pell trial.

The piece also had a crack at, among others, former Prime Minister Julia Gillard, for establishing the child abuse Royal Commission; Vivian Waller, the lawyer who advised former choirboy 'Witness J'; and my publisher, Louise Adler, so-called 'darling of the luvvies'.

The whole thing was completely mad, but also deeply offensive to the serious record of Wallington and Ferguson in particular.

This is just a very small taste of some of the stops that are pulled out on behalf of a white male with the right friends. The fatwa from Anglo-Saxon older male commentators on anyone who came up against Pell would drag on for a good five years.

Wallington stayed the course. She carried on with her job and committed Pell to trial. Even though the DPP would later drop the charges, for him, for me, for the complainants, the process was far from over.

THE SECRET HEARING

After your day in court is done, you walk mechanically across the road and perch on a bar stool. Your husband buys you a glass of champagne. You stare at the tiny golden bubbles, fizzing to the top. You're wired and mightily relieved. You stood your ground. You feel like you have survived. His arguments did not win the day.

But the next morning, you wake to feel like a Mack Truck has powered through the walls of the room and flattened you. Every single bone in your body aches in the way it does when you have done a particularly gruelling workout for the first time in months. You lie, unable to get out of bed. Your mouth feels glued shut. Your body hums with a strange, invisible trauma. Your children walk into the room, but, seeing you, close the door behind them and scurry back downstairs.

It's not a case of intellectually processing what has just happened. Your mind is too scrambled for that. You are not thinking 'woe is me', or 'that was terrible'. It just is what it is. It takes days to snap out of it.

Even years later, you walk past the building where he has his chambers, and you flinch and pick up your pace. You fear running into him in the street. You are given your court transcript, but you can't bear to look at it.

Disclosing this is uncomfortable – it admits vulnerability. It's genuinely annoying to admit that this person had this effect. But being treated with such unnecessary derision has a surprising impact on a person that we don't often hear much about in public discourse. It's instructive to be honest about what it does. It's not by any means a plea for sympathy, nor to in any way say that what was endured touched the sides of the profound trauma of people who have been raped or abused and then had to go through this too.

Being able to show what this is like, from a deeply personal perspective, gives an insight into the impact of a style of cross-examination that, for some criminal defence barristers, in a sex trial, is all in a day's work. It gave me an overwhelming surge of empathy for the people – not just Pell accusers, but all of the people I'd come to know – whose stories I had been covering for the past few years.

Because, the journalist privilege was, for me, not just something set out in a section of the *Evidence Act* to protect confidential sources, but everything that came with who I was – journalistic training, legal education, access to the best advice, understanding of the issues, socio-economic advantages. These combined privileges were the sorts of things only a tiny handful of the people who have endured the horrible traumas in the first place might hope to have.

Often, the reason victims had none of these advantages in life was directly attributable to the trauma they had suffered and the course it had set them upon.

I thought of how one Ballarat complainant always called but never replied to my text messages and how it was only much later down the track that I discovered the reason was that he had poor literacy. And how Rob Walsh, the St Alipius victim whose brothers and cousin had died, had only learned to properly read and write when he was twenty-five. 'That's okay,' he told me, not wanting sympathy, 'I get by.'

Walsh, who came to court the day of my evidence, told me afterwards that facing a barrister as a witness was the 'hardest thing I have ever done'.

'Physically, and emotionally exhausting,' Walsh told me.

These people are at a strategic, educational and financial disadvantage. The power difference between them and the well-resourced defendant could not be more profound. Not to mention the power difference between them and the barrister cross-examining them.

We rarely get to know what happens to them now, because, in order to protect them, the law in Victoria says they should give their evidence *in camera* – that is, the public gallery must be emptied of journalists or members of the public.

So there they are, in the box, far more alone than I was, with no lawyer and no one independent outside the judicial officer and the Crown watching over what defence counsel is doing.

It's horrible to imagine what happens to such complainants.

They have no Hugh Bennett to spring to his feet in the public gallery, nor Jack Rush QC or Peter Morrissey SC to advise them.

In the Pell case, some of the complainants elected to have, in their remote witness room, a support dog – in this case, a black Labrador named Coop.

The child abuse Royal Commission made recommendations that these dogs provided real comfort to some witnesses and, since that time, jurisdictions including Victoria have adopted the program.

For some complainants, Coop really eased their anxiety about giving evidence.

As sweet as Coop was when he laid his head on their lap and looked up at them with large hazel puppy eyes, he could scarcely replace a Queen's Counsel giving sage advice about how to give their best evidence.

As Michelle Epstein, a Sydney psychologist whose work is almost exclusively with survivors of childhood sexual abuse, notes, so often these people are, with best intentions, infantilised by the system.

'It is just another example of where someone has tried to do something that they believe is really helpful, but they don't realise how incredibly offensive it could be to some people to have a dog offered to them [when they don't have a lawyer],' Epstein says.

The accused is free to sit in court through the entire proceedings, to take notes and provide feedback to counsel. If they are well-resourced, they'll engage a renowned QC whose price tag is many thousands of dollars a day, a junior barrister and a team of solicitors.

On the other side of that ledger is the complainant, described as a 'witness' even though this proceeding wouldn't exist without them; in a remote witness facility, with a box of tissues, a support person who has no legal qualifications, and, well, a dog.

Unbelievably, Richter in the case in which I was a witness, even questioned the need for the complainants to have this dog.

'I always thought dogs were there for children and very old people,' Richter told Wallington in a way that was reported by media at the time to be 'derisively'.

It brought to mind the teddy bear Georgie Burg told me about in Canberra that the children weren't allowed to bring into the witness box, lest it reminded the jury of the fact that they were little kids.

'They're also for *vulnerable* people,' Wallington replied to Richter's jibe about the dog.

Belinda Wallington allowed the dog. Coop did his level best.

So many lawyers have said, in my research for this book, that it is up to the judge to ensure that the barrister doesn't resort to improper questioning. But the child abuse Royal Commission found that, often, judicial officers are pushed to the limit. And, when they do admonish a barrister, they find themselves the subject of an appeal point.

Former director of the Tasmania Law Reform Institute, Terese Henning, gave a submission to the Royal Commission that was about children and witnesses with cognitive impairments, and how they are questioned at trial. It could equally apply to any complainants in sexual cases, who are, I would argue, inherently almost always vulnerable.

'The nub of the problem appears to be that these groups of people are generally questioned inappropriately,' Henning wrote. 'Questioning can be abusive, hostile, repetitive and overly lengthy.'

She said that such questioning intimidated witnesses 'into silence, contradictions, or general emotional and cognitive disorganisation'.

Henning said there was evidence to show how exploiting witnesses' limitations and vulnerabilities could 'hamper their ability to recall and recount events' and that the Australian Law Reform Commission had characterised these sorts of practices as 'clear examples of legal abuse'.

Again, she was talking about children and people with additional needs. But I can see so clearly how all of these comments could easily apply to a vulnerable adult complainant.

'Ultimately, even though judges understand these problems and are empowered to intervene to impose standards of questioning on counsel that eliminate these problems, for various reasons they may not do so,' Henning said. 'Primarily, they appear to fear rendering the trial unfair for the accused.'

Henning also pointed out that the law reforms hadn't displaced judges' traditional reluctance to intervene in cross-examination because the defence could use it to garner sympathy from the jury by casting the judge as a 'partial advocate'.

'More prosaically and somewhat regrettably, intervention has been frowned upon for interfering with the flow of questioning ...

'It has also been observed (and this represents one of the biggest and most intransigent obstacles to intervention by both judges and counsel), the conventions of cross-examination are so entrenched and intrinsic to the adversarial trial and to conceptions of what fairness to defendants demands, that they actually prevent trial judges and counsel from recognising or rejecting questioning that is unfair ...'

There is a sense, therefore, that judges or magistrates can be 'worn down' by persistent or aggressive defence counsel.

In another submission by University of Sydney Law School Professor Judy Cashmore, in conjunction with the advocacy group Survivors and Mates Support Network, the authors noted a key theme in feedback from complainants and other witnesses about their experience was that they were 'harassed and intimidated' by the defence and wanted more protection from the Crown and from judicial intervention from 'oppressive and humiliating questioning'.

The authors cite one adult complainant of a child sexual offence who said he felt 'bullied' during his evidence and he elected to stay in a psychiatric hospital during the process 'as a safety strategy'.

'I continue to experience nightmares and flashbacks about cross-examination,' the survivor said.

Another survivor told them, '... we secured a conviction, but it wrecked my life'.

Judy Cashmore cited difficulties for the complainants during cross-examination, including capacity to manage anxiety and embarrassment, lack of knowledge about the legal system and 'legal jargon', power imbalance and susceptibility to leading and complex questions.

I thought about how, at some point during the anus/sphincter/
rectum business, I had actually gone along with one of Richter's
questions because in the split-second heat of the moment, I was
too embarrassed to admit that I didn't really understand the
anatomical definitions.

My mind was swirling with his loud voice and the disturbing
mental pictures he repeatedly drew. I thought about how that sort
of questioning could completely bamboozle someone who was
reliving the worst moments of their life, especially if they had other
difficulties like poor literacy or substance abuse arising from their
trauma, and how, potentially, it could throw the whole thing.

And that's where we come to that oft-repeated phrase from
victims – that the cross-examination was as bad, if not worse, than
the original abuse.

Psychologist Michelle Epstein says her patients who go through
the court process generally say they would recommend others not
to do it.

'And that's everyone from high-powered CEOs to those who are
unemployed and unable to work,' Epstein says. 'Regardless of who
they are, the vast majority of patients say to me, "If I knew then
what I know now, I would not do it. I wouldn't go through the
legal process."

'Now that is a shocking indictment on our legal system.'

Epstein says that going to the police is often not the starting
point for her clients and that she works 'with people for years or
decades to get them to the point where they *can* go to police'.

And then they go through the court process.

'You have two layers – the original abuse, then the subsequent
years of secrecy/not being believed and then the added layer of the
court case,' Epstein says. 'Clinically, it's such a complicated picture
and such an interwoven trauma.

'What they go through is utterly, utterly disgraceful.

'So many people are completely crippled by the court case.'

She says many people she sees are suicidal after the trial. 'And we
have to spend a lot of time working with them to not be suicidal.'

Epstein says the reason the court case can often be worse than
the original sexual abuse as a child is that because now, they
are being brought to a place where some people infantilise and

disbelieve them – all the worst things for a person whose sense of trust has been utterly betrayed at a fundamental developmental age. They feel like a child again because they are being treated as one. A naughty child.

'Not only is it a traumatic experience, but it parallels the experience of being sexually abused,' she explains. 'It's a retraumatisation, in so many ways, and on so many levels – that it really often causes people to disintegrate.'

So it is, she says, 'psychologically devastating'.

Georgie Burg, the survivor of Anglican paedophile John Aitchison, says she had never in her life been spoken to in the way that the defence counsel in her case spoke to her and 'you don't ever forget it'. And she says one of the most problematic parts of being scolded by barristers in court is that, for many victims, that's what their perpetrator did to them when they *were* a child.

'And I think they,' Georgie says, referring to defence counsel, 'know that. I think for all they argue that they are defending someone, and that it's part of their job and all of that kind of thing, people know how to make someone feel small.

'If you are part of an abusive system, you know how to strip away someone's dignity and reduce them to almost someone that you're looking at like they're an animal,' she says. 'Like ... their whole life, everything about them, deserves to be viewed with contempt.

'... Ordinary people don't talk to other people like that.'

When she thinks of the sneering tone and the dismissive approach employed by some defence counsel, Georgie says 'the best word I can think of is inhumanity'.

'They are not looking at it from a human perspective – they are looking at it from an academic, removed, "this series of facts" [perspective].

'And I can understand, in theory anyway, that it's the only way they can do, or they believe it's the only way they can do the job that they're being paid to do,' Georgie says. 'But I think that they can do better.'

So do I.

Judge Meryl Sexton, a currently-sitting judge of the Victorian County Court who headed up its sex offences list for thirteen years until 2018, tells me in an interview for this book that she too has often heard it said that cross-examination was worse than the abuse.

'I know that some of my colleagues, when that first started being said with the Law Reform Commission report back in 2004, they found that very hard to believe,' she says.

'They understood how bad the abuse was, and they just thought that the court process could not be put into the same category.

'I think that view has changed.

'There may still be some that have some scepticism about it, but we know that that's the way some victims felt and can still sometimes feel.'

It's one of those things that doesn't make sense and seems somehow melodramatic when first expressed. How on earth could a barrister asking questions in court compare to, for instance, a Christian Brother raping a young boy? How is that even vaguely comparable?

Well, if the boy for years and years either held on to his story because he was too afraid to come forward, or was bullied into silence by a religious community, or dismissed by his parents, when he finally comes to court, he is plunged into the moment of his most profound childhood trauma.

In that place, he is treated by defence counsel with disrespect, which reminds him of the disrespect his perpetrator gave him. His perpetrator is sitting right behind the defence counsel watching how he responds to the descriptions of what the perpetrator did to him.

Like, potentially, others in his community, he is not believed. And inside of him, he just feels like that little kid again. Who no one would believe. And who kept his trap shut for decades as a method of self-protection. No one could doubt him if he never told them what happened.

Judge Sexton takes her responsibilities to protect the complainant witnesses who come before her court very seriously. She does concede that 'I'm sure there have been times when I would have not managed something as well as I would like to.'

'And I'd like to think that it doesn't get to the point of me thinking that the witness has been badly served by the system,' Judge Sexton says. 'But generally speaking, if a witness sees the judge calling on the barrister to do their job in a different way, be clearer, not speak in that tone, then I think [the witness realises] they are being supported. And that may help with the experience,' she says. 'But on the other hand, the very fact that we've got voices being raised – the level just goes up, and that's anxiety-provoking for me, so it must be for the witness as well.'

Well, yes, from personal experience, I can attest that it is.

'But I'd like to think that generally, doesn't matter who they are, barristers don't get away with that worst possible stuff in my court – I might be wrong!'

I wonder if that's the same in every court. I tell her that's not a criticism of the judges trying to manage it – actually, it's a criticism of people who think they can behave that way in the first place: the defence counsel. Why do these people think that that's an appropriate way to speak to someone?

'I don't know the answer to that,' Judge Sexton tells me.

'It seems to me that it is a very old-fashioned view about dealing with witnesses – any witness – that way,' she says.

'I think that there is a huge responsibility on judicial officers to maintain a proper approach. But some judicial officers would see it as not their role.

'And whenever I get the opportunity, and I present a lot of judicial education, I repeatedly raise the fact that we have the legislative responsibility under the *Evidence Act* to disallow improper questions.

'... This law now applies to *all* witnesses, it is no longer restricted to vulnerable witnesses,' she says of the ban on questions using an offensive, intimidating, repetitive or confusing tone.

'That is a legislative signpost that cultural change is required to rid court cases of such questioning where barristers still seek to employ that "style".'

She does, however, admit that there is 'still work to be done'.

'It is, I know, a problem for some judicial officers that they don't want to go over the line in intervention.

'Well, no one wants to go over the line – but I think, sometimes the line, they don't understand, can go further than they think it does.

'Again, it's a matter of saying, "Where is our authority coming from?"'

She also presents education on vulnerable witnesses for
barristers and she cautions that the principles you can apply to
vulnerable witnesses apply to any witnesses.

'It is, in fact, good practice to be polite, clear and ask simple
questions of any witness,' she says. 'And if you do that, the judges
are going to thank you, the juries are going to understand what
you are getting at and, certainly, the witnesses will thank you.'

Judge Sexton thinks that the message is spreading upwards,
from new members of the legal profession – the young ones coming
through. She admits that there are, however, the recalcitrants.

'Some of the ones who have been around for a long time, we
will not change.'

And there's the rub. This is a profession disproportionately
dominated by older men who used to be able to question rape
victims about their sex lives. It's a profession where those older
men used to be able to treat children's evidence as inherently
unreliable and to require mandatory corroboration of a crime
so often committed in secret. Where there was no such thing as
rape in marriage, where the fact that a priest had been of 'good
character' in every other part of his life (note: because he was
grooming not just his victims, but also the community) meant that
he got a discount on his sentence. And where having a bible hurled
across the courtroom at you was a badge of honour.

In that sort of profession, by those sorts of men, witnesses are
still being subjected to the sort of curial bollocking I received. If the
barrister is persistent enough and not intimidated by the judicial
officer – in fact, prosecutors tell me the barristers often intimidate
the judges – then the witness still has a terrible time. As so many
stories in this book prove.

As I write these words tonight, a message flashes up on my
phone to say that a lovely lady, the mother of a friend, has died.
My eyes well up. The daughter will be absolutely bereft. The
daughter is a survivor of childhood sexual abuse. She was my first
introduction to the fundamental havoc that this sort of abuse can
wreak on a child's brain.

The suicide attempts began when she was a teenager. Poorly
executed, but distressing, nonetheless. The signs of a girl who was
crying out for help but didn't quite know how to do it. The poor

choices in men started up pretty early too. Her mother and father patiently tried to steer her through as she lurched from crisis to crisis. It affected her mental health, her relationships, her friendships. If her heart was worn on her sleeve, it was a pulsating, shiny, veiny muscle. Confronting all she met with its desperate need for love.

She was a naturally bright, bubbly and imaginative person who didn't have a bad bone in her body. I had lost count of the times I had thought, 'She's better now, she's doing so well.' And then she wasn't. She rarely spoke of her abuse, but it was always there.

The thought of her now, rudderless, without the unconditional love of her kind mum, is devastating. I don't want to paint her as an unreconstructed 'victim' – she has had many achievements in her career and more generally. She has made a courageous fist of life, getting up repeatedly after it knocks her down, but she is, undoubtedly, indelibly marked by what happened to her. This is sexual abuse. These are the people who come before our courts to tell their stories, in the hope that they are believed, and their perpetrator is called to account.

I suspect my friend would have been a disaster in the witness box with a bullying defence counsel. I can't even bring myself to think of it, it's so distressing. I believe passionately in going to police, but would I encourage her to come forward, were her perpetrator still alive? I'd think long and hard.

* * *

Kelsey Hegarty is a GP who is recognised by the World Health Organization as an expert in domestic and family violence.

'I've got one hundred and thirty publications. I've got large grant monies. I run a whole [National Health and Medical Research Centre] Centre of Research Excellence. I don't think that there's any doubt that I'm an academic expert,' Hegarty explains to me.

But, like me, none of that mattered when she found herself on the receiving end of a cross-examination. She had gone to court as an expert witness, expecting to give that evidence in a fairly straightforward way, as she had many times before.

But not so long ago, Hegarty found herself being cross-examined by a defence counsel who decided to completely rip her apart – her credibility, her expertise, her academic contributions. I have seen the transcript. He did not ask her anything substantive about what she had been called to give evidence about – but rather, decided he would shoot her reputation down in flames. Over and over again. It was like a blood sport.

Her evidence, like mine, went for the better part of a day.

'"I never want to appear again," is how I felt at the time,' Hegarty tells me. '"I never want to put myself through that again" ... I definitely said that to my friends, my work colleagues, to my family.'

'What does that say to you about the adversarial system?' I ask her.

'It makes me extremely worried,' Hegarty says, 'because it is this idea that people are just fighting and quibbling over split hairs.

'My experience of being in [that] court hasn't felt like it is trying to get at what happened.'

'It's not trying to get at the truth?' I ask her.

'No.'

'That's a fairly damning insight,' I say. 'What did you do when you walked out?'

'I think I burst into tears,' Hegarty says. 'Yeah, I think I did.'

'And what was the dominant emotion as you were crying?' I ask her.

'Anger,' she says. 'I was angry that people are allowed to do this to witnesses. I was probably swearing as well.'

She also felt that, from an older male barrister, it was gendered.

'It just felt that way,' Hegarty says. 'It felt belittling. And that's a common technique to reduce women, isn't it? And people mansplain. There was a lot of mansplaining going on ...

'I was angry that he couldn't be stopped. Yep – that he couldn't be stopped and that I just had to stand there and take it.'

Like me, it was strange for Hegarty to find herself in this situation, because, in her professional life, she had read the transcripts of women who were survivors and who had been put through the same pattern of 'trying to break the person down'.

'The questions they're being asked are ridiculous questions,' Hegarty says. 'They are really ridiculous questions about what happened first and second and third, ten years ago, three years ago. At a time [in the complainant's life] of fear-inducing, terrifying actions.'

The colour of the clothes, the position in the room, the scarifying anatomical details – the anus, the sphincter and the rectum.

'Yeah, it's just totally unrealistic,' Hegarty says, 'I don't know why anybody's allowed to ask those questions.'

She can't quite believe how traumatised survivors make it through the endless criminal justice process under these circumstances, or how they actually manage to withstand the slings and arrows they must endure.

'It's a miracle that they stick with it,' Hegarty says. 'And I take my hat off to them, because it's so hard.'

Based on her own experience, and through reading the transcripts of the women she has seen, and speaking to survivors, I ask Kelsey Hegarty what she thinks about the system as it currently operates.

'I wouldn't recommend anyone to do it,' Hegarty shoots back, firmly.

'Really?' I reply.

'I just don't know how anybody does it,' she says.

'Wow,' I return. 'Which means that perpetrators get away with it.'

'Yep,' she replies.

* * *

In March 2018, I was enormously relieved that my own evidence was over, but it was just the committal proceeding. There were still two trials planned. I often thought of the dread I would have felt if that had meant reliving a terrible trauma perpetrated upon me by a trusted adult when I was a little kid.

The fight over my confidential sources also made me concerned that the defence team was not finished with me. I was right.

Three months after my March evidence in the committal, we got word from the Crown that the first trial was to proceed in August.

This time Peter Morrissey would be acting for me. The Crown told Peter the so-called 'Swimmers Trial' (which ultimately never proceeded because charges were withdrawn after the Crown failed in an application to use tendency and coincidence to link the complainants' cases) would run first.

However, this also meant that the 'Cathedral Trial' – the one in which I had confidential sources – would be heard in public.

I felt comforted by that. As an investigative journalist, I didn't want to be having these arguments about journalistic rights behind closed doors.

The first trial would be bound by the law prohibiting *sub judice* contempt of court, meaning it could not be reported by media until there was an outcome in the second trial, or the second trial did not, for whatever reason, proceed.

The principle behind this is that jurors' minds should not be contaminated by the information they have received in the public domain that the accused was found guilty in another trial. To try to ensure a fair trial for Pell, the court had also imposed an extremely wide suppression order which prevented media from reporting on the trial – even, unusually, those working outside Victoria.

I felt that if I was to argue for my rights to protect my confidential sources that should be a transparent process, ventilated in public.

The stakes, as it happened, were high. If I was to protect the sources, the judge might disagree with my reasons for doing so, using his or her discretion under the *Evidence Act* to compel me to disclose the sources and the information they had provided because, the judge might consider, the public interest and the administration of justice outweighed my right to protect these people's anonymity.

If that happened, I was in a spot of trouble.

For journalists, protecting sources is sacrosanct.

Television current affairs stories and non-fiction books require many, many people to go on the record and that is always, emphatically, my preferred position. People had taken great risks to go public and speak to me on the record and for that, I will be eternally grateful to them.

Having said that, some people inform your journalism, but are not the subjects of your journalism. They help you to put the pieces together, but it's far from integral that they be named. And for all sorts of reasons – for example, they are whistleblowers for whom the stakes are just too high – they elect to stay off the record.

For complainants, the law grants them automatic anonymity to protect them, so it is understandable that they, too, might seek confidentiality.

Also, we were talking about a community of people scarred by betrayal. People for whom trust was paramount. It would be completely unconscionable to breach that trust.

The Media, Entertainment and Arts Alliance Journalist Code of Ethics states:

> Where a source seeks anonymity, do not agree without first considering the source's motives and any alternative attributable source. Where confidences are accepted, respect them in all circumstances.

So protecting my sources in these circumstances meant going all the way. And if the defence team pushed for me to release the material from my sources, I would have to stay the course.

If I stayed the course, I would have to bring on a hearing.

If, during that hearing, the judge sided with the defence team, I'd have to choose to protect my sources and I'd be in contempt in the face of the court.

If that happened, I risked criminal conviction, a fine, and, worst-case scenario, jail. It was a sobering and frightening prospect.

I did not want those decisions to be made behind closed doors. I thought it was a PR disaster for the defence if it took place in public – and it therefore might give up on the material from my confidential sources. So I was mightily relieved that Peter Morrissey had been told the Swimmers Trial was first.

On 5 July 2018, after Peter Morrissey spoke to the Crown, the new subpoenas arrived from the defence. They were not giving up. They had also asked for new material which we would have to locate and identify. It was Groundhog Day. It felt like another fishing expedition.

Again, I was expected to dictate a new set of shorthand notes into a recorder. We were given fifteen days to comply. For most of this time, I was on a four-week story shoot across four states. I frequently had conversations with lawyers as I walked up and down airport terminals, sitting in the passenger seat as the producer drove up country roads to the next shoot, scanning through documents on my phone in a hotel room, or, if I happened to be home, long into the night after the kids had gone to bed. I had another nasty cough that had lingered for weeks. I was getting by on painkillers and caffeine.

About that time, I recall sitting on my bed one day as the phone rang. It was Crown solicitor Ailsa McVean. The prosecution had decided that there were good forensic reasons for the Cathedral Trial to go first.

I was expected to give evidence for the first time in four weeks. The second, Swimmers Trial, was set down for November. McVean knew that I was desperately hoping that the Swimmers Trial would be first.

'I'm so sorry, Louise,' she said.

My stomach hit the floor. I was going to spend the rest of the year immersed in this. And second, what possible reason would the defence have to not pursue my sources, if the entire matter were to be held in secret?

I knew that my needs or wishes were completely ancillary to the criminal justice process, that none of this was about me, but it did throw up some disturbing possibilities.

Could a journalist in 2018 be pursued by the defence team in a sex offence trial to betray her confidential sources, to have this matter addressed in a secret hearing? To have her fate sealed by a judge whose decision could not be reported? What then? A secret prosecution?

In Victoria, if a court orders a witness to answer a question and he or she refuses, the witness can be found guilty of the common law offence of contempt in the face of the court. It is open to the judge to adopt a 'special summary procedure'. As the Victorian Law Reform Commission recently pointed out, where this is alleged, 'the court can, of its own motion and without any formal proceedings being instituted,' order that the person committing the contempt – the 'contemnor' – be kept in custody or released on bail, and 'adopt thereafter such procedure as in the circumstances the court thinks fit to try the charge'.

'The special summary procedure ... allows the presiding judicial officer to effectively place themselves in the position of prosecutor, witness, jury and judge,' the Law Reform Commission noted. 'The consequence is that the procedural safeguards adhered to in ordinary criminal proceedings are not expressly guaranteed.'

The case law says that the power should be used sparingly. It was more likely the judge would refer the matter to the Director of Public Prosecutions (DPP) to consider the merits of prosecution. Note, the DPP has not shied away from prosecution for contempt in the Pell matter – at the time of writing, there are a number of Australian journalists charged and still before the courts for breaching the suppression order when Pell's jury conviction (which was, of course, eventually overturned by the High Court) was announced internationally, but still not permitted to be disclosed in Australia.

If found guilty, contempt is punishable by imprisonment, a fine or both. It is open for the contemnor to apologise and for the charge to be dropped, but how could I apologise for something that I was doing according to my conscience and my journalistic principles?

The fact that these matters would be settled in a secret hearing was absurd, but also chilling.

Some people wondered whether I should ask one particularly vulnerable source to waive the privilege. Could he bring it upon himself to release me?

I didn't think about that moral dilemma for a second.

'I think it is entirely inappropriate,' I said, 'and goes against all our ethical foundations as journalists to ask someone to waive this privilege under these circumstances.

'It's not a fair position to put him in,' I said.

'He asked me for confidentiality and I promised it from day one. To ask him to change his mind during what is undoubtedly the most stressful thing he has ever endured is not right.'

I was supported at the ABC by managers right up to the director level. That was comforting.

Peter Morrissey engaged a junior barrister. To my eternal gratitude, he chose Sarala Fitzgerald. Fitzgerald is about my age, smart as a whip, super-organised and extremely competent. Morrissey chose her because she has expertise in cases which involve Victoria's Charter of Human Rights and Responsibilities and, in his words, 'she's a very good operator'. By any definition, this case raised clear questions about human rights.

Sarala Fitzgerald represents the new face of the Victorian Bar that Matt Collins and Wendy Harris are so keen to present. She has razor-sharp short hair to match her razor-sharp pant suits and razor-sharp wit.

She likes to wear neckties. And my favourite fun fact about her is that sometimes, just to mess with the heads of the blokes in the room, she'll wear a Melbourne Grammar old boys' tie, pinched from her husband. Melbourne Grammar is the all-boys alma mater of the city's establishment. Fitzgerald likes to keep them all on their toes, watching the cogs turn as they spot the familiar tie. 'Isn't that …? I don't … Did *she* used to be a *he*?'

Both she and the ABC's doggedly capable solicitor Kathryn Wilson worked with Morrissey like demons to get our submissions together in time.

Between 20 July and 1 August, we had a dizzying task of things to do – in my case, to somehow fit around the monster hours I was pulling for *Four Corners*.

We had to find witnesses to give evidence about the importance of the journalist privilege. Among those who offered to do so were Walter 'Robby' Robinson, the head of *The Boston Globe*'s 'Spotlight' team featured in the film of the same name; *Four Corners* presenter Sarah Ferguson; Gold Walkley winner Joanne McCarthy, whose work had prompted the child abuse Royal Commission; writer David Marr; reporter, academic and erstwhile political prisoner, Peter Greste; Professor of Journalism Matthew Ricketson; and survivor, author and barrister James Miller.

'I was personally very moved by the stories told to me by the people who I gave those undertakings to,' I swore in the affidavit about the sources. 'I would lose all respect for myself if I betrayed the trust that I intentionally elicited from those vulnerable people.

'I built that trust knowing how fragile those people are … It would be a heinous breach of faith on my part to breach that trust.

'Whilst I genuinely mean no disrespect to this Court, for which I wholeheartedly do have respect, I do not believe I could comply with an order that required me to breach that trust.

'That is not because I do not fear going to jail, quite the contrary.

'That prospect makes me feel extremely anxious, not least because I have a much-loved husband and two young children ...'

In the days before the court hearing, a meeting was called with some of the most senior people at the ABC to inform them that if we lost the case, I faced potential criminal charges. They gave their unanimous support for our course of action.

On the Saturday and Sunday, I was to appear at an interstate writers' festival, a commitment booked months in advance. My phone kept ringing with lawyers on the other end trying to save me from criminal prosecution.

I had two sessions at the festival. The last one was with legendary ABC broadcaster Margaret Throsby. I wasn't permitted to discuss anything to do with the allegations about Pell. I talked about the damning history of sexual abuse in the Catholic Church.

Throsby asked in a careful way about the impact of my journalism. I told her and the crowd that, the next day, I was going to have to go to a court to protect my confidential sources. I didn't identify the case, the court, the accused or even the location. All I said was that 'my sources come from a community of people that had been profoundly betrayed by an institution'.

'And I will not betray them.'

There was a standing ovation, I looked out, bleary-eyed, at the crowd, trying to stop my hands from shaking. People were weeping. As I walked off the stage, people gripped my hands and hugged me and told me to be strong, they'd be thinking of me.

The events I spoke at were always sombre occasions. And there were always survivors. Standing up the back, looking haunted. Little old ladies clutching my arm as tears rolled down their powdery cheeks, whispering 'some of us never tell' and just nodding meaningfully and walking away. Weary parents of people who had died because of what this did to them, the parents, not able to let go, wondering if I could do some checking on Father So and So.

These events always drew these wounded people. Most had lived with the pain but had never been through the legal process. It was all too much. Meeting them always reaffirmed the sense of doing all of this for the right reasons. Thinking of them now reaffirms why I am writing this book.

I got home that evening to find defence submissions had been sent to Sarala Fitzgerald just before 8 pm. I wondered how anyone was supposed to adequately prepare for court under those circumstances.

The late hour might have accounted for the word 'SUBPEONAS' (*sic*) in the title, in bold black type.

The document contained factual errors and assumptions and its main thrust was that in my book I was not engaging in 'journalism' at all. I was acting as an author, in my spare time, on 'literary' work.

A novel stance, given that the Walkley Awards for Excellence in Journalism, the most prestigious awards for our profession, had awarded me the prize for Book of the Year. One of the requirements for entry is that the book be a work of 'journalistic non-fiction'.

There was an underlying implication in the defence's submissions that I was a low-rent hack. It reheated their trope of me as, essentially, not an investigative journalist, but a nuisance who interfered with the course of justice.

This distortion painted me as being some sort of stalker when, in fact, I was doing my job – finding people involved in a very big breaking story and asking them, very politely, if they would like to be involved. The same sort of work done by Walter Robinson's *Boston Globe* colleagues featured in the *Spotlight* film. And, in fact, when pushed on this question, a source said – quoted in their own submissions – that I was just being a 'prudent journalist'.

The defence team alleged that my opposing their subpoena was an abuse of process.

I read it open-mouthed and tried not to think too much about it and to get some sleep that night before the hearing in the morning. Meanwhile, Sarala Fitzgerald and Peter Morrissey beavering away. They had come up with a masterstroke: lodging a section 35 notice that we intended to submit an application to the Victorian Attorney-General under the State's Charter of Human Rights and Responsibilities.

In it, we intended to explore the conflict between the administration of justice for the accused and the erosion of my civil liberties by the suppression order in the trial. The Victorian Charter recognises both freedom of expression and access to a fair and public hearing. I was, in these circumstances, being denied both. The defence team was attempting, in secret, to have me reveal confidential sources, a matter of great public interest.

In submissions prepared for the application by Fitzgerald and Morrissey, they argued, 'Ms Milligan's right to freedom of expression, and the rights of others in Victoria to receive information about the application to have Ms Milligan disclose her sources, should weigh heavily in the court's consideration of whether the current suppression order is necessary to ensure the accused gets a fair hearing.'

We sought to have the breadth of the suppression order attached to the Pell case narrowed so as to allow me to disclose what was happening to me in these proceedings. And we argued that this would have no impact on whether or not there would be a fair trial.

The notice was sent to the Victorian Attorney-General, the Equal Opportunity and Human Rights Commission, the Chief Judge of the County Court, the Director of Public Prosecutions and the defence.

The next morning, Nick and I made the journey again to the court district – this time to Peter Morrissey's chambers. My former boss Jo Puccini was there, and Louise Adler, Andy Burns and solicitor Kathryn Wilson. The ABC's Director of News, Gaven Morris, would also come along to court to show support.

The time for advice was over. I remember Peter Morrissey turning to me and saying that it was one thing for us not to give the material to the defence, but what if the judge decided that in order to determine whether I had the journalist privilege, His Honour must first inspect the documents?

I paused for a while and then said it would not make a difference to my decision. A County Court judge might be the very kind of person that my sources didn't want to see their material. So I had to hold the line. I wasn't giving up the material under any circumstances. Off the record is off the record.

I turned to Jo Puccini, who is a very strong and principled woman, in whose journalistic judgement I have huge faith.

'I'm right, aren't I? I'm right?'

Jo looked back at me, nodded her head really slowly and deliberately, saying, 'Yeah … Yeah.' I think it's the first time I've ever seen her look nervous or hesitant.

Peter cleared them all out. He is a kind man and I felt I was in sound hands. He was very supportive, but also emphasised the possibility of the jail term again. The criminal conviction, how serious that was, as a mother of young children. 'Comrade, you can pull out at any time. You just let me know, pal.'

I wasn't pulling out.

* * *

You cross the road to the big silver County Court building, flanked by Morrissey, at a steady clip. Your legs are made of jangling pins and needles. You glance up at the giant Lady of Justice sculpture on the court's edifice, depicting the figure known to the ancient Romans as Justitia. She's blindfolded, with one foot forward, her left hand holding aloft the scales of justice, her right hand holding her sword at the ready.

You think of all the souls who have passed through here, contemplating reliving their darkest hours.

Upstairs in the courtroom, Paul Galbally, *sans* Richter and Shann, gives you and yours an awkward polite smile – the kind of too-wide expression where the eyes don't match the mouth. Where the eyes seem to say, 'Let's all pretend this situation isn't monumentally fucked. How about it?'

The barrister who wrote the thunderous submissions is young. His mousey hair has the barest hint of ginger.

From the gallery, you straighten your back in your seat. Neutral pleasant court face, Milligan.

'It's going to be okay,' you think to yourself, mentally clicking your ruby slippers together three times.

The prosecutor, Mark Gibson, is there too – he's pleasant in that restrained way he has.

On the bench is Chief Judge Peter Kidd, who will be hearing the trial. Kidd has a shiny pate and a sensible demeanour. From the moment he comes in, you start to allow yourself to think that maybe it's going to be all right after all.

'The submissions which have been foreshadowed are extremely complex,' Chief Judge Kidd says, 'and I'm being invited to make a ruling on a particular provision as it applies to a criminal proceeding which will seemingly be novel in the sense that there are very few, if any, rulings and certainly not appellant guidance as to the approach to be taken.' Which basically means there are no precedents in appeals courts that could help him make his decision.

Then he raises the issue of the notice to proceed under the Charter of Human Rights and Responsibilities. 'Any arguments advanced upon the footing of the Charter are complex,' Kidd says.

But then he starts to have a go at the defence and the prosecution – note – not us, saying the case isn't 'trial ready' and it wouldn't be starting on time the following Tuesday.

'And I will need to discuss that with the parties as to where we go with that, because these weighty matters need to be properly considered.'

He says he's not 'looking to blame anyone' but 'this issue concerning the journalist contest and the subpoena is a weighty issue and that was never foreshadowed'.

The defence barrister's ears seem to start to redden.

'... Ms Milligan, who I assume is in court, Ms Milligan's in court?'

'She is present,' says Morrissey. You nod and sit up straighter, trying not to look too much like the kid you once were at the front of the class, shooting up her hand for teachers' questions.

Kidd continues. He needs to hear the 'lion's share of the argument', so he can understand the issues, but it seems to be 'fruitless' to put Ms Milligan in the box 'this early in the process'.

He's taking it seriously, you start to think.

He also says he hasn't had time to read the submissions filed the night before.

The judge says he wants to read all the material. 'So, where do we go from here?'

The defence seems thrown by all of this.

'The accused will not take a step in this proceeding that involves delaying the trial,' the defence barrister says.

'So, I will need to take some instructions in light of what's fallen from Your Honour.'

Good grief. Is he caving?

'The second thing is this: the accused will not take a step that results in the already great difficulties in him obtaining a fair trial by reason of publicity being added to.'

Your instinct was right – they would not have pressed this so hard had it not been in secret. It's not good PR for them. And so Morrissey and Fitzgerald's idea to press to lift the suppression order for this hearing was also a masterstroke.

'The third thing I will say is this: that we are very much conscious of the court's time ...'

He really does seem to be caving. You exchange meaningful glances with the others.

Kidd reinforces how much is still to be done in preparation for the trial. You get the impression that while he takes your matter seriously, he'd be just as happy if it disappeared.

'We're conscious of the court's time,' the barrister manages. '... [W]e will not take a step – and I expect that includes calling on the subpoenas today – that will result in this court's time being diverted so that the trial is delayed.'

Kidd makes it clear that's 'just the reality of the situation' – he now has, just a week before the trial, a 'very significant matter' brought before him.

'I certainly make no criticism of the ABC of taking issue with it. That's their right,' he says. You nod again. 'But it's a very weighty matter, as is the issue of the Charter [of Human Rights and Responsibilities].'

The objective reality, he says, is the case is 'far from trial-ready. And it's an important trial, obviously enough, and I'm not going to have it begin on the run.'

The barrister says he'll need to make a phone call. Morrissey catches your eye. This is all very promising indeed. And completely unexpected. The barrister's riding instructions are very clear that the trial will begin the following week, come hell or high water.

Chief Judge Kidd stands it down for fifteen minutes.

You huddle into a room with your team and you all stand there, wide-eyed.

All of that extreme stress and nonsense and they appear to be caving at the first hurdle. You all gasp and shake your heads a bit.

You file back into court.

'Your Honour, the position is this, for reasons Your Honour will appreciate,' the barrister begins. 'We will not call on the two subpoenas to the ABC and to Louise Milligan.'

'Well, in that case I don't think I've got any orders to make,' Chief Judge Kidd says, looking, frankly, relieved. 'All right. Well, in that case, that concludes the matter for today. So, ten o'clock tomorrow?'

The tipstaff says, 'All stand,' and you all bow to Chief Judge Peter Kidd. And in all your years of bowing to judges, you've never done it with more meaning.

The secret hearing is done.

'Good luck with the trial,' you say to Mark Gibson on the way out. You try not to sound like you are singing. He gives you a kind nod.

And it feels like that moment in *The Wizard of Oz* when Dorothy dumps the bucket of water over the wicked witch's head. And 'poof!' She's gone.

Not for the community of people you came to this place to stick up for, though. Not by a long shot.

A BOY LIKE PARIS

The County Court trial of *DPP v Pell* was also carried out without the media being permitted to report on any of it. It was open for members of the public or journalists to attend, but because of the strict suppression order that Chief Justice Kidd had imposed, they could not report on it at the time. Most people had no idea it was taking place. As a potential witness in the next trial, I was asked not to attend.

Two teenagers with an interest in the matter got wind that the trial was proceeding. At some point during the evidence, they began to slip into court.

Paris Street and Finley Tobin were alumni of St Kevin's College, the elite Catholic school to which the choirboys who were being discussed in the Cathedral Trial were given their choral scholarships. Paris and Finley hadn't known those boys. One, the key witness known only as 'J', was now in his thirties; the other had died of a drug overdose four years earlier. They had only attended the school for a short time in the 1990s, before Paris and Finley were even born.

Paris and Finley were eighteen. Both were blond, and both had an unassuming prettiness about them. The sort of boys whose faces and necks still flushed a hot crimson when they were nervous. Terribly well-mannered. Well brought up. Studious and thoughtful, both were in their first year at the University of Melbourne. Paris was living at Newman College, the Catholic halls of residence. Something about him and Finley reminded me of characters from an Evelyn Waugh novel.

They were conspicuous, in the public gallery of that secret trial, Paris remembers, because they were the only 'shimmer of youth'.

As they entered the courtroom on one of those days, Paris and Finley heard a sound from the dock. They turned around to see Pell, motioning to them.

'Good morning,' Finley remembers the accused saying, with a broad smile. Finley said he thought Pell looked like he was lonely, and he just wanted to talk to someone. 'Sorry …?' Paris says he started to say. Finley heard his friend stammering as Paris tried to answer Pell. He sounded shocked and uncomfortable. Paris, meanwhile, could feel the blood rushing to his head, his heart thumping in his chest.

Finley had by that time learned to read Paris' signs of when he was triggered. When he would meet with his friend, often a cloud would come over Paris. Finley observed that while they were at the trial, Paris constantly seemed to be in a 'tense' state.

So Finley shuffled Paris into a seat away from the dock and Paris composed himself.

As a St Kevin's alumnus who was interested in the law, Paris was keen to see the trial. But he was also there for another reason.

Paris Street had unfinished business with Robert Richter.

He remembers catching Richter's eye one day as he was sitting closest to the aisle in the row of courtroom seats. They clocked each other, Paris says, for a moment in time somewhere 'between a look and a gaze'.

'Not so short that it was innocuous,' Paris says, 'but not so long that it was hostile.'

'I'd say he knew me.'

Paris would later write a letter to Richter, which he shared with me, and sent to the silk.

Paris Street was the boy whose desperate mother, Caroline Redmond, had contacted me the year before, when her son was still finishing year twelve. The mother whose correspondence I, in the daze of complying with the Pell subpoena, travelling for *Four Corners*, and receiving eleventy-billion emails a day, had simply forgotten.

Paris hadn't forgotten, though.

* * *

Paris Street started at St Kevin's College when he and his brother were nine.

'The first day in the quadrangle at the junior school, everyone was out there,' Paris remembers. 'I was with my twin brother. It was probably one of the happiest days of my life.

'I think as soon as you put the blazer on, you feel like you belong somewhere and you're part of something.

'And I think that's what makes it so appealing.'

'He absolutely loved it,' Caroline Redmond says of her son at the school. 'Absolutely. Absolutely loved it up until year nine, really.'

St Kevin's is a sprawling Catholic school for boys set on Melbourne's Yarra River. It was established by the Christian Brothers in 1918 and had in years gone past been a more modest place. But, based as it was, among the mock-Tudor mansions of Toorak, the city's priciest real estate, it had developed a brilliant reputation. St Kevin's boys would regularly top the state in English exams.

St Kevin's motto was *Omnia Pro Deo* – All things for God. Alumni and teachers told me that the-then headmaster, Stephen Russell, who had been there for more than two decades, had styled the school after the likes of Eton. The boys were all expected to rise for him as he walked into assembly.

During special assemblies, like graduation presentations, a senior teacher would call them all to attention. 'Quiet, boys. Please be upstanding for the entrance of the official party,' Finley Tobin remembers the teacher saying. Russell would walk creakily across the wooden floorboards of the stage, followed by the rest of the school's leadership team. They'd all be wearing academic gowns.

'You'd think they were royal,' Finley says.

A teacher remembers, during one of these processions at a speech night at the end of the year, that they entered to the thunderous tones of 'O Fortuna' from *Carmina Burana*.

A student turned to the teacher and whispered, 'You'd think he was God!' of the headmaster.

'Here, he is,' the teacher whispered back.

The Director of Studies, who was largely responsible for encouraging the brilliant English marks, would also wear his academic robes as he strode through the halls. Women teachers would complain of sweltering feet in summer because they were not permitted to wear open-toed shoes. There was also a ban on three-quarter length trousers. Accessories were expected to be 'appropriate'. It was, in some ways, like a place from another time.

Be that as it may, the leadership team had managed to garner an enviable reputation for the school. Its parent body included people from the highest echelons of the law, politics, policing, media. Many of the fathers and grandfathers were old boys.

The annual fees were $20,000 – so beyond the means of most Melbourne families. But that was still significantly lower than comparable schools for boys, like Xavier College, Melbourne Grammar or Scotch. The combination of that, with the convenience of being on the train line, in a central location, with fantastic academic results, was irresistible.

In a city where the first question often asked is not, as it is in Sydney, 'Where do you live?', but, even into your middle age, 'What school did you go to?', parents clamoured to get their sons into St Kevin's College. Finley Tobin says they'd put boys on waiting lists 'as soon as they're born'.

'St Kevin's promotes a belief that you're very privileged and lucky to have your son go there,' Susan Lackner, whose two sons went to the school, tells me.

Luke Macaronas, a brilliant student from the year above Paris and Finley, says it was high stakes for the boys, who were expected to behave.

'Because it is a private institution, and because it has to keep these promises that it offers to parents about good grades and good performance and strong students, reputation is everything at a place like this,' Macaronas says.

The reputation was attractive to prospective parents. St Kevin's seemed to turn out nice boys. As someone who has met many of its young, recent alumni, they have been, to a person, intelligent, respectful, beautifully mannered and thoughtful.

Another parent, Jo O'Brien, says your son was 'basically guaranteed a good result'. Her boy, Ned, who was close friends with Paris Street at school, is now doing a law degree.

'Great teachers, especially in year twelve, the English teachers are the best in the state,' Jo O'Brien says. 'Great sporting reputation. Accessible. It's in Toorak. Everybody wants to go there.'

The school's sporting reputation rivalled the academic excellence. St Kevin's boasts ample playing fields and rowing sheds. First thing in the morning, the four- and eight-boy crews can be seen, in their emerald, gold and blue rowing uniforms, gracefully edging their boats through the glitter of the Yarra in the morning sun.

But in recent years, the school has become best-known for its athletics prowess. Talented runners who can't afford the fees are offered scholarships to keep up the college's reputation.

At the athletics and football meets for Melbourne's most prestigious private schools, known as Associated Public Schools (APS), all two thousand or so St Kevin's boys would be required to attend, and they would bellow their time-honoured school chants in thunderous unison:

Where we come from?
So we tell them (So we tell them)
We are from Toorak (We are from Toorak)
We are the army! The mighty Skevies army! (The mighty Skevies army!)
We are the army!
The mighty Skevies army! (The mighty Skevies army!)
The mighty, mighty, mighty Skevies army!

Teachers, who were also required to attend, would feel somewhat embarrassed at the display. None of the other schools would have compulsory attendance for all students, so St Kevin's sea of boys yelling their chants with guttural aggression always felt a little over the top, given no one else could possibly compete.

'It's definitely a show of our dominance and the fact that we have the pride to come en masse like that is definitely part of our culture,' Finley Tobin told me.

'And at the same time, that turns into a bit of a hive mind or a bit of a frenzied state where people think it's okay to shout in public and yell at other schools.'

'Exactly what makes St Kevin's so celebrated,' Luke Macaronas reflected, 'is exactly its Achilles heel as well.

'It has a fantastic culture of collegiality, of community and that is also where this idea of pride and shame is located too.

So, absolutely, when you're among this crowd, it is an incredible feeling of bravado and strength. That is also the feeling of being in an army and going to war. And parents say that. And when you watch boys run onto a field or when you watch boys sing these kinds of things, they do sound like they're going to war.'

The school would later become notorious when a large group of St Kevin's boys, on their way to an APS carnival, was filmed on a tram singing a highly misogynistic chant, which Finley Tobin agreed was 'definitely evidence of a toxic culture' at the school.

> I wish that all the ladies (I wish that all the ladies)
> Were holes in the road (were holes in the road)
> If I was a dump truck (if I was a dump truck)
> I'd fill them with my load (I'd fill them with my load).

Paris Street was disgusted when he saw the boys chanting on television, although, like all of the St Kevin's alumni I spoke to, he remembered that they had been singing that particular chant for some years. He was an excellent student who had won awards for academic excellence, was in an 'extended thinking' class and doing maths extension. But he loved, more than anything, to run. Tall and rangy, he excelled at middle-distance and spent his weekends representing the school. When he got into his teens, running was about all Paris wanted to do in his spare time.

As he moved into years eight and nine, his mother began to notice that the obsession was taking on a worrying dimension. Paris was ten kilograms lighter than his twin. She started taking him to see a dietician because she was concerned he wasn't eating sufficiently for the amount of running he was doing. By the March of his year nine year, she described him as 'a greyhound on speed'. She contacted the school psychologist and a coach.

'He was thin, he wasn't putting on weight, I took him to the doctor,' Caroline remembers.

The doctor reassured her Paris was okay, but her mother's intuition told her otherwise.

She discovered that her son was being privately coached, without her knowledge, by a man named Peter Kehoe. Kehoe was an old boy who had been training students at the school for forty years. But he had been let go after a falling-out with a teacher – the school's cross-country coach, Brosie McCann. McCann never had any suspicions of a sexual or criminal kind about Kehoe, but, as a teacher, McCann thought the dismissive way Kehoe spoke about some of the boys and other staff at the school was at times inappropriate and unprofessional.

Kehoe had sent a 'strange' email to Caroline and her husband about a falling-out he'd had with Brosie McCann over the fact that McCann insisted that Paris train with the school team, not just with Peter Kehoe. Kehoe had written a long and rambling email to the headmaster, Stephen Russell, about why Paris should be allowed to train with him alone.

What raised Caroline's suspicion was that Kehoe claimed to have discussed this arrangement with 'the Streets' and that the headmaster seemed to be, according to the email, abreast of these individual training sessions, even though she wasn't.

'I have made it clear to the Streets that in my discussions with you, you indicated that you were more than happy for any students to train with me,' Kehoe wrote.

Kehoe was oddly critical of McCann, who, unlike him at this point, was on the payroll at the school, and the 'inordinate risks Mr Brosie subjects his athletes to'. The risks Kehoe was speaking of were about McCann's training style, which was different from his.

The claims about McCann's coaching style were completely unfounded and self-serving. Everyone I have discussed this case with who knew McCann has spoken highly of McCann's character and his methods. What wasn't apparent at this stage was that the real risk to Paris Street was Peter Kehoe.

Caroline says this was the first time she had discovered that Kehoe was now training her son exclusively, through the St Kevin's Amateur Athletics Club (SKAAC), which was affiliated with the school.

SKAAC used the St Kevin's facilities for training, but Kehoe had started to train Paris elsewhere, alone.

Paris was fourteen. 'I said [to the school], "I haven't given him permission to train Paris, he's just taken it upon himself to start training,"' Caroline remembers.

She found it odd. The man seemed to have control of her son, even when he wasn't there. For instance, when the family went to Noosa for a wedding, Paris kept going to the local track, 'running in the rain', she says.

'We couldn't get him down to the beach. It was like Peter had control from a distance.'

Caroline Redmond rang the school to voice her concerns. She says a senior teacher at the school rang her back and said, '[the headmaster] Mr Russell wants you to know that Peter is a person of good character and you have nothing to worry about.'

Caroline says she made it clear that Peter Kehoe was not to drive her son to training. She bought Paris a $500 public transport ticket to ensure it didn't happen.

But she would later discover it did happen.

Caroline was also completely unaware of the disturbing messages that Kehoe had begun to send her son, who was, at the time, only in year nine.

Photographs show a skinny teenager, with dark blond hair and a smattering of freckles on his nose. He didn't seem to be one of those boys who look sophisticated or wilful or knowing. This didn't seem to be a kid who might smoke behind the rowing sheds, taunt girls on the train or send spitballs from the back of the bus. He wouldn't have a sip of alcohol until he was sixteen.

'Paris was a pretty reserved and quiet kid,' his friend Ned O'Brien remembers, 'who came out of his shell once you knew him for a while.'

In his year nine school photo, Paris' large eyes, the colour of cornflowers, smile artlessly back at the camera. He looks so young.

The messages from Kehoe started in about March 2014, when Paris was still in year nine and crept up on Paris the way the work of any clever groomer does. Subtle, at first. Friendly, encouraging, jokey.

'Awesome plan for an awesome guy!'

And then, little by little, they became slightly more suggestive.

Of Paris running on a warm day, Kehoe texted, *'Hot stuff. I bet you would have won a wet [t]-shirt competition!'*

Paris had no idea what a wet t-shirt competition was.

'*Maybe you need to run quickly, just to keep warm. Maybe you need another hug from me.*'

'*Every time I get the circle pop up on my screen with your Facebook photo in it, I get all excited! I think, "Yay, it's Paris!"*'

'*Cheers and love you muchly.*'

When Paris would ask an innocuous question about running, the answers would be just too much.

'*Sure. Whatever you wish is my command.*'

Or when Paris politely said it was nice seeing him, '*I can assure you, it was very nice seeing you.*'

When Paris was recovering from being unwell and 'living under a rock for the past week and a half', the response was, '*How was the rock? Snuggly?*'

Peter Kehoe was, at the time, fifty-nine years old. Short, jowly, unremarkable in appearance, well-spoken. He lived alone in a rented modest unit in a leafy suburb not far from where Paris lived with his parents. He drove a navy Mercedes Benz which he named 'Morticia' after the gothic matriarch in the 1960s television sitcom *The Addams Family*.

Kehoe had been a scholarship boy at St Kevin's, from the class of 1971. He came from a large family with a widowed single mother. One former member of SKAAC who had known the family for decades remembered them as parishioners at St Michael's, Ashburton. The man always remembers Kehoe as 'troubled'. He said he'd always felt sorry for him.

At the time when Kehoe was training Paris, Kehoe was, unbeknownst to Paris, on a cocktail of psychiatric medication prescribed for a major depressive disorder. He'd been in therapy for years and had been hospitalised for his condition.

He was a retired public servant who now devoted all of his time volunteering as an athletics coach. Some families, who told me they didn't want to owe something to an older single man who was coaching their young boy, insisted on paying.

He trained a handful of boys, including one who was from a very humble family, about whom some other members of the club had had some concerns because Kehoe had organised his scholarship to St Kevin's, was often paying his way and was travelling with him when they went to running meets. The boy never, to my knowledge at the time of writing, made any complaints, and, when asked, was defensive about Kehoe. But the arrangement concerned some of the parents around the club.

As 2014 wore on, Kehoe's messaging with Paris continued and became more concerning. But the boy didn't really understand the true meaning or intention of the 'little offhand, sexual comments' that he can now clearly see were thrown into the correspondence.

When Paris sent Kehoe a list of results from a meet at which St Kevin's boys had been running, Kehoe replied, referring to his nemesis Brosie McCann, '*Ha ha ha! Fantastic! Suck on that, Brosie, you wanker.*'

When Paris replied that he didn't know how a certain runner did it, he was '*so poised*', Kehoe returned with, '*You mean Brosie is poised while he is sucking on it?*'

Grooming or otherwise, it is unbelievably inappropriate commentary from a running coach who had been recommended, Caroline Redmond says, by the headmaster of a prestigious, fee-paying school, to a fourteen-year-old boy. Sexual, off-colour, not least defamatory of McCann, who staff, parents and alumni have told me was decent and well-liked and was just wanting to enforce proper protocols about how and where the boys trained, including that it was perhaps healthier for Paris to train with his school mates than with some single older bloke, no matter how good a coach Kehoe was, at a fairly deserted park nowhere near the school.

In a later reference to McCann as a '*fuckhead*', Kehoe said, '*Actually, I should stop calling Brosie fuckhead, because that is certainly one head I wouldn't fuck.*'

'He's not a fuckhead,' Paris says of McCann. 'Like, it was just really weird. Like yeah, it was inappropriate, because I'm a student. Does he want a response out of me? I'm not going to comment on one of my teachers like that, and I had no problems with Brosie whatsoever.'

Meanwhile, Kehoe stepped up the affectionate texts. Facebook, the 59-year-old told the now fifteen-year-old, had picked Paris as his '*best friend*'.

During a discussion about which athletics singlet to wear, Kehoe told Paris he looked '*great in both*' and '*God, you don't need to try*'.

This information is even more off-putting when you see how young Paris looked at the time. Tall, but by no means one of those boys who appears older than he is. He was still a child.

Kehoe thought it was 'weird' that, when Paris checked, Facebook did not think he was Paris' best friend.

'*Well, I must say I am terribly disappointed. Ah, the pain of unrequited love!*'

'Very creepy,' Caroline Redmond now says about the messages she had no idea this man was sending her boy. 'Obviously, you could see what he was trying to do.'

'*I think you're the best thing since sliced bread ...*' Kehoe later told Paris. When Paris referenced peanut butter (about which there had been discussion between them in a conversation about diet because he'd been eating peanut butter and gaining some weight), Kehoe replied, '*So all I'd have to do is add peanut butter and I'd be edible?*'

Paris, he now says not quite understanding the double entendre, answered '*Quite possibly*'.

Kehoe replied: '*Oh GOODY GOODY DO I WANT TO CONTINUE THIS CONVERSATION!!! ... Love you. Xxxxxxxx*'

'I just thought it was odd – just [a] weird, quirky, strange way to communicate to anyone,' Paris remembers.

'I didn't think it was, at that point, illegal, criminal. I didn't understand the true intentions ... It's difficult because, looking back in hindsight as a twenty-year-old, I just think, "Jesus, like how did I meet this guy?"

'But as a fourteen-, fifteen-year-old, I think that's how they get away with it, because they don't expect a fourteen-, fifteen-year-old to come to that conclusion, that this is, what? Like, he's doing what grooming is.

'They do it because fourteen-, fifteen-year-olds can't really grasp that ...'

As the brittle Melbourne winter of 2014 began to thaw into September spring, Peter Kehoe became emboldened.

* * *

Despite having no idea about the Facebook messages, Caroline Redmond was, nonetheless, becoming increasingly concerned. On one occasion, she blanched at a conversation between Paris and Kehoe in which Paris had said *'running is the best thing ever'*.

Kehoe responded, *'Oh, running is not the only thing. There are other great things, and I wish I could teach you that.'*

On 2 September 2014, when Caroline went to pick up Paris, she noticed that Kehoe was wearing her son's St Kevin's jacket.

Two days later, on 4 September, it became clear that Caroline's inklings that something was not quite right were well-founded.

Paris woke that day with a nasty bout of hay fever. He decided not to go to school. But by the afternoon, the symptoms had cleared. It was a training day with Kehoe and so he decided to stick to his schedule.

Because he wasn't coming from school, he decided to ask Kehoe if the coach could pick him up. Not surprisingly, Kehoe gladly agreed.

As Paris was on his last round of the track, he says Kehoe mentioned that he had some St Kevin's yearbooks back at his place, and if Paris wanted to, he could look at them. Paris looked back at the coach.

'I said that I had a Japanese oral presentation that I needed to finish,' Paris says.

Kehoe came back with the sort of smutty comment you might have heard on *The Benny Hill Show* or *Are You Being Served?* in the 1970s.

'He said, "That's not the only oral you'll have to do,"' Paris remembers.

'[I] felt very uncomfortable. Yeah. But I felt like I was in a position where I couldn't do anything ... I just sort of had to listen to it.'

Peter Kehoe was Paris' ride home. You can get to his place by public transport from Stradbroke Park, but it's not that convenient.

A few minutes later, Kehoe asked Paris if his parents were home. Paris told him 'no'.

'Oh, I can bring you to my house and I can show you the photos,' the coach said.

Paris tried again to fob him off. 'I asked if he could bring them to training, like, another training session.'

'Because you didn't want to go to his house?' I ask Paris.

'Yeah. Yeah,' he says. As Paris says this, he has this faraway look in his eyes. Paris Street's eyes don't look artless and happy-go-lucky anymore. They often have a glassy and spacey appearance – you get the impression that at times he's not really there. He's off thinking, pondering, dwelling.

Kehoe persisted. Paris then went to have his customary chocolate milk recovery drink.

'And he said, "Oh! The sight of that dripping down your face,"' Paris remembers. Paris didn't know what to do, so he laughed nervously.

Kehoe asked about the yearbooks a third time, and this time Paris acquiesced, got in the passenger seat of Morticia the blue Mercedes, and went to Kehoe's place.

They pulled up in a driveway off a tree-lined street at a low-roofed blond brick mid-century unit block. Kehoe's place was up at the back. When they made their way through the entrance into the living spaces, the pastel, embossed late sixties and early seventies yearbooks were waiting for them on the kitchen table.

'And it was a bit of an odd spot, to have the yearbooks, just in – in the kitchen,' he would later say. 'I – I thought he would've had [them] in his room or something.'

Kehoe started flicking his fingers through the yellowing pages, and pointing to grainy black and white photographs of himself, with the somewhat bouffant hairstyle of the time. He commented on other old boys that meant nothing to a Generation Z kid, who was bored but politely going along with it.

Then things took a darker turn. 'He pointed out four people and said – he mentioned these people had committed suicide,' Paris would later tell police, 'and in the same photo he pointed out a student – who would later become a psychiatrist.'

The fifteen-year-old Paris' memory of what Kehoe then told him was that the psychiatrist had informed Kehoe that the suicides had 'something to do with the priesthood'. Given that the Christian Brothers ran the school at the time, I expected that it was more likely Kehoe had referred to them, instead of priests, and Paris agreed it was probably right. St Kevin's had, like so many Catholic schools of the era, a history of paedophiles in its ranks and the Christian Brothers were prolific offenders.

Kehoe would later say that he 'felt quite depressed when I saw that photo'. And 'just felt like sharing it, ah, with somebody'.

I wonder what Paris thought was going on. He says he wasn't really sure what to think at the time, but he started to feel uncomfortable. He has thought about it over and over since then.

'The only explanation I have for that would be that he was trying to justify what he was doing,' Paris says.

Whatever it was, it was chilling. Even more so because of what Kehoe said next. Kehoe pointed out a boy in the photographs.

'[H]e said, "Oh, this person was a cutie. I wish I would've put my hand on his butt," or something like that.

'And at that point I was feeling pretty uncomfortable and – because I just didn't know what to think.'

Paris had 'no idea' what to say.

'There was this incredible tension in the room, that I needed to get out of, and I tried to sort of break that by just sort of laughing. Not because I found it funny, obviously. Just because I wanted to, you know, break that tension a little bit because it, you know, the stress and the anxiety was intense.'

So Paris tried to make his excuses to leave. 'I said it was nice visiting the "Kehoe Crib",' he says, referring to the unit.

'This is me … after hearing things like that … I just want to get out of there.'

But Kehoe wasn't letting him go so soon. He told Paris he'd only seen 'half of it'. Did he want to see the other half of the Kehoe crib?

'The other half' was just Kehoe's bedroom. That was all the coach showed Paris.

'I had no idea what was going on,' Paris says. 'Like, I just want[ed] to get out of there. Yeah. Probably one of the most scary times of my life.'

When Kehoe opened the door to the bedroom, all Paris could see was a half-made bed. He had no idea what to say. 'Like, I have no interest in seeing his bedroom or anything,' he says.

'So I said, "That's a big bed."' Kehoe told the boy he could 'jump in it whenever you like'.

Paris just laughed uncomfortably and made his way back to the kitchen to get his bag. But as he was picking up his bag, Kehoe started at him again.

'And then he said, "Do you know why I was looking forward to today's training session?"

'Then I said "no". Then he said, "Because on Tuesday," so, two days before … [he said] that he had got an erection, and that he pre-cummed.'

Kehoe then asked Paris Street if he knew what 'pre-cum' was.

'And then I said, "No".' Paris continues, 'Then he said, "It's the premature stages of ejaculation." Then he said, "You can lick it off whenever you like."'

Paris winces as he remembers the scene.

'One thing that was very difficult and I'll never get it out of my head, was not only what he said, when he said, "You can lick it off whenever you like," but just his facial expression.

'It was like eagerness. It was like, "Oh god."' Paris recoils and then demonstrates a grotesque eager beaver expression.

'Anticipating that something was going to happen?' I ask him.

'Yep,' Paris finishes.

He had now come to understand why Kehoe had shown so much interest in him.

'I just wanted to run,' Paris now tells me.

'I didn't really understand the severity of what he was saying, until that day. That was sort of the tipping point for me.

'I had put all my trust and faith into this one person to train me, and improve my running, and to come to understand that that was just all false, was heavy.'

To the fifteen-year-old's eternal relief, his mother then called, which gave him an excuse to leave. As he was on the phone to Caroline, Paris says Kehoe held the door handle like he didn't want Caroline to hear the door being opened. Paris surmised it was because Kehoe didn't want her to hear the sound and ask questions about where he was.

When Kehoe dropped Paris off that afternoon, he told the teenager, 'Keep looking good.'

Twenty minutes later, the coach sent a winky face emoji.

And later, '*Can't wait to see you again on Saturday at 4pm.*'

Paris sat with this information for a couple of days, not quite knowing what to do. He sent Kehoe some mundane information about a teacher at St Kevin's agreeing to a training regime.

'*God I hope so. I am not sure I could cope with Paris deprivation … Fucking beauty, I'm soooo wrapped. To be able to just coach you in peace will be such a joy.*'

And then, a little later, a love heart emoticon followed by three kisses.

And then, '*I've just closed the blinds, it makes me feel safe from the world.*'

And the last message, when Paris decided never to correspond with this man again, '*Your thighs, gorgeous as they are, are not fully defined at present. My god, when they are, they will be spectacular.*' Winky face emoji.

I ask Paris how he felt about himself when he put it all together in his mind.

'Terrible, yeah,' he says in that trailing off way that he has now. 'It just felt like a complete waste of, like, a year. And even my childhood.'

Paris decided to tell his friend Ned O'Brien, who was also coached by Kehoe. He said that he thought Kehoe might be 'gay'. At recess or lunch on the St Kevin's playground, Paris showed Ned the Facebook messages.

Ned O'Brien was, at this point, still fourteen. He was a tiny kid, still towered over by his friend Paris. His voice still hadn't broken.

'He was up to here,' his mother, Jo O'Brien, motions with her hand, indicating a small kid.

'He was a little boy. He hadn't had his growth spurt yet – squeaky voice. Yeah, he was a little boy.'

But he was a pocket rocket of a runner and he had a good head on his shoulders. Little Ned O'Brien knew that this wasn't just 'gay'. Despite the fact that he'd had no problems himself with Kehoe and he was a 'respected coach', Ned O'Brien thought this was creepy.

'I said to [Paris], "I think it's a bit more than that. I don't think you should be concerned as to his sexuality, [but] as to if he's coming on to you in a predatory sense,"' Ned remembers.

'I was pretty shocked. I didn't really believe it either – I couldn't really picture it happening, but obviously the evidence was right there – I had to believe it.'

He thought the Facebook messages were 'very sexual in nature, and in no way could be passed off as a joke'.

When Jo O'Brien picked up her son from athletics that Saturday, she noticed he seemed very down. Jo O'Brien is a no-nonsense woman with a wicked sense of humour, who talks with her hands and has a well-developed sense of what is right and wrong.

Jo doesn't care much about what other people think. She rolls her eyes at some of the more pretentious St Kevin's establishment types and thumbs her nose at people who tell her what to do. She was a devoted athletics mum and remembers asking her boy about running that day.

'He said, "I don't want to talk about running, Mum,"' Jo remembers. '"I need to tell you something. I think Paris is in danger. Peter's been saying some really weird things to him and I think that I need to tell you because he could be in danger."'

I think every mother of a boy just wishes that when he gets into his teens, he'll have the wisdom of Ned O'Brien.

'My response was, firstly, shock,' Jo remembers. 'I was proud that Ned could talk to me about this, that he cared enough about his friend to tell me.

'I tried to calm Ned down. I told him he did the right thing by telling me, and this was something that I needed to talk to Paris' mum about.'

Jo O'Brien picked up the phone and called Caroline Redmond. Caroline missed the call. The pair weren't in the same friendship circle, so when Caroline saw the missed call from Jo, she knew it must be something to do with Paris and Ned. She turned to her son and asked him why Jo O'Brien might be on the phone.

Paris 'fessed up. His mother, who is calm in a crisis, told him to go to his bedroom and write everything down.

Then she and Paris' father, Neil, took Paris Street to see Victoria Police. Peter Kehoe was charged soon after.

THE CROSS

Paris Street's case is instructive because it is an example not just of what happens to a person, in this case a child, when they find themselves making a complaint in the criminal justice system, but also how the institutions and people in positions of authority around them fail to respond. It shows how the intersection of a bruising trial, even when you get the outcome you desired, and a betrayal by an institution and its adults who are supposed to know better – can sometimes account for as much of the ongoing trauma as the original crime.

While what Peter Kehoe did was disgusting, inappropriate and certainly criminal, it is at the lower end of the spectrum of sexual offending. What happened to Paris after the crime is reprehensible.

It's a pattern that victims of sexual crimes repeatedly see – the inability of people to see that their colleague, their friend, their employee, their ally, could be a perpetrator. They fall in together and talk about 'allegations' and 'innocent until proven guilty' and that the accuser must be 'mixed up' or 'troubled'. It's the jumping to that conclusion first, before even countenancing the other possibility, and the damage that this does to the accuser in their community, that's hard to understand.

Innocent until proven guilty does not have to mean gaslighting the victim, and indeed, ignoring child protection measures.

It's incredibly damaging for a victim to see people who do not know the circumstances of the offending make wrongful assumptions about what took place. If someone has been betrayed, a continued further betrayal of this nature is crippling for their prospects of recovery.

And this was 2015, not 1975. It was happening at the very same time that the Royal Commission into Institutional Responses to Child Sexual Abuse was in the middle of its five-year process. Every day, institutions like (and in fact, including) St Kevin's – schools and sporting clubs too – were confessing to and atoning for their terrible histories of child sexual abuse. This sort of spectacular institutional betrayal was considered to be something in the past. It would never happen now. We had such robust child protection practices, in part informed by the Commission and, in Victoria, the parliamentary inquiry's *Betrayal of Trust* report.

As Paris Street's indomitable lawyer, Judy Courtin, would later say of the debacle: 'I mean, what planet are we on?'

Courtin points out that this was at the time when the Royal Commission was very much in the public focus. 'The knowledge was out there. These crimes were being exposed. The responses from the institutions such as St Kevin's were being exposed, they were horrific.

'Where's the lesson here? Nothing's been learned. Nothing has been learned.

'And all at the expense of someone like Paris. It's just shocking and appalling. Where are the words?'

And yet it happened. Paris Street's trust was betrayed. Paris Street was, in 2015, thrown under the bus. The support for the man he accused, and who would be convicted, was considerable.

Jo O'Brien was friendly with the St Kevin's cross-country coach, Brosie McCann, who would remain a great support to her son Ned. She rang McCann and told him what she knew. McCann made phone calls to inform the leadership of the school. He was no fan of Kehoe's. Jo thought that now that the management of the school was informed, it would reach out to her son to support him. That he would hear from the headmaster about such a significant matter. She was wrong. When Ned came home from school the following day, she says he had nothing to report.

'Oh, he just came home and said, "Mum, nobody spoke to me about what happened with Paris. I thought Mr Russell would have called me into his office and acknowledged what I did, but he didn't. I think I've done the wrong thing and I think I'm in big trouble,'" Jo remembers.

Both Ned and Jo felt, from that time onward, that his stocks had fallen at St Kevin's College. Stephen Russell denies that Ned and Paris weren't supported.

On 19 September, the president of SKAAC, Peter McGarry, had a conversation with the school's Dean of Sport, Luke Travers, who happened to be a long-time club member.

Records kept by the club and a letter to the school headmaster record the conversation. In it, it's alleged that Travers told McGarry about the Kehoe allegations, disclosing that there had been 'a previous incident in approximately 1986' involving Kehoe and a (then) young athlete who was coached by Kehoe. I will call him 'Douglas'. Douglas had left the club abruptly.

McGarry was taken aback, and immediately disclosed the conversation to two other committee members, including barrister Patrick Noonan.

Douglas' real name was reasonably common, and he was difficult to find. He was not a St Kevin's alumnus – he had been brought in to the club by Kehoe himself. But, eventually, Paris Street's lawyers were able to track him down.

A file note from the lawyer's conversation shows that Douglas said he did 'not have a bad word to say about Kehoe'. He said that Kehoe had been really good to him and had introduced him to classical music. He told the lawyer that he had known Kehoe since 1978.

Douglas told the lawyer that, when he was eighteen, in the early 1980s, he went on to share a house in Richmond in inner Melbourne with Kehoe, who would have been, by that stage, in his mid-to-late twenties. But then Douglas makes a rather large and glaring admission.

'K had obviously become attracted to him and asked him to have sex,' the file note says. Douglas said 'no' to Kehoe and, in his words, 'that was the end of it'.

The point is that this was a record of a person who was a teenager (although technically an adult), also younger than Kehoe, also coached by Kehoe, also clearly the subject of Kehoe's sexual attention.

Luke Travers hotly denies that he ever raised the subject of Douglas with McGarry.

But McGarry only joined the club in the 1990s, that is, long after Douglas had left. He had never heard Douglas' name before and, as he wrote to the school, 'Luke's mention of this incident was the first time that I had ever heard of that incident.' McGarry wrote that he had made further inquiries to try to determine who Douglas was. He even made further inquiries with Travers. He says Travers indicated to him that he 'did not know anything else about the incident'.

Peter Kehoe was charged by Victoria Police on 30 September 2014.

Caroline Redmond says that soon after, on 15 October, Luke Travers was again informed of details of the crime. Caroline Redmond told Travers in detail what had taken place with Paris.

'Everything,' Caroline says, 'I told him everything.'

'[H]e said to me, "Well, Peter says he didn't do anything,"' she says. 'And I said, like, "Well, he hasn't been charged with grooming and stalking because he didn't do anything. The police have got better things to do with their time than charge people just randomly for not doing anything."'

Despite Travers' long-term friendship with Kehoe, Caroline expected that he would now support her son, given what had taken place.

That's not what happened. Luke Travers, the Dean of Sport, would be a key supporter of Peter Kehoe's in his attempt to beat the charges and to rehabilitate his reputation. There is no suggestion that, at the time, Travers knew of or supported any illegal or abusive or grooming activity on the part of Kehoe. And there is no suggestion that, in providing evidence to the Court in Kehoe's trial, he in any way approved of the actions of which Kehoe was found guilty.

Two days after Caroline Redmond says she spoke to Luke Travers, he wrote an employment reference for Kehoe.

'I have known Peter Kehoe since 1975 and, in the nearly forty years since our first meeting, I have come to know Peter well in a variety of relationships and capacities and I am therefore able to make judgements regarding his qualities as a person and in the field of athletics,' Travers wrote.

The reference spoke of Peter's excellent history of coaching athletics and his string of achievements.

'Hallmarks of Peter's coaching are his commitment, enthusiasm, reliability, and his level of planning. In all of these areas, he is faultless,' Travers wrote.

He noted that Peter was a life member of the club and an inductee into its Hall of Fame. 'These honours indicate the high esteem and repute in which he is held in these communities.'

It is breathtaking to consider that the man he spoke of was, at the time, the subject of charges by police of grooming a teenage boy who had been one of Luke Travers' own students at an elite Catholic school which, in its public statements, prided itself on its protection of children. Travers denies that he knew at this point that Kehoe had been charged.

When I ask former SKAAC committee member and barrister Patrick Noonan what he makes of this unqualified endorsement of Kehoe if Caroline Redmond's recollection is correct, Noonan is deadpan.

'Well, I think that in the context, it certainly lacked some critical information that someone wanting to potentially employ Peter to work with children would have wanted to know,' Noonan replies. 'In that sense, it was potentially misleading to any employer.'

'That he was being accused of a child sex offence?' I counter.

'That is probably a relevant factor if you're employing someone to work with children, yes, you would think,' Noonan replies.

But later, once it's indisputable he definitely did know Kehoe was charged, some of his friends attached to the club then exchanged a series of bitter emails about the fact that the club wanted to expel Kehoe because of the charges.

I include this because it shows the lengths that people will go to, to protect someone who is accused of serious crimes against a child, rather than to demonstrate support for the vulnerable young person who has gone to police.

The criminal law might require that a person is 'innocent until proven guilty', but that is not, however, the standard applied to school or sporting settings, where a mandatory reporting regime means any whiff of a complaint must be reported and acted upon swiftly. This is how children are protected from further crimes, how they are protected from institutional cover-up, how their community avoids retraumatising them at an extremely vulnerable time through disbelief and lack of support.

Kehoe's supporters at the club included Ray Mooney who, incidentally, many decades before had been convicted of rape and jailed for eight years.

In the 1960s, Mooney had driven a woman to a clifftop, beaten her about the face, knocked her to the ground and twice raped her. He had for many years lived his life as a reformed man. He had been a playwright and university lecturer, who had written about progressive causes, such as prisoners' rights, and made many media appearances. On his Facebook page, he was vocal about issues around protecting victims of child sexual abuse. But in this case, he stood with the (then) alleged perpetrator, arguing that he should be stood down pending the case and have no contact with under-16 athletes, rather than expelled from the club.

'Whatever happened to "innocent until proven guilty"?' Mooney posted on Facebook.

'During my incarceration and upon my release I was 100% supported by SKAAC and proudly competed under her banner despite many offers to compete for other clubs,' he wrote.

Should someone be '100% supported' by a club when there were children in its care and the person had been charged with child sex offences?

'Today I'm ashamed to be associated with an organisation that denies a person of Peter's dedication and generosity to be treated as an equal.'

People can be dedicated and generous and they can also be groomers. In fact, it's clear that often the two go hand in hand. Groomers groom communities, not just children.

In a fairly restrained post, Patrick Noonan asked Mooney to take down his comments about Kehoe because they had been seen by a family member of one of the affected boys (that is, Paris and Ned).

At this stage Noonan was prepared to give Mooney the benefit of the doubt and said, 'it is clear from aspects of your post that you are not fully aware of the circumstances'.

He urged Mooney not to do anything that might 'inadvertently prove prejudicial'.

Mooney replied that the decision to expel Kehoe from the club was 'totally prejudicial to the case' and their 'approach to censorship is something from the middle ages'.

Kehoe himself began writing furious emails to the club too.

'There is no way that you could know anything about the case other than the bullshit that has been put out there by the other side [the "other side" being Paris and his family],' Kehoe wrote. 'That's why, as you should know, we have the system we do, where evidence is tested under cross-examination, and bullshit is shown to be what it is.'

'Bullshit' claims by a fifteen-year-old boy to whom he'd sent text message kisses, whom he told in writing, *'love you muchly'*, and had written of the boy's teacher *'that is certainly one head I wouldn't fuck'*. Travers would later admit in court that Paris Street's mother had told him all about the allegations that were read out to him.

Mooney described the SKAAC expulsion of Kehoe as a 'star chamber', saying, 'They've made fundamental legal and moral blunders and are now covering their arses.'

'I stand by [my comments] and have no problems defending them in any arena,' Mooney later wrote to me.

'If Paris felt traumatised by [my comments], then I'm not certain what I can say, other than I sympathise for his emotional and psychological trauma – and that's coming from someone who knows more about sexual abuse than most people on this planet,' he says, adding that he went to St Patrick's College Ballarat – a centre of clergy abuse in the town.

'I live with the "trauma" of never having had the guts to return and even the score,' he says of St Patrick's.

It is worth wondering whether Mooney would apply the same steely standards of innocent until proven guilty beyond reasonable doubt to the perpetrators at St Patrick's College with whom he wished to, as he says, 'even the score'. And just how tirelessly those men worked for their community, and indeed, how vigorously they were defended in courts of law.

Mooney told Patrick Noonan that he'd been advised that Noonan's comments bordered on 'professional misconduct' and had implied to the world that Peter Kehoe was guilty before he had been convicted of the crimes. 'I would be advised to speak to the Legal Services Commissioner to have it put before the Ethics Committee of the Victorian Bar Council,' Mooney said.

It is still hard to understand why friends, colleagues and acquaintances of people charged with or convicted of sexual crimes will so vehemently speak up to protect people who volunteered to train boys and young men at clubs and sporting associations only to groom them. Why choose this hill to die on?

After decades of bitter history laid bare in its *Betrayal of Trust* report, Victoria has an extremely strict child safety regulatory regime.

As the Kehoe issue was taking place at the club, the state was in the process of passing through its parliament strict legislation which would make it a criminal offence for people within an institution (and this included a sporting club) to fail to protect children.

Under the child safety protocols governed by the Commissioner for Children and Young People, organisations must now also show their commitment to risk management and fulfil multiple requirements to demonstrate that they are doing so. Their approach is supposed to be 'child-centred'.

Patrick Noonan had an understanding of these processes, as he had acted in the child abuse Royal Commission. He knew that a commitment to the safety and protection of the children who trained with the club – including, but not limited to, Paris – was paramount. But furthermore, he knew that it was the right thing to do. To say that for doing this, he should be reported to the Legal Services Commissioner, was really quite something. Needless to say, Noonan never heard from the Legal Services Commissioner. And, after Kehoe was convicted, neither he nor the club heard from Mooney. Mooney confirms to me now that he never actually went through with his threat to report Noonan – that the course of action was advised to him by a 'prominent' lawyer, but he eventually decided not to proceed with that advice.

Mooney says he was the one who recommended that Kehoe hire Robert Richter to defend him against Paris Street's allegations because 'Richter was the go-to lawyer police used'. It is his understanding that Kehoe, a retiree who lived in modest rental premises and did not own property, paid for Richter and he was 'not cheap, I promise you'. He says Richter's fee was even more than what Kehoe had had to pay Paris Street in Paris' later civil claim against Kehoe and the school.

I ask Mooney whether he now regrets his defence of Kehoe, given what has transpired.

'I'm aware that whatever answer I give it's an argument that I'm never going to "win" given his conviction,' Mooney writes to me. 'It's important for you to know that from the outset I asked him what happened – he never denied the inappropriate remarks, but denied his intention was in grooming Paris,' he says, adding that grooming was a relatively new offence at the time. He later asked me to apologise to Paris on his behalf. It seemed that since we first corresponded he'd been dwelling on the hurt his correspondence to the club about Kehoe might have caused. He was 'saddened' to think about this. He wished Paris well for the future.

There was no contrition in Peter Kehoe's correspondence to the club. He was on the warpath in his efforts to defend himself against those charges. His group emails to club members made arcane submissions about the precise contents of the club's constitution, urging members to vote down the proposal to expel him. It's quite an extraordinary insight into the self-belief of the man, and the unwavering support of those around him who chose to side with him over a teenage boy and the safety of other children at the club.

One of those who weighed in was Luke Travers, who wasn't just subject to one child safety protocol – the club's – but also the protocol covering the school, which was responsible for the care of students like Paris and Ned. Travers advised Kehoe that if he hadn't been given written notice of the expulsion then the club was unable to expel him. 'They have not acted in accordance with the rules of the Club,' he declared.

How the rules of an amateur athletics club could trump the rules that govern institutions around child protection is mystifying.

Travers did advise Kehoe to voluntarily relinquish membership until the case had 'settled'. His assumption seemed to be that the court case would go Kehoe's way.

'I would have thought that I would be given a second chance,' Kehoe said. A second chance at what?

Paris Street says he had decided to leave St Kevin's for a time during this incident and the lead-up to the court case, taking a scholarship at Trinity Grammar. He remained there for about six months, before returning to the more familiar environment of St Kevin's.

Paris Street says he heard nothing from St Kevin's from the moment that police charged Kehoe at the end of September, until the court case the following April.

* * *

In April 2015, Peter Kehoe's trial began in the Melbourne Magistrates' Court.

It was a closed court because the victim, Paris, was only fifteen. Paris was the primary witness, and Ned O'Brien would also give evidence for him.

The morning that Jo O'Brien was packing her boy off to court, she received a phone call from a member of St Kevin's administrative staff wanting to know why Ned wasn't at school.

'I said, "Well why don't you go and ask Mr Russell?"' Jo remembers. 'He knows where Ned is right now.'

Jo put down the phone and several minutes later, it rang again. The St Kevin's headmaster, Stephen Russell, wanted to speak to her.

She says when Russell got on the phone, he distanced himself from Paris Street, emphasising that Paris was a former student of the school. It's worth noting that Paris' twin brother was still at St Kevin's. And, she says, he also distanced himself from Peter Kehoe, who was just 'a former athletics coach of the school'.

Jo O'Brien narrowed her eyes at this comment.

'But I know for a fact that Kehoe had been coaching there for thirty-eight years,' Jo says. She says that one morning, at cross country, the pair were chatting, and Kehoe had introduced her to Russell.

'I would say that Mr Russell was distancing himself, sweeping things under the rug.'

Her suspicions were aroused even further when Stephen Russell asked if Ned would be wearing his school uniform to court.

'I thought, "Wow, you really do want to cover this up,"' Jo says. '"You really do want to keep this quiet."'

Caroline Redmond had also heard nothing from the school until not too long before the court case. This time, it was a woman who was at the time a senior member of staff. Caroline says she asked if she had a court case coming up and wanted to know if Caroline wanted counselling for Paris' twin brother at school.

'And I said, "No, well [his twin is] not actually going to court."' Caroline says she told the woman, adding that her other son didn't need counselling.

Caroline couldn't believe that the woman was asking about her other son, and not the boy, Paris, who had actually made the allegations. She said she was 'surprised' the woman didn't know about the case because 'Luke Travers knows all about it'.

She was taken aback by what she says the woman told her next. 'She said, "Well, you've got no comeback over this."' I ask Caroline what she took this to mean.

'Well, to be honest, suing, I would think that's what she meant … It was really inappropriate – because it wasn't even something that crossed my mind at the time.

'I had no intention of having any comeback towards them except having support … It wasn't on my wavelength to think about any comeback really. I was just managing a child who was unwell.'

Sometimes, in this journalism job, you grow accustomed to a story when you have been working on it for a long time. But each time I come back to the long list of individual failures in Paris Street's case, it's no less shocking than the last. How did this happen?

* * *

In preparation for giving evidence in the trial of Peter Kehoe, the police informant, Lauren Richards, came over to Paris Street's house to hand him some court paperwork. Clipped to the documents was a five dollar note – which is always given to witnesses so they can get to court by public transport. Paris put it in his back pocket.

On another occasion, Paris was also introduced to the police prosecutor. The prosecutor had shown him what Paris describes as a sort of diorama of the structure of the court. Little figurines showed where everyone sat. The man ran through the basic mechanics of how a case works.

On the day of the hearing, Paris was ushered up into the remote witness facility. The facility was across the road from the Magistrates' Court where the trial would take place. Paris remembers children's drawings on the walls and seeing other families supporting other kids.

'I just wanted to get in there and get out,' he says. 'I didn't really want to talk to any other family who was in there or socialise with people.'

Ned O'Brien was sent up there too, as he was to give evidence. The two boys waited and waited in that cheerless room as the hearing was delayed with a bail application from a previous matter.

Paris doodled aimlessly on a whiteboard. Ned played on his phone.

Ned took a selfie of the two of them at one point, which the boys sent to Finley Tobin. Ned looks so young. His hair is gelled to the side in a very 'nice' way that looks like Jo fixed it for him that morning for his day in court. He's in the foreground and his eyes sparkle in that playful, unwearied way teenage boys' eyes do. He's wearing a cheeky but endearing grin.

Paris is in the background, leaning back on a chair. He's wearing a blue shirt. He is very pale. His face is thin. He has big dark circles under his eyes. The corners of his mouth are turned up, but it's more of a grimace than a smile. It reminds me of the sort of photo you see of a cancer patient when you go to visit them in hospital. They smile dutifully for the camera, but their eyes look right through you.

Paris just planned to tell the truth that day. And once he had done that, they would be finished with him and, he believed that on the strength of the evidence, Kehoe would be convicted.

'All that's on my mind is "How the hell can this guy even plead not guilty? How is that possible?"' Paris remembers.

'In my head, I'm just, one hundred per cent, "You've just completely wronged me and so what is all this about?" I didn't get it at that point.'

While Paris and I are very different people, I can relate to him at that age. An A-grade student and an A-type personality, the type who would shoot up his or her hand to answer a question in class. A nice kid at a good Catholic school who came from a decent family where things had gone fairly well in life to that point. Paris thought that if you just did the right thing in this world, if you told the truth, things would go as they ought to. Justice would be done.

Paris was coming forward only because he wanted to protect other kids. He was fairly certain he knew what Kehoe was capable of, and he wanted to stop that happening to any other boy. He wasn't looking forward to talking about it again, in court, but essentially, he thought he was doing a good turn. He thought that he might be asked a few questions. That it would be over with reasonably soon.

'I didn't want to have to prepare to justify what I know happened. I didn't want to have to think about it,' Paris says. 'I only wanted to say what happened like I did in the police [interview]. Regardless of who cross-examined me, I just wanted to get in and out.'

He had no idea what was really about to happen – when he entered the remote witness room, the screen snapped on and there was Robert Richter QC.

No one told Paris what Richter would be like. Paris had discovered he was the defence counsel shortly beforehand and remembers the witness liaison people being impressed that Kehoe was to have a QC of his standing.

'I remember when they first mentioned that there was a QC defending him, and I didn't know what that was,' Paris says.

He detected some excitement in the room that it was to be Richter. He remembers looking up Richter's profile on the Victorian Bar website. He remembers discovering that Richter had successfully defended Mick Gatto in an underworld trial.

No QC, nor any solicitor, gave Paris Street encouraging tips on how to handle himself. No one described to Paris the style of cross-examination he could expect.

'I had no idea, no idea. I thought it was going to be, like, easy-going – relaxed,' he tells me.

He says people from the witness support service were very sympathetic during the breaks in cross-examination. But by the time they got to him, the damage was already done.

Magistrates' Court proceedings like this one are not typically transcribed. So when Paris Street applied to the court for a copy of his evidence, all that was available was an audio recording. Accordingly, the first introduction I had to Robert Richter's cross-examination of Paris was not the barrister's words, typed out, but his voice. His tone.

I was aghast to discover that the tone he employed with this fifteen-year-old schoolboy sounded incredibly similar to the tone he employed with me. Sarcastic, belittling, disbelieving, derisive. It rarely changed. And in that first morning, everything that Paris Street had come to understand about the world disintegrated.

The first thing that occurred to Paris when that screen snapped on was that he thought that Richter looked like his perpetrator. That threw him.

Richter went in hard, straight out of the blocks.

'Paris, um, you understand that in the current climate, to call someone a paedophile is, ah, about as nasty a name as you can put to someone?'

Subtext: *Naughty boy. Tarnishing this good man's name.*

The only thing worse than calling someone a paedophile, one might think, is being the victim of one.

Richter would try to imply that Paris was conflating this innocent man's behaviour with rumours that the barrister pushed Paris to admit he'd heard at St Kevin's in light of the Royal Commission, which was taking place at the time. But Paris, a year nine student from a generation that didn't really read newspapers, watched television on demand and got snippets of news here and there from social media, didn't know what he was talking about, saying he didn't hear 'any of that'.

'Never? Not a word?'

'Never.'

Richter's demeanour, just as it was with me, was sceptical and scolding, exasperated at this boy, coming before this court to waste its time by besmirching his client's good name. He frequently raised his voice: '*When?*' '*Why?*' 'You *did*, did you?' '*You just made that up!*' '*No, no, no!*'

He asked questions until he pigeonholed Paris into answering in the affirmative, and then, would say, with a note of mild irritation in his voice, 'Right. Thank you.'

When, for instance, he asked Paris about typing up what had happened to him for his parents and police, Richter employed the exact same strategy he did with me – asking Paris if he was to examine the metadata, would it show it hadn't been altered? Paris, to his credit, didn't blanch.

He frequently tried to verbal Paris, to put words in the teenager's mouth. He laughed when referring to some of the evidence of Kehoe's disgusting comments that Paris was there to complain of.

'I remember when he was speaking and cross-examining me, it's like, they weren't questions, they were very twisted statements to try and get a final response out of me,' Paris tells me.

'[Y]ou thought he was just joking on the fourth of September when you went to his house,' Richter, for instance, insisted to Paris during the cross-examination.

'You thought he was just joking! Can I suggest this to you?' (Paris: 'No.')

'Can I suggest to you that whatever happened in the house, you thought "This is a joke"? That's what you thought.'

Paris didn't. 'I thought what he was doing was wrong,' he said.

Richter wanted to know why Paris didn't then ask, 'Why are you saying these things?'

'I was scared,' Paris began.

'Scared of *what*?' Richter countered, incredulous.

'Scared of Peter.'

'What do you mean, "scared of Peter"? What would he do to you?' Richter returned.

'It's like I was just punching back, and his words were the gloves and my brain was the bag,' Paris now remembers of the style of questioning.

'At the time, in my mind, from like, the very first question he asked me, like, it's almost like Richter wanted me to rethink what I already know and challenge my own knowledge, so he could break me,' Paris says.

'That's what it felt like he was trying to do. And if he didn't get it at that point, he'd already prepared for that, for the next one.'

Paris tried to explain to Richter that the reason he was scared was he wasn't sure what Peter might do. Richter mocked that, pointing out that Paris was fifteen and taller than Kehoe, 'pretty strong, right?'.

'Whaddya mean you were scared of what he would do?'

'I-I was scared. I- didn't …' Paris stuttered. 'I was, it was just, suddenly, happened. And I didn't know what to do.'

'*Oh* no,' Richter replied, by this time his tone was deeply sarcastic. He then said that in Paris' police interview, Paris had said that he didn't want to query Kehoe about the comments he had made 'because of course he would deny being a paedophile'.

'That's, that's what you said in your … statement, isn't it?' (Paris: 'Yes.')

'Well, that's very, very different from saying "I was *scared*", isn't it? You see the difference?'

Paris was confused, he remembered he must have said something like that he was scared to the police. He *was* scared.

'Look, why didn't you say that to the police?' Richter pressed.

'I did say to the police that I was scared.'

'Look, you didn't say to the police that you were scared at the *time*! What you said to them is you didn't ask him if he was joking,' Richter said, raising his voice. 'Because you said to yourself, "Well, if he's a paedophile, of course he'd say he wasn't."

'That's what you said to the police! Correct? [Paris: 'I can't remember.'] Well, it's in the transcript and that's the way you said it to the police. Were you trying to tell the truth? *Then?* [Paris: 'Yes'.]

'Okay, so the reason you didn't ask him "Are you joking?" is because you thought he'd say, "Of course I'm joking! Don't be silly! I'm not a paedophile!" That's the actual reason you didn't ask him if he was joking?'

'Ye-s,' the teenager answered, confused and somewhat cowed.

This is a skewed way of interpreting Paris' police interview. Paris is asked by police to go over the incident at Kehoe's house several times. Each time he describes it, he says that he was feeling 'really just unpleasant', that he 'thought "this isn't right"', that he thought, 'what's wrong with this person?', that 'there's something going on here', that it was 'a bit weird', that he felt 'really uncomfortable', that he 'just wanted to go', that he 'didn't wanna be around him any more', that he 'didn't know if he was dangerous or what he was going to do, because [he] knew of child predators and people like that', that he 'didn't want anything to happen', that he 'thought it was along the lines of [paedophilia]'.

Paris told police he thought that Kehoe was 'genuinely trying' to 'do what like, a child predator does'.

'I thought he was trying to make me do what he said,' Paris said in the police interview, 'Like, suck his – well, well, his cock.

'He wasn't joking about it, and I felt just uncomfortable and powerless,' Paris told the detectives.

He then explained further to the officers that if he asked Kehoe about it, Kehoe would say he was joking, that he wouldn't just say he was a paedophile. And so he, Paris, 'didn't really have any, anything to say'.

When police asked Paris why Kehoe wasn't his coach anymore, Paris replied: 'Because I'm just scared to go … to be around him and I'm also scared for others that – what he could do and what he might have done before …

'I'm scared just 'cause he might take things further with – in terms of sexual behaviour and – yeah. I'm just scared that he might do anything like that.'

It is clear from reading the police interview that the Richter characterisation of Paris Street's feelings and his motivations is distorted. But, because of the hectoring way he asked it, Paris answered 'yes'.

Paris Street did not at that point give his best evidence – that is, he was hectored into giving an inaccurate response. Paris Street's answer wasn't exactly true.

Richter also tried to imply that Paris couldn't have been scared, because he didn't go home and tell his mum that night, because he still had plans, at that stage, to train with Kehoe.

'Why?' Richter asked, again raising his voice.

'I- didn't decide to,' Paris said, sounding uncomfortable.

'No, no, no, no, no, that's not a reason!'

Again, this is unfair. He did tell his friend Ned O'Brien the next day. And he told his mother very soon after. And he never trained with Kehoe again. Given that, at the precise time Richter was asking these questions, the Royal Commission was hearing stories

of how many child victims took decades to come forward, a matter
of a day or two seemed completely immaterial. A child was still
formulating in his mind what to do about something that made
him very uncomfortable and concerned.

'You couldn't have been scared,' Richter pressed.

'I was scared.'

'*How*? If you were scared, you wouldn't say, "I'm going to train
with him on Tuesday." Would you?'

'Truthfully, I was scared.'

One of the things that Paris found most disconcerting about the
cross-examination was how Richter laughed when he was talking
about things that made Paris feel sick. Paris much later wrote
about this in his letter to Richter, saying that he would never forget
Richter's 'scornful laughter'.

'And he was saying he was a cutie, right? [Paris: 'Yes.'] And he
was saying,' Richter laughed, '"I should have put my hand on his
bum!" He was telling you,' Richter continued, his voice breaking
with mirth, 'that that'd really rub the Christian Brothers in a funny
way! Wasn't he? In relation to the Christian Brothers? That would
have really sent them spare! Ha!'

'Could you repeat that?' Paris managed.

'Ye-s!' Richter chuckled. 'When he was saying, "I should've
put my hand on his bum," he was saying, "That would've really
sent those Brothers up!"' Richter forced out the words between
sniggers.

The magistrate would later comprehensively find that this
wasn't what Kehoe was implying.

But even at its most timid interpretation, the one that Richter
was trying to spin – *those crazy kiddy-fiddling Christian Brothers,
that would've really sent them up the wall* – it's still an unbelievably
inappropriate thing for Kehoe to have joked about with a fifteen-
year-old in his care, in his home. It doesn't bear scrutiny and it
isn't remotely funny. It's not something a QC should be laughing at
when cross-examining a teenager.

'He never proposed to you that you commit a sexual offence
with him, did he? Never? In all fairness? ['No.'] And he took a
fatherly interest in your wellbeing, you agree with that, don't you?
['Yes.'] To the point where he said, "I love you." Right? ['Yes.']

Whenever he said I love you, it was in the context of a fatherly interest, I suggest to you. He was not asking you to reciprocate by saying "I love you too" or to do anything about it?'

'It could have been but I'm not sure,' Paris replied.

In fairness to Richter, this 'fatherly' madness was an instruction from his client – it was something Kehoe himself had argued in his own evidence. I have spoken to many defence counsel who say you must bring the case that your client instructs.

But, as I read it, I wondered what sort of creepy father would text to his son, in capital letters '*OH GOODY GOODY GOODY*', or talk about wet t-shirt competitions, or about having him with peanut butter, or sign off with multiple kisses.

But what was so apparent when I listened to the recording was the tone that Richter employed throughout the cross-examination. As if the teenager in front of him is either a delusional idiot or a conniving fraud. The 'you *did*, did you?' What came across as the bored but sceptical, '*Yes?*' What came across as the mocking tone when he repeatedly doubted that Paris was scared.

Paris tells me his impression was that Richter would do whatever it took to get an acquittal for his client. He felt terribly alone.

'And being in a closed court, the only people who could hear it were me, the magistrate, the prosecutor and, like, Kehoe.

'And [Kehoe] was probably laughing at it. He was probably, like, "High five, this guy is going to get me off."'

As the day wore on, you could hear in Paris Street's voice an increasing adolescent sullenness in tone. His answers became very short and clipped. That's not the sort of person Paris is at all. But he felt cornered and totally confused about what was happening to him. As his defence mechanisms started to kick in, he became monosyllabic. As Bernie from the ABC documentary *Revelation* said, it's that sense of '*I'm not the villain*'. It's that feeling in the person who is coming before that court to complain of these ugly things that happened to them, only to be belittled and doubted and scorned.

I see an unusual venom in Paris, who is normally assiduously polite and reasonable, as he remembers this.

'I just wanted to SHOUT at him,' Paris tells me. 'I just wanted to shout "Who the *FUCK* ...?"

'I just wanted to, but I knew that I couldn't because I'm in this really formal environment and I've just been told by a magistrate, do I understand what's going to happen here?

'No! I don't prepare myself for this kind of stuff.

'It's like, in my head, [I'm] like, "I know exactly what happened and how I felt at that exact time. Nothing can change that. Not even a QC. I don't care if it's a QC or if you've gotten all these people off beforehand"...

'I probably should have been thinking, "This is a courageous thing to do, you've come all this way." But instead, I was completely *broken* after that first day. My whole shirt was just covered in sweat. Not my armpits, my whole shirt.'

Paris didn't understand why the barrage of questions had to be so unrelenting, delivered with such scorn. And why would he? No one had explained to him that this was going to take place.

The police prosecutor – notionally grossly out-matched by one of the most senior and bombastic criminal silks in the country – made a good fist of intervening. He was helped by the evidence – particularly the Facebook messages – which was overwhelmingly stacked against the accused and would ultimately lead to Kehoe's conviction. The magistrate intervened at times too.

But when it came to how Paris Street was treated by the defence counsel, as with every complainant of this sort of crime, essentially, no one was fighting in his corner. He wondered why Richter couldn't show some form of understanding of what he was going through.

'Just have *some* form of human sympathy,' Paris tells me he wanted to say to Richter, his eyes widening sharply. 'Like, or empathy? "You've been a child yourself."'

And that's the thing that, as I listen to the audio of the Kehoe case, I keep thinking. Paris was, at law, a child. The cross-examination would go for two days. I thought about how mine had gone for one and how completely spent I was after that one day.

How can we allow a teenager to be spoken to like this, without warning or assistance about how to manage it? Paris didn't have Jack Rush QC or Peter Morrissey SC or Sarala Fitzgerald, Kathryn Wilson or Hugh Bennett. He had a run-through of the mechanics of the proceedings, a diorama and a five-dollar note to get him to court. He had, in the witness assistance program, someone to hand him tissues when he got upset. But he did not have any legal agency in this process.

'Up to that point, I was like, "I really want to tell my story,"' Paris says. 'But then when he was cross-examining me, I was like, "Far out, why have I done this?"'

'It was the most painful thing. Mentally and physically. I was physically like, exhausted. I don't think I ate over two days. Sweating. I looked so tired.'

The first time the magistrate asked if he wanted a break, Paris replied that he would.

'And as soon as the screen turned off, I just bawled my eyes out. Just absolutely like, cried,' Paris remembers. 'This is like, in the time frame that I'm meant to be collecting myself and having a break and I'm just bawling my eyes out.'

'Paris was fifteen at the time,' says Dr Judy Courtin. 'Now to be cross-examined by Mr Richter is a gruelling experience for anyone, but a child who had been sexually abused and not being supported by his school, that's quite a remarkable experience and can be potentially a devastating experience.'

At the time, Paris opted not to write a victim impact statement. He was just too spent.

'I had little energy to write,' he tells me now, 'let alone think about the impact the crime had on me.'

It's a decision he now regrets. 'I could have written a victim impact statement on the cross-examination alone.'

So, five years down the track, still psychologically smarting from that process, Paris Street wrote to Robert Richter, more or less to get his feelings down. He agreed to share it with me for this book because he wanted not just Richter to see it, but every defence counsel in a sexual case, especially where the complainant is a child. He wanted every person involved in the court system to know what it's like to be a kid like him, subjected to that barrage. He wanted it because he, like every person I have spoken to who has gone through this unrelenting system, hopes for change.

'Hello Robert

'*Unfortunately, I won't forget you. Your face on the screen in the remote child witness facility room when it first switched*

on, I will never forget that. Your scornful laughter when I was
being cross-examined by you, I will never forget that either.
The rest breaks from your cross-examination that I had spent
crying, I won't forget those. Your ridicule towards me, the re-
traumatisation of me and the psychological pain you caused me, I
just can't forget that.

'*At the beginning of your second day of cross-examination, the*
first words you said to me were: "Paris, I won't be very long. It
can't be easy for you."'

Pausing here for a moment, it's true that Richter did say those
words. They are pretty much the only time over the two days of
cross-examination that he paid lip service to Paris Street's anguish.
Paris continued:

'*Had it not been for your vain and condescending, brutal and*
dictator-like cross-examination of me, I would have appreciated
this.

'*To contextualise this letter for you, I was fifteen years old*
when you cross-examined me at Peter Kehoe's trial. Seven
months before that trial, Peter Kehoe had driven me to his home,
pointed at boys in his year level at St Kevin's who had committed
suicide, told me he thought their suicide had "something to do
with the Christian Brothers", shown me to his bedroom, said I
could jump in [to his bed] whenever I want, told me he had an
erection at training two days earlier, told me he had pre-cummed,
asked whether I knew what pre cum was, told me that it was the
premature stages of ejaculation and told me I could lick it off
whenever I like. You defended the grooming charges of Peter
Kehoe and cross-examined me over two days. Those two days
opened a healing wound in my mind.

'*Your cross-examination of me was a cognitive annihilation of*
my fifteen-year-old brain. On the first day of cross-examination
and after I had told you that, at the time he coached me, I didn't
suspect anything you responded:

'"*Yeah, well, we are talking about at the time, we're not talking*
about what you put together in your head afterwards."

'*Deplorable, heartless.*

'*Shortly after this, I told you I did not tell the police that*
Peter Kehoe had asked me to delete Facebook messages because

I couldn't remember to do so off of the top of my head, and you responded:

"Yeah, you just made that up, didn't you?"

'I am unsure whether a question in a cross-examination of a fifteen-year-old can be more tactless than this. You are a Queen's Counsel barrister.

'I live with a scar in my mind from your cross-examination.

'It couldn't have been easy for me, Robert, could it have been?'

Paris Street vividly remembers the sick feeling, sitting in the passenger seat of his mother's Lexus, as she drove him home from that first day of his evidence. A song was playing on the car radio – 'King', by Years and Years. And every time Paris hears its dancey beat and its lyrics now – about being a king 'under your control', and asking to be 'let go' – he's catapulted back into that Lexus and how awful he felt after that day.

Because the day had been so relentlessly adversarial, and he had been so comprehensively doubted, and even though, in fact, he had stood his ground and had been an excellent witness, he had come to doubt himself and wonder if he had squandered his evidence.

'[I was thinking] could this guy get off because someone has the ability to shape questions in a way that distorts?' he tells me.

'When I got home after the first day of being cross-examined, I just smashed my ... was kicking my door.'

Then he cried into his pillow.

Fifteen-year-old Paris did what fifteen-year-old boys do when they don't know how to express their rage. He began to punch and elbow the walls in his bedroom. Later, as he would be betrayed by the school he had loved, he punched and elbowed some more.

'I mean ...' he trails off as he remembers. 'The holes in my wall aren't fixed yet.'

The bedroom door has recently been repaired. But alongside the flags and the trophies for his running, behind whiteboards and his desk, the punch holes in his bedroom wall remain as Paris Street's grim testament to what happened to him.

Paris sent his letter to Robert Richter in August 2020. Richter replied promptly, saying he was sorry to have caused Paris 'distress', but, he added, 'alas it came with the territory which was that I had a job to do which I did based on instructions'.

'That,' he declared, 'is what a barrister does.'

'It may not comfort you to know that I have known people – my family included – who have been through trauma and suffering unimaginably greater than you can imagine and have made up their mind to construct a life on the basis that they were not responsible for suffering inflicted on them and needed to live on and make a life in the best way they could knowing they were innocent,' Richter wrote.

Paris was horrified when Richter urged him to do 'the same, rather than construct a life based on the proposition that you are no more than a victim'. When did he ever do that? What did Richter know about Paris' life?

Richter reminded him that the criminal justice system does not start with the presumption that 'a complainant IS a victim' because it would be a reversal of our system of justice. He added that Paris' victim status had been 'upheld by the court' and said 'all I can do is to urge you to gather whatever strength of character you have to make something of your life rather than to define yourself as a victim and as someone with no agency over your future'.

'I wish you good luck,' he said, signing off the email with a PS complaining that he had been 'falsely accused' in the media of being a 'monster' and it had been inaccurately reported that he had tormented Paris for '4 days'.

The email was sent six months after 'Boys Club', a *Four Corners* story we broadcast on St Kevin's and Paris Street. It never accused Richter of being a monster, nor anything remotely similar. Nor indeed did it say that Paris was cross-examined for four days.

Paris Street isn't defined by his victimhood. And according to hundreds of people who wrote to and about him after the program went to air, with just some of their responses compiled for him into a 72-page booklet by a kind viewer, he is 'courageous', 'impressive', 'remarkable', 'gutsy', 'articulate', 'forthright', 'all class', 'compelling', 'an inspiration', demonstrates 'moral clarity', is 'a legend'. And, so often, 'a hero'. Paris Street is, they said, a hero.

At first blush, Robert Richter's letter to Paris Street made my heart sink and Paris Street's blood boil. But then, as I scanned through it again, it just crystallised in seven crisp paragraphs all of the reasons why this book needed to be written.

* * *

Ned O'Brien was still a very small kid at the time of the trial. He had an impishly amiable quality – just one of those kids you are instantly drawn to. Even though he got some facts mixed up in the heat of the moment, he had his moments where he bested Robert Richter.

'It was pretty surreal,' he says of his cross-examination by the most feared QC at the Victorian Bar.

Ned's mother, Jo, was very stressed at the time, but she now chuckles at her son's mental toughness. As we're sitting in her kitchen, she mimics Ned's still childish voice giving it up to the silk, exaggerating the squeakiness in his voice for full comic effect.

'I was so proud of him,' she tells me, still giggling a bit, but her eyes shining with love for her boy. Ned watches on from the corner, a bit bashful.

When Richter implied that the reason Paris had gone to him to disclose what Kehoe had done was because Paris 'wasn't sure whether Peter was serious or not', little Ned O'Brien piped up immediately.

'Joke or not, sir, that's inappropriate to say to an underage person.'

'Go Ned O'Brien,' I thought.

The magistrate chuckled at the feisty kid in her midst. Richter adopted a patronising jokey tone.

'*Very* good! They teach you *well* at St Kevin's!' he said, then changed his tone. 'It may have been inappropriate,' he continued, 'but Paris was uncertain as to whether Peter was serious.'

'I sort of feel like he tried to put a lot of words in my mouth,' Ned remembers, 'and I had to constantly make sure that I was saying what I wanted to say and what I believed.'

Richter tried to trip Ned up on, for instance, the fact that he had written down that Paris had said Kehoe talked about how he had 'pre-ejaculated', which later changed in Ned's police statement to 'pre-cummed'.

It was to become one of those Richter specials in which he bamboozles the witness with gross sexual detail, trying to mine the evidence for an inconsistency.

'Do you know what ejaculation is?' Richter asked.

'Yes, sir,' Ned said, softly, with a note of sourness.

'Do you know what cum is?'

'Yes. Sir.'

'So, were you reporting what Peter had – what Paris had told you, or, what?'

'Yes, I was reporting what Paris told me.'

'Paris used the word pre-ejaculated to you?' Richter continued, sceptically, and the way he said it, you could almost *hear* his eyes narrowing.

'One or the other, sir, I don't think that really matters,' Ned countered. Go Ned.

Richter pressed that Paris must have said 'pre-ejaculated', Ned said he believed that Paris said 'pre-cummed' and that he couldn't remember that fine detail when he wrote it down.

'Well if you couldn't remember it that soon afterwards, how come you remember it now?'

'Because I'm thinking back on it now, sir.'

'*Are* you?' Richter sneered.

'Yes,' Ned deadpanned in return.

Richter comes across, during this exchange, not as brutal as he was with Paris, but he still comes across as sceptical, patronising, sarcastic. And, the thing that struck me was how horrible this sounds – this raking over disgusting detail about ejaculate versus cum – the same way he'd raked over the anatomy of the anal canal with me – when it is a young boy answering him. When it is a young boy sticking up for himself. Yes, this subject matter was not pretty. But when combined with the tone he employed, it takes on a bullying edge.

The most surprising parts of the trial wouldn't be from Ned O'Brien's evidence though.

They would come courtesy of Paris Street's discovery that St Kevin's Dean of Sport, Luke Travers, had taken a day of leave from his teaching duties to go and give character evidence for Kehoe.

In his evidence, he described Peter Kehoe as an old friend, a 'very charming person', and 'very reliable'. He said there had never, to his knowledge, been a complaint about Kehoe, the charges were completely out of character.

'I've never had someone come up to me – a parent come up to me and complain about, you know, something inappropriate,' Travers told the court. 'If anything, I've had people who have spoken wonderfully about ... what he has done for them.'

But what is extraordinary is Travers' response, in light of the seniority of his teaching role at St Kevin's at the time, when asked about the messages Kehoe sent to Paris.

'Would you accept that as a teacher it would be inappropriate to send a Facebook message to a student with words of "I love you", or something similar to that?' the police prosecutor asked Travers.

'It depends upon the context,' was Travers' somewhat jaw-dropping reply.

When asked what about a message with a love heart, he reiterated that, again, 'I guess you have to contextualise it, I suppose.'

'What about,' the prosecutor continued, 'x's – you know, kiss, kiss, kiss, kiss?'

'Same as before – depends upon the context.'

The Magistrate, Michelle Ehrlich, intervened at several points, asking if Travers would send a message saying, 'I love you', 'full-stop'.

Travers responded that he personally wouldn't, but 'as I say, I could, in the right context, see it as appropriate, but I wouldn't do it myself, no, and certainly not to a student and not to a male student, no'.

It's hard to imagine what on earth the context would be in which it was okay to send kisses, love hearts, 'I love you' to a student.

'There can be no other interpretation,' Judy Courtin, who would later bring a civil action on Paris' behalf, would say. 'I'm sorry, there is only one context – and that is of a sex offender grooming a child.'

When Magistrate Ehrlich asked why Travers wouldn't personally send such a message, Travers' first response wasn't about appropriate conduct with a child, or child safety. It was about homophobia.

'Oh, well, the connotation of perhaps being, um, can I use the word "gay"?' he began. 'I suppose, you know, being a bit homophobic, I suppose, in that respect.'

When the prosecutor asked Travers if he would send messages with a 'sexual connotation', Travers replied that he would not. He conceded that it would be completely inappropriate, agreed with the prosecutor's assertion that there was no professional or personal reason to do it.

Was there *any* reason, as a teacher or a coach? Travers replied 'well, certainly as a teacher, no'. The magistrate clarified whether this extended to a coach.

'Ummm …' was Travers' reply.

'Jesus Christ, this is absurd!' Richter said.

I'm not sure whether it is Richter's customary courtroom etiquette to speak in that way, but when the magistrate replied that 'you called' Travers, Richter said 'sorry'.

Travers, meanwhile, continued to prevaricate, saying sometimes that it was not appropriate to act in this way towards a junior athlete, but then continuing to insist that it depended upon the context and the relationship. He saw no problem with inviting a student back to his place to look at yearbooks and deemed it 'appropriate'.

As for inviting a student to jump in his bed, Travers said it was something he 'wouldn't do' – 'I'm not necessarily saying it's appropriate'.

The magistrate intervened and asked Travers if he had seen any of the detail of the allegations against Kehoe. Travers replied that he hadn't and he 'only [knew] the charge'.

'Do you know any of the specifics?' the magistrate pressed.

'Um, no,' Travers replied.

'Not even one?'

'I only know what the mother has claimed happened, so that's my only knowledge of the very specific details of the case,' he said.

But later in his evidence, when he was read the details of some of the messages by the prosecutor, Travers volunteered, of his own volition, that he actually did know.

'I can say pretty much what has been read to me is what was said to me by Paris' mother, so I am aware of the content, so it didn't come as a surprise to me what was said.'

'What do you mean?' Magistrate Ehrlich asked him.

'Oh, well, certainly what was said to me almost word for word is what Paris' mother informed me of.'

Importantly, Travers was admitting here that he knew of what Paris' mother had told him, she says *before* he wrote an employment reference for Peter Kehoe. He knew it before he decided to get up and give this evidence in support of him. One of the most senior teachers at St Kevin's College knew all of this, he admitted on oath, but chose to give evidence for his old friend Kehoe, instead of a fifteen-year-old student.

'I was a student at the school and to have someone personally and professionally endorse him and support him, as I read in the emails and as I heard in Luke Travers' evidence in court, supporting him, yeah, it makes you feel betrayed,' Paris Street told me.

Robert Richter's best efforts on behalf of Peter Kehoe came to nothing. Magistrate Ehrlich found Kehoe guilty of grooming.

'I have no hesitation that Paris was a credible and reliable witness,' Magistrate Ehrlich found. 'He was honest and had a clear memory of events. His account was consistent with the tenor of the Facebook evidence and was corroborated by Ned O'Brien and his mother [Caroline], both of whom I also had no difficulty in believing. I cannot say the same for the defendant ... The defendant was not being honest when he gave evidence.'

Like Saxon Mullins and so many others, Paris Street did not celebrate the verdict. When his mother read him a text message informing them, he just said, 'Of course he is [guilty] – exactly.' Paris had only been surprised that Kehoe had pleaded not guilty in the first place. He says he felt nothing.

'I came out of that process no better than I was beforehand – and probably worse. In fact, a hundred, a hundred per cent worse, in terms of the cross-examination ...

'What do I get out of this? Just a five-dollar note.

'Like, I literally get *nothing* out of this – that's what it felt like. What happened, happened.'

I can attest that, five years later, it is the cross-examination and the institutional betrayal by his school that seems to cut Paris Street to the bone just as much as the disgusting behaviour by Peter Kehoe. Paris still really struggles with all of this. It severed his faith in the institutions he thought were supposed to protect him at a critical age. His mental health still suffers because of it.

While Robert Richter failed to achieve an acquittal for his client, he was more successful on the sentencing front. During the plea, he spoke of Kehoe's 'spotless character'. Magistrate Ehrlich sentenced Kehoe to a non-custodial community corrections order. He was to remain on the sex offenders' register for eight years.

'Number one, he is not a sexual predator and has not been a sexual predator,' Richter told the court. 'Number two, he is not a paedophile and has not had paedophiliac tendencies,' the QC said, and the magistrate agreed.

* * *

I do always find it strange in courts that pronouncements are routinely pleaded about a convicted person's past, when, in fact, we don't *know*. We only know about what has come before the courts. To me, it should be qualified as such, given the low rates of victims making complaints to the courts. I've heard it pleaded and referred to in sentences in artificial examples, some of them extremely high-profile, where there has been a string of other allegations against the offender which have not, for various reasons, yet been the subject of a conviction.

There was, towards the end, a very strange exchange between Richter and the magistrate.

'So we come to think about how this could [crime] come about, consistent with Your Honour's findings?' Richter mused. 'And the only thing I can think of is relating back to the work of literature and films.

'If one thinks of Thomas Mann's *Death in Venice* – or the movie, *Death in Venice*, in particular, one can put it down to a one-off infatuation with a young man.'

'I was going to say that,' the magistrate replied, to my mind, astonishingly, 'it's love.'

'Correct,' Richter replied.

Love? Correct? This man has just been convicted of grooming a fifteen-year-old boy and we call it 'love'? Doesn't that minimise the intent of the parliament in drafting what was then new legislation to safeguard against grooming of children? And why did the parliament enact that legislation? To prevent future physical sexual crimes against children. To prevent indecent assaults. To prevent abuse. To prevent child rape.

Preventing crimes like that from taking place had been foremost in Paris Street's mind when he resolved to go to the police. When Paris much later heard the exchange between the defence counsel and the magistrate on the audio recording of the hearing, he says he had no idea what *Death in Venice* was. He discovered the plotline was about an older gentleman, visiting Venice when it was blighted by a cholera epidemic, who became infatuated with an extraordinarily beautiful Polish boy.

'So I looked it up,' Paris says, letting out a disgusted guffaw. 'It was ... "*WHAT?*"'

But there was to be another extraordinary blow for Paris from this trial. After Kehoe was convicted of grooming, and before Michelle Ehrlich delivered the non-custodial sentence, Robert Richter got up and said he had a reference to give her on behalf of Kehoe.

Paris discovered later that this reference was written by the headmaster of St Kevin's College, Stephen Russell.

'[I felt] just gutted,' Paris said of the moment he realised that the headmaster had gone in to bat for the sex offender.

'Yeah, gutted and just, like, flicked off. Like, "This is how we think about you, we don't care". Like we, yeah ...' Paris trails off again and he looks so wounded.

Judy Courtin says it's 'quite extraordinary that a Headmaster and the Dean of Sport in particular, will basically disregard the vulnerable student and support an offender' – emphasising again that this happened when the Royal Commission was in the news every day.

Every single evening, as you drove home from work during that era, the late Mark Colvin would say 'Welcome to *PM*' on ABC Radio, and then we'd hear another terrible story of abuse in, often, a Catholic institution like St Kevin's. The assumption was that this sort of institutional support of perpetrators was something from the 1970s and 1980s. Surely this couldn't happen again? That reference showed that it could.

'I definitely think that St Kevin's were trying to sweep the whole situation under the rug,' Ned O'Brien tells me. 'And that, yeah, because it was in a closed court, that it would never really come out.

'I think Mr Russell was trying to save face at the school, with heavily skewed priorities.

'How did you feel about the fact that Stephen Russell wrote that reference?' I asked Jo O'Brien for the *Four Corners* story we would ultimately put together on the St Kevin's scandal.

'That says it all,' Jo returned, shaking her head. 'He should not be the headmaster. That's all I – honestly. That's just not on. Why would he want to get involved in that? It's crazy.' When we broke the St Kevin's scandal on *Four Corners*, Stephen Russell issued a statement saying the reference was 'limited' and 'factual'. The statement also said, 'However, people make errors of judgement … today, I would not provide a reference. I sincerely regret that I did so in 2014.'

One of the big unanswered questions I have about this is why the leader of a large and wealthy institution like St Kevin's would protect a minnow like Kehoe, when one of its boys was at stake. Apart from being breathtakingly insensitive to the victim, Paris, it also seemed incredibly short-sighted.

The long game played spectacularly badly for Stephen Russell. When our *Four Corners* story ran almost five years after he wrote that reference, his whole castle came tumbling down.

BOYS' CLUB

In a jarring irony, at the very same time that Stephen Russell was writing his reference for Peter Kehoe, St Kevin's then–Head of Faith, Michael McGirr, was preparing to apologise to the child abuse Royal Commission for doing the same thing in a historical case.

Just seventeen days after Paris' case, McGirr got up and made his apology to the Royal Commission for his own character evidence for a paedophile Christian Brother, Stephen Farrell, in a trial involving nine counts of indecent assault on minors.

'In 1997, I gave character evidence on behalf of Stephen Farrell ... I now deeply regret having done this,' McGirr wrote to the commission. 'In fact, it was a source of great regret for me very shortly after it happened, when I found out more about Stephen Farrell and what he had done.'

McGirr said he was 'sure' that he had 'swayed the outcome'.

In 1997, McGirr, at the time a Jesuit priest himself, had also written an article about Farrell in the Jesuit publication, *Eureka Street*. It had shown some measure of sympathy for Farrell. McGirr's piece did show the perspective of the victims, but as McGirr himself admitted, he was 'far too willing to lay the blame at the feet of an inadequate institution and not willing enough to see either the personal responsibility of an abuser such as Farrell, or the shocking effects of such abuse on those abused. I regret those failures of understanding on my part.'

One of Farrell's victims was Phil Nagle, a survivor from Ballarat I've come to know quite well. Phil was furious when he saw McGirr had apologised to the Royal Commission. He telephoned the commission to say that he did not accept the apology and he wished for that to be read out.

Whatever the outcome of McGirr's apology, it is difficult to imagine that he did not in some way consult Stephen Russell before he made it. The apology was unequivocal and humble in tone. There would be no such apology from Russell to the Royal Commission or in any other forum for the reference he wrote for Peter Kehoe until after *Four Corners* exposed it, at which point he expressed 'regret'.

In July 2019, a Christian Brother who was a former member of staff at the College, John Laidlaw, was sentenced to four and a half years in prison for historical charges of sexually assaulting six boys, aged between twelve and seventeen, between 1963 and 1984.

The President of the St Kevin's Amateur Athletics Club (SKAAC), Peter McGarry, happened to be in court to support one of the victims.

McGarry sat quietly and watched the row of Laidlaw's now ageing and broken victims, heartbroken at the carnage this man had clearly wrought on the men's lives.

'Every single board member of every single school should be made to sit in on a sexual assault trial to see what it does to people,' McGarry would much later tell me.

Interestingly, Stephen Russell would say in correspondence to the St Kevin's community about the Laidlaw conviction that the school 'emphatically denounces any crimes against young people and has zero tolerance for child sexual abuse or child abuse'.

'Our duty of care to our students, present and past, is our top priority,' Russell opined. 'The care, safety and welfare of students are embedded in our current policies and procedures to ensure a commitment to zero tolerance of child abuse.'

I ask Ned O'Brien what he thought of the Laidlaw letter.

'I think that it's incredibly hypocritical given what he did in 2015,' Ned replies.

'Do you think that his actions match his words?' I ask.

'Definitely not.'

As for Luke Travers, he dug in. And as he did so, the undermining of Paris Street by St Kevin's that began during the legal process, continued at the school. Luke Travers would say that he never meant to hurt the student, but what on earth did he think might be the result of his actions?

Peter McGarry wrote to Stephen Russell eighteen days after Kehoe's conviction, expressing his 'disgust' that Travers had given character evidence for Kehoe instead of supporting Paris and Ned. McGarry had gone along to watch some of the trial and taken notes. The club also wrote to Travers himself, asking him for more information about his evidence.

McGarry had a boy at St Kevin's. Patrick Noonan, an old boy, had his son's name down at the school too, to start at the commencement of the 2020 school year. In light of Travers' support of Kehoe, they both requested that Luke Travers have nothing to do with their sons. It was a bold stand. The commitment was given by St Kevin's.

'*In supporting Peter Kehoe against the evidence of the [St Kevin's] boys and their families,*' McGarry wrote to Russell, '*Luke has put his groomer friend first, with no regard whatsoever to the wellbeing of the [St Kevin's] students involved, to whom he owed a duty of care.*

'*Worse, he used his position and title as Dean of Sport [at St Kevin's] to protect a groomer against the completely true evidence of two honest and courageous [St Kevin's] boys, helping to needlessly subject those boys to a more difficult and traumatic process.*

'*As a parent, I am concerned that such conduct by a senior staff member should not occur and that the care and safety of [St Kevin's] students should never be displaced by a staff member's loyalty to an accused sex offender.*

'*Condoning conduct of this nature, creates a real risk that inappropriate conduct by sports coaches may not be promptly disclosed by students in future, due to a culture in which there is a general expectation that they may face active opposition and [disbelief] by senior school staff.*'

It has to be said that the actions of a group of volunteers at an amateur athletics club outshone those of the leadership team of an elite boys' school to which parents paid $20,000 a year and taxpayers contributed richly. SKAAC stood up for Paris and for Ned. St Kevin's remained all but silent.

Luke Travers stayed on at St Kevin's. I contacted Mr Travers when I was investigating this story. We spoke at length but he told me his comments were off the record. I am honouring his request. Everything in this book is on the public record.

He sent emails defending himself to the club, saying, 'bugger off and mind your own business' and threatening legal action.

In the email, Travers described Paris' mother's conversation with him as 'hearsay evidence', and he was 'not too sure why, having heard her version of events, I would be prevented from giving character evidence for Peter'.

He minimised his role, saying he had described Kehoe's Facebook messages as 'inappropriate'. But he neglected to give the full picture – that he had said in court, it 'depends on the context'.

Reading the email, knowing it was written by a teacher in relation to his friend who was now on the sex offenders' register, is just astounding.

'The Club's continued obsession with the case, using the justification of duty of care issues, has now become clearly prurient,' Travers declared.

'The Executive would be better spending its time on athletics issues like getting people to run ...' Really? Why? What about the children in the club's care? Or in the school's care? Where did they fit in?

'He was threatening us for having spoken with the Headmaster, which really meant that we couldn't raise concerns with the Headmaster without being subjected to threats,' Patrick Noonan remembers of the correspondence.

'He was very aggressive in saying that he would come after us legally if we pursue the issue any further.'

'This is a substantial slur on my professionalism and my character,' Travers said of McGarry's letter to the headmaster.

'I warn the Executive that should this be repeated or inferred [sic] in any setting either by the spoken or written word I will seek legal redress.'

During this period, as headmaster Russell was on leave overseas, acting in his position at St Kevin's was his deputy, a man named Bill Doherty, who has now moved on to become principal at Xavier College, possibly Australia's most exclusive Catholic boys' school.

The centrality of Xavier to the life of Melbourne's elite and its power structures cannot be underestimated. Its alumni include former governors, an archbishop, judges, ministers of the Crown, premiers, a federal opposition leader, Olympians, AFL stars and even a former private secretary to the Duke of Edinburgh. It is the pinnacle of the Catholic establishment in Melbourne.

Since we exposed the Paris Street story in *Four Corners* in February 2020, Bill Doherty has sought to distance himself from the scandal. But his involvement in the handling of its aftermath, as it happens, was not inconsiderable. For a city that is obsessed with where you were educated, a Xavier angle on this story is irresistible. After my story aired, although we hadn't mentioned a Xavier link, my phone was abuzz for weeks with people asking me when I was going to publish about Xavier's connections to this scandal.

On 23 February 2015, before the Peter Kehoe court case had commenced, Doherty told SKAAC that 'the blanket "no comment" will be the way SKC wish to play this'.

After the conviction, the club members wanted more. But that was not forthcoming. Bill Doherty wrote a letter informing St Kevin's parents of the conviction. But it was sent *only* to parents of cross-country and middle-distance runners. The smallest circle possible. Paris Street's family were not consulted about its contents. Five years down the track, when we were investigating the case for *Four Corners*, many parents at St Kevin's had no idea about what had happened.

Patrick Noonan received the letter and he pointed out that it emphasised that, at the time of the conviction, Paris was no longer a student of the school.

'The letter very much seemed to be trying to distance the school from it and just absolve the school of any responsibility,' Noonan says.

Two months after Kehoe was sentenced, Peter McGarry and his wife, Rachael, who has since been president of the school's mothers' association, went to meet with Doherty and other senior school staff members.

The McGarrys wanted to know what the school would be doing in response to the letter they had sent the school about Travers.

They were dismayed by the reaction of one staff member, the same person who Caroline Redmond says had told her the family had 'no comeback against the school'. They say that the staff member told them a teacher like Travers was 'well within his rights to act as a defence witness in the case'.

Peter McGarry pressed further: '... [Y]ou have no problem at all with an SKC teacher acting as a defence witness in a case of sexual abuse allegedly perpetrated against an SKC boy at the time?'

'No, I don't see any problem with it,' he says the staff member replied, adding that Doherty said nothing to contradict this position. McGarry said Doherty distanced the school from Kehoe.

I was told repeatedly from numerous sources that this senior staff member would consistently be named in allegations of not adequately dealing with complaints of a sexual nature – whether they be made by students or staff.

When Stephen Russell returned to St Kevin's later in the year, he admitted that there had been an investigation into Luke Travers, carried out by the school's parent body, Edmund Rice Education Australia (EREA). The members of the athletics club who had been on the receiving end of Travers' heated emails in support of Kehoe, and, in McGarry's case had witnessed his evidence in court, were never contacted for the investigation.

The outcome was that EREA would simply put a note on Travers' employment file. He remained at the school and he remained Dean of Sport. The investigation remained secret and no one was given a copy of its report.

The point is, the headmaster and the Catholic lay body which took over the governing of fifty-five schools around the country when the Christian Brothers proved themselves unfit for that task, the body which was in receipt of more than $440 million in government funding and $356 million in fees, was kept up to date with what was going on at St Kevin's College with Paris' complaint.

It knew about Russell's reference for a convicted sex offender who had offended against one of their own teenage students. And it knew that Travers had gone to court to support Kehoe. The question is: why did an organisation which outwardly prided itself on its child protection policies (brought in after the Christian Brothers were dragged kicking and screaming into admitting to their horrifying history of child sexual abuse) allow this to happen?

Paris Street had been at Trinity Grammar for some months, but with all of the upheaval of the court case, with his brother still at St Kevin's along with all of his friendship circle since he was nine, he decided to go back to the school. He was vulnerable and lonely at Trinity and both he and his parents thought that, despite everything that had taken place, it would be best for his mental health to be at a school which was familiar. They were not, at that point, aware of the extent of the protection Kehoe had been given by the school.

Bill Doherty welcomed Paris back to St Kevin's, but Paris says there was a condition given to him by Doherty and a senior staff member that he maintain 'corridor relations' with Luke Travers.

'I took it to mean that they didn't think that I would be friendly in the corridors with him – I just think they wanted to minimise any risk that I would cause a stir or something,' Paris says.

The 'corridor relations' ultimatum was, Paris says, given to him in a meeting with these two senior staff members where he was alone, without the support of his parents.

'It felt like I had no other option but to say yes,' he says.

'For him to be told to maintain corridor relations with the man that supported the offender is mind-blowing,' Judy Courtin says. 'It is really mind-blowing.'

She says Paris was 'basically being told' that he was 'the one who has to do the right thing to maintain the integrity and credibility of St Kevin's'.

'It was put on Paris to protect the reputation of St Kevin's in circumstances where he had sexual offences, sexual crimes, committed against him,' Courtin says.

'The Catholic institutions and others are expert at trying to protect their brand.

'And we know now, particularly through the Royal Commission, that protecting their brand has been going on forever at the expense of their victims.'

The school's leadership team pressured Paris to have what they and Travers would describe as a 'restorative justice' meeting with Travers.

Patrick Noonan, the barrister from the athletics club, got wind of this and in his words, thought it was 'just ridiculous'.

'I just could not see that ending well,' Noonan tells me.

Noonan, a highly intelligent man who is in my experience of the utmost integrity, had gained, through acting for the institution in the Royal Commission, substantial insight into best practice when it came to child protection policies.

Noonan thought St Kevin's might welcome an approach from him to offer assistance in putting the school's leadership team in touch with the right people who might help them strengthen their child protection policies in response to the case.

He contacted Bill Doherty. He kept contemporaneous notes of the conversation in which he cautioned Doherty that the Peter Kehoe matter hadn't been handled well so far.

'At the moment,' Noonan records himself as saying, 'looking at a headline any day, "School backs paedophile against students".' Precisely the sort of headlines that our Four Corners story would ultimately generate.

'In what way?' the note says Doherty replied.

'Travo supported all the way through,' the notes record. 'Attacked people who tried to exclude Peter Kehoe. Gave evidence … at trial. School gave evidence on sentencing …'

Noonan, thinking he was helping, says he asked Doherty if St Kevin's had any training on sexual abuse.

'On the legal liability side,' Noonan's note records that Doherty replied.

'Not on the child protection side?' I ask Noonan, much later, as he recounts the conversation.

'Well, that seemed to be his response, yes,' Noonan drily replies. 'He just really was very much in denial throughout the whole conversation.'

He says that Doherty said the school leadership was concerned that the case would be revealed 'via a third party' – which Noonan took to be the media. But Noonan was much more concerned about the ongoing approach by the school to child safety.

'I said to Bill, "The most expensive QC in Australia can't help you, as Peter Kehoe found, if the facts are against you. And, for example, things like [words to the effect of] 'looking at you, I have pre-cum on my dick'."

'And what I was trying to convey was that, really, the interests of the school and the institution and the interests of the kid are completely aligned, they are the same thing, that helping the kid helps the school.

'Because even being a cynical – even being a complete psychopath about it, if you just want to help the school, the best way that you can do that is to help the kid.

'On a long game, on a short game, on any game, it just can't help the school to harm the child.'

But that message didn't seem to sink in.

When Noonan offered in the phone call to put Doherty in touch with experts who could help the school revamp its child protection policies, he says Doherty showed little interest.

Bill Doherty's conversations with parents who made complaints about his role in the way St Kevin's handled the Paris Street case have not, until now, been fully exposed.

In his discussion with Noonan, Doherty brought up the so-called 'restorative justice' meeting plan between Travers and Paris, which Noonan thought was a terrible idea.

'"Luke is a teacher and an adult, Paris is a kid at school,"' Noonan says he told Doherty. '"He calls him 'Mr Travers' and 'Sir' and they're not on an equal footing."

'Luke, from what [the club] had heard was very much supportive of the perpetrator.

'It really isn't on the kid to try and sort things out – he's done nothing wrong, especially in that imbalance.

'That seemed fraught to me. I thought that was going to end very badly.'

It did end badly. It ended with Travers telling Paris Street that he was still friends with Peter Kehoe, and that when he first heard about the matter he thought it was a 'storm in a teacup'.

'As a friend,' contemporaneous notes by the St Kevin's school psychologist on Paris' file record, 'I didn't want him to be convicted.'

'Now, to do that to a victim or a survivor of sexual abuse, it's hideous, it's totally hideous,' Judy Courtin says. 'And I find this extraordinary too because one of the very, very clear salient messages from the Royal Commission was that the child's needs must be paramount over and above everyone else. And that did not happen.'

But it got worse. When Paris Street's relationship with the school had soured to the point that he eventually launched legal action against St Kevin's, the college's lawyers at first refused to give him the records of his own psychiatric notes.

Courtin says the school's solicitors delayed handing over the notes for months. Courtin is a gregarious and dogged solicitor who came to the law late in life because of her passion for the issue of clergy abuse – about which she had written her PhD. She doesn't give up. As Margaret Thatcher once said of herself, 'The lady's not for turning.' Judy Courtin does not tend to turn.

Eventually the notes were released. Then, Courtin was horrified to realise that ten pages of Paris' own counselling notes had been blacked out by the school. When, after more months of persisting, the school finally handed over the entire set, she realised that some pages had simply been left out.

But it was when Courtin and her colleagues laid the two sets side by side that they were shocked at the hide of the college. The notes show that the redactions included Paris' description of the meeting with Luke Travers in which Travers spoke of his continuing friendship with Kehoe, the *'storm in a teacup'* and his desire that Kehoe not be convicted.

They left out a page which said Paris *'feels that they had the power to do a great deal and chose to protect the school ahead of P's wellbeing'*.

'Well, it's another example of trying to protect themselves,' Courtin tells me. 'Trying to protect the name of St Kevin's College.'

The college psychologist, who had by then left the school, was horrified. The notes had been removed from a locked cabinet without seeking permission from him or Paris and given to the school's leadership team, seeming to defy guidelines set down by the Australian Psychological Society.

Stephen Russell didn't answer written questions about this before our *Four Corners* story, 'Boys Club', was broadcast. But after the program went to air, he told parents in a statement that the redactions were made in accordance with a 'usual provision in the legislation to protect the privacy of others' – including the school's psychologist.

'When it became a court matter, the full versions without any deletions were given to his [Paris'] lawyers.'

But privacy clearly wasn't an issue here. They were Paris' own notes of his own discussions with the school psychologist. The psychologist did not object to them being released – in fact, he supported it. They were simply a record of what had been said.

The actions of the school's leadership team caused Paris Street's mental health to spiral significantly.

'He went from being an A-grade student to having great difficulties in his work,' Courtin says. 'He started to suffer terrible anxiety and panic attacks. He ended up being hospitalised, needing psychiatric care. He transitioned from a very confident, caring young man into a psychiatrically very unwell young man. He was crushed by the institution. He was crushed.'

'I was appalled,' a parent of a former student Susan Lackner says, 'Absolutely appalled. This could have been my son. This could have been anybody's son.'

Lackner is a psychological therapist who has worked with many people who have been victims of sexual abuse. Her son was friends with Ned O'Brien and she was so horrified when she discovered what had happened to Paris and, indeed, Ned, that she refused to give any donations to the school after that point.

'I would go to assemblies and, before this event, I would sit there and think, "This is an amazing school, I'm so grateful my children have got the opportunity to be going here, that I am giving them this opportunity."

'And I would sit there afterwards and just say, you know, "This feels like propaganda to me. I just don't believe anything that I'm hearing. They don't walk their talk.'"

As he drove along Melbourne's Yarra Boulevard, approaching the giant cross on the school's chapel overlooking the river, Paris tells me he'd 'just get triggered and would have a panic attack and would not want to go to school'.

'I wouldn't want to sleep at night because I wouldn't want to get up in the morning to go to school,' Paris says.

Years down the track, the combination of a legal process for which he was brutally ill-prepared, a cross-examination that I found to be unnecessarily demeaning, the fact that the institution that was supposed to protect him instead supported his perpetrator, the ham-fisted way they went about trying to mop up and conceal the aftermath, the 'corridor relations', the 'storm in a teacup', the redaction of his own psychologist's notes, all of those things, combined to keep Paris Street from really being well.

Paris is a sensitive, thoughtful soul. I'll always admire how he stood up to both his perpetrator and the institution that had so shaped his identity. St Kevin's is such a powerful network of people. Calling it out was immensely brave. Paris knew that, by doing so, he might alienate people who had been his school mates.

His life, now, is not what it might have been. Anxiety is a constant presence. He's very bright, but at times he struggles to focus on his university work. His ability to trust has been sorely tested and that sometimes affects his friendships.

I will never forget the Friday before our *Four Corners* story was due to go to air, after months of preparation, a tabloid newspaper had seen our promo and tried to scoop us with some bones of information they had from the case. No one from the paper had the common decency and journalistic ethics to contact the person who was most affected – Paris Street. He was just a vehicle for a 'big yarn'.

Paris called me to alert me to the tabloid story and, for the first time since I met him, he just sobbed and sobbed. He felt like they had taken away his voice, his first opportunity to seize back control after years of feeling powerless. I comforted him and told him not to worry, it would just mean that on the Monday night, more people would watch our show and more people would hear the real story – the message he really wanted to deliver.

The promotions for our story on the ABC in those days before its broadcast sent the St Kevin's community into a tailspin.

A tearful Stephen Russell was given a standing ovation at the mothers' association lunch on the Friday before. Many of those mothers have since been in contact to say how betrayed they felt, and how disgusted they were at Russell, when they finally sat down to watch the program on the Monday night.

Russell infamously posted a prayer by poet John O'Donohue from his poem 'Time to be Slow' on the school's website:

'This is the time to be slow
Lie low to the wall
Until the bitter weather passes.'

Lying low to the wall didn't work out so well for Russell. The bitter weather turned out to be an almighty electrical storm.

It was hard to believe that this happened despite the school having had advice from a crisis management company a few months before.

My phone practically melted with parents, alumni and current students contacting me to express their disgust. That intensified when the story actually went to air.

Social media exploded in derision towards the school's leadership.

'If Stephen Russell and Luke Travers think they can lie low to the wall,' Paris' friend Finley Tobin tweeted, 'they are mistaken.

'The bitter weather has already passed for the one person that should have been, but never was, their priority: Paris Street.'

Russell refused to apologise to Paris or anyone else. He sent out a long, defensive, and in part, factually incorrect, statement to the St Kevin's community the night our program aired. It landed after midnight. It appeared to be hastily prepared – even bearing the wrong date.

The next day, the Executive Director of EREA, Wayne Tinsey, got up in assembly and backed Russell. This time there would be no academic gowns or rousing classical music as Russell and the leadership team filed in. And this time, many brave St Kevin's boys refused to stand for the headmaster. They went home and expressed disgust to their parents. Their parents started organising to force Russell out. I was contacted by many families who wanted to know what they could do to make change. They were organising online to take on the school.

Within two days, it became clear that Russell's position was completely untenable – he resigned. Tinsey recanted and apologised to Paris Street for the distress he and the school had caused him.

Then, another member of the senior leadership team left following allegations of bullying that resulted in legal proceedings that have since been settled.

That teacher was also removed. So was another senior teacher whom I had disclosed in the story as being accused of sexual harassment. The investigation into those claims by the school was substantiated. The Commissioner for Children and Young People was contacted about concerns about that teacher and there is an investigation currently being conducted into his behaviour which will determine whether he is ever allowed to teach in Victoria again. Travers was also removed, and, at time of writing, the school has commissioned a reportable conduct investigation under the Victorian *Child Wellbeing and Safety Act 2005* to determine whether his actions amounted to 'significant emotional or psychological harm to a child'. If upheld, his registration to practise as a teacher could be removed by the Victorian Institute of Teaching. Paris was interviewed by a barrister for this investigation in June 2020. Travers' attempts to allege unfair dismissal came to nothing when, confronted with the audio recording of his own evidence in support of Peter Kehoe, he backed down. John Crowley confirmed to staff that Travers was not given a financial settlement from St Kevin's.

As for Xavier principal Bill Doherty, he told *Four Corners* in a statement that he remained 'content with the actions and communication that I offered on this matter at the time. I will always act for the care of students for whom I am responsible.' With the rumours of his involvement swirling around his own school community, he fired off a letter to parents and alumni saying that 'at all times, may truth, integrity and courage prevail'.

'The victims of abuse, in any form, historical or current, must be recognised, heard and supported,' he wrote.

He said he had written to St Kevin's parents regarding the Kehoe matter when he was acting headmaster but didn't qualify that the vast majority of parents at the school were told nothing – and that he chose, or was directed to, write to only the middle-distance and cross-country students' parents.

'People who speak up to address the unacceptable behaviour of others help to ensure that our society and our organisations are centred on good values rather than poor behaviours and are to be applauded,' Doherty wrote.

The Chair of Xavier's College Board was given the full back story of Doherty's involvement, both verbally and in writing. And in a letter to the chair from Peter McGarry, it was pointed out that members of SKAAC *had* spoken up – directly to Doherty – and he 'did not applaud us. In fact he did nothing.'

'So we are writing to you, so that you may have the truth, which will hopefully allow integrity and courage to prevail.'

At the time of writing, there has been no more correspondence from Xavier College about the matter.

In another link to the George Pell case, a former senior teacher at St Kevin's was removed from the Catholic boys' school Mazenod College, where he was by that time working as dean of their junior college. As former choir master of the St Patrick's Cathedral choir, this teacher had given evidence for Pell. He had reached into the dock and shaken the cardinal's hand after his evidence finished. That had angered Chief Judge Peter Kidd, who instructed witnesses not to walk past the dock from that time forth.

Victoria's Commissioner for Children and Young People had referred four sets of allegations to Victoria Police for investigation. In March, Victoria Police confirmed to me in a statement that it was assessing those referrals and we published the development in an online story.

I remember when Paris Street had first told me about his case and I had seen the documents associated with it and I had said to him, 'This is going to be like a Shakespearean tragedy after the story goes to air, with bodies littered across the stage.' But you never really know how a story, or its issues will be received. This story was received by an educated, wealthy, powerful parent body with fury. They demanded immediate action and they got it. It was a bloodbath.

Most importantly, Russell was replaced with John Crowley, who had been principal of St Patrick's College in Ballarat, George Pell's alma mater and scene of, in the 1970s, a ring of paedophile Christian Brothers. Crowley had set about making genuine change at the school and making child protection his number one priority. When, for instance, Pell was convicted (later to be acquitted by the

High Court), Crowley set about taking down the plaques at the school which honoured Pell. A month after Pell was acquitted, and the Royal Commission's redactions about him were removed from its final report – revealing that the commission found he knew that priests had offended – the school decided to keep the plaques down.

Crowley also removed Pell's 'Legends of St Patrick's College' honour – given to old boys who had made a mark in the community. And instead of, as was historically customary, honouring an alumnus who was, say, a doctor or lawyer or footballer, Crowley honoured Peter Blenkiron – a survivor of a Christian Brother's abuse who had worked hard for those in his community who had been blighted by this scourge.

Blenkiron, a dear and humble man, invited me to the ceremony. I spoke to Crowley and he told me that he didn't want the boys going into that school every day seeing a plaque honouring a person like Pell. He couldn't talk to them about feeling safe and do such a thing.

Crowley's appointment to St Kevin's marked the beginning of a monumental shift in culture. Some months down the track, he sent a letter to parents saying that he had elected not to take up the permanent principal's position, but he oversaw the ousting of a list of teachers about some of whom there had long been complaints and suspicions – which in some cases had either been ignored or minimised or swept under the carpet. On the last day of winter 2020, as jasmine was beginning to burst into bloom along the suburban fences Paris Street would run past as he tried to put it all behind him, St Kevin's College made an announcement. For the first time in its 118-year history, the school had appointed a woman to be its principal. Deborah Barker had come from an all-girls' school, Santa Maria Northcote.

The maddening part of the scandal at St Kevin's is how so much of it could have been avoided.

Did Richter pause to think that perhaps he could have achieved his forensic purpose without treating a teenager so? Has he done this to other teenagers? Why didn't anyone warn Paris about what he was up for?

Why does the court system allow adults who should know better to speak to kids in a way that might see them dismissed from a job if they treated a young person like that in the workplace? Why does it strip kids like Paris of their dignity in this way?

Why couldn't Luke Travers see what he was doing to this young kid? Where was his empathy? Why, in the minds of Kehoe's mates, did 'innocent until proven guilty' trump child protection?

How could the headmaster Stephen Russell think it was okay for him to write in support of the perpetrator who had so disturbed his student? Where did he think he was going with that? If, as he said in a statement after the story went to air, he consulted with EREA, why on earth did no one stop this train from coursing off the tracks at high speed?

Dr Wayne Tinsey of EREA would write to me a week after the *Four Corners* story to thank me for my 'brave and compassionate advocacy for Paris' and to apologise.

'The thought that extraordinary, brave and innocent people would feel that I allocated any responsibility for the culture that has been exposed, is abhorrent to me,' Tinsey wrote.

It seemed, on the face of it, a humble and heartfelt letter, but it rang hollow for me. EREA had known about all of this before. The organisation had been a party to Paris' civil action – which outlined everything about Stephen Russell and Luke Travers. Tinsey had refused to engage when our team repeatedly tried to get him to speak to us on or off the record. In his brief and anodyne statement, he hadn't answered any of our questions.

He had gone in to bat for Russell, and, when that turned into a PR disaster, he had recanted. It could be argued that he had a serious conflict of interest because both his wife and son were employed at the school, by Russell. He sent his apology letter to me just minutes after I had forwarded to the school yet another sexual harassment complaint made by a young language assistant about a senior male member of staff who has been the subject of numerous complaints by staff, parents and students and has now been removed.

Tinsey and the EREA have supported and overseen all of the work John Crowley has done to remove problematic teachers. But there is still a long way to go before they can completely restore confidence in the organisation and the school's commitment to student safety.

Why do powerful people so often place reputation and superficial damage control before doing the right thing?

Why show support for an alleged predator by writing references in court without thinking about how it might affect their alleged victims? Why redact the psych notes? Didn't the lawyers pause to think?

Yes, Tinsey, Stephen Russell, St Kevin's and EREA played a foolish long game. Their strategy of trying to protect the school's reputation only, eventually, tarnished it far more.

It will take a long time for the school community to recover from this debacle – something that could all have been so easily avoided.

But, most importantly, on the other side of this whole mess was a teenage boy, who just wanted to see the good in his world and now, five years later, sees it through a sickly, distorted filter.

THE OTHERWISE
BLAMELESS LIFE

If only St Kevin's College was a weird anomaly. It's not. This phenomenen of powerful people supporting the perpetrator instead of the victim, in the courtroom and beyond, is jarringly common.

As Paris Street found, it's most disturbing, though, when the very people a young person might have thought were there to protect them instead decide to back the convicted criminal over the victim.

Such was the extraordinary case of Robert Sharwood, an Anglican priest who taught at one of the most exclusive schools in Brisbane: Anglican Church Grammar School, most commonly known as 'Churchie'.

At the time of Sharwood's conviction for repeated sexual crimes against a boy who was fourteen when the offending began, no fewer than twenty people of high esteem in his community wrote letters of support to be provided to the court after he was convicted.

'My wife and I have known Robert Sharwood for some thirty-five years,' one correspondent, an officer in the Royal Australian Airforce, wrote to the court. 'We are writing because we have learned that Robert has now been convicted of some offences committed thirty years ago.'

The euphemisms in the letter run thick and fast.

'At that time we were informed of the trouble and to our knowledge it was dealt with and was then put to rest.'

'The trouble'? 'Put to rest'?

These were crimes on the statute books. Indictable offences. Sharwood pleaded guilty to seven charges of sexual assault. He was also found guilty of sodomy, permitting sodomy and two charges of indecent assault.

All against a teenage boy. The prosecutor had told the court there had been at least three hundred occasions on which the boy had been abused between 1974 and 1976.

Prosecutor Ron Swanwick noted that by contesting the four offences, Sharwood had ensured his victim was subjected to the ordeal of cross-examination and forced to relive the details of the abuse he had suffered.

But none of that seemed to matter to the correspondents who wrote the glowing character references about Sharwood. And, in their correspondence, not one of them demonstrated any sympathy, nor, indeed, empathy, for the victim.

Eleven of the character references were written by people who were or had been associated with schools – mostly Churchie. Teachers, a house master, chaplains, tutors, a member of the school council.

A female teacher who had been at Churchie and was then at a prestigious Sydney Uniting Church school described Sharwood as 'an honourable and inspiring priest', a 'loving father and husband and entertaining host'.

Her only fleeting reference to his crimes was that she was 'aware that sex charges had been made against' Sharwood. She makes no reference to the victim.

Another one, from a church musician and former tutor at an elite Anglican girls' boarding school, listed Sharwood's many achievements and accomplishments and then said, 'whatever Robert may or may not have done amiss in the 1970s and of which he now stands accused I am firmly of the belief that these sorts of incidents are not part of his present life'.

It's worth noting at the point of this reference being written, Sharwood had already pleaded guilty to many of the offences and had just been found guilty of others. Sodomy of a young boy in his care is not 'amiss'.

'If he strayed then, he is now completely rehabilitated.' *Strayed*? How did this person know?

Another, from a teacher at Churchie, extolled Sharwood's virtues by praising all the time he devoted to the 'Gifted and Talented camps run by the school each year'.

It is hardly surprising that someone who was found guilty of repeated crimes against a boy might be the first to volunteer to give of his time at a schoolboys camp.

A former member of Churchie's council – indeed, another Anglican priest – was 'convinced that there has been no blemish on Robert's record since [his marriage] and his effectiveness as a teacher and chaplain at [Churchie] was highly valued and appreciated'.

Another Churchie teacher said he was 'aware that Robert Sharwood has been charged with serious offences, some of which he has pleaded guilty to'. Nonetheless, this educator confidently concluded, 'With respect, I suggest that, if convicted of criminal misbehaviour in the 1970s, Robert Sharwood, from my observation, is now a completely rehabilitated person.'

How did he know?

A 'Reverend Canon', who had known Sharwood since 1959, also extolled his virtues. He did admit that the majority of his colleagues back in 1972 'considered him too immature and opposed his ordination'. He did disclose a 'surprise visit' from Sharwood in 1976, where he admitted that a letter from Sharwood to the victim referring to a sexual relationship that 'may have exceeded the bounds of a professional relationship'.

He said that Sharwood was 'very remorseful' and 'greatly chastened'. 'In my opinion, Robert has grown in maturity since the indiscretion,' he said.

Anal sex with a teenage boy is not an 'indiscretion' or a 'relationship'. The court heard that the victim bled from the anus, and that Sharwood had been very angry with the victim for going to the doctor. Sharwood committed a crime which would have lifelong consequences for his victim. The fact that an Anglican priest in no way acknowledged the pain of that victim is profoundly disappointing.

The priest talked about how Robert and his family 'have suffered greatly as a result' of the rumours about his crimes. There was zero said about the suffering of Sharwood's victim.

The last sentence is devastatingly dismissive of his victim: 'If Robert were to be sentenced to imprisonment, the church and the wider Australian community would also be penalised through the loss of his exemplary and faithful service, so evident since 1976.'

Who cares about his faithful service? He had damaged a child for life. He should have been removed from the priesthood in 1976 when his offending was reported to the diocese.

Numerous family members were brought in too. And while it is not surprising that they might have supported him, when they referred to what had taken place, they also used euphemistic language like 'a short-term waywardness in human nature', or a 'close involvement' as the result of 'sexual immaturity'.

Sexual immaturity on the part of the teenage victim, perhaps, but not on the part of Sharwood, who was at the time of the crimes in his thirties.

These referees didn't come forward in the dark ages. The trial and sentencing took place in 2006.

But not one of these people, so many of them educators responsible for children, showed a single bit of empathy for Sharwood's victim in their letters to the court.

The boy in question, the boy whom the prosecutors told the court had been abused at least three hundred times by Sharwood, was shocked by the parade of powerful people who stood up to protect the perpetrator, without apparently caring about the effect this might have on him.

The victim was part of the Anglican community that rallied around Robert Sharwood.

'That's a quite schismatic thing, is it not?' he tells me of the fact that the people writing these references for a paedophile were educators of children.

'That's the understatement of the century,' I say.

The survivor continues. 'They have abrogated the primary responsibility of their profession,' he says. 'Which is the care and concern of children.

'Here they have evidence of a child who has had criminal activities performed upon them, and they have shown no care and concern for that child.

'And, *ipso facto*, any other child – because the potential is that there are other children.

'Rather, they are showing care and concern for the criminal.'

As it happens, one other person did make allegations about what he said Sharwood did to him when he was a teenager. He grew up to be a man called Bruce, who made a police statement and had several conversations with the other victim's wife, who happens to be an investigative journalist.

In the police statement and correspondence with the wife, as well as correspondence with the Anglican dioceses of Brisbane and Melbourne, Bruce alleged that he had been abused by a priest from Brisbane – Robert Sharwood – with another Anglican teacher, Ian Bridge, when he had met them at a Royal School of Church Music summer school in Launceston. Sharwood has, independently, admitted to having a sexual relationship with Bridge.

Bruce said the pair had called his mother and asked to take him on a holiday after the camp to Hobart. She, a devout Anglican, thought her son couldn't be safer than with a priest and a teacher from an Anglican school.

As it happened, it seems that Bruce was deeply unsafe. During the following few days, as alleged in Bruce's statement and being investigated by police during the time of the other victim's case, the pair had sex with young Bruce several times a day. I have read his statements and the details are too horrific to write here. I won't forget them soon. They had a heartbreaking and lifelong impact on Bruce.

'I felt pressured and coerced into doing these things because they were members of the church, they were trusted by my family, they were school teachers and a priest, and they were in a position of authority,' Bruce wrote in his police statement.

'They took advantage of their power and my age. Because of me being so young, once I was in that situation I couldn't get out ... I was also absolutely petrified of telling anybody about it, including my parents. This was because of a feeling that I was going to get into trouble.'

Bruce said he thought if he did disclose, he would be accused of 'just telling tales'.

'I didn't think anyone would believe me,' he told police.

The teacher, Ian Bridge, would later be shot dead at a gay beat.

A month after Sharwood was convicted of the abuse of the other victim, and while police were still investigating Bruce's case, Bruce's partner wrote to the other victim's wife to tell her that Bruce had died. He'd taken his own life. Bruce's partner found him surrounded by lit candles.

So all of the Sharwood referees – people responsible for the care and safety of children, who had waxed lyrical about all of Sharwood's great qualities, assumed that his rape of the teenage victim was just some sort of temporary aberration – should know that another man made similarly awful allegations.

They should know that he tried to get the church to listen. That he was prepared to go to the police. And for that other man, it had been all too much. He was no longer able to live with the memories of the abuse he swore in a police statement that he had suffered.

The fact that four of the Sharwood referees were Anglican priests – including one who had at one time been the Dean of Brisbane – was further retraumatising for the victim, who had lived his life as a member of the church.

After Sharwood's conviction, the church conducted an investigation into removing Sharwood's holy orders, and, extraordinarily, wrote to the victim, inviting him to give evidence to the church's professional standards board, but noting that he may then be cross-examined directly by Sharwood.

The letter referred simply to 'charges', ignoring the fact that Sharwood had been convicted. And further, if Sharwood was to be given the opportunity to cross-examine the victim, did this then indicate that the church did not respect the findings of a court of law?

The survivor wrote back to say that he found the use of the word 'charges' instead of 'convictions' 'offensive and insulting to me'.

'It is inexplicable to me that the Board considers it suitable to afford the respondent power to cross-examine me who is the survivor of his criminal actions which have been convicted in a court of law. I will not be cross-examined by a convicted criminal or any of his representatives,' he wrote.

'It makes you feel devalued,' he tells me now. 'It makes you feel angry, and sort of tossed aside like a commodity – not valued as a person. When the whole point of the religion is supposed to be that every person is of equal value.'

The referees for Robert Sharwood were devastatingly effective in their purpose: reducing the sentence for his crime. Sharwood was sentenced to two years and nine months in prison for his crimes against his victim but received parole after serving just one year. Sharwood still lives in Brisbane.

Character references are just another problematic element of the criminal justice system for complainants of sexual crimes. To see upstanding citizens – teachers, priests, politicians, even prime ministers – speak glowingly of the people about whom they make accusations is extraordinarily retraumatising.

In the Royal Commission into Institutional Responses to Child Sexual Abuse's Criminal Justice Consultation Paper, it recommended legislative reforms which excluded good character as a mitigating factor for judges sentencing child sex offenders.

'[A]llowing good character as a mitigating factor can be highly problematic in sentencing for child sexual abuse offences,' the commissioners said. 'In particular, offenders may use their reputation and good character to facilitate the grooming and sexual abuse of children and to mask their behaviour.

'This may be particularly so in matters of institutional child sexual abuse.'

As psychologist Michelle Epstein wrote in *New Matilda* about these sorts of references after our *Four Corners* story on St Kevin's was broadcast, 'Of course all these character references speak of a person who has dedicated their life to working with children.

'Surely only a really nice person gives up their weekends and spare time helping children? In their own home?

'It's laughable.

'By systematically placing themselves in positions of trust and authority with children and within institutions, the paedophile not only gets extraordinary, unfettered access to potential victims, he/she also develops an impressive CV and a long and illustrious history of being a "really good person".

'This is the modus operandi of the charismatic sociopath; leaving a very visible trail of good deeds and high-status referees. Many will be awarded medals, honorary positions, lifetime memberships and Orders of Australia. They will position themselves to be beyond reproach and above the law.'

Epstein makes the salient point that it's not only children who are groomed – it's also 'neighbours, friends, parents, teachers, headmasters, sports masters, clubs, communities, organisations, institutions, parishes, popes, politicians, prime ministers and shock jocks'.

'Tragically, when high-status people give character references for convicted paedophiles, they do not realise they have been groomed over many years or even decades for the precise moment when the paedophile is found out, and is in great need of people in high places to vouch for him …

'All who are groomed to clear the way for paedophiles, are victims of deception. Unfortunately, people in positions of authority do not even want to think about the possibility that they were used, duped, manipulated and befriended for the sole purpose of aiding and abetting sexual crimes against children.

'It's unthinkable and unbelievable, so they don't think about it and they don't believe it. If it helps their denial, they don't believe the victims either.'

New South Wales and South Australia legislated several years ago to remove good character as a mitigating factor in sentencing, but it remained in other states until recently.

In Queensland, where Sharwood's case took place, Premier Annastacia Palaszczuk's government has drafted a bill which would ensure that the court must not have regard to a child sex offender's good character if it assisted the offender in committing the crimes.

The wife of the Sharwood victim wrote to Premier Palaszczuk to commend the proposed legislation and to ask that the Sharwood case be referenced in parliament when the bill is being debated.

At the time of writing, the legislation has been postponed by the coronavirus pandemic.

A report by the Sentencing Advisory Council of Victoria in 2016 chaired by Professor Arie Freiberg which examined cases of sexual penetration of a child under the age of twelve, found cases in which superior courts had, despite previous good character facilitating access to child victims, taken it into account as a 'weighty mitigating factor'. In one such case, in the Court of Appeal in 2013, the court overruled the findings of the trial judge, Judge Elizabeth Gaynor, who 'emphasised that the offences involved a gross breach of trust and exploitation of the position that he (the child's uncle) occupied'.

'It was error in these circumstances to have diminished the weight to be given to the appellant's good character,' the Court of Appeal found.

'It is one thing to describe the offending as a breach of trust – so much cannot be gainsaid – but it is another thing to diminish the weight to be attributed to good character which a person is otherwise possessed of at the time when an offence is committed. If a person is otherwise of good character, he or she is entitled to have that taken into account at the time of sentencing.'

The court reduced the accused's sentence from eight years maximum in prison with a six-year non-parole period, to five years maximum with a three-year non-parole period. So the offender was to spend half the amount of time in prison he originally faced.

In another case examined by the Sentencing Advisory Council, a pastor's 'excellent' reputation and no prior convictions were taken into account when sentencing him for abusing three sisters.

'Yet this "excellent" reputation was the very reason that the offender was entrusted with the girls in the first place,' the report said.

The Sentencing Advisory Council found that there had been a number of cases where 'the offender's good character or good prospects of rehabilitation were emphasised in mitigation, despite the presence of representative charges indicating factual circumstances to the contrary'. 'Representative charges' are where multiple offences are added together to form one charge. It means, basically, that there were far more crimes committed than the charges really suggest.

The report cites one such case where otherwise good character was taken into account when the perpetrator was a friend of the child's family who had offended against her over a seven-year period – from when she was seven years old to when she was fourteen.

'The judge did not highlight this as giving context to the offending and in fact described that context in different terms,' the report said.

Those terms were that the offender had a marriage breakdown, was separated from his sons, never re-partnered and lived a lonely life.

Astonishingly, the judge also said, 'I accept that the affection you received from and gave to your young victim enhanced your emotional life with love.' He went on to qualify that it did not excuse the man's conduct, which was 'predatory', but why even say it in the first place?

'I accept that your vulnerability gives context to your offending,' the judge said. He sentenced the man to six years and six months, with a minimum non-parole period of four years.

Depressingly, the Sentencing Advisory Council report found that 'in cases of sexual penetration with a child under the age of 12, it appeared that considerably greater weight was given to mitigating factors that were personal to the offender, such as prior good character or the burden that imprisonment would impose, than to aggravating factors based on harm to the victim'.

'This was so despite strong language acknowledging the range of physical, mental, and emotional harms suffered by the victim or victims and their families, as well as current authority about the breadth and depth of the harms inherently caused by the offence of sexual penetration with a child under 12.'

Remembering that this involves sexual penetration of primary school–aged children, it's horrible to contemplate that these crimes exist at all, let alone that the courts seem more concerned with their perpetrators than the victims in their sentencing practices.

These little kids deserve so much better.

Victoria enacted legislation in 2018 – after the child abuse Royal Commission's final report – to prevent good character from being taken into account as a mitigating factor if it was 'of assistance in the commission of a child sex offence'.

But character references are still used in some child sex offence cases. For example, before George Pell's convictions were quashed in the High Court in April 2020, a slew of character references were produced to the court – from a university vice-chancellor, from former staff, a head of a charity, and friends.

Most famously, one came from former Prime Minister John Howard. Another former Prime Minister, Tony Abbott, also made public statements of support in the media, saying the verdict was 'devastating ... for the friends of Cardinal Pell' – one of whom was him.

'Cardinal Pell is a person of both high intelligence and exemplary character,' Howard wrote. 'Strength and sincerity have always been features of his personality. I have always found him to be lacking hypocrisy and cant ... Cardinal Pell is a lively conversationalist who maintains a deep and objective interest in contemporary social and political issues. It is my view that he has dedicated his life to his nation and his church.'

County Court Chief Judge Peter Kidd noted the numerous character references. 'They speak of a man who dedicated his life to service, in particular to vulnerable members of the community,' Chief Judge Kidd said. 'They describe a compassionate and generous person, especially to those experiencing difficulty in their lives; someone who has a deep commitment to social justice issues and the advancement of education for young people. 'I note that these references were not challenged or contradicted by the prosecution.' Chief Judge Kidd made 'substantial allowance for [Pell's] good character and otherwise blameless life'. Pell had been found to be far from 'otherwise blameless' in his life by another body – the Royal Commission into Institutional Responses to Child Abuse. Three commissioners assessing two of the case studies which concerned Pell – including two judges, Jennifer Coate and Chair Peter McClellan – had found in 2017 that Pell, in direct contradiction of the evidence he had given to the commission, had knowledge of allegations about clergy offending in the Diocese of Ballarat and the Archdiocese of Melbourne.

While in some cases his evidence about notorious allegations was accepted by the commission, many of his submissions in relation to what he knew about offending in Ballarat and Melbourne were described as 'implausible', 'inconceivable' or 'not tenable'.

The commission found he wasn't lied to by the notorious Bishop Ronald Mulkearns about why they were moving Father Gerald Ridsdale – one of Australia's worst paedophiles – from parish to parish to abuse ever more children. That, said the commissioners, was 'inconceivable'.

Ridsdale's movements were discussed at Bishop Mulkearns' meetings with his priestly consultors, one of whom, from July 1977, was George Pell.

The commission was satisfied that Bishop Ronald Mulkearns told his consultors about Ridsdale's offences.

'We do not accept that Bishop Mulkearns lied,' the commissioners found, directly contradicting the key plank of Pell's evidence. 'It is inconceivable in these circumstances that Bishop Mulkearns deceived his consultors by not telling them the true reason. There would be little utility in doing so. The secret was out ...

'We are satisfied that Bishop Mulkearns told the consultors that it was necessary to move Ridsdale from the Diocese and from parish work because of complaints that he had sexually abused children. A contrary position is not tenable.'

The report says the 'conduct of any consultor who did not advise against' Ridsdale being moved on 'and who knew the reason Ridsdale ... was being moved, is unacceptable'.

Pell was a consultor. That is, Pell's conduct was unacceptable.

'The lives of dozens of children and their families, likely to be more than a hundred, were devastated by [Ridsdale's] conduct,' the commission found.

The average age of Ridsdale's victims was ten for girls and eleven for boys.

'There was a catastrophic institutional failure which resulted in many children being sexually abused,' the royal commissioners said of Ballarat.

'The welfare of children was not the primary concern of Bishop Mulkearns and other senior members of the Diocese when responding to complaints and allegations of child sexual abuse against their priests.

'There is no doubt it should have been.'

The Ridsdale case is just one example of Pell's knowledge found in the report – others include Fathers Peter Searson and Nazareno Fasciale in Melbourne and Brother Ted Dowlan in Ballarat.

As I wrote in *Cardinal*, all of these men did enormous damage in abusing multiple children in their care.

The commission's report is ruinous for Pell. It hardly paints a 'blameless' picture. But because the law requires that the minds of a jury in a criminal trial must not be 'poisoned' by adverse publicity about the accused – the law of '*sub judice*' – the Royal Commission had elected to redact all of these references in its report, with those redactions to be removed when Pell was convicted or acquitted.

So Chief Judge Kidd was bound not to take this into account in sentencing Pell. It is unlikely he knew about any of these findings as they were not in the public domain. He sentenced Pell to six years in prison, with a three-year and eight-month non-parole period.

It's in some ways academic now, because the High Court decided that a jury, acting rationally, should have entertained a reasonable doubt in Pell's case.

But had the High Court upheld the conviction, Pell's sentence would have remained artificially lower than perhaps it might otherwise have been. Victoria has, after all, introduced a crime of 'failure to protect a child under the age of 16 from a risk of sexual abuse'. The law does not have retrospective application – however, if Pell were to do what he did in the 1970s and 1980s now, that is, not report allegations of sexual abuse in children, he could quite conceivably be charged and, if a jury found him guilty beyond reasonable doubt, convicted.

But according to the law, he led an 'otherwise blameless life'.

LONE WOLF

Perhaps the most surreal part of navigating complainants' journeys through the legal system is finding yourself, inadvertently, becoming a complainant too.

I say those words and then I scold myself. Every complainant of a crime is an inadvertent participant in this process. No one asks to be involved in this ordeal. And most of those I write about endure trauma I will never experience. So I tell the following story simply to illustrate how, no matter how well-resourced you are, the system can still mightily let you down. To demonstrate how surplus-to-needs you end up being, even though you instigated the whole thing.

On a steamy Saturday night in January 2020, I discovered a series of direct messages from a couple of journalists in my acquaintance who had been trying to reach me for a few hours.

They had discovered that a lawyer with whom they had been having a disagreement had posted an intervention order on Twitter and it had my name and date of birth on it as the person who has taken out the order. They were worried for me and alarmed that a lawyer would do such a thing.

I was alarmed too. I had never had anything to do with the lawyer. Why was she tweeting an intervention order I presumed she knew nothing about – which was designed to promote my safety?

I felt sick and my heart started pumping. How exactly was this thing out there?

This thing related to a guy who called himself 'Lone Wolf'.

A guy who had repeatedly made threats to kill me or have me killed.

* * *

Lone Wolf first fleetingly caught my attention in 2018. I noticed a tweet from someone whose profile photo was a picture of me. It was creepy.

Women journalists and commentators are frequently subjected to online hatred and vitriol and, for that reason, I have always attempted to keep my public discussion controlled and professional.

I can't remember much about it, but it was creepy enough for me to block the guy. I remember that his Twitter handle was something to do with a Lone Wolf. You don't forget a menacing name like that when they are using your own photo as a profile picture. But then, you just push the memory to the back of your already overcrowded brain.

* * *

When Pell's conviction was made public on 26 February 2019 and well before that conviction was overturned and Pell was acquitted by the High Court, I was informed by a high-profile tweeter that she was reporting a man to Twitter for his violent comments about me. He used the avatar 'Lone Wolf'. She thought I should also report it to the police.

One tweet was directed to the Australian Federal Police Commissioner:

'Commissioner you know that anger I was talking about yesterday? The anger enough to kill people? I don't like hearing @milliganreports boasting about an injustice. If George Pell were a relative or friend of mine, she'd be dead. I'd find a way.'

On Twitter, if you use someone's 'handle' in a tweet, the user will see it unless they have blocked the person. Because I had blocked him, the tweets hadn't come up in my feed. But the site allows you to check what blocked users are saying about you. In another tweet, which linked to a Facebook post, he said:

'*I have some real issues with the continued employment of Louise Milligan by the ABC. You can't have someone damage journalistic integrity and the justice system in the way she has by indulging lower-class individuals in their hatred for a religious figure.*

'*Hatred begets hatred. I want this woman to pay for what's [sic] she's done. I need her to pay for it. You're making me angrier and I have no idea where this anger is going to go.*'

'*@Victoria Police have questions to answer here as well. If you harbor [sic] hate … what do you think happens? It pushes people closer and closer to the edge.*'

He also made threats to kill Pell's accuser.

'*If he cared about his family at all he wouldn't have done this – because there are guys out there like me who do have the strength of will and mental capacity to kill him for this if we are sufficiently incensed.*'

I thought I should inform my bosses and they advised me to report it to my local police station. I did that on 27 February.

At the police station, the constable who saw me was very friendly and sympathetic. I explained everything to her in great detail. She assured me there would be an investigation. I was asked to go in and make a formal statement to another very nice and professional officer. I felt relieved.

Naïvely, I believed that the police would now monitor this individual. But that never happened.

As the weeks wore on, his threats grew more dangerous. He talked about killing me or having me killed. He referred to a lecture I was delivering at the ABC and published text messages with a friend to arrange to stay with her while he was in Melbourne.

I started to feel sick. Nothing seemed to be happening. The head of security at the ABC was extremely nervous about the night of the lecture, which was coming up. The threats continued.

'*… She should be gone already given that the case was thrown out. This can and will happen again if action isn't taken.*'

'*And @milliganreports, how dare you throw the word justice around. I'm a hero … and you are not fit to lick my boots. HOW FUCKING DARE YOU. YOU ARE GONE IF THE APPEAL FAILS. THAT IS A PROMISE.*'

'If that appeal for Mr. Pell is unsuccessful, what makes you think I won't confront this woman? My girlfriend and I broke up and I'm in a very dark place right now.'

'You stop this nonsense now or if it isn't me someone else will be doing the killing.'

My bosses at the ABC intervened and contacted the superiors at my local police station. They were most sympathetic and explained that they had put a detective on the case.

Again, I thought it would be taken seriously. Again, it wasn't.

The detective telephoned me and, during that conversation, she spoke to me in a voice I felt was rehearsed from countless other conversations with women who were enduring threats of violence. The tone was, I felt, 'no need to get emotional'. She was superficially professional, but had a hardened quality, an unsympathetic air, and a completely unsophisticated understanding of social media.

She kept referring to Twitter as 'Tweeter'. Each time she did it, my jaw clenched.

She may not have realised, but she made me feel like I was a waste of her time. I understand that police have a lot of very difficult work to do about very serious matters, but I felt that my matter warranted proper attention. She was also of the view that finding an IP (Internet Protocol) address attached to the Twitter account – which could track down where the man was – was nigh-on impossible.

'The thing is, Louise, we will need to write away to Tweeter [cue jaw clench] in the US and it could take them up to a year to get back to us,' she said.

Then Lone Wolf changed his profile photo.

The new profile photo was a picture of me, which he had clearly snapped from his television or computer screen, giving an interview to another journalist outside court. In front of it, he held up a sign which said, 'I will find you'.

That's when I became quite distressed. The detective agreed to meet me at the station. It was decided that John Lyons, the ABC's head of investigative and in-depth journalism, would join in via conference call. I was so glad that John was on the call. He was taken aback at her attitude and became quite agitated at her continued assertion that it would take a year for the police to determine the identity of someone who was threatening to kill me on a public platform.

'If Louise was the prime minister,' John said, 'you'd be outside this guy's place right now.'

'But, John, Louise isn't the prime minister,' was her reply.

No, I was not the prime minister. I was a person whose life was being threatened by a clearly disturbed individual who I had never met. I didn't know where he was. I had young children at home. I was a public figure who was readily identifiable because I regularly appeared on television. And, on a rapidly approaching date, I was giving a lecture at a large auditorium and this man had threatened to kill me at that event.

John, in very unvarnished language, made exactly those points.

Modern police have been discouraged from having personal accounts on forums like Facebook and Twitter because they can compromise their personal security and their professionalism. That makes sense. But it sometimes has the effect of meaning that they are not in step with the community they are serving. I think it's something that urgently needs to be addressed by police hierarchy.

A couple of days before I met the detective, a man called Brenton Tarrant killed fifty-one worshippers at two mosques in Christchurch, New Zealand. He live-streamed the first attack on the online message board, 8chan. He had been making threats on the site directly before the attacks.

The publicity around the Christchurch attacks jolted police in both New Zealand and Australia into the realisation that so-called 'keyboard warriors' could actually carry out what had often in the past been assumed to be idle threats. As more information about the case became public, I became increasingly worried.

Eventually, in desperation, during a conversation about something else with a politician I knew professionally, I asked his advice about what I could do. He was concerned because of the Christchurch situation.

Within hours, Victoria Police swung into action. I had a profuse apology from the detective's superior at my local police station. He was fantastic. The man was located in New South Wales. The NSW Police counter-terrorism squad were involved.

Shortly after, I was told Lone Wolf lived in a small town in New South Wales. Local police had arrived at his home, arrested him and charged him with State and Commonwealth offences. His computer equipment was seized, he was served with an intervention order and placed on bail with very strict conditions that included not using computers or social media in any form. He was not to come near me, nor to attempt to contact me.

That was April 2019. The very friendly and seemingly helpful New South Wales senior constable from the man's local town told me there was to be a court hearing later in the year. I would be told when that would take place.

I felt that, given all of this, I was probably reasonably safe. I trusted that I would be kept informed and justice would take its normal course.

As it turned out, my trust was misplaced. I was not informed. I did not receive justice.

I didn't hear about Lone Wolf again until the journalists warned me in January 2020 – nine months later – that he was tweeting again.

Because I had blocked him, I hadn't realised what he was up to. Once or twice after the previous April, I checked Lone Wolf's account, and there was nothing there. He seemed to be abiding by the bail conditions and the intervention order. I assumed that the legal process would take some time and that I would be told when the court date was to take place.

The night I discovered, in January 2020, that screenshots of the intervention order were being published on Twitter, I sat up for some hours and looked back through Lone Wolf's history, capturing screenshots as I went.

I discovered that he had been tweeting furiously again about me – trying to reach people who I assume he thought might contact me because he couldn't, as I had blocked him.

As I scrolled back, I realised that the tweets had commenced again back in October the year before – three months earlier. He alluded to a court hearing of some sort. He was saying that the judge had believed him and thrown out my case. He was saying he had been exonerated, and it was a malicious prosecution by myself and the ABC. He was angry at us for what he perceived was unfair persecution and said, at one point 'Violence is the answer.'

He threatened to breach the intervention order, said, of the Pell appeal, *'It's gonna be overturned and is gonna be the fucking end of her. If it is not ...'*

'What?' I thought. 'Why the hell don't I know about this? Why was it thrown out?'

Less than an hour after the court hearing had taken place, he had gone home and fired up Twitter again.

And from his first tweet since leaving court, he used the same profile picture with the photograph of me and the sign: 'I will find you'. He said he was doing this to prove that he had done nothing wrong in the first place. He went home and he breached the order from day one. And no one noticed.

He was now completely emboldened.

The morning after I discovered the tweets, I immediately called the local police station in Lone Wolf's town. A senior constable returned my call. He sounded fairly young, and he was sympathetic. He wasn't terribly formal in the way some cops can be.

It turns out he had helped do the raid on Lone Wolf's house the previous April, when they removed his computer equipment. He knew all about the case.

I told him what had been going on. He said it was a clear breach of the intervention order.

I asked him what happened to the case. Why was Lone Wolf out and posting on Twitter again? How could this happen?

He looked up the file and he told me he didn't have much information, but he could say that the case went to a local court the previous October.

I told him no one had informed me of that.

'You didn't get a subpoena to appear as a witness?' he asked.

No, I did not. Not only that, I didn't get any word from NSW Police that the case was proceeding on that day. I didn't receive any notice of the outcome. I had been waiting and I assumed that it must have been delayed the way these things often are. I thought they would tell me when it was going to court.

It transpired that the offences had been found as 'conviction not proved [sic]' by way of section 32(3) of the NSW *Mental Health Act 2007*. Lone Wolf had been discharged into the care of his mother.

Scoffing sourly, I told the cop it was hilarious that I had not been informed of any of this.

He said it was not hilarious at all and he apologised profusely.

I told him I was working on a book and it was about what happens to complainants who are victims of crimes when they come forward to the criminal justice system and how it lets them down so bitterly.

He cut in and said, sincerely, 'I am *so* glad you are writing that book, Louise. That book really needs to be written. We see really awful things happening to complainants.'

I told him that I knew. My heart was racing now.

'That is what's happening to me right now,' I began. 'I'm being shut out of the process.

'So if this is what happens to me, what hope does anyone else have?'

The senior constable just kept apologising. He was sweet, and he was embarrassed.

'It's wild,' I continue. 'I can't describe it any other way.

'I was the victim in this matter, and I've been so thoroughly shut out of the process that I haven't even been told the outcome.

'No one consulted me on how it was to proceed. No one gave me the opportunity to give oral evidence. No one asked me what I thought of this plea bargain. No one informed me that it was happening. No one wrote, apologetically or otherwise, to say this is what had taken place.'

Lone Wolf went to court on the morning of 10 October 2019. Just before midday that day, he started tweeting again for the first time since he had been granted bail earlier in the year.

His first subject was the Pell case. He tweeted about that directly to Victoria Police and to its Chief Commissioner, Graham Ashton. With the picture of me.

Within five days, he was actively disparaging me again, accusing me of being in a conspiracy against Pell. No one noticed.

I didn't either because I had long since blocked him. So he chose another person to whom he'd deliver his weird and confused manifesto. The first person he chose to target in this renewed campaign against me was Saxon Mullins.

As I re-read his comments over the next couple of days – his endorsement of the idea of a mass shooting, his threats to go the full 'Arthur Fleck', his lies about me, his vitriol, his paranoid conspiracy theories, as I looked over and over at that picture of me with that sign, 'I will find you', the anger rose through me.

I thought about those comments from the barristers about how the system wasn't perfect but there were checks and balances in place. I thought about all complainants in all cases, endlessly tormented because their case was intentionally delayed or just didn't go ahead, feeling like they'd wasted their time and been put through the wringer for it.

I thought about Saxon and how she never gave up and politely called me every now and then to make sure I hadn't forgotten her, and she wasn't going away because it was burning inside her. I thought of Paris Street, going along to the Pell trial just because he wanted to look Richter in the eye.

I thought of how all of these people felt, and so many others felt, when the High Court said 'no jury, acting rationally' could have reached the conclusion it did to find Pell guilty. I thought about the chilling effect that this pronouncement about a jury – effectively, that they didn't know their own minds, that they didn't matter – would have on any person coming forward against a powerful and connected man.

I later found out that it had had a profoundly chilling effect on one woman who had planned to come forward against another high-profile man. She told all of her friends she was devastated. Two months later, she took her own life.

How can this all keep happening? Doesn't this system warrant change?

I rang a Pell complainant and I told him what had happened with Lone Wolf. I hadn't spoken to him for ages at that point. He had had an incredibly rough time. Life had dealt him a series of crushing blows – many of which had had nothing to do with his complaint to police or the case that followed. He was a likeable guy.

I just knew that he would understand what I was going through. He was angry but not surprised that the system had let me down.

He told me he wanted to expose the 'terrible' way complainants were treated by this process.

He said he wanted me to say he was someone who would not advise a complainant of sexual abuse to come forward to police.

'My life is fucking ruined, Louise. I am not the same.' He rarely left the house now. I felt desperately sad for this man, whom I had become fond of through this process. I just wanted his life to be better. I've refrained from naming him here just because he's had enough. He needs his life to be better too.

My rational self told me that a trial would have been horrible for this complainant. But yet the process had taken nearly four years of this man's life and then ... nothing. He was just expected to walk away and resume his life.

The system so often builds complainants up and then, at crucial and unexpected moments, it tells them they don't matter that much. They're left reeling. The nice local cop's words rattled around in my brain again. 'That book really needs to be written.'

Nothing I had endured – not the months of stress, not Richter, not the prospect of being prosecuted for contempt of court, not the secret hearing, and not the mishandling of the Lone Wolf business – held a candle to what all of the people I have written about have suffered. I wrestled with whether to include this Lone Wolf business in this book at all because I don't want to imply that I am a victim. I don't want pity – others are so much more deserving of that. But it so perfectly illustrated the flaws in the system, that it fails even someone like me, that in the end I figured it had to be told.

I looked in the mirror, wiped the mascara off the skin under my eyes, where it had collected in smudges as if a little kid with poor fine motor skills had drawn all over me with a stubbed grey-lead pencil.

And I pulled out my laptop and I began to write.

* * *

It would take NSW Police almost three months to charge Lone Wolf after my first conversation with the young constable. In the meantime, Lone Wolf would escalate, repeatedly referencing the Christchurch shooter Brenton Tarrant, talking about causing 'an international incident', saying he was a vigilante and was 'ready for the end of [his] own life', threatening my friends – in the case of one of them, a well-known journalist, calling her a 'fucking fat fucking bitch' and brandishing the intervention order at her, saying, 'Maybe you should get one to [sic]'. '*I FUCKING HATE HER. I FUCKING HATE HER,*' he said of me in a direct message to my friend.

He made disparaging comments about Saxon Mullins and Paris Street.

'*Paris Street, you're a fucker. Boo hoo I got harassed by a gay guy in year 7 dude. Don't see me crying like the little bitch you are.*'

He eventually started to also threaten the ABC Managing Director, David Anderson. Anderson, a genuine and decent man, was very supportive. Yet again, for the second year in a row, it was high-level intervention that finally got the police to act. And at that time, the hierarchy of Victoria Police was incredibly supportive and helpful in assisting the young New South Wales constable to bring Lone Wolf to justice.

Lone Wolf was charged again in the week in April 2020 that George Pell was acquitted by the High Court. The hearing was repeatedly delayed because of COVID. Lone Wolf eventually pleaded guilty in August. He was sentenced to a one-year community corrections order and, thanks to the efforts of the nice young cop, the intervention order will remain in place until 2025. I was not, however, given the opportunity to give a victim impact statement that might assist the magistrate in sentencing him. That horse has now bolted, but I hope that all involved will read these pages. I hope Lone Wolf can get some help and focus his attentions on something more worthwhile.

The entire episode caused me enormous stress, fears for my safety, and serious concern at the lack of training for many police in these sorts of cases. But most of all, if the system can let me down – with all of the privilege and resources that come with the job that I do – no wonder far more profoundly hurt victims are let down too.

THE FIX

The issues examined in this book cause me to reflect that we must do better. We must do better by children, by the men and women they grow up to be. By the adult victims of sexual crimes who also come before the courts, expecting a far fairer system than what they ultimately encounter.

As the Victorian Law Commission noted, in 2016, the focus on the contest between the Crown and the accused perpetrator has 'eclipsed the recognition of the victim's inherent interest'. The victim becomes a bystander in the action that has often, tragically, defined their life in ways they desperately wish it hadn't.

In 2019, Victorian Attorney-General Jill Hennessy burst into tears in State parliament talking about the legacy of institutional child sexual abuse, and legislation she championed to compel religious leaders to report knowledge of these crimes.

'People took their lives because they could not bear to live with the consequences,' Hennessy said, breaking down and bending her head in tears. She sobbed for a few seconds, before tilting her head up again and continuing, defiantly, through sobs, 'They could not bear to live with the consequences of being a victim of child sexual abuse.

'When no one believed them. And no one protected them.

'And if we don't start taking our obligations seriously, around the protection of children, then we don't deserve to sit in this parliament.'

I don't think I've ever seen such a moving speech by a politician in a parliamentary chamber. It signalled that Hennessy genuinely does care.

But in August 2020, survivors and advocacy groups were dismayed to discover that Hennessy's department had overseen a change in Victorian law – quietly enacted the previous February. It would now mean that where there was a guilty verdict for a crime of sexual penetration, a victim would have to get a court order to be able to speak out under their own name about the case.

The news was broken by activist journalist Nina Funnell, a director, with Saxon Mullins and a group of criminologists, of the group Rape and Sexual Assault Research and Advocacy (RASARA). It was splashed on the cover of the *Herald Sun* newspaper. It seemed to be the result of some very poor drafting. The law had been designed to actually assist victims who had seen suppression orders attached to their case to be able to apply to the court to have it removed so that they could speak out after conviction if they so wished. Instead, it meant that now *all* victims had to apply to the court. It meant, for example, Ballarat Catholic Church clergy abuse survivors who had been advocating on behalf of their community for years could not speak out in their own names. It was absurd, silencing, horribly paternalistic.

Reading it, in the *Judicial Proceedings Reports Act*, the relevant sections can only be described as legislative soup. I spoke to three separate lawyers for victims who experienced real difficulty in determining on first and second reading, what it really meant.

Both Hennessy and Premier Daniel Andrews swiftly reacted to Funnell's story and the subsequent outcry it provoked by survivors, saying that the law would be urgently amended to fix the problem and indicating that the effect of it was unintentional. It was certainly not in keeping with the Victorian government's previous stance on these issues.

But Swinburne University criminologist and RASARA director, Dr Rachael Burgin, told me that the RASARA group had been warning the Attorney-General's office for some time about the problem with the law. They were annoyed that it took a story on the front page of a newspaper for the government to take notice. At time of writing, it seems the law will be changed soon, but it was another disempowering moment for survivors who have already had enough. RASARA is currently campaigning to reform sexual assault laws around the country.

The Victorian Law Reform Commission is currently conducting a review of improving the response of the justice system to sexual offences. Included in the terms of reference will be an examination of how to better support complainants in the criminal justice system and defamation and civil claims, including reducing trauma to them.

At the time of writing, there are a slew of inquiries being conducted and legislative proposals considered to try to wrestle with these issues: New South Wales is still finalising its Law Reform Commission Report into consent laws sparked by Saxon's case. Attorney-General Mark Speakman has also, in the wake of the Dyson Heydon findings in the High Court investigation, announced a departmental review of the way New South Wales courts and tribunals handle sexual harassment complaints. Queensland is still toying with the implementation of its legislation which would mean that child sex offenders' good character cannot be taken into account in sentencing.

The Victorian Law Reform Inquiry report on Victims of Crime made a number of recommendations – some of which, such as the bans on improper questioning, and a pilot intermediary scheme for child and vulnerable witnesses (discussed below) have been implemented. But others have not. It recommended that the State's Charter of Human Rights and Responsibilities be amended to include provisions that victims are acknowledged as participants (but not parties) to criminal proceedings, that they be 'treated with respect at all times' and that they be protected from 'unnecessary trauma, intimidation and distress when giving evidence'. That has not happened. The charter continues to protect, at length, the rights of accused people – as it should. But victims enjoy no such protections.

Submissions to a Victorian Law Reform Inquiry into committal proceedings by the Office of Public Prosecutions, which released its discussion paper in June 2020, have also recommended no cross-examination of victims of sexual offences prior to trial – to avoid the trauma of having to go through this process twice. It proposes abolishing a committal proceeding altogether and replacing it with a 'case management hearing' to ventilate the more procedural issues rather than raking over issues that will be raised at trial. Many lawyers have said to me that committal proceedings are often improperly used as a way of destroying witnesses, when there is no risk of upsetting a jury, before they get to trial. This proposal seems sensible. It would also minimise the length of time before both the complainant and the accused get finality in their case. The average time for a case to be completed from time of charge to completion was 19.9 months.

In 2017, the child abuse Royal Commission also made twelve recommendations to State and Territory governments to implement measures to improve the experience of giving evidence for victims and survivors in child sex cases. An analysis in March 2020 of ninety-eight projects of States and Territories to implement those recommendations found only eighteen of the projects had been completed. The analysis, by knowmore Legal – which is funded by the Commonwealth Government to give advice and information to survivors of abuse – found half of the projects had achieved no clear progress at all.

There have been many other parliamentary inquiries, Law Reform Commission reports, media exposés and scandals. And yet, we are where we are. And where we are is far from good enough.

For me, the single biggest issue is that victims are, essentially, legally, at sea. They have no one advising them on how they should navigate this system. Unlike me, they don't have Jack Rush QC or Peter Morrissey SC or Sarala Fitzgerald, or the lawyers at the ABC. They don't have a management team and sympathetic colleagues and a publisher behind them. In many cases, their families are not supportive of their chosen course, or at the very least, try to convince them they shouldn't come forward.

They come before the court to be cross-examined, potentially by a fierce advocate, with years of experience, completely alone. To have to relive their disgusting trauma and to have it doubted again, with no one to make sure that their human rights are not being abrogated, that the *Evidence Act* is not being breached, that the barrister isn't acting in a way that breaks the rules he or she is bound by.

Yes, there is a judge and a prosecutor, but so often, for a multitude of reasons, they do not protect the witness or at least, they do not do it as well as they might.

'The reluctance to recognise victims as anything more than a prosecution witness,' writes Dr Mary Iliadis, a criminologist from Melbourne's Deakin University, in a paper from 2019 on the subject, stems from a concern that victims 'will invite potentially subjective and thus prejudicial submissions on matters of state concern' which could compromise the 'objective and public nature of the criminal justice system and hinder an accused person's due process rights to a fair and impartial trial'.

Essentially, this means that the law is concerned that elevating the role of complainant witnesses – victims – will give an unfair advantage to the Crown in proving the prosecution case beyond reasonable doubt and that people accused of, say, child rape, won't get justice. But the flow-on consequences of these concerns are not good for victims.

Iliadis says that the law has tried to give 'greater credence to victims' rights', but in doing so, the desire to protect the right to an accused's fair trial has resulted in 'conservative adversarial reform' relating to things like more information to victims and providing victim impact statements.

But even that process has been extremely clunky and paternalistic. The young woman I called 'Sophie' in the Weston Airbnb case was horrified by the way her victim impact statement was received. Unlike many victims who feel too broken to have the energy to read their statement aloud, Sophie was determined to deliver hers in the court.

Sophie understood that it was rare for rape cases to have the outcome hers did – that is, with a conviction – but said, 'I feel no victory and no justice.

'As time goes on, everything seems to be getting harder and I can see how it has affected me in so many ways that it is hard not to be disappointed in myself,' Sophie told the court.

'I have been suicidal; I have been depressed and I suffer severe anxiety ...'

She said her experience of the legal system had just 'added to the trauma'. 'My relationships have been damaged, I don't meet or trust new people and I have put a strain on the ones I already had,' she said.

These words had great poignancy for Sophie. She tells me when we speak on the phone that during the court case, her-then partner flew to Melbourne, and, in her words, 'dumped' her, then flew home.

She speaks of her financial troubles, her lost happiness, her lack of self-confidence, the experience of reading about incredibly intimate details about her own body in the media, feeling disempowered and paternalised and kept in the dark about a case that wouldn't have existed without her.

'I hope these aspects of the system can evolve so that the experience of attempting to get justice isn't so painful,' Sophie read from her statement to the court.

'The scary thing is, I don't get a release date; I don't get to start over – I am just left to make the most of the person I am now.

'I am yet to discover the full impact of how this will affect me, and while right here, right now, I would rather be doing anything else, I am doing this for the future woman I will become, who will never get her day to speak in court again, but will suffer the consequences of this trauma for the rest of her life.'

I can only imagine what it was like for Sophie to deliver this speech in that intimidating place, the courtroom, but she did it. In my experience, she is a spirited and impressive young woman who refused to back down and managed to stare down the criminal justice system. I salute her.

But Sophie tells me that after her statement, bearing in mind that her rapist had at that time been convicted, she felt the judge gave her no words of comfort.

'The judge just replied that you should not look for any closure from this,' Sophie tells me now.

'It made me so angry – I had just read out a page and a half about how this affected my life and he just says, "don't look for closure from this". He didn't give me any sympathy – he didn't say "sorry this happened to you".

'I trusted the process, even though I knew it was flawed, [but at that moment] it was basically like I had handed in an essay and I got my constructive criticism and I was, like, [thinking] "Shut the hell up – it's your chance to say that I am heard and the court has heard me."'

Sitting in a neighbourhood restaurant with Paris Street, he describes to me his whole experience of the legal system as 'like I was in after-school detention'.

For Paris, because of all of the resources devoted to defending Kehoe, it felt like, instead of him, his perpetrator was being protected – 'the person who should've, could've *didn't* protect me'.

'It felt like, "Where's hope?"' Paris says, looking off into the distance in that way that he has.

He felt utterly confused when Richter started at him – like he had done something wrong, when he'd only reported to police behaviour that, as a fifteen-year-old boy, concerned him.

'And that's the point where I needed someone like a lawyer who understood what was going on,' he says.

'The support people who were there were very comforting, and supportive,' he says, 'but if I had someone who was powerful and influential in their own right, supporting me, a person who I could have built trust with, that would have been so much better.'

'If I had a lawyer or someone on my side ... If I had Judy there,' he says, referring to his indomitable solicitor, Judy Courtin, 'she would, it would, be someone supporting *me* and not just defending or prosecuting Kehoe.

'That's something I could tell was missing. That's what was missing. Like, in the breaks when I was bawling my eyes out, they were comforting, but they couldn't ... they couldn't offer any advice.'

The way Saxon Mullins describes it, it was like being just a 'bystander' in the criminal justice process.

'One hundred per cent,' Saxon says, 'and a bystander throughout this whole ordeal that turned on me.

'I get no say, no information, just "thanks for doing your bit" and that's it.'

Michele Williams QC, the former senior Crown prosecutor and first head of the specialist sex offences unit at Victoria's Office of Public Prosecutions, says witnesses should be better informed. And that, says Williams, is up to the prosecutor. Interestingly, in my interviews with women who have been prosecutors or judges, they are all proudly interventionist. But Williams says that in her experience, some of the older men didn't think it was part of their job to intervene.

'I think there's still this old hangover of, "Oh well just let the witness go and it'll be better in the end because we don't want to interfere, we don't want to look like we're trying to protect them,"' Williams says.

'But I don't think,' she says, pausing to qualify that this is a 'big generalisation', 'I don't think the blokes get it, that it's not about that, and it is still about at least trying to treat witnesses with respect.

'It's not meant to be this whole traumatic experience, but it is.

'And I just wonder, as I say, how far we've come?'

She says the point is, that all of the reforms in the world about remote witness evidence, legislative reform about improper questions and judicial directions, don't mean anything if the prosecutor doesn't intervene and the judge or magistrate isn't in control of the courtroom.

'They don't carry their job out, you see,' she says of some judicial officers. 'They've got to control their own courtroom.'

But she also says it's about prosecutors properly conferencing their witnesses – and, in fact, during her time at the Crown, she tried to make it mandatory for prosecutors to do this.

'And people used to say to me, particularly the older males, "Ah, no, no, I can't have a conference with the complainant, they might say something,"' Williams says.

'And I said, "Well, you know what? If you want to continue with this work, you will conference the complainant and I'll understand if you don't want to – we will take you off the list of barristers who are interested in doing this work,"' she says.

She says the barristers' response was, 'Oh my God!'

'So I started a bit of a revolution in that lane. I dragged all the older blokes kicking and screaming into the modern era.'

But she laments that you 'need someone to lead in that space' – meaning the sexual offences space. 'You need someone who is proactive in that space. I might be falling foul of the current heads in the prosecution space at the moment, but they don't lead on those aspects,' Williams says.

'And it's absolutely vital. It's vital not only for the witness, in this case we are talking about a complainant of an often horrific, pretty much always, sexual offence against them.'

She says this is about preparing the victim for exactly what the courtroom process is about, what giving their evidence will involve.

'I used to always say, "I'm being very selfish here, I want to get the best from you. I want to win."'

Hearing this passionate, tough woman speak is heartening. I just think of the many people to whom I have spoken over the years who didn't have someone like her to lay it all out for them, to encourage them, to lift them up.

'"I want you to be able to give the best evidence that I know you are able to do, because I can see – it's in your statement,"' Williams would tell the complainants.

She is very clear that this is not about 'coaching' witnesses – a practice which takes place in the United States but is not permitted in Australian law.

'But I used to always say,' she explains, '"Look, we're going to have … Let's call this a practice run. I've got your statement, I need to get the evidence from you."' She would then run through some of the questions in the statement to ensure that the witness could answer her questions in a logical fashion. She'd also give them an indication of the types of questions they might be asked.

'I often said, "Look, I will do my best but you're not going to like a lot of the questions and it's going to be difficult. I can object, and I will object if I think it's insulting, or it shouldn't be asked, and so on and so forth."'

For Williams, it was 'totally' about 'forewarned is forearmed' and being 'well and truly prepared'. She would have a conference with the witness, but not just hurriedly, the same day as their evidence, before they went into court.

'You see, some [prosecutors] go, "Oh well, yes, I'll conference them on the morning and I'll spend fifteen minutes with them." And everybody's rushed … That's not preparing the witness.'

Instead, she recommended preparing the witness the previous week. And spending a whole day with several witnesses 'so that we had plenty of time to prepare them for not only the evidence that they could give but the emotional journey that they were inevitably going to go on'.

Sally Flynn QC also advocates for very careful conferencing of complainants.

'Don't lie about it, don't lie about anything. If you don't understand the question, don't answer it. If you don't know, or don't remember, don't make up anything. Don't guess, don't speculate. If you don't know, you don't know.'

She says she then discusses, without, again, resorting to coaching, who the defence barrister is and the types of questions he or she might ask, that they might 'thump the table', or raise their voice, if that happens to be their style.

'And I'll say, "He might ask you a question where he sounds absolutely like he knows what he's talking about and he's holding a piece of paper in front of him and it's written on there,"' Flynn says.

'But if your evidence was the car was red, and he says to you, in a really confident voice, "But the car was *blue*, wasn't it?", you don't agree with it. Don't agree with anything you genuinely don't agree with.'

She says the problem is that, otherwise, witnesses 'go in there and they just go along with it, because they think, "Oh, this guy must know."'

'And it's just *so* frustrating,' Flynn says. 'And you talk to them afterwards and say, "Well, why did you agree with that? Why did you agree that it was in the back bungalow and not in the bedroom?" [and they will reply] "I don't know, I just got flustered, and I just wanted it to be over with."'

Unprepared witnesses do not give best evidence – they give evidence against themselves, or against the case, even when it's not true. They are tied in knots, confused, led into saying things that, in any other forum, they know not to be true.

Barristers who have done prosecutions well acknowledge that some of their colleagues do not necessarily prepare the witness the way they do. Some prosecutors conference the witness in a far more careful and bland way. They worry about overstepping the mark.

'Some are lazy,' Williams begins, 'some don't care enough ... Some don't want to do it.' And some, she adds, think this is not the job of the prosecutor at all – that it's the job of the social workers in the Witness Assistance Service program who should be preparing the witness. The problem is, the social workers can't really explain exactly who defence counsel are and what they are about to do to you. They didn't for Paris Street. And neither did the police prosecutor. I describe Paris' experience to Michele – the complete surprise that defence counsel would speak to him in that way, the lack of significant preparation or understanding, the sobbing when the screen snapped off, the punching of the bedroom walls, the fifteen-year-old's world coming tumbling down.

'I mean it's ...' Williams trails off. 'The system, it seems to me, hasn't come that far in many respects, and it just needs people to really be able to take control.

'And I keep saying it and I will repeat it; it has to be the prosecutors because they're the ones who have to ... It's their case.

'Now, it is their job to present the evidence in the best light, and also, as far as I'm concerned ... it's not about protecting the witnesses; it's about ensuring that they are treated with respect and, as much as possible, the process doesn't retraumatise them.'

A Centre for Independent Justice report from 2019 on victims' experiences found, in interviews with victims, that while many prosecutors advocate the kind of consultative approach that Williams advocates, some did not. Some found lawyers treated them in ways that were 'cold', 'clinical', 'unapproachable' or 'rude'. They said that one of the most striking examples of poor communication by lawyers towards victims was when lawyers failed to demonstrate empathy. Some said they were intimidated in pre-trial meetings and didn't know what to ask. Prosecutors interviewed for the study expressed their concern that there was a tension between fully informing the complainant and not coaching a witness.

'... It did make it feel somewhat tokenistic, and certainly in that meeting there was that sense of it being a token, "Okay, we have to tick this box, like we have to tell the victims about this and try and explain it and it doesn't matter what you say because I'm the expert here," one victim said.

'... You can't help but feel like you're just another number who's been put through the wringer.'

The social workers from the Witness Assistance Service program who liaised with victims expressed similar concerns to the victims themselves about some prosecutors.

'People in conferences where they just struggle to have empathy. They just come in with this really clinical ... with what they need to talk about.'

'It's okay for people to cry. It's okay for people to get angry, you know, but ... I get that look ... like, "Make them stop," ... I can't make them stop.'

'... As soon as a victim cries, you get the whole table of people staring at you like, "Fix this problem ..."'

Felicity Gerry QC is a British advocate who operates both in Melbourne and in the United Kingdom. She has specialised in sex offences, mercy petitions and international human trafficking cases. She's an incredible, effusive, tornado of a woman who has chambers on the same floor as Robert Richter, Phil Dunn and Peter Morrissey.

She's tall, striking, with dark hair highlighted with a sweep of silver at the front. She sports vermilion lipstick, winged eyeliner, cobalt nail polish and statement clothes. She talks at a rate of knots. You can't miss her. She's so different from all the blokes around her in the most excellent possible way. But apart from that, Gerry has been a fierce advocate for women's and children's human rights. She is passionate about victims taking up the power once denied them to come into the courtroom and make themselves heard. She has worked both as a prosecutor and as a defence counsel.

'Because when I started twenty-five years ago, hardly any women and children gave evidence as witnesses, even then,' Gerry tells me.

'I have a thing about women being visible – come and tell your damned story, because we've had to put up with this for centuries,' she says. 'We used to be property. We could be beaten with a stick. We could be raped. Our children were abused. If you don't stand up and tell those stories, then people don't hear those stories.'

The issue is, Gerry concedes, that the courts are now making up for lost time.

'So now you've got courts dealing with not just the new cases but all those historic cases from thirty years ago that nobody ever did anything about,' she says. 'So you've got the courts full, absolutely full, of vulnerability, no recognition of it in the dock, loads of it in the witness box, and learning along the way, "How do we get this right?" And I would call it, the only way you can get it right is with dignity and respect.'

Gerry is the first to allow that sometimes the dignity and respect goes out the window when cross-examination becomes heated. And she concedes that the system is still learning how to manage 'this stuff'.

'The system, it's a slow beast. It's a very slow beast,' she says.

Defence counsel are searching for reasonable doubts that they might offer to the jury. Victims are horribly retraumatised by doubt. It's a very difficult balance to strike. Gerry thinks that, on the whole, it is achievable.

'Look, you don't have to shout at a witness,' she says. 'You don't have to bully a witness. You don't have to be sarcastic. You have to, weirdly, enable them to give their best evidence about the stuff that you're challenging them on, if you're cross-examining.

'So, it's always going to be a challenge. And you get a mixed bag of reactions.

'Some people will say, "Oh, that was so cathartic. I don't care, win or lose, I've told my story."

'And other people will say, "That was worse than what happened in the first place."'

She thinks that, from the outset, witnesses need to be given a better understanding of what's going to happen to them.

'That's the choice you have to make when you go to the police, the moment you step through that door. I think that's where people don't necessarily get that advice,' Gerry says. 'There are two things that I think go wrong. One is the moment you step through the door it's not private anymore. It is not private. You're going into a public zone because it's a police investigation. That's the state.'

But she also thinks that the advice witnesses are given about how to behave is often wrong and sets them up for failure.

'[E]verybody advises them, "Be strong. You can be really strong." So, they sort of get themselves het up to be strong and they're not. They're simply not strong.'

That leads to problems with how the witness presents – and can, ironically, make them less believable for a jury. It's something I've often seen as a television reporter. People can at times be so worried that they are going to cry that they don't open up and then the audience doesn't feel empathy for them.

'So you then get … a terrible witness who's sort of wooden and being strong, and they're given the wrong advice by their friends, "Be strong, you can do it", and they're not.

'Don't be strong, just tell your story.

'I think that people don't understand that you cannot be strong about this stuff. You are going to break because it's the worst thing that's happened to you anyway and you're reliving that worst experience.'

For Gerry, prosecutors and those around witnesses need not to sugar-coat the experience of being a witness.

'They're just alone. They're just on their own. That witness box is a very lonely place, whether you're in a room doing video or in a courtroom, you're on your own because it's your story.

'I sometimes think, "Maybe that's what we need to teach people. You've got the power to go and tell your story."

'It's going to be bloody hard, and you've got to know that you can cope with that. And you might not know until you actually do it.

'It's okay that you can't do it, or you couldn't do it as well, or it devastates you afterwards, that's okay because you still have the power to do it.'

But just because reliving this experience is going to be, by its very nature, awful, Gerry says that doesn't give legal advocates carte blanche to treat witnesses as they like. She says barristers also need to take some responsibility for what is happening in the court – and that means trauma-informed practice.

'Achieving best evidence is good language,' she says. 'Dignity and respect is good language. It's all about courtesy … That sounds so old-fashioned and patriarchal now – "it's courtesy" – but it's absolutely what it is.'

Courtesy doesn't seem so old-fashioned to me. And it doesn't seem like too big an ask.

The problem is, how do you regulate courtesy? What if you have a steamroller of a defence barrister who just refuses to employ it? What if it's all in the tone and defies the transcript and, therefore, is difficult to assess should an appeal be lodged alleging that, for instance, the judge has an apprehended bias?

Gerry has been involved with a program in the UK called The Advocate's Gateway, which provides 'toolkits' for both Crown and defence counsel on how to get best evidence from vulnerable witnesses such as children, witnesses with autism or ADHD, or other disabilities.

The scheme pioneered the use of intermediaries – independent and neutral third parties who come into the courtroom to assist these witnesses.

Police or prosecutors refer the complainant to the scheme if they assess that there is a need. Some extremely competent teenagers have been granted intermediaries, but at this stage it is by no means a catch-all for every child who comes before the court. For that reason, I'm not at all certain that Paris Street would have been granted one for his case.

These programs were discussed in the child abuse Royal Commission and, as a result, are now being piloted across Australia. The Victorian County Court has just completed a trial program with intermediaries and, for anyone who has experience of someone close to them with a language or communication disorder, they are a marvellous introduction to the courts. I don't quite know how they managed before – and can only conclude that many injustices ensued.

County Court Judge Meryl Sexton is proud of the intermediary program, which she says isn't just about what questions barristers can ask a witness, but 'managing those witnesses, from all perspectives'. The process starts with a 'ground rules hearing' where the special requirements of the witness are heard, and the style of questioning is settled to meet their needs. In courtrooms like this, defence counsel simply aren't allowed to ask questions that confuse or intimidate the witness. Language is required to be direct, bullying the witness is anathema to this process.

'The intermediary program has been well-received. It's such a different way of doing things, though, it's still going through teething problems,' Judge Sexton told me.

'I have yet to have a practitioner who hasn't said, "I agree with all of the recommendations of the intermediary, they all seem completely common sense, what a great idea, and I have no trouble doing any of that,"' she says.

'However, when we come to the hearing the next day, they can't help themselves but ask questions without taking the witness' needs into account, and as laid out in the ground rules.

'And they just forget – partly because they haven't taken to heart that they have to prepare ahead of time – they can't just stand up and have a list of topics and just ask the question off the top of their head – they have to actually think about their questions. Preparing questions in advance is alien to the way barristers operate.'

Judge Sexton maintains the barristers aren't motivated by 'ill-will', they just haven't quite realised that they have to prepare very carefully for these hearings in advance and think about what they ask.

'And that's something we're still having to work through,' she says.

For instance, she notes that where the intermediary establishes that there has to be a pause between asking a question and expecting an answer because the witness needs time to cognitively process their thoughts on a question, the barristers often don't get that cue.

'And barristers will often read the witness taking the time to respond as "Oh, they didn't understand what I said", so they'll ask a follow-up question,' Judge Sexton explains. 'Which means the witness has to think about the follow-up question, and they still haven't processed the first one.

'So, that's a bad habit, but it's a habit that barristers find difficult to break.

'... and that's where we [as judges] have to say, "No, remember you have to wait, count five seconds, count to five in your head, before you ask, 'Do you want me to ask that a different way,'" rather than just going in with a different way of asking it, and without giving the witness time to process.'

Another example is barristers asking so-called 'tag questions' phrased in the negative – 'he didn't do it, did he?' which is, Judge Sexton says, a 'very complex question' for a vulnerable witness who has a communication issue. Barristers are required to instead ask direct questions, phrased in the positive.

'That's [barristers'] favourite question, putting something in the negative,' Judge Sexton says.

'And so this has been a very hard process for them ... This is a whole different way of doing things.'

That is the understatement of the century. I think about this polite, ordered setting, where the witness' needs are discussed and met, rather than what, for example, Paris was subjected to.

Sexton cites an example of where there was a ground rules hearing with an intermediary's report in one of her cases and the barrister did a 'fantastic job'.

'It was slow, it was measured, it was, for him, apparently, unutterably boring,' Sexton says. 'But he didn't break out – he stuck to it,' she says.

'And the feedback, later, was that he had never felt so impotent as a barrister. He just thought that it wasn't getting the message across to the jury.'

When a witness who was related to the complainant came to be interviewed, there had been no intermediary arranged for her because the court wasn't aware that, as became immediately apparent, she, too, had a disability.

And so what happened?

'The barrister did revert to type,' Judge Sexton remembers. She says he wasn't 'being mean' to the witness, but he was asking questions too quickly, posing them in the negative.

'And I had to just intervene on almost every question,' she says. 'And I happen to be an interventionist judge ... I'm sure some barristers don't like that. But, I've just had so much experience of this over so many years, that I just know how important it is for a vulnerable witness to be asked appropriate questions in an appropriate way that recognises their communication needs. Despite my intervention, I still felt she was not able to give her best evidence because she did not have the benefit of being prepared. She couldn't have an intermediary, who would have ensured that the court was aware of her communication needs, because she wasn't a complainant witness, but I recognise that we could well have managed her much better.

'The moral of the story is that, in the end, the accused did get acquitted. So, the result for the barrister was, "I did the job of questioning the complainant, within the ground rules, and I got the outcome for my client that I was seeking to get." You could not say that his client had not had a fair trial with those rules being strictly adhered to for the complainant witness.'

Judge Sexton is making the very valid point – which desperately needs to be heard by defence counsel – that just because you treat a witness with the care and respect that they deserve, and tailor your questioning to meet their needs and vulnerabilities, doesn't mean that the accused won't get a fair trial.

But I must say, I came away from that anecdote feeling dispirited. I pictured the complainant, with their cognitive impairment, making all that effort to make a complaint to police, going through this intimidating process (however better designed) and my heart sank for that vulnerable person.

It also sank for the female relative who was trying to help the complainant but who didn't understand what the barrister was saying to her, who was trying to formulate understanding in her mind of what a question meant, only to have the barrister whip on to the next question.

I'm glad that she had Meryl Sexton, an interventionist judge, in that courtroom to protect her. But I thought of those two vulnerable people and I felt very sad.

While intermediaries are being used in this pilot scheme in cases where the witness is vulnerable or is a child, I wonder what magic thing happens between the age of fifteen when Paris gave evidence and the age of eighteen when Saxon Mullins gave evidence, that makes someone suddenly able to withstand a withering cross-examination?

Ground rules hearings are time-consuming and probably tiresome for many barristers, but shouldn't there be more ground rules and more protections more generally? I think there should.

Saxon Mullins says adults – remembering in her case she was a teenager – are both infantilised and disempowered by the system.

She goes back to the witness room at the Downing Centre District Court – with the ridiculous game of Cluedo.

'There [are] no magazines, or books even, so that even from the word go, it's not catering for adults [who] are going through something traumatic,' Saxon says.

'The way I saw it at the time is … it's like they're saying, "You're upset by this, so you're like a child." I'm not in charge of this and I have no choice over which way this goes. I have no choice over what I know or what I can do, so there's no other way to feel than like a child.'

But at the same time, while victims feel infantilised and like a child in this environment, the environment conversely, the next moment, regards them as a knowing and distrustful adult. It addresses them as 'madam'; defence counsel put 'some age' on them.

Politician and former solicitor advocate Trevor Khan says it's hard to avoid things getting 'ugly' in a criminal sex trial.

'It is, by its nature, a form of combat,' Khan tells me. 'Combat involves the shedding of blood at some point by one side or the other. That may be a fundamental problem with our system of justice. But that's the nature of it.'

There are some concessions to victims' vulnerability. These come in the form of a series of measures which were introduced around Australia after several Law Reform Commission inquiries, parliamentary inquiries, the Royal Commission, etc.

These include, for example, the right to give evidence in a remote witness facility. This means that victims don't have to be in the same room as their perpetrator, which is an enormous relief for many victims as that is an intensely retriggering and intimidating experience.

It has reached the point, certainly in Victoria, where this is the assumed position. Certainly, from the point of view of both defence counsel and prosecutors to whom I have spoken, most concede that it is far better for the Crown case if the complainant appears in the courtroom in person. Because it gives the opportunity for the jury to see, first-hand, just how distressed they are by what has taken place.

'I think it's disempowering,' Peter Morrissey SC tells me of complainants being removed from the courtroom and giving their evidence via video link.

'And can I tell you one thing? Defence barristers want them up on the screen. If there's one thing you want, it's to have them up on a screen – absolutely.'

Trevor Khan agrees that a complainant giving video evidence was, in his experience, 'always a plus from the accused's point of view'.

So while the complainant is being 'protected' by removing them from the courtroom and showing their evidence via video link, it is arguable that they are, simultaneously, being disserviced.

Sally Flynn QC says her practice as a Crown was 'always' to get the complainant in court if she could.

'I think it's so much better for the jury to have a real person in front of them,' Flynn says.

She concedes that the 'default position' of many prosecutors is to simply have the witness on video link, but Flynn thinks that's a mistake.

'What I do is, I say, "Come and have a look at the court,"' Flynn says. 'And I talk them through very carefully what's going to happen. I think they are so much more powerful if they are in court rather than on that video screen.

'Similarly, if you have a second trial and the accused has to be retried and witnesses recalled, it's always better to have them in court than simply playing the tape of their previous evidence. If the jurors are watching the tape, it can be like they're watching a movie.

'But a lot of prosecutors would not even ask the complainant to do that. A lot of them would not even raise it. And I think that it's a mistake to not even try.'

Flynn has a line that she uses for the jury if the complainant does elect to be in court: '"He stood there in that witness box and he faced you and he told you what happened to him," and you hope the jury realises that the complainant did not have to do that,' Flynn says.

I can imagine that that might have a powerful impact on a jury. The bravery of it speaks for itself. Flynn cautions that she has to be 'mindful of the impact' on the complainant, but 'I think that if you prepare them well, then it can be effective'.

One thing that has repeatedly occurred to me is why not take the accused out of the courtroom instead of the complainant? Why not give the complainant some purchase in the situation by actually putting them in the place where the proceedings that they initiated – the proceedings that *would not exist* without them – are taking place? Why should they be the one who is infantilised and subjected to this paternalistic idea that they can't stand up for themselves in this place?

If they are properly briefed, as Flynn and Williams describe, if the prosecutor is on his or her toes and doesn't shrink away from intervening when the defence counsel crosses the line, if the judge does his or her job and stops curial bullying from taking place, the only thing standing in the way of the complainant feeling awful about this process is the person they say sexually attacked/abused/raped them at a time when they were vulnerable. It makes total sense that they would not want to be in the same room as them, why not remove the accused?

Some of the barristers I speak to are immediately concerned that this will indicate that the accused, who does, of course, have the presumption of innocence, is, in the minds of the jury, someone who is to be feared by the complainant.

But if it was, as a matter of course, something that happened, what is the difference between putting the complainant in another location to protect the complainant and putting the accused in another location to protect the complainant? Surely the judge could give a very clear warning to the jury that they are not to make anything of the fact the accused is on video link for this evidence, that this always happens in these cases?

John Desmond is fairly open to these sorts of ideas if it makes the complainant comfortable – and says he doesn't see a problem with it, in principle, if it was carefully managed and if the accused had the opportunity to communicate with counsel if necessary – which would mean that the case would have to have a brief adjournment while they had a conference.

'If they want it as easy as possible, in terms of the window-dressing, fine,' Desmond says. 'Pillows, blankets, therapy dogs … whatever. I don't care.'

Judge Meryl Sexton says it would be a 'radical change' to remove the accused when the accused had not exhibited misbehaviour – and 'may incorrectly send a message to the jury that they have done so'.

'The point is that allowing the witness to give evidence in court while removing the accused may provide for some witnesses a greater "purchase in the process", but allowing that would need to be balanced against the potential for unfairness to the accused person who has not engaged in misbehaviour generally, or specifically towards the witness,' Judge Sexton says.

She does say that there is capacity for the accused to be behind a screen if the complainant wishes, but wonders whether in the post-COVID world, where all cases are being done online anyway, the 'shape of trials to come' might change.

Victoria's Victims of Crime Commissioner Fiona McCormack agrees that removing the accused is a 'really interesting concept' and something she'd like to have explored from a policy position.

Trevor Khan thinks it's a very good idea and he can't see 'a lot of argument against it'.

Khan agrees that any issue of it being seen to prejudice the accused's right to a fair trial could be dispensed with by way of a judicial direction to the jury '… To indicate that it's the practice that the accused not be present during the giving of the evidence. It's the sort of thing that happens in our courts now – it doesn't really make any difference.'

There are many, many proposals to consider. Some, such as the restorative justice model advocated by RMIT University's Centre for Innovative Justice, involve a complete overhaul of the way we run sex cases. That involves a presumption in favour of a process of the victim and the perpetrator coming together so that the victim can be heard. It avoids the pain of the criminal justice proceeding and may provide some sort of reconciliation. I can imagine some cases where, if the perpetrator was willing, that might work. But there would also be many examples in which it would not. Given the sociopathic profiles of, for instance, recidivist institutional child sex offenders, I think that would be a dangerous idea in those sorts of instances and it would do away with the hard-won notion that these are crimes and they – and women and children and now adult men – should be taken seriously.

Criminologist Michael Salter has real problems with restorative justice.

'There is no passion for restorative justice from victims and survivors,' Salter says. I must say, I tend to agree. I can think of few victims I have ever met wanting to be in the same room as their perpetrator.

'The biggest advocates for restorative justice are advocates of restorative justice – I just don't hear it from victims, ever,' he says. 'It's always advocated by, frankly, nice, white, middle-class people.

They like the conferencing process. They like sitting in a room with their clipboards.'

Desmond, too, has reservations about this model working in practical reality because it requires an admission of guilt by the accused and, with his experience of his clients, 'they're just not going to admit that it happened'. He says he would not advise his clients to do it.

'They're saying they didn't do it,' he says. 'And I wouldn't countenance the thought.

'There are barristers who don't run trials, and plead [guilty], and good luck to them, they can go down that path.'

* * *

I am not a lawyer, nor a politician, nor a policy-maker. I don't have the answers to what can fix this. But almost all of the victims I speak to say that having a lawyer in court to protect them would make an enormous difference to their experience.

A complainant having their own lawyer is something that has traditionally been considered anathema to criminal proceedings under the common law in which it is the State, not the complainant, that brings the case. It's something that many victims struggle to understand, and, when raised as a possibility to criminal lawyers, involves much eye-rolling that the person suggesting it just doesn't understand the criminal justice system.

'There's also something called "magic legalism",' Salter says, 'where people take the underlying principles of the criminal justice system and create a metaphysics out of it – where certain procedural rules and regulations for assessing or adjudicating matters in the justice system become these, kind of, Ten Commandments, that are supposed to guide human reasoning more generally.'

These received wisdoms may have, in relation to the right of the accused to have a fair trial, considerable merit. But they also allow the system in which complainants are bullied to be perpetuated.

The feedback to the Centre for Innovative Justice's 2019 report on victims demonstrated this widespread failure of understanding on the part of victims. Often, the report found, the system was not adequately explained to victims. It's not their fault that they don't know. It may be, for many, the first time they have ever turned their mind to the operation of the criminal justice system. And that is more likely if they come from vulnerable circumstances.

Even today, before writing this paragraph, I spoke to a bright and otherwise fairly well-educated survivor of sexual assault who, in error, described the prosecutor as her 'defence' lawyer. While she thought that the prosecutor was empathetic and good at her job, she didn't always understand the distance that was necessarily employed because the prosecutor serves the court and the administration of justice, not the complainant.

'If you compare how the defence handles themselves in court versus the prosecution, it is, on one hand you've got the defence really driving home messages, and on the other hand, you seem to have this very meek and mild and sort of not argumentative approach from the prosecution,' one victim told the Centre for Innovative Justice report authors.

'I never felt like we had someone 100 per cent in our corner fighting for us,' said another.

'He [the accused] had someone in his corner, fighting tooth and nail that would do anything. I never felt that we had that in any way because they [the Crown] just want to see the law upheld ... I don't know, you just want getting the best outcome for you to matter more than getting the right outcome for the law ... I never felt that. Ever.'

For many complainants now, still, it's a matter of getting a support worker who is very sympathetic, but not legally trained, a box of tissues, a perfunctory chat with the prosecutor before their evidence, and, if they want one, a dog.

Like me, Melbourne silk Julie Condon QC understands that sometimes the dog can be supportive for a complainant and 'that's their choice in difficult circumstances', but in the absence of better instruction about what the complainant is about to go through, the idea of a dog is 'risible, really'.

'It's just, there's something really unsophisticated about it,' Condon says.

'On a more philosophical level, it's pretty ...' she raises her eyebrows and exhales slowly, 'yeah ...'

But her reservations about the dog don't mean she supports giving these people a lawyer. Condon – who has in fact seen all sides of a sexual criminal trial as defence counsel, prosecutor and judge – says providing lawyers for complainants is 'anathema to the adversarial system'.

'Look, personally, I must say I would be intuitively, instinctively, resistant to the idea of a complainant having a lawyer that's present, that is there to advise them,' she says.

I ask Condon what if it was strictly defined, but Condon says that if you give someone a lawyer, you cannot then place constraints on the type of advice that lawyer gives the person.

Again, she says it is the role of the Crown to inform complainants effectively. I counter that complainants tell me that, often, that is not happening.

'To me that's a failing,' Condon says, 'that is absolutely a failing of the DPP and their Witness Assistance Service, because that is what they're there for.

'… It is my assumption that they would be doing it. They should be doing it. That is their job so that exactly somebody doesn't come out completely shell-shocked and say, "You didn't warn me."'

But as to having a lawyer in the court, Condon is very concerned it amounts to 'adjusting the burden of proof', referring to the fundamental principle underlying the criminal justice system – that the job of proving a case beyond reasonable doubt rests squarely with the prosecution.

The defence in a criminal trial doesn't have to prove the facts or issues in the case. The defence doesn't have to prove that their version of events isn't true – they simply have to show that there is a reasonable doubt that the Crown's case is not true. They reach for the bottom drawer and they find something that might just make the jury have a little doubt about the complainant's story. An inconsistency. A suspicion that the person might not quite be 'credible', a niggling concern that something is not quite right and therefore, in all conscience, they cannot convict the accused beyond reasonable doubt.

In a conversation with a highly educated professional woman in my circle of acquaintance who was on a jury in a sex trial, she volunteered to me that everyone on her jury was convinced that the accused had committed the crime, but they could not say that there was not a reasonable doubt. And so, with very heavy hearts, they set him free. She thinks about the victim in that case all the time. A person she knows in her bones is a victim, but who the law told her she was not permitted to believe.

Condon says that in a sex trial, where the burden of proof lies with the prosecution, it means believing the word of the complainant. It's word against word. And that's what makes it so difficult.

'Most other trials don't stand or fall on one witness,' she says.

She believes that if a lawyer was acting for the complainant, as well as the Crown, it would mean that the complainant would have more of a stake in the proceedings than they should, and they would be, implicitly, more sympathetic to the jury.

'It's that subliminal effect thinking,' Condon says, 'from the point of view of the jury – who are the ones who make the decision, ultimately, on the facts – "Hold on, why has that complainant got a lawyer sitting at the Bar table and we've heard from ten other witnesses and none of them have lawyers?"'

Surely, because without the complainant, these proceedings would not exist? Because it's artificial to think of the complainant as just 'one of eleven witnesses'. Because, as Saxon Mullins says, she didn't stand outside her own body and watch this happening. Yes, it is just an allegation at this point – because the accused is innocent until proven guilty – but no one is under the illusion that the complainant is just another witness, however the defence might like to treat them.

'Personally, of course they have a great stake [in the proceedings], but legally they don't; whereas, of course, for an accused, they've got the personal *and* the legal,' Condon says, adding that she is aware this is of no consolation to the complainant.

The stakes, she is essentially saying, are so much higher for the accused because they face such horrendous consequences if they are found guilty – loss of liberty in prison, moral opprobrium, shame, difficulty in later securing employment. All of those things would be devastating for an innocent person and that's why the system is as it is.

But I just feel that we are throwing the baby out with the bathwater. And the high stakes for the complainant – particularly in a high-profile case where, if the accused is well-resourced, can go for years through the appeal process – are forgotten or minimised. The complainant can be absolutely forgiven for thinking that the system is comprehensively stacked against them.

Condon concedes that in historical child sex cases in particular, it's almost impossible for the jury *not* to have a reasonable doubt because of the 'effluxion of time', the fact that it's usually word against word – that sex offenders don't routinely do what they do in front of witnesses.

'There's something, really, I think, about the structure of those particular allegations that makes it difficult?' Condon concedes. 'It's not just that everything, in your view, is against the complainant; it's also the factual context in which the allegation arises for the jury – it makes it difficult, doesn't it?' she says.

That's what, I say, I'm trying to get to the bottom of, because I feel that we lead victims up this garden path, where we encourage them to come forward with their complaint to police, in the hope not just that they, individually, receive justice, but also that they might prevent their perpetrator from ruining more lives.

'Those things weigh heavily upon people who have been through this and seen their own lives destroyed, or very, very poorly affected,' I say to Condon, 'and they don't want that to happen to other children and so they have that motivation. But then the system –'

Condon cuts in, 'Fails them?'

'Fails them,' I repeat, nodding. It fails them.

* * *

Slowly, some of the people who have been working in this system for decades are coming to see that there may be some merit in the proposal of granting a lawyer to victims.

Mark Tedeschi QC is perhaps one of the most famous prosecutors in Australian history. The former New South Wales senior Crown prosecutor ran notorious murder cases such as Kathleen Folbigg's, who killed her four children. As a young court reporter for *The Australian* in the early 2000s, I watched him prosecute that and many other homicides, and I have to say I have never seen more magnetic performances before a jury by a Crown prosecutor.

He, like everyone who has practised as a Crown prosecutor, has seen witnesses subjected to bullying behaviour by over-zealous members of the defence counsel old guard.

'There are some older barristers whose methods of aggressive cross-examination in sexual assault cases have not changed since they were young men,' Tedeschi tells me. 'And because of their reputation, they won't change.

'They are a product of a bygone era and they should not be able to get away with what they do.'

Tedeschi is one who has come around to the idea of having a lawyer in court for complainants in sex trials to combat this kind of questioning when it is not being addressed by the prosecutor or the judge.

'The witness is not a party to the proceedings, but there is nothing to stop them having a lawyer at the back of the court who could intervene if their client is at risk, in the same way that we sometimes see lawyers in the public gallery whose clients are witnesses and who are, for example, at risk of self-incrimination,' Tedeschi tells me.

'I can't see any reason why there couldn't be a similar situation where a witness felt that they might be bullied, that they too might have a lawyer in court in the public gallery.

'There's nothing to prevent the lawyer from standing up and saying, "I represent the witness" and words to the effect of "I am entitled to insist that the witness not be harangued" or "the questions are demeaning [and] in breach of the *Evidence Act*".

'Why not? I don't have a problem with that.'

Trevor Khan says 'defence counsel would hate' the proposition, but he agrees that if it were explained very carefully to the jury that the complainant had a lawyer in the room to protect their interests, then, in a limited way, it might work. He says that if these lawyers did raise objections based on a complainant's human rights being abrogated, or improper questioning not picked up by the prosecutor or the judge, the issues would have to be dealt with in the absence of the jury.

'Yes, I think it could happen,' Khan says, 'I think it would certainly bring the Crowns to heel very quickly in terms of being more active in support of the complainants.'

Former Supreme Court Judge Marcia Neave was a Law Reform Commissioner who proposed many changes to Victoria's legal system to make it more victim-centred. She is also open to the proposal but says, like all of these things, it's a question of finding the money in a tight budgetary climate.

Despite being a self-described 'old-school' advocate, John Desmond also does not have a problem with complainants having a limited form of representation in court and says that it 'should be fine with any defence barrister'.

'I don't see that changing the system significantly, and if it makes it easier for them, [that's fine],' Desmond tells me. 'I don't have a problem with that whatsoever. It's just someone else I can have an argument with! That's what I get paid to do. Let it go another day – I'll make more money!'

He cautions that a barrister like him putting a prior inconsistent statement to a complainant is going to be no less traumatic, lawyer or no lawyer.

'Make it as easy as you can, but they're still going to struggle when that prior inconsistent statement's put to them,' he says with the confidence of someone who has realised that people almost always make errors in the re-telling of their stories.

'That's the trauma. That's the trauma ... The trauma is really being asked to explain the inexplicable.'

The Irish criminal justice system had boldly gone where others in the common law world have feared to tread, introducing a limited form of independent legal representation for victims in sex trials that allows, for instance, sexual assault complainants to seek state-funded representation to, as Dr Mary Iliadis from Deakin University notes, 'oppose a defendant's application to introduce a victim's sexual history evidence in court'.

'It also enables victim interests to be acknowledged and included,' Iliadis writes, 'thereby recognising a "triangulation of interests" among the accused, state and victim.'

Iliadis found in her research that defence teams seemed to find 'work-arounds' to bypass the legislation and there were 'significant discrepancies' in the exercise of judicial discretion about sexual history evidence. Similarly, in Scotland, research showed that legislative attempts to prevent arbitrary use of defendants' sexual history questioning of victims actually led to more defence counsel questioning victims about sexual history.

It should be noted that the Irish system does not continue beyond the application to question about sexual history stage – as Iliadis notes, 'the victim has no further legal assistance and must go on to endure the cross-examination about their prior sexual history without representation'.

In essence, the Irish proposal seems insufficient in its scope and flawed in its drafting. '... These findings are not unique to Ireland, but reflect trends in other adversarial jurisdictions that exploit loopholes in safeguards to prevent the introduction of victims' sexual history,' Iliadis writes.

But just because Ireland got it wrong doesn't mean that we can't get it right.

* * *

I sit down with Peter Morrissey in his chambers to talk about these issues. I want the man who defended me to see what it's like from the point of view of the victims he has cross-examined. I wonder what he thinks of victims having their own lawyers.

'I guess what I'm saying is, when you put it all together, why shouldn't they have a seat at the table?' I ask Morrissey.

'Because it's not their case,' he replies, emphatically. 'See, they're not running the case. Give them a seat at the table? "Okay, you can bring the witnesses."'

I agree with him that it's not their case, but I wonder why that stops someone from defending their interests when the line is being crossed by defence counsel. Morrissey can see why I'm asking this – because, as he saw through representing me, I had, in his words, 'been through the wringer' myself and could identify with these people.

But I remind him that I knew what to do. I didn't have a substance abuse problem, or a truncated education, or a mountain of trauma or, without putting too fine a point on it, an anal rape I was trying to blot out of my brain.

'Yeah, I get all of that,' he says.

'I mean, I'm not talking about the system being completely overhauled,' I tell him. 'But could you have [some form of legal representation] as an option?' I ask, adding that it would be a qualified option. What I envision is not a lawyer who is a party, sitting at the Bar table, but a lawyer who is present in court in the way, say, Hugh Bennett from the ABC was for me. Who could spring to his or her feet in very limited and controlled circumstances.

'I would, myself,' Morrissey answers, 'politically, I'd be one hundred per cent against it. I don't want them in the court.'

'Why?' I ask him.

'Because it's a public process,' he replies. 'It's a public proceeding. It's brought on behalf of the public. They [the witness] might be a liar.'

'But even if they are a liar,' I respond, 'if they are being treated in a way that is inappropriate, and no one's actually looking out for them …'

'But are they really being treated in a way that's inappropriate?' he asks.

'Yes,' I reply, immediately. Of course not always, of course I have seen transcripts where defence counsel did the job that was required of them in as respectful a manner as they could muster, but yes.

Morrissey tells me that it's not always bullying that wins the day in a sex case – sometimes it's because a barrister does a good job. He, for instance, has only lost one sex case since 2002, and he's 'never yelled at anyone'.

I suspect that yelling rarely happens these days. It's not about yelling, *per se*, it's about treating someone with derision. I find it hard to imagine Morrissey doing that and I don't know about the sex cases he's referring to, but it depresses me nonetheless that he's only lost one sex case in the better part of twenty years, given the statistics for false complaints are so low.

I ask about the Royal Commission's Criminal Justice Report, how it outlines at the start that many victims reported that being cross-examined was as bad as being raped. Then that meant, did it not, that broadly speaking, something was really wrong?

'But the question is,' Morrissey replies, 'is it as bad?'

'The point is,' I tell him, 'that's how they feel.'

Morrissey wonders how they got to that point. Who got them to say that? Who led them? I know it's a terrible thing for a genuinely decent man like him to confront – the possibility that he might have left a person feeling that way. It's hard to reconcile the idea that a man who has been there for me in my darkest legal hours, and to whom I will always be grateful, might ever have done that to a victim. But I've now lost count of the number of victims of these crimes who have said it to me about other barristers.

'Can I say to you, afterwards, after *him*,' I say, referring to my own evidence, 'I lay in my bed the next day, and I could not move. I couldn't move. I couldn't get up to get a glass of water.'

'I'm not demeaning how the victim feels,' he quietly says.

I tell him I know. And I do know. I honestly don't think he demeans how victims feel. And I think he knows that I know.

'But the point is,' I continue, 'it was extremely traumatic, extremely.

'And I held my own. Right? So imagine what it's like for someone who doesn't have the ability to hold their own?'

I carry those people who didn't have the ability to hold their own around with me. Not in a 'woe is me' way, but 'woe are they'. I don't forget them. They are always summed up in those words of the tearful Bernie in the *Revelation* documentary, dropping out of his evidence at that eleventh hour because he was in such a state of anxiety about how he was 'due to get grilled, like I'm the fuckin' villain. I'm not the villain, mate'. *I'm not the villain.*

I keep ploughing on with Morrissey and I say what is true. What I'm sort of embarrassed to admit, but it's true.

'I,' I begin, 'the only thing in my life that was as bad as that day was when my first husband died. And I had to go and identify his body at the morgue.'

Morrissey swallows and says, quietly, 'I've done that. Not for a husband, but yes.'

He continues, nodding his head empathetically.

'No, no, I get you, I get you. That's traumatic. That's traumatic.'

I feel for him in this moment and I really, really don't want him to think that I'm personally having a go at him. I just need him to know. I need one of the good guys to know. And maybe if he knows, one of those victims might not have such an awful time. Not because he is the king of the awful times. But because these barristers just need to know. And the reality is, without situations like mine, which are incredibly rare, they never get this kind of feedback.

'No, no, no, it's good to have the … it's good to discuss,' Morrissey says, nodding his head again. 'And I completely get that it's traumatic.'

I never got to speak to Robert Richter and I daresay I never will. I have no desire to ever be in his company again and would probably walk out of any room he entered. But at that moment, in Peter Morrissey's messy chambers, on Peter Morrissey's Chesterfield, just across the way from Robert Richter's messy chambers and Robert Richter's Chesterfield, I felt like I was saying, for what it was worth, what needed to be said.

ACKNOWLEDGEMENTS

How do I even begin to find adequate words to thank the people who have been marked by trauma, took that trauma to the criminal justice system, who then, despite being badly let down by it, let down in general, trusted me with your stories?

I am just in awe of your courage. I thank you all. You, and your families, are all in my heart, every day. I'll never forget you.

To those I knew who are no longer here and those I never met who shouldn't have died so young. And to your families, left behind. You should not have been left behind.

To all of the people who stuck out their necks to protect the vulnerable – thank you. Especially those who acted against their own immediate interest to tell the truth because they knew it would mean that women and children in the future would be protected. You impress me endlessly.

To all of the excellent sources behind the scenes – you know who you are – who helped me stand up for survivors and for child safety.

To every single member of the public who has contacted me over the past few years to send messages of support. Every single time it meant something. Thank you.

Thank you to all of the lawyers who also trusted me with their honest reflections about the system. Especially those of you who were not afraid to show your own vulnerability or were willing to countenance change.

Thank you especially to Peter Morrissey, Jack Rush and Sarala Fitzgerald, for getting me out of a jam. For being sensitive, kind and smart. I'll forever be grateful to you. Thank you also to Kathryn Wilson and Hugh Bennett for all of your dogged months of hard work.

To Sally Neighbour and Morag Ramsay, for believing in my journalism, always having my back and for inspiring me with your relentless and forensic commitment to our craft. You are the best in the business.

To the team of *Four Corners* producers and researchers who worked so hard on those stories that originated on our program. Mary Fallon, Sashka Koloff, Lucy Carter, Lauren Day, Peter Cronau, I love working with you all. You are incredible professionals.

To John Lyons for going out of your way to support me time and time again through some of the more difficult times I've faced over the past few years.

To Jo Puccini for making the effort to come to Melbourne to support me during my legal cases and for your wise counsel. To Sarah Curnow for your forensic attention to the craft, your excellent commitment to proper discovery and for being on the other end of the phone with wise counsel. To Gaven Morris for your support during my case and for backing important journalism. To David Anderson, thank you for going out of your way to ensure my safety. And thank you for your decent leadership and your general kindness. To Richard James, for in those bleak weeks, standing out the front of my place, making it feel okay.

To Andy Burns for your unwavering friendship, love, journalistic integrity and phone calls every other day to chew the fat and compare notes.

To all at Hachette for believing in this book.

And to Louise Adler, my fearless publisher, my dear friend. You know how grateful I am to you for the risks you took for me, for always believing in what we did and never wavering or blaming anyone else, for never being anything other than a warrior woman despite how hard these past few years have been. Thank you also for pestering me to write this second book, after the ordeal of the aftermath of the first.

And to Mum, Dad and my whole family. I couldn't ask for better. Love you all to bits. I come from good stock. My people are good people.

If you would like to find out more about Hachette Australia,
our authors, upcoming events and new releases you can visit
our website or our social media channels:

hachette.com.au

f HachetteAustralia

🐦 **📷** HachetteAus